READING INTERVENTION CASE STUDIES FOR SCHOOL PSYCHOLOGISTS

Reading Intervention Case Studies for School Psychologists provides vivid, real-world examples of school-based interventions targeting students' phonological awareness, phonics, fluency, and comprehension in reading. This book offers a rich variety of applied reading interventions in school settings, spanning strategies such as incidental teaching, word boxes, peer tutoring, taped words, story mapping, and beyond. Each case includes thorough descriptions of the specific area of concern, detailed intervention protocols, data collection and analysis methods, and tips for ensuring social acceptability and treatment integrity. School psychologists, along with related professionals in special education, general education, and speech-language pathology, will come away with new insights into this comprehensive set of well-researched and frequently applied reading interventions.

Melissa Coolong-Chaffin is Professor of Psychology in the School Psychology Program and Co-Director of the Academic Intervention Clinic in the Human Development Center at the University of Wisconsin – Eau Claire, USA.

Renee O. Hawkins is Professor of School Psychology and Director of the School of Human Services at the University of Cincinnati, USA.

Michael I. Axelrod is Professor of Psychology in the School Psychology Program and Director of the Human Development Center at the University of Wisconsin – Eau Claire, USA.

READING INTERVENTION CASE STUDIES FOR SCHOOL PSYCHOLOGISTS

Evidence-Based Implementation and Analysis

Edited by Melissa Coolong-Chaffin, Renee O. Hawkins and Michael I. Axelrod

Routledge
Taylor & Francis Group
NEW YORK AND LONDON

Designed cover image: Shutterstock

First published 2024
by Routledge
605 Third Avenue, New York, NY 10158

and by Routledge
4 Park Square, Milton Park, Abingdon, Oxon, OX14 4RN

Routledge is an imprint of the Taylor & Francis Group, an informa business

Library of Congress Cataloging-in-Publication Data
Names: Coolong-Chaffin, Melissa, editor. | Hawkins, Renee O., editor. | Axelrod, Michael I., editor.
Title: Reading intervention case studies for school psychologists: evidence-based implementation and analysis / Edited by Melissa Coolong-Chaffin, Renee O. Hawkins, and Michael I. Axelrod.
Identifiers: LCCN 2023020001 (print) | LCCN 2023020002 (ebook) | ISBN 9781032227573 (hardback) | ISBN 9781032231112 (paperback) | ISBN 9781003275749 (ebook)
Subjects: LCSH: School psychology. | Reading--Remedial teaching. | Response to intervention (Learning disabled children) | Reading disability.
Classification: LCC LB1027.55 .R44 2024 (print) |
LCC LB1027.55 (ebook) | DDC 370.15–dc23/eng/20230502
LC record available at https://lccn.loc.gov/2023020001
LC ebook record available at https://lccn.loc.gov/2023020002

ISBN: 978-1-032-22757-3 (hbk)
ISBN: 978-1-032-23111-2 (pbk)
ISBN: 978-1-003-27574-9 (ebk)

DOI: 10.4324/9781003275749

Typeset in Sabon
by SPi Technologies India Pvt Ltd (Straive)

This book is dedicated to the education professionals who work tirelessly to help their students improve their reading skills.
To my colleagues and students in the School Psychology Program at the University of Cincinnati (R.O.H.)
Thanks to Dave and Will for making life adventurous and thanks to the students who inspire me daily (M.C.C.).
To my family and friends for being there to cheer me on (M.I.A.)

CONTENTS

FIGURES

TABLES

CONTRIBUTORS

Kizzy Albritton, Ph.D. University of Texas at Austin, Austin, TX, USA

Michael I. Axelrod, Ph.D. University of Wisconsin, Eau Claire, WI, USA

John C. Begeny, Ph.D. North Carolina State University, Raleigh, NC, USA

Alexis Blackmon, M.Ed. University of Cincinnati, Cincinnati, OH, USA

Matthew K. Burns, Ph.D. University of Missouri

Caitlyn C. Chambers, Ph.D. University of Cincinnati, Cincinnati, OH, USA

Tai A. Collins, Ph.D. University of Cincinnati, Cincinnati, OH, USA

Melissa Coolong-Chaffin, Ph.D. University of Wisconsin, Eau Claire, WI, USA

Felicia L. Davidson Helps Education Fund, Raleigh NC, USA

Jesslyn M. Durling, M.S. North Carolina State University, Raleigh, NC, USA

Josalyn A. Foster, M.Ed. University of Cincinnati, Cincinnati, OH, USA

Douglas Fuchs, Ph.D. American Institutes for Research and Vanderbilt University, Nashville, TN, USA

Jessica L. Hagaman, Ph.D. University of Nebraska – Omaha, Omaha, NE, USA

Stephanie Hammerschmidt-Snidarich, Ph.D. University of Florida, Gainesville, FL, USA

Renee O. Hawkins, Ph.D. University of Cincinnati, Cincinnati, OH, USA

Stacy-Ann A. January, Ph.D. University of South Florida, Tampa, FL, USA

Lakeisha Johnson, Ph.D. Florida State University, Tallahassee, FL, USA

Laurice M. Joseph, Ph.D. The Ohio State University, Columbus, OH, USA

Devin M. Kearns, Ph.D. University of Connecticut, Mansfield, CT, USA

Virginia C. Kessler, M.Ed. The University of Tennessee – Knoxville, Knoxville, TN, USA

Cheryl P. Lyon, Ph.D. University of Connecticut, Mansfield, CT, USA

Kathrin E. Maki, Ph.D. University of Florida, Gainesville, FL, USA

Kandace W. Mossing, M.Ed. University of Cincinnati, Cincinnati, OH, USA

Shobana Musti, Ph.D. Pace University, Pleasantville, NY, USA

Natasha K. Newson, M.S. North Carolina State University, Raleigh, NC, USA

Michele M. Nobel, Ph.D. Ohio Wesleyan University, Delaware, OH, USA

Alana Oif Telesman, M.A. The Ohio State University, Columbus, OH, USA

C. Shannon O'Neal North Carolina State University, Raleigh, NC, USA

Brian Orr, Ph.D. University of Wisconsin, Eau Claire, WI, USA

Shawna Petersen-Brown, Ph.D. Minnesota State University, Mankato

Jordan Pollard, MSW, M.Ed. University of Cincinnati, Cincinnati, OH, USA

Jessica Schloth, B.A. University of South Florida, Tampa, FL, USA

Christopher H. Skinner, Ph.D. The University of Tennessee – Knoxville, Knoxville, TN, USA

Melissa V. Stalega, M.Ed. University of Connecticut, Mansfield, CT, USA

Mary Stepanek, M.Ed. University of Cincinnati, Cincinnati, OH, USA

Angela Stokes, M.S., M.Ed. Eleva-Strum School District, Eleva, WI, USA

Amy Trayers, M.A. University of South Florida, Tampa, FL, USA

Mary E. Tusing, Ph.D. University of Wisconsin, Eau Claire, WI, USA

Patricia F. Vadasy, Ph.D. Oregon Research Institute, Eugene, OR, USA

Dana Wagner, Ph.D. Minnesota State University, Mankato, MN, USA

Tabitha N. Wandell The University of Tennessee – Knoxville, Knoxville, TN, USA

Joseph Wang, Ed.S. University of Cincinnati, Cincinnati, OH, USA

Chelsea Wilson, M.S. The University of Tennessee – Knoxville, Knoxville, TN, USA

Nicole Wyckoff, M.A. University of South Florida, Tampa, FL, USA

ACKNOWLEDGEMENTS

We would like to give credit to the many people who helped make this book possible. Thanks to Daniel Schwartz from Routledge/Taylor & Francis for his guidance, support, and patience throughout this project. Special thanks to Dr. Mary Beth Tusing for sharing her knowledge and providing guidance and friendship over the years and to Toni Volbrecht who manages all of the details so that we can concentrate on other things. We would also like to acknowledge Emma Shortreed for her assistance with editing tasks. Finally, this work would not have been possible without the inspiration from the countless educators, students, and families with whom we have worked throughout the years.

1

INTRODUCTION

Melissa Coolong-Chaffin
University of Wisconsin Eau Claire, Eau Claire, WI, USA

Renee O. Hawkins
University of Cincinnati, Cincinnati, OH, USA

Michael I. Axelrod
University of Wisconsin Eau Claire, Eau Claire, WI, USA

Dana Wagner
Minnesota State University, Mankato, MN, USA

Introduction

It is axiomatic that reading is a fundamental skill required for success in school, work, and society. Yet despite decades of research regarding effective instruction and intervention strategies, many students in this country are not proficient readers. For example, the most recent results from the National Assessment of Educational Progress (2022) found that 37% of fourth graders and 30% of eighth graders failed to meet basic standards. Both groups also showed a significant decline in performance relative to 2019—presumably due in part to the disruptive impact of the pandemic. The results are even more stark for students from minoritized groups (National Center for Education Statistics, National Assessment of Educational Progress, 2022). In addition, reading problems are the number one reason students are referred for special education (National Center for Education Statistics, 2022). Recent policy updates (e.g., Every Student Succeeds Act, 2015) have called for evidence-based practices (EBP) in schools to address the issue, but barriers to the implementation of these practices such as limited time and resources, and limited EBPs for some problems have hindered their success (Scheibel, 2023).

DOI: 10.4324/9781003275749-1

Multiple contributing factors to the reading epidemic have been described, including familial poverty, limited experience with language or reading prior to entering school, limited time and material resources in schools, and inadequate teacher training and preparation to name a few. Another long-lamented explanation for the poor reading performance of students in the US is the *research to practice gap* in which the most validated approaches to instruction and intervention and findings from cognitive science fail to find their way to the classroom. Another important reason that is less discussed is the *practice to research gap*, in which the research itself fails to address the needs of those charged with bringing the promise of these findings to reality. Educators need strategies and interventions to address reading skill deficits that are effective and practical to implement. However, it is not enough to have a list of interventions from which to choose—educators also need to know what to select, for whom, under what circumstances, how to support implementation, and how to evaluate whether or not those interventions are working—and what to do if they are not—for the actual students in their classrooms. This book attempts to meet these needs by providing educators with strategies and interventions to address common reading challenges. This is not a 'one-size-fits-all' cookbook approach; interventions are described in the context of many typical scenarios encountered in schools with practical ideas about how to implement them effectively within a broader decision-making framework. It bears mentioning that intervention cannot occur in a vacuum. Supplemental interventions must be layered on to generally effective core instruction, and, as such, the interventions presented in this book should be seen as supplemental to a comprehensive reading curriculum delivered with fidelity in the classroom. This introductory chapter will provide a brief description of reading skill development to aid in the selection of the appropriate skill(s) to target for intervention, as well as a description of the problem-solving model as a guide for decision-making in the intervention process. Assessment approaches for problem identification and problem analysis, considerations for intervention plan development, progress monitoring, and strategies to ensure treatment integrity, measurement fidelity, and social validity will be presented.

Reading Development

Put simply, skilled readers can effectively and efficiently derive meaning from text (Scarborough, 2001). This simple definition belies the complexity of the process of becoming a skilled reader, however. Many elegant and illustrative models of reading development exist in the literature, and a thorough description of these models is beyond the scope of this book.

One such model is Scarborough's Reading Rope (2001) in which the multiple strands woven together that result in skilled reading are depicted. One set of strands represents word recognition skills. Word recognition requires the understanding that spoken words are comprised of syllables and individual sounds (phonological awareness). This awareness of the sound structure of language is a fundamental prerequisite to mapping the spoken sounds (phonemes) onto the written letters on the page (graphemes). The general understanding that spoken sounds are represented by written letters is the alphabetic principle. Readers must apply this knowledge of letter-sound correspondences to decoding words on the page. Readers must also draw on a repertoire of words that are read automatically, or sight words. The store of sight words builds with exposure and practice.

Of course, simply being able to correctly identify and pronounce words encountered on the page is just part of the process of skilled reading. The other set of strands depict language comprehension skills. These skills include an understanding of vocabulary, background knowledge about the topic, understanding of syntax (how words are arranged in phrases and sentences) and semantics (meaning of words and sentence structures), familiarity with text conventions and structures, verbal reasoning skills, among other skills.

Scarborough's model can help us identify component skills readers may struggle with in order to select appropriate targets for intervention. Another commonly used resource for identifying component skills that might be targeted for intervention is the National Reading Panel Report (2000). To understand which instructional strategies and approaches are most effective in helping students achieve the goal of reading proficiency, the National Reading Panel (2000) identified effective strategies in five key areas from the extant literature.

The first area is phonemic awareness in which students learn to identify and manipulate the sounds in spoken words. Systematic, explicit instruction in phonemic awareness tasks, such as having students manipulate phonemes with written or printed letters, had a significant impact on phonemic awareness, reading, and spelling skills. Phonics is the teaching of letter-sound correspondences for use in reading and spelling. The most effective phonics approaches teach these skills in a systematic way, meaning that the skills are delineated and taught sequentially. Synthetic phonics instruction in which students are taught to read letter sounds and blend them into words is particularly effective.

Fluency is the ability to read quickly, accurately, and with proper expression. Fluency supports comprehension as students who read fluently are able to devote cognitive resources to understanding what words *mean*, as opposed to focusing on what the words *say*. Fluent readers are also able to read more in less time, a process that facilitates not only efficiency, but also builds further fluency. Strategies involving repeated practice with guidance and feedback build fluency.

Understanding the meaning of words is critically important for overall comprehension. Vocabulary can be taught incidentally, as new words are encountered when reading, or directly, such as preteaching new words before reading a text. Finally, effective comprehension strategies support understanding when students actively engage in the process of reading, connects the content to their background knowledge and previous experiences, and create mental representations of what they are reading. While some readers may do this automatically, these reading comprehension strategies can be taught directly as well.

Information from models of reading development and the available evidence for effective approaches to teaching the components of skilled reading have guided the selection of skills and strategies we have highlighted in the subsequent chapters.

Problem-Solving Process

As mentioned previously, it is not enough for educators to have a list of interventions from which to choose, intervention selection and implementation is best guided by a decision-making framework. The problem-solving model is a useful framework for informing this process. While there are several variations of the problem-solving model, all share a common process (for example, see Pluymert, 2014). The first step in the model is *problem identification*, in which the problem to be addressed is operationally defined relative to some expectation. One way of defining a problem is to consider the discrepancy between what is expected and what is occurring (Deno, 2005). Once the problem is clearly defined in clear, observable, measurable terms, the problem can be further analyzed in order to develop testable hypotheses. Why is the problem occurring? What can the student do/what can the student not do? Is the observed performance the result of a skill deficit or a performance deficit? Is the problem unique to the student, or does it affect a larger group of students? What are some possible contextual factors related to the problem? Effective *problem analysis* leads to the identification or development of an intervention that is likely to close the gap between what is expected and what is occurring.

Following problem analysis, a detailed *intervention plan* is developed and implemented. Crucial questions to consider during this stage are related to implementation. Which intervention shall we implement? What is the goal and how will we monitor progress toward that goal? Who will do what, when, for how long, and with what materials? How do we support buy-in and proper implementation of the plan? When will we check back to see if the problem has been solved? Effective problem solving requires ongoing data collection and analysis. The final stage is *plan evaluation*—did the plan work? If not, why not? Did we select the right target behavior? Was the plan implemented as intended? Should we continue with the plan? Modify the plan? Terminate the plan?

The remainder of this chapter will describe each step in the problem-solving process in more detail. Subsequent chapters will use this process to frame the presentation of case studies of evidence-based reading interventions implemented in classroom settings.

Problem Identification

School-based prevention and early intervention models (e.g., multi-tiered systems of support, or MTSS) are based, in part, on correctly identifying which students are in most need. Most schools employ a universal screening process to identify students at-risk for reading problems (Jenkins, Hudson, & Johnson, 2007; Mellard, McNight, & Woods, 2009). Universal screening serves to accurately predict a student's success or failure within the curriculum using an evaluation paradigm that emphasizes brevity (i.e., 1–3-minute probes), widespread reach (i.e., assess all students), multiple administrations across the year, and adequate psychometric properties (Albers & Kettler, 2014; January & Klingbeil, 2020).

Albers and Kettler (2014) highlighted three universal screening approaches commonly used by schools. A broadband universal screening is designed to broadly assess certain critical areas, such as academics, behavior, and mental health, with the purpose of understanding students' general functioning. Narrowband universal screening targets specific skill domains (e.g., early literacy skills, decoding, oral reading fluency) to provide detailed information about target skills. Broadband and narrowband screening approaches are considered direct-route approaches, as students are identified for services based the results of the screener.

However, using one screener score alone may lead to too many false positives and negatives (VanMeveren, Hulac, & Wollersheim-Shervy, 2020). To improve accuracy, schools might employ a multiple-gate approach, where students pass through a series of screening assessments to eventually identify those most at-risk. Gate 1 might involve the teacher identifying students who, based on classroom assessments and observations, are struggling most with learning to read. For Gate 2, a student's state test scores in reading would be examined for performance patterns.

Finally, Gate 3 would involve administering specific CBMs to those students performing below a certain cut point on the state test. According to Albers and Kettler (2014), a high number of false positives is acceptable at Gate 1, as screening at the other gates is intended to identify those students in need of reading intervention.

Research on the use of universal screening as part of a larger MTSS has generally been positive. For example, Grapin, Waldron, and Joyce-Beaulieu (2019) found that elementary school students exposed to a Response to Intervention (RTI) framework that included implementation of universal screening procedures had higher reading comprehension scores than students in the control condition. The authors concluded that a comprehensive prevention and intervention model that emphasizes data-based decision-making and the use of universal screening data to identify students for intervention can have a profound impact on students' reading achievement.

One common assessment approach used within the problem-solving process is curriculum-based measurement (CBM). CBMs are available for multiple reading skills (e.g., letter sound fluency, nonsense word fluency, oral reading fluency, vocabulary matching, maze) and are brief, easy to administer, sensitive to student growth, linked to classroom performance, and have good psychometric properties (Albers & Kettler, 2014). Hintze, Christ, and Methe (2006) highlighted two important features of CBM that make the assessment model ideal for measuring students' academic performance: (1) CBM's focus "is on broad, long-term goal objectives (i.e., end of year), rather than short-term mastery objectives" (p. 51) and (2) CBM is able to assess the "retention and generalization of learning" (p. 51) because it focuses on the curriculum more broadly. CBMs can serve to both understand students' reading skills and monitor their progress (Deno & Fuchs, 1987; Fuchs, 2004). CBMs can be used to identify which students are at risk for reading difficulties, identify skills to target for intervention, and monitor progress.

When considering an individual student's performance and need for intervention, the first question to ask is whether the problem is unique to the student, or whether it affects a larger group of students. This can be answered by examining the percentage of students who perform below a cut score on a screening measure. If more than 15–20% of students fail to meet the screening benchmark, the problem should be analyzed at the grade or classroom level with a focus on the core curriculum—specifically, the evidence base for the core curriculum, teachers' level of implementation fidelity of the program, and student engagement and performance within the curricular materials.

If the problem is relatively unique to the student, more information is needed to further define that problem. Reviews of the literature and research syntheses highlight the fact that correctly identifying skills to target for intervention is a crucial first step in developing an effective intervention (see Shapiro, 2010; Swanson, 1999; Vaughn, Gersten, & Chard, 2000). Not surprisingly, when a student is referred for academic problems, educators often first ask, "What skills should we target for assessment and intervention?" Although on the surface this question might seem simple, the fact that reading represents a complex skill set comprised of many subskills makes selecting a target a potentially involved task. Moreover, transactions between the student, the instruction, the tasks, and the learning environment suggest reading problems may be multifaceted, thus complicating the problem identification process. Consequently, the next step to developing an intervention is *problem analysis* which involves assessing both the student's skills and the context in which the student's reading problems occur.

Problem Analysis

The purpose of the second stage of the problem-solving model, problem analysis, is to gain a more in-depth understanding of the problem, so the team can develop a testable hypothesis and align intervention with individual need. The problem-solving team should examine existing student data, gather additional diagnostic data, and consider alterable instructional variables. The information should come from multiple data sources, including informal and formal tests, direct observations, and reports from teachers and other educators who have worked with the referred student (Christ & Aranas, 2014). In addition, it is important that the team incorporates knowledge of existing evidence-based reading interventions throughout the process. As a result of decades of rigorous and productive research aimed at improving reading outcomes for all students, particularly those with reading challenges, educators have access to research validated intervention programs that include well-developed scope and sequence of skills, assessment and instructional materials, and carefully designed teacher lesson plans with scripts and guidance for providing feedback and reteaching. Published intervention programs targeting a range of skills and levels are widely available (e.g., see National Center on Intensive Intervention, 2021). Just as a medical doctor considers multiple test results, patient reports and available treatments when making decisions with a patient, educators should have a good understanding of potential interventions in the context of student data during the problem analysis stage.

Review Existing Student Data

Educators arrive at the problem analysis stage for an individual student after examining screening or progress monitoring data. If fewer than approximately 20% of students in a school or classroom score below the screening benchmark, then the problem can be analyzed at the individual level. When it is an initial problem identified by screening results, teams start with limited data about the student's performance. For students who have been receiving intervention and are failing to make sufficient progress, teams typically have access to data from multiple sources, including screening, progress monitoring, and diagnostic data. Teams should begin the analysis process with a file review to determine what data are available and what are still needed.

Screening and progress monitoring data. Screening and progress monitoring data can be valuable sources of diagnostic information for use in analyzing a problem. Results from both types of assessments can show if there is a problem of accuracy and/or speed. For example, a student might read 90 words correct per minute with no errors on an oral reading fluency measure but fall below the benchmark of 135 words correct per minute. Another student with the same score of 90 words correct per minute might have made 15 errors. These data would help the team select an intervention aligned with an accuracy versus an accuracy and speed problem. Another way screening tools can provide diagnostic information is by illustrating which subskills within a domain a student has mastered and which are developing. For instance, phonological awareness screening assessments might measure onset sounds, rhyming, blending, and segmenting (Illuminate Education Inc., 2021; Sodoro et al., 2002). A student could meet the benchmark for onset rhymes and rhyming but fall below expected performance for blending and segmenting. The team could then target those two subskills in an intervention. Progress monitoring data can provide information about subskill mastery and development over time as well as show types of persistent errors in student performance. Several oral reading fluency progress monitoring probes might show a student's error pattern of meaning preserving mistakes on mostly phonetically regular multisyllabic words. This could suggest the student is relying too heavily on context and needs targeted intervention in multisyllabic word reading.

Placement tests and mastery monitoring data. In reviewing existing data, problem-solving teams might have access to placement test results and mastery monitoring data from core instruction and intervention programs. These results can provide valuable information about a student's acquisition of specific skills. For example, within the early reading intervention program *Sound Partners* (Vadasy, 1997), a placement test will show a student's level of acquisition on phonological awareness and phonics skills. A mastery test will demonstrate the student's acquisition of specific skills at the end of every unit or ten lessons. Examination of those test results could reveal a pattern of relative strengths and weaknesses, such as a student consistently reading phonic elements and decodable words correctly but making errors on irregular words.

Gather Additional Skill-based Data

Placement tests can also be used to gather additional data about a student's needs. A problem-solving team could give a placement test for an intervention or interventions aligned with the student's targeted skills to obtain data about skill level and intervention appropriateness. Imagine a team has screening information for a secondary student that indicates a problem in the domain of reading comprehension. Knowing the research validated Learning Strategies within the Strategic Instruction Model (University of Kansas Center for Research on Learning, n.d.) target a range of specific comprehension skills, such as finding the main idea, summarizing, and making inferences, the team could give placement tests for each of those strategies. The test results would indicate what specific skill instruction the student needs. During the problem analysis stage, the team may also decide a formal, standardized diagnostic assessment of a particular skill or skills is needed. For example, the Test of Phonological Awareness—2nd Edition: PLUS (TOPA-2+) (Torgesen & Bryant, 2004) would illustrate specific strengths and weaknesses in phonological awareness, and the CORE phonics assessment (Consortium on Reading Excellence, 2008) would show the student's acquisition of a range of phonic elements. At this stage in the problem analysis process, it is important to have team members with expertise in reading development, essential subskills and expected scope and sequence of instructional targets and skill acquisition to determine what additional information is needed to make the best possible decision regarding target skills.

Consider Instructional Variables

Several goals direct the assessment of the instructional environment, which serve to assist in problem analysis. First and foremost, assessment should help determine the extent to which classroom environmental factors are contributing to the student's reading challenges. Environmental variables found to influence learning include academic engaged time (e.g., scheduled and allotted time to learn, time on-task, frequent practice, opportunities to respond), arrangement of instruction and presentation of learning content (e.g., lesson begins with brief review of previous learning, presentation of new material, clear and detailed instructions), frequency and specificity of performance feedback, teacher management of behavior, classroom structure, and assessment methods (see Martens, Daly, Begeny, & VanDerHeyden, 2011; Rosenfield, 1987). Second, assessment should contribute to understanding the degree to which the student's reading problems represent a skill deficit (i.e., "can't do") or performance problem (i.e., "won't do"). A skill deficit implies the student does not have the specific reading skills being taught (i.e., inadequate mastery). A performance problem implies the student has the reading skills but does not use the skills consistently. Finally, assessment for reading problems should establish where in the curriculum the student has achieved proficiency. This assists in understanding whether the student's reading problems are a function of failing to master prerequisite skills.

Identifying relevant environmental variables (e.g., instructional, curricular) allows for a more thorough appreciation of the problem. Reading problems are often a function of the interaction between environmental variables and student-specific factors (see Shapiro, 2010). In addition to assessing the student's reading skills, a thoughtful evaluation of the instruction, frequency of performance feedback and reinforcement, and classroom organization is necessary to better understand the problem and design appropriate interventions.

As stated, the problem analysis stage requires educators to evaluate why a problem is occurring by considering alterable variables within the teaching and learning environment. Utilizing a framework to guide this level of analysis is imperative as it provides focus on important variables that can be changed by educators. One such framework is described by Daly and colleagues (1997). They illustrate a method of brief experimental analysis for choosing academic interventions based on a functional explanation of the skill deficits. This paradigm involves experimentally evaluating several different interventions by measuring their impact on student performance in specific skills in short-test conditions. Each intervention is designed to evaluate one of the following hypotheses: 1. The child does not want to do the task; 2. The child has not had enough practice to do the task; 3. The child has not had enough help to do the task; 4. The child has not had to do it that way before; 5. The task is too difficult. By manipulating each independent variable successively (i.e., incentive, practice, modeling, rehearsal and feedback, and task difficulty, respectively), while measuring the same dependent variable (e.g., oral reading fluency), and then replicating the results, the most successful intervention can be chosen for an individual student. The hypotheses are arranged in ascending order from least intrusive to most intrusive, and when tested in that succession, allow the interventionist to determine the most simple, effective intervention for the student. This framework allows educators to select promising interventions for individual students which then can be implemented over time.

Another useful framework comes from a recently published textbook in which Wanzek et al. (2019) describe eight critical intervention elements—those which have empirical evidence of positively impacting reading outcomes—that can be intensified within any reading intervention. This framework fits well within the problem analysis stage. The dimensions are categorized as organizational or instructional and listed below.

1. Organizational
   a. Time
   b. Group size
2. Instructional
   a. Explicit instruction
   b. Systematic instruction
   c. Opportunities for active student engagement
   d. Teacher feedback
   e. Cognitive processing strategies
   f. Support with transfer

Although there are several ways to adjust these elements, we offer just a couple of general examples for each. Time can be intensified by increasing the number of minutes within a session or the number of sessions per week. Group size is intensified when the student to teacher ratio decreases, which can be accomplished by reducing the total number of students within a group or adding an interventionist to the group. Explicit instruction within an intervention can be strengthened by making the description and demonstration of a reading skill or strategy more clear, coherent, and unambiguous than what is standard and by increasing the number and types of examples provided. A more systematic approach might involve providing students with additional incremental steps to master a complex skill and increasing the guidance and support needed to effectively practice, then gradually releasing them. Active student engagement can be intensified by increasing the total number, type (verbal, action and written; group, partner and individual), timing (throughout the session), and quality (direct alignment with the targeted skill) of opportunities for every student to respond within an intervention session. Teacher feedback can be adjusted by increasing the amount, immediacy, and specificity of positive and corrective feedback on student performance. Cognitive processing strategies, such as a mnemonic for remembering a set of steps or positive self-statements to support persistence and focus, can create a more intensive intervention. Explicit and systematic instruction and support (such as examples across materials or cue cards in other settings) for the transfer of a skill or strategy can also strengthen an intervention for an individual. Direct observation and teacher reports regarding student performance during reading instruction is important in thinking about what organizational and instructional variables might be prioritized and modified within an intervention. Teams should generate a hypothesis regarding student need for intensification in one or more of the eight dimensions and develop an intervention plan aligned with this hypothesis and the targeted skill(s) identified from the analysis of the skill-based data.

Plan Development

Progress Monitoring. Regular monitoring of students' reading performance has been linked to improved outcomes (Jung et al., 2018) and determining a progress monitoring schedule is a key step in plan development. Just as the intensity of intervention is matched to student need, so can the schedule for progress monitoring. At Tier 1, for schoolwide programming, universal benchmarking 3–4 times a year is appropriate for gauging the overall effectiveness of instruction and screening for students who may need additional intervention support. At Tier 2, when students are receiving strategic intervention, often in a small-group format, problem-solving teams should collect more data to ensure that students are making progress and resources are not being wasted on ineffective interventions. Tier 2 progress monitoring may occur monthly, bi-weekly, or weekly, depending on the resources of the system (i.e., personnel to collect the data), as well as the significance of the needs of the students. At Tier 3, where services are individualized to support students who demonstrate the highest level of need, even more progress monitoring data may be collected. Collecting data at least weekly can help teams quickly determine plan effectiveness and implement changes as needed.

Goal Setting. A variety of data sources may be considered by problem-solving teams to establish performance goals. Normative data, including local and national norms, provide information regarding the performance of same-age or same-grade comparison groups. Local norms offer valuable insight as to the performance of peers learning in the same context. While normative data do offer comparison points, local and national norms may not reflect the performance levels required for students to meet overall achievement goals. That is, a student may be performing at the 50th percentile as compared to local norms but, if the local norm is equivalent to performance well below an empirically derived benchmark, the student is not on track. Empirically derived benchmarks represent another important data source for goal setting and are based on a criterion- or competency-based approach to assessment. Research-based benchmarks are minimum scores that are predictive of successful future performance. In reading, Acadience Learning (Acadience Learning Inc., 2021) and Dynamic Indicators of Basic Early Literacy Skills (DIBELS; University of Oregon, 2020) are two examples of assessment tools with empirically derived benchmarks that can be used for goal setting.

Intervention goals should be ambitious. Typically, in the context of reading, the goal is for the student to "catch up," which requires an accelerated rate of learning. To help establish these expectations, teams should consider the typical rate of improvement (ROI) for expected benchmark scores. For example, to determine the typical ROI on a measure across the school year, you would subtract the beginning of year benchmark score from the end of year benchmark and divide by the number of weeks of school. To determine the ROI needed for the target student to meet the end of year benchmark, you would subtract their current level of performance (score) from the end of year benchmark and divide by the number of weeks left of instruction. These same calculations can be done for any given benchmark period (e.g., fall to winter, winter to spring). The resulting goal ROI can be used to create an aim line for progress, with this line being used to aid in evaluating student progress and adjusting intervention plans.

While ultimately the goal is for students to demonstrate performance at benchmark scores, if a student's skills deficits are significant, it may not be reasonable to expect them to meet goals in a benchmark period or academic year. That is, the ROI required for the student to meet the goal may be so high that even with the most intensive support, it may be unrealistic to expect that the student will meet the goal in a given time period. In situations such as this, teams may consider setting both short- and long-term goals, still establishing an accelerated ROI but also allowing the appropriate time for learning to occur.

Decision Rules. Decision rules can add accountability to the problem-solving process by setting predetermined guidelines for making decisions about when to intensify or modify an intervention based on a student's lack of progress or when to fade or remove intervention support when a student met the intervention goals. Decision rules can be based on time, trend estimation, or some combination of the two. An example of a time-based decision rule is "If the student has not met the goal after 12 weeks of intervention, the problem-solving team will meet and modify the intervention plan." Decision rules based on trend estimation would consider the ROI needed for the student to meet the goal in the form of an aim line on a graph of progress. The trend line of the student's actual progress is then compared to the aim line. An example decision rule is "If three data points fall below the aim line, the team will modify the intervention plan." Considering both time and ROI, another example of a decision rule is "If after at least 8 weeks of intervention, three progress monitoring points fall below the aim line, the team will consider changes to the intervention plan."

Detailed Intervention Scripts. Problem-solving teams can further support intervention plan development and implementation by creating detailed intervention scripts. First, detailing what exactly will be involved in each intervention session in a script ensures that everyone on the team understands the plan and can express questions and concerns that can be addressed before implementation. Second, the script can be used to support training for the person responsible for intervention implementation and can increase treatment fidelity. Next, the script can also be used as a checklist to be completed by the interventionist and/or by an observer to document treatment fidelity (discussed below). Finally, scripts can be saved as a resource to future problem-solving teams considering the same strategy, increasing the problem-solving efficiency of the system.

Treatment Fidelity. To determine whether or not an intervention plan has been successful, problem-solving teams first need to establish that the plan was implemented as planned. An important part of intervention planning is establishing methods and a schedule for collecting intervention adherence data. Both intervention adherence and treatment fidelity refer to the degree to which an intervention was implemented as intended. Methods for collecting adherence data include self-report on the part of the interventionist; direct observation of intervention sessions by a trained observer; and permanent products resulting from the sessions. Typically, self-reports and direct observations are documented by the individual noting the steps that were completed using a checklist of key steps included in the intervention. Observers may also rate the quality of implementation as well. Also, the frequency and duration of all intervention sessions should be documented as indicators of adherence to the intervention schedule or planned "does" of support. In determining how often adherence data are collected, teams may consider factors such as the experience of the interventionist, the complexity of the intervention plan, the significance of the skill deficit being addressed, among others. If an intervention is complicated and/or the interventionist is inexperienced with the methods, more adherence data may be needed initially, with the schedule thinning once the team is confident that the procedures can be followed accurately. For intense interventions, addressing significant skill deficits, a think schedule of monitoring adherence may be appropriate so efficient decision-making can occur, either continuing with the intervention as it is having the desired effect or moving on to an alternative intervention to increase the likelihood that the student makes progress and access effective services in a timely manner.

Monitoring Inter-observer or Inter-scorer Agreement. It is important for problem-solving teams to have confidence that decisions made based on progress monitoring data are valid. There are a few ways to increase this confidence. First, teams should select progress monitoring measures with reliability and validity evidence documented through prior research. Second, the team should be sure that those collecting the data have been properly trained on how to administer and score the particular measure being used. Training may occur through a variety of ways (formal university coursework as part of professional training, continuing education workshop, in-house professional development) but is important for ensuring that the data collected are accurate. In addition, monitoring the inter-scorer agreement of evaluators can establish the reliability of data collected throughout intervention implementation. During plan development, problem-solving teams should establish a schedule for collection such inter-rater agreement data, which involves having two individuals score the same assessment and compare their scores. In research, the minimum standard for collecting inter-observer or inter-scorer agreement is 20% of assessment sessions. This standard represents a starting point for teams to consider as they determine how much inter-scorer agreement data may be needed to establish confidence in the data, which may be more or less depending on a variety of factors similar to those that may be considered when determining the schedule for monitoring adherence, such as the experience of data collector and the significance/stakes of decisions to made based on the data.

Acceptability and Collaboration. Throughout plan development, it is important to gauge the acceptability of the strategies developed to vested partners, particularly the person who will ultimately be responsible for intervention implementation. Although treatment acceptability alone is not enough to ensure accurate implementation, engaging in collaborative intervention development can be a key to effective problem solving by the team. In addition, researchers have developed questionnaires such as the Usage Rating Profile-Intervention (URP-IR; Chafouleas et al., 2011) and Children's Usage Rating Profile (Briesch & Chafouleas, 2009) to evaluate factors including acceptability, understanding feasibility, family–school collaboration, system climate, and system support—all which impact intervention implementation. Ratings from the URP-IR or similar tools can help inform plan development and subsequent plan evaluation, offering critical insights when implementation issues arise.

Plan Evaluation

Visual Analysis

Visual analysis of time series graphs of student performance should be the primary approach to evaluating the effectiveness of the intervention plan. Graphs should include all progress monitoring data across baseline (pre-intervention) and intervention, with vertical phase change lines, indicating when intervention implementation began and any significant changes to the intervention plan. Graphs should also include an aim line of the target ROI needed to meet the goal, which should also be labeled on the graph. While such A-B accountability designs help teams make judgements regarding intervention effectiveness and student progress, it is important for teams to remember that they do not provide causal evidence and other factors, particularly any environmental changes that may have co-occurred with intervention implementation, may influence outcomes (Riley-Tillman et al., 2020).

As they examine the graphed reading performance data, problem-solving teams should consider the level, trend, and variability of the data (Riley-Tillman et al., 2020). First, the team is looking for the level of the data to increase, getting closer to the goal over time. Second, the trend of the data is particularly important as it relates to ROI. Ideally, the trend line of the data is consistent with, if not steeper than, the aim line, reflecting the accelerated ROI needed for the student to meet intervention goals. Finally, there should not be a great deal of variability, particularly in the intervention phase. Significant variability may be related to issues with the assessment, such as unreliable scoring or variable student effort/engagement, or issues related to treatment integrity, such as inconsistent implementation, among other factors that should be explored by the team. If performance data are not improving in level and/or not improving at the ROI needed to meet the goal, the team should rule out issues related to plan adherence and data reliability and then develop modifications to the existing plan or new intervention strategies to meet student needs more effectively.

Conclusion

The purpose of this chapter is to provide an overview of reading skill development and orient the reader to the problem-solving process that serves as the organizing structure for the case studies described in each of the remaining chapters. The purpose of this book is to provide school psychologists and other educational professionals with practical, real-world examples of how to implement reading interventions targeting problems with phonological awareness, phonics, fluency, vocabulary, and comprehension. This resource goes beyond descriptions of theory and research by providing step-by-step examples of how to implement evidence-based reading interventions in school settings. Vivid case examples illustrate all the necessary elements of effective academic interventions including rich descriptions of the specific area of concern, analysis of student and contextual variables in order to match the intervention to the problem, detailed intervention protocols, data collection and analysis methods, and tips for ensuring social acceptability and treatment integrity.

References

Acadience Learning Inc. (2021). *Benchmarks and composite scores*. Retrieved from https://acadiencelearning.org/wp-content/uploads/2021/11/Acadience-Reading-K-6-Benchmark-Goals-handout_2021_color.pdf

Albers, C. A., & Kettler, R. J. (2014). Best practices in universal screening. In P. L. Harrison & A. Thomas (Eds.), *Best practices in school psychology: Data-based and collaborative decision making* (pp. 121–131). Bethesda, MD: National Association of School Psychologists.

Briesch, A. M., & Chafouleas, S. M. (2009). *Children's usage rating profile (Actual)*. Storrs, CT: University of Connecticut.

Chafouleas, S. M., Briesch, A. M., Neugebauer, S. R., & Riley-Tillman, T. C. (2011). *Usage rating profile – Intervention (Revised)*. Storrs, CT: University of Connecticut.

Christ, T. J., & Aranas, Y. A. (2014). Best practices in problem analysis. *Best Practices in School Psychology V*, *2*, 159–176.

Consortium on Reading Excellence. (2008). Core phonics survey. In B. Honing, L. Diamond, & R. Nathan (Eds.), *Assessing reading: Multiple measures for kindergarten through eighth grade* (2nd ed., pp. 63–80). Novato, CA: Arena.

Daly III, E. J., Martens, B. K., Witt, J. C., & Dool, E. J. (1997). A model for conducting a functional analysis of academic performance problems. *School Psychology Review*, *26*(4), 554–574.

Deno, S. (2005). Problem-solving assessment. In R. Brown-Chidsey (Ed.), *Assessment for intervention: A problem-solving approach* (pp. 10–40). New York, NY: Guilford Press.

Deno, S. L., & Fuchs, L. S. (1987). Developing curriculum-based measurement systems for data-based special education problem solving. *Focus on Exceptional Children*, *19*, 1–16.

Every Student Succeeds Act, 20 U.S.C. § 6301. (2015). https://www.congress.gov/bill/114th-congress/senate-bill/1177

Fuchs, L. S. (2004). The past, present, and future of curriculum-based measurement research. *School Psychology Review*, *33*, 188–192.

Grapin, S. L., Waldron, N., & Joyce-Beaulieu, D. (2019). Longitudinal effects of RtI implementation on reading achievement outcomes. *Psychology in the Schools*, *56*, 242–254.

Hintz, J. M., Christ, T. J., & Methe, S. A. (2006). Curriculum-based assessment. *Psychology in the Schools*, *43*, 45–56.
Howell, K. W., & Hosp, J. L. (2014). Best practices in curriculum-based evaluation. In P. L. Harrison & A. Thomas (Eds.), *Best practices in school psychology: Data-based and collaborative decision making* (pp. 121–131). Bethesda, MD: National Association of School Psychologists.
Illuminate Education Inc. (2021). Psychometric evidence of FastBridge Universal Screening & Progress Monitoring System. Retrieved from https://www.illuminateed.com/wp-content/uploads/2021/07/Psychometric-Evidence-of-FastBridge-Universal-Screening-Progress-Monitoring-System-2021.pdf
January, S.A., & Klingbeil, D.A. (2020). Universal screening in grades K-2: A systematic review and meta-analysis of early reading curriculum-based measures. *Journal of School Psychology*, *83*, 103–122.
Jenkins, J. R., Hudson, R. F., & Johnson, E. S. (2007). Screening for service delivery in an RTI framework: Candidate measures. *School Psychology Review*, *36*, 560–582.
Jung, P. G., McMaster, K. L., Kunkel, A. K., Shin, J., & Stecker, P. M. (2018). Effects of data-based individualization for students with intensive learning needs: A meta-analysis. *Learning Disabilities Research & Practice*, *33*(3), 144–155.
Martens, B. K., Daly, E. J., Begeny, J. C., & VanDerHeyden, A. (2011). Behavioral approaches to education. In W. W. Fisher, C. C. Piazza, & H. S. Roane (Eds.), *Handbook of applied behavior analysis* (pp. 385–401). New York, NY: Guilford Press.
Mellard, D. F., McNight, M., & Woods, K. (2009). Response to intervention screening and progress monitoring practices in 41 local schools. *Learning Disabilities Practice*, *24*, 186–195.
National Center for Education Statistics. (2022). Students with Disabilities. *Condition of Education*. U.S. Department of Education, Institute of Education Sciences. Retrieved February 17, 2023, from https://nces.ed.gov/programs/coe/indicator/cgg
National Center on Intensive Intervention. (2021). Academic Intervention Tools Chart. U.S. Office of Special Education Programs. Retrieved from https://charts.intensiveintervention.org/aintervention?_ga=2.256797774.470499586.1676768926-711311827.1673633710
National Reading Panel. (2000). *Report of the National Reading Panel. Teaching children to read: An evidence-based assessment of the scientific research literature on reading and its implications for reading instruction*. Washington, DC: US Department of Health and Human Services.
Pluymert, K. (2014). Problem-solving foundations for school psychological services. In P. L. Harrison & A. Thomas (Eds.), *Best practices in school psychology: Data-based and collaborative decision making* (pp. 25–39). Bethesda, MD: National Association of School Psychologists.
Riley-Tillman, T. C., Burns, M. K., & Kilgus, S. P. (2020). *Evaluating educational interventions: Single-cased designs for measuring response to intervention*. New York, NY: Guilford Press.
Rosenfield, S. A. (1987). *Instructional consultation*. Hillsdale, NJ: Lawrence Erlbaum.

Scarborough, H. S. (2001). Connecting early language and literacy to later reading (dis)abilities: Evidence, theory, and practice. In S. Neuman & D. Dickinson (Eds.), *Handbook for research in early literacy* (pp. 97–110). New York, NY: Guilford Press.

Scheibel, G. (2023). Addressing barriers to evidence-based practice: Using evidence-based decision making and high leverage practices to meet student needs. *Teaching Exceptional Children*. https://doi.org/10.1177/00400599221143471

Shapiro, E. S. (2010). *Academic skills problems: Direct assessment and intervention* (4th ed.). New York, NY: Guilford Press.

Sodoro, J., Allinder, R. M., & Rankin-Erickson, J. L. (2002). Assessment of phonological awareness: Review of methods and tools. *Educational Psychology Review*, *14*, 223–260.

Swanson, H. L. (1999). Reading research for students with LD: A meta-analysis. *Journal of Learning Disabilities*, *32*, 504–532.

Torgesen, J. K., & Bryant, B. R. (2004). *Test of phonological awareness (PLUS)*. Austin, TX: Pro-Ed.

University of Kansas Center for Research on Learning. (n.d.). SIM: Strategic instruction model. Retrieved from https://sim.ku.edu/sim-instructional-tools-interventions

University of Oregon. (2020). *DIBELS 8th edition benchmark goals*. Retrieved from https://dibels.uoregon.edu/sites/dibels1.uoregon.edu/files/2021-06/DIBELS 8thEditionGoals.pdf

Vadasy, P. F., & Pool, K. (1997). *Sound Partners: A one-to-one tutoring program in phonological and early reading skills for first graders*. Seattle, WA: Washington Research Institute.

VanMeveren, K., Hulac, D., & Wollersheim-Shervy, S. (2020). Universal screening methods and models: Diagnostic accuracy of reading assessments. *Assessment for Effective Intervention*, *45*, 255–265.

Vaughn, S., Gersten, R., & Chard, D. J. (2000). The underlying message in LD intervention research: Findings from research syntheses. *Exceptional Children*, *67*, 99–114.

Wanzek, J., Al Otaiba, S., & McMaster, K. L. (2019). *Intensive reading interventions for the elementary grades*. New York, NY: Guilford Press.

2

ONSET-RIME, ALLITERATION, AND INCIDENTAL TEACHING

Kizzy Albritton

University of Texas at Austin, Austin, TX, USA

Lakeisha Johnson

Florida State University, Tallahassee, FL, USA

Introduction

There is overwhelming evidence outlining the importance of early literacy development during the preschool timeframe. Often referred to as emergent literacy skills (Whitehurst & Lonigan, 1998), these skills are multifaceted and include areas such as oral language, conventions of print, letter knowledge, phonological awareness, linguistic awareness, emergent writing, phonological memory, and rapid naming. Empirical research examining early literacy development has significantly increased over the last two decades with many studies developed in response to the seminal report by the National Early Literacy Panel (2009). In this report, researchers identified specific skills that have been found to be strongly associated with reading success in the later years. Specifically, researchers concluded that alphabet knowledge, phonological awareness, name writing, and phonological memory are strongly predictive of a child's ability to effectively decode, read fluently, comprehend written text, and successfully write and spell. As a result, researchers have significantly increased their efforts to improve children's skills in these areas, particularly in the area of phonological awareness.

Phonological awareness is an umbrella term that describes the awareness of the parts of spoken language at several levels: word, syllable, onset-rime, and phoneme. Whereas words and syllables are considered larger units of spoken language, phonemes are the smallest unit of sound that make a difference in a word's meaning. Skills in this area are foundational,

DOI: 10.4324/9781003275749-2

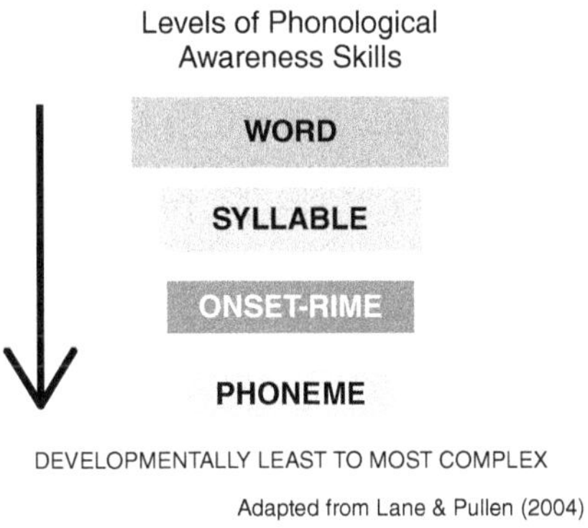

FIGURE 2.1 Levels of Phonological Awareness Skills

as they lead to strong decoding skills (Honig et al., 2018). While breaking words into syllables, rhyming, and alliteration (initial and final sound sorting) are some of the earliest phonological awareness skills children master, onset-rime and blending, segmenting, and deleting phonemes are more complex skills (known as phonemic awareness).

Many skills taught in early childhood classrooms utilize incidental teaching, a strategy that provides unstructured learning opportunities by following the child's lead and interests in the natural environment. Incidental teaching optimizes learning opportunities that occur naturally between the adult and the child. As learning is led by the child's interest, there is motivation to communicate, participate in activities, or practice new skills and behaviors. Utilizing principles of applied behavior analysis (ABA), the premise behind incidental teaching is that when a child uses a skill, and gets rewarded for it, they are more likely to do it again. As the skills are targeted in a wide range of natural environments (e.g., home, school, playground, etc.), they are more often generalized (McGee et al., 1999).

To maximize learning opportunities between the adult and child, several things must happen. First, the adult must follow the child's lead. This may mean going along with the object the child is currently playing with, or by identifying developmentally appropriate toys, materials, and objects that are motivating to the child. In turn, the child is more likely to continue engaging in the communicative interaction. Second, it is important that the adult has the child's attention before initiating or teaching a new skill that requires a response. Being face-to-face, at eye-level, may help ensure the child is attending. Third, having the adult arrange the environment is important as the activities are child-led. Placing the glue out of reach for an art project, or not offering a large enough portion, creates a natural opportunity for the child to make a request. Finally, repetition is imperative in incidental teaching as it allows for more interactions and communicative requests from the child (McGee et al., 1999).

Components of incidental teaching include watching and listening, engaging, waiting, supporting, and confirming. Through watching and listening, the adult can respond appropriately to the child's initiations for communication. Once the child initiates, the adult engages them by prompting them to elaborate leading to a contingent response (i.e., I do something, you do something). It is extremely important to give the child enough wait time to respond or demonstrate a behavior or action. At least five seconds of wait time are recommended so that the child processes the language used by the adult. Support the child, if necessary, by scaffolding, providing choices when there is no response or when the response is inappropriate or incorrect. Finally, the adult confirms the child's behavior or response through reassurance, praise, or a reward (Florida Atlantic University Center for Autism and Related Disabilities, n.d.). Figure 2.2 demonstrates an example of the incidental teaching strategy to help a child request more.

One particular intervention that may assist children's acquisition of rhyming and alliteration skills is Read It Again! PreK (RIA; Justice & McGinty, 2008). RIA is a supplemental early language and literacy intervention developed for use with preschool-age children. RIA may be delivered in a whole-class format or in small groups and is available at no cost to educational professionals (https://crane.osu.edu/our-work/read-it-again/). Self-study materials and videos are also freely available to assist educators in effectively implementing RIA. Materials are also available in Spanish, Danish, and French indicating its feasibility for use with young children from culturally and linguistically diverse backgrounds.

The entire intervention package includes a total of 60 lessons that span four domains and include both language-based (vocabulary and narrative domains) and code-based skills (print knowledge and phonological awareness domains). For the purposes of the current case study, the teacher utilized lessons from the phonological awareness domain since these lessons focused on skills that supported students' rhyming and alliteration. Each lesson is approximately 20 minutes in length and includes a script that may be used to assist in the delivery of the intervention. Teachers are also provided with recommendations to scaffold lessons to accommodate students who have varying needs (i.e., more support or less support). Teachers are encouraged to use the eliciting, co-participating, or reducing choices strategies when children are having difficulty with a particular skill and use the

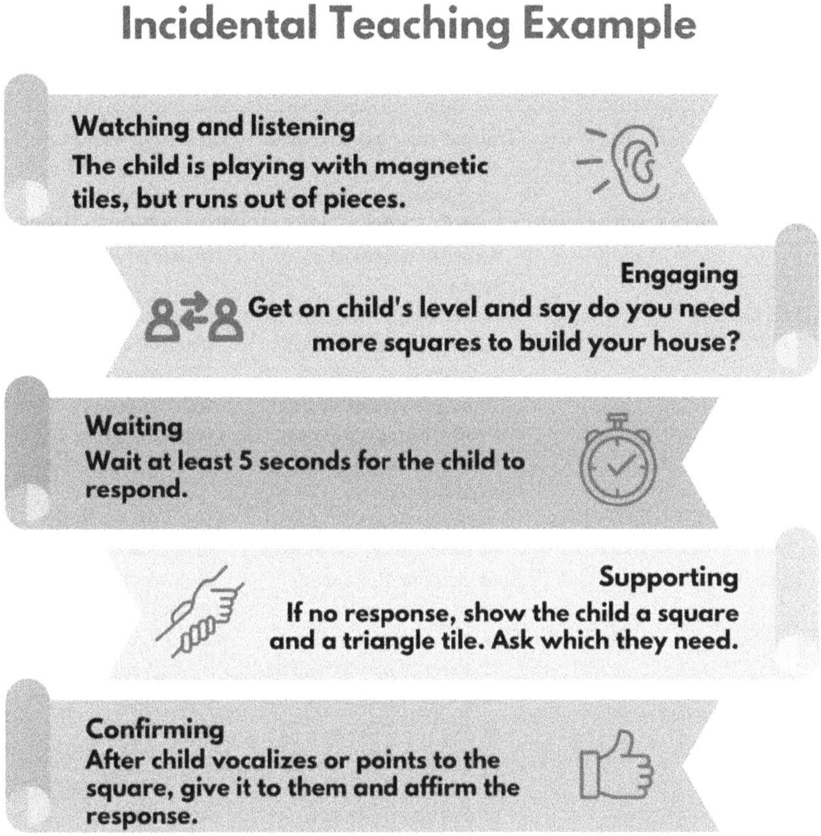

FIGURE 2.2 Incidental Teaching Example

reasoning, generalizing, and predicting strategies when a particular skill is too easy. Table 2.1 provides a description and example of each strategy.

Several studies (e.g., Albritton et al., 2018; Bleses et al., 2018; Justice et al., 2010; Mashburn et al., 2016; Piasta et al., 2020) have examined the efficacy of RIA with a range of students from varying backgrounds (e.g., students from economically marginalized backgrounds, students with disabilities, students from rural backgrounds). Using a quasi-experimental design, Justice et al. (2010) implemented RIA with 137 preschool-age children and 20 early childhood professionals across 11 experimental and 9 control classrooms. Results indicated that children who received RIA demonstrated better performance on early language and literacy outcomes (i.e., vocabulary, phonological awareness, and print awareness) than students who did not receive the intervention. Bleses et al. (2018) implemented

TABLE 2.1 Scaffolding Strategies Suggested in the Read It Again! – PreK Curriculum

Strategy	*Type of Strategy*	*Description*	*Example*
Reasoning	Too Easy	Teacher may ask children to provide an explanation regarding why something happened or will happen.	*These two words do not rhyme. Why do you think it is important to learn about rhyming?*
Generalizing	Too Easy	Teacher may ask children to provide additional information about a topic presented in the lesson using a past or future personal experience.	*On yesterday, we discussed rhymes. Do you remember what it means when words rhyme?*
Predicting	Too Easy	Teacher may ask children to offer their description of what will happen next.	*What do you think they will see when they arrive to their grandparents' house?*
Eliciting	Too Hard	Teacher may provide children with the correct response in an effort to provide a model.	*What rhymes with man? Can rhymes with man. Tell me: man, can.*
Co-participating	Too Hard	Teacher demonstrates the correct response by allowing children to complete the task with another individual (e.g., teacher or classmate).	*Man and can rhyme. Let's say it together: man, can.*
Reducing choices	Too Hard	Teacher reduces the number of choices available to assist children identifying or providing the correct response.	*What rhymes with man? Let's see – can, boat, ran – which two rhymed?*

Note: Strategies adapted from Notari-Syverson et al. (2007).

a modified version of RIA with approximately 5,300 children in Danish preschools. Educators used RIA to provide small-group instruction and children who received RIA exhibited stronger phonological awareness and letter knowledge when compared to children who did not receive RIA small group instruction.

Case Study

Impact Preschool is a public preschool program supporting young children between the ages of 3 and 5. The school district recognized the need to provide preventative and early intervention support to young children and families and established the public preschool program approximately five years ago. The program is housed within one of the larger and centrally located elementary schools within the school district and due to 5-star quality ratings from the state's department of education, the program has seen a tremendous increase in enrollment over the last two years. Current enrollment numbers range between 50–60 students each academic year, with class sizes ranging from 18 to 20 students and two teachers per classroom (lead teacher and assistant teacher). Given the demand, the school district is considering the opening of another early childhood program. All teachers are provided with multiple professional development opportunities throughout the school year.

Given the program's focus on prevention, as well as early intervention, special education services are also available to students and their families. Students receiving early intervention special education services have an individualized education plan (IEP) that allows teachers and parents to develop annual goals and objectives, as well as monitor progress towards those goals and objectives. The early childhood program also has a dedicated school psychologist, a speech-language pathologist, and an occupational therapist. The early childhood program implemented tiered frameworks to ensure all students' academic, social-emotional, and behavioral needs were being met. During the previous academic year, school personnel began closely monitoring students' early literacy development, as all agreed they could be doing more to support these foundational skills. This decision was in response to a new state-wide kindergarten readiness assessment that all students must complete prior to kindergarten entry. This decision was also influenced by data from the school district's report card indicating that a large percentage of kindergarten children were not considered "on track" based on district benchmarking. By increasing the focus on students' early literacy development during the preschool years and providing appropriate early intervention, fewer children will enter kindergarten exhibiting early literacy difficulties.

It was mid-November and Ms. Baker was leading her 4-year-old class in a large group lesson on identifying the first sound in a word. For the past several weeks, the class received several lessons regarding letter-sound correspondence and Ms. Baker provided many practice opportunities. Several of the students were demonstrating appropriate progress in their ability to identify all 26 letters of the alphabet and orally indicate the corresponding sounds for each letter. However, Ms. Baker noticed that while some students are able to identify the letters of the alphabet, many demonstrated some difficulty with orally providing the correct letter sound. As a result, the students were also demonstrating some difficulty in initial sound fluency and orally providing words that have the same onset and rime. She tried teaching alliteration in fun ways, such as songs and silly tongue twisters to help improve their sound awareness. For example, she asked the class what is the first sound we hear in each word: Pat picked peppers. Several students had difficulty segmenting the /p/ sound in the initial position of each word. Additionally, she was concerned that when she reads books or sings songs with lots of rhyming, there are a few students who are unable to generate additional rhyming words. Ms. Baker understood how important letter-sound correspondence, rhyming, and understanding of alliteration are to developing more complex phonological awareness skills, so she met with the school-based problem-solving team to share her concerns about the class progress. Since the school-based problem-solving team had been in place for quite some time and Ms. Baker was familiar with the process, she gathered several data points for the team to review when she met. These data included performance on letter identification, letter-sound correspondence, initial-sound detection, and onset-rime tasks. Ms. Baker was looking forward to teaching other more complex phonological awareness skills like segmenting and blending but did not want to move ahead too quickly for those who were struggling.

Problem Identification

At the onset-rime level, the first skills to develop are recognizing, generating, and categorizing rhymes (Honig et al., 2018). In the classroom, recognizing rhymes may show up as giving children a pair of words and then determining whether they rhyme or play rhyming bingo (Listen to these pairs of words and tell me if they rhyme: *bat, cat; fin, fan; rock, lock*). Next, children may be asked to generate rhymes on their own. For example, when singing *Down by the Bay*, children could fill in the ending rhyming word of the lyric (Did you ever see a bear, combing his *hair*). Teachers could also gather objects or pictures in a basket and have each child pull out an item and come up with a word that rhymes with it. When categorizing rhymes, children have to determine the word that does not fit when given a set of words (Tell me which word does not belong with the others: *boot, hoot, hook*).

More complex onset-rime skills include blending and segmenting (Honig et al., 2018). The onset of a word is the initial sound (e.g., /m/ in *man*) and the rime is the sounds that follow, which are usually a vowel and final

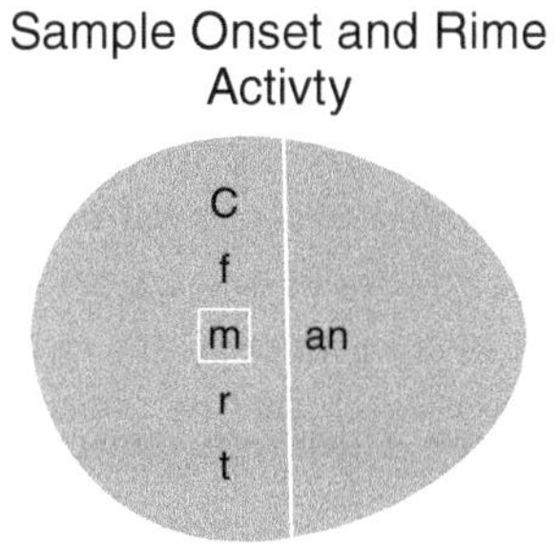

FIGURE 2.3 Sample Onset and Rime Activity

consonant (/an/ in *man*). Teaching this skill is foundational, as it allows children to recognize word families and common chunks within words. Children can blend onset and rime by putting together two units of sound (e.g., When you put /s/ and /un/ together, it makes…*sun*). When segmenting, children are given the whole word and then asked to segment it into onset and rime (Let's break apart the word *push* into two big parts - /p/…/ush/) (Reading Rockets, 2022). Additional onset and rime activities include creating word sorts where children have to categorize words that have the same rime and writing a rime on one side of an Easter egg and several onset options on the other side of the egg to make complete words (see Figure 2.3).

Just like rhyming, alliteration also helps children practice word awareness and listening skills. Alliteration tasks help children understand the links between letters and sounds and is one of the first skills acquired in phonemic awareness. In the classroom, an alliteration task could be identifying the initial sound in silly phrases (e.g., *Bob bakes biscuits*) or playing I Spy, and children have to find items that start with the same initial sound (e.g., I Spy something that begins with the /b/ sound just like Bobby's name—*board*).

Research has shown that 80–90% of typically developing children enjoy rhyme and alliteration activities by age 4, while they are able to recognize rhyme and determine words that do not rhyme by age 5. By age 5½, children are able to blend onset and rime, generate rhymes, and match or isolate initial sounds in words (Moats & Tolman, 2009).

Members of the school-based problem-solving team included Ms. Baker, the speech-language pathologist, the school psychologist, and the director of the early childhood program. During the meeting, the team discussed the class-wide early literacy curriculum currently in use across all preschool classrooms. The team also discussed any potential social-emotional and/or behavioral difficulties that could be impacting students' performance. Ms. Baker indicated that the current early literacy curriculum has been effective in previous years; however, she believed that her current students appeared to need some additional support given interruptions to their educational experiences caused by the COVID-19 pandemic. Additionally, Ms. Baker explained her current classroom management system and indicated that most students are demonstrating developmentally appropriate social-emotional and behavioral skills within the classroom. Lastly, Ms. Baker reviewed the results of her initial data collection which further support her concerns regarding students' phonological awareness skills, particularly in the areas of rhyming, alliteration, onset-rime, and letter-sound correspondence. After an extensive discussion of potential intervention programs, the school-based problem-solving team recommended that Ms. Baker implement a class-wide intervention to further support students' phonological awareness skills at all developmental levels. The team recommended the Read It Again! -PreK (RIA) curriculum given its strong research evidence base and free accessibility to educators. All teachers received an 8-hour training on the curriculum at the beginning of the school year. The training included an opportunity for teachers to practice implementation of individual lessons and receive feedback from training facilitators. Overall, initial feedback from teachers regarding the RIA training was very positive with most teachers commenting on the ease of use and how quickly they could get through the lessons daily, as they only take about 20 minutes. Although the curriculum includes multiple domains, Ms. Baker will focus on providing lessons that allow her to focus on students' phonological awareness skills. The school-based problem-solving team also recommended that Ms. Baker begin collecting baseline data on all students' performance to establish current levels of functioning.

Problem Analysis

Given Ms. Baker's concerns about students' phonological awareness skills, particularly in the areas of rhyming, alliteration, and letter-sound correspondence, she decided to utilize the results of the school-wide universal screening data analysis to better understand the difference between their current levels of performance in relation to their expected levels of performance. Several years ago, the school's leadership team had an opportunity to receive professional development regarding the implementation of tiered frameworks. The school also received ongoing technical assistance from several professors in the local university's College of Education as they implemented a tiered framework in their school building. After extensive research and meetings with teachers and parents, the leadership team selected the Individual Growth and Development Indicators (myIGDIs; McConnell et al., 2013), as the universal screening measure to progress monitor students' early literacy development. The myIGDIs subtests are administered to all preschool students during the Fall, Winter, and Spring of each academic year. All subtests are administered one-on-one and administrations typically last approximately 10–15 minutes for each child. The early literacy myIGDIs includes five measures: Picture Naming, Rhyming, Alliteration, Sound ID, and "Which One Doesn't Belong". Given Ms. Baker's concerns regarding students' phonological awareness skills, she decided to focus on data from the Rhyming, Alliteration, and Sound ID subtests from the myIGDIs. On the Rhyming subtest, students are presented a stimulus of different pictures and must select the two pictures that represent the pair of rhyming words. On the Alliteration, subtest students must name the picture that has the same first sound provided by the examiner (e.g., *fan, dog—which one starts with the /f/ sound*?). The Sound ID subtest requires students to point to the letter that matches the sound provided by the examiner (e.g., *which one makes the /b/ sound*?). The students' expected level of performance was determined using the age-based norms provided within the myIGDIs administration manual.

Measurement of Target Reading Skill, Data Collection Strategies, and Progress Monitoring

Members of the school-based problem-solving team along with Ms. Baker met to review the data from the Fall and Winter administrations of the Rhyming, Alliteration, and Sound ID subtests. The team used the recommendations outlined by the publisher to assess students' performance. Specifically, students who scored in the Tier 2/3 cut range were deemed as in need of additional support. After review of the classroom data, approximately 53% of students' scores were in the Tier 2/3 cut range for the Rhyming subtest, 57% for the Alliteration subtest, and 51% for the Sound ID subtest further indicating the need for class-wide intervention.

Since RIA had been selected as the class-wide intervention, the school-based problem-solving team discussed potential data collection strategies that could be used to monitor students' progress during intervention implementation. Progress monitoring during intervention implementation is important as it serves as an indicator of intervention effectiveness. The discussion regarding data collection strategies included the importance of a brief measure that could be easily administered to students and that aligned with the targeted reading skills (i.e., rhyming and alliteration). The RIA intervention provides two tools that can be used to monitor students' progress: the pupil progress checklist and implementation notes. While both tools can be beneficial, they each have limitations. The pupil progress checklist is designed for use three times during the academic year and therefore is not intended to be used as a continuous progress monitoring tool. Furthermore, although the implementation notes are designed for use after each lesson to allow teachers to make qualitative observations about the lesson and how well students responded to the lesson, it is not designed to quantitatively measure students' performance.

Given these limitations and the need for continuous and proximal progress monitoring probes, the school psychologist and speech pathologist conducted a review of the existing research literature to determine the availability of probes designed to briefly measure preschool students' rhyming and alliteration skills. Previous studies indicated the use of probes specifically designed for the intervention. Therefore, the school psychologist, speech pathologist, and classroom teacher collaborated to create alliteration and rhyming probes using a pool of 48 CV, CVC, or VC words. Twelve word sets were created for the rhyming probes and twelve word sets were created for the alliteration probes using the pool of 48 words. Each word set included eight words (alliteration) and eight sets of pictures (rhyming). This process was consistent with previous research involving preschool-age children and examining the effectiveness of interventions targeting phonological awareness skills (e.g., Koutsoftas et al., 2009). Probes were administered by Ms. Baker, the school psychologist and/or speech pathologist to all students once per week for two weeks prior to the start of the intervention, once per week during intervention implementation, and once per week for two weeks post intervention. This allowed the school-based problem-solving team to collect baseline, intervention, and maintenance data for all students in the classroom.

The team also decided it would be important to have a distal measure of students' progress and agreed that the school psychologist would administer the Print Knowledge and Phonological Awareness subtests from Test of Preschool Early Literacy (TOPEL; Lonigan et al., 2007) to all preschool students in Ms. Baker's class prior to the start of the RIA intervention and once again at the end of the academic year. The TOPEL is a norm-referenced, standardized assessment designed to measure areas deemed to be critical for early literacy development (i.e., print knowledge, vocabulary, and phonological awareness). The TOPEL can be administered to young children between the ages of 3 years, 0 months to 5 years, 11 months. The Print Knowledge subtest includes 36 items and measures children's alphabet knowledge and understanding of print language conventions. The Phonological Awareness subtest includes 27 items and measures children's ability to blend and segment parts of words. Since Ms. Baker's concerns and the intervention were primarily focused on students' rhyming and alliteration, the team decided that the Definitional Vocabulary subtest of the TOPEL would not be administered to students.

Intervention Plan

After discussing the selected intervention and progress monitoring measure, Ms. Baker collaborated with the school-based problem-solving team to develop an intervention plan for the students in her classroom. When developing the intervention plan, the team discussed target goals for the class. These goals were based on students' current levels of performance (i.e., the results from the myIGDIs Rhyming, Alliteration, and Sound ID subtests), as well as expected benchmarks for the students at this time of year.

Since the results of the Fall and Winter administrations of the Rhyming and Alliteration subtest revealed that students were performing in the Tier 2/3 range, the short-term goal was for each student to increase their score by 25%. This goal was selected since "a short-term improvement of 25% would demonstrate strong initial progress" (Newman & Rosenfield, 2019, p. 108). A 25% increase in improvement would also potentially move most students out of the Tier 2/3 range to the "cut range" indicating that students are making moderate progress but additional information and/or support may be needed.

Ms. Baker provided class-wide supplemental language and literacy instruction using phonological awareness lessons from the RIA. Ms. Baker implemented a total of ten sequential lessons from the curriculum two times per week, across a 5-week period. She implemented each lesson as outlined, while also providing the necessary scaffolding and differentiation. For example, when Ms. Baker observed that some students in the class needed more support during a lesson, she used the eliciting strategy. She began by providing two words that rhyme and asked the student to repeat the two words ("paw" and "jaw"). She then provided two words that did not rhyme and asked the student to repeat those words ("paw" and "corn"). Conversely, Ms. Baker noticed that a few students were demonstrating a strong level of competency in identifying words that rhyme. In this instance, she asked students to refer to another rhyming activity that occurred during the day and asked what other times the student heard rhyming words. Each lesson included a shared book-reading opportunity which provided students a chance to practice the rhyming and alliteration skills taught during the lesson of the day. She used the incidental teaching strategy during the shared reads to allow children to have more opportunities to practice skills. For example, when reading *Even Superheroes Have*

Bad Days, each child had to come up with an adjective that described their personality and started with the same initial sound in their name (e.g., Patient Payton, Quick Quinton). Additionally, Ms. Baker used rhyming books like *Chicka Chicka Boom Boom* to select words from the text to separate into onset and rime. She supported children who needed scaffolding by providing wait time and choices. The incidental teaching strategy was especially helpful for her students whose IEP focused on increasing conversational turns, making requests, and improving overall expressive language skills.

Intervention Fidelity and Interobserver Agreement Plans

Members of the school-based problem-solving team collaborated with Ms. Baker to develop an intervention fidelity checklist that was used to monitor the fidelity of implementation for each lesson. Copies of the intervention fidelity checklist were placed in a binder so that they could be easily accessed by Ms. Baker. Prior to the beginning of the lesson, Ms. Baker placed a copy of the checklist next to her lesson plans materials so that it was visible. At the end of each lesson, Ms. Baker completed the checklist as the students in the class assisted with putting away materials and transitioned to the next activity for the day. Additionally, the speech-language pathologist and the problem-solving team lead, conducted classroom observations on 20% of the intervention lessons conducted by Ms. Baker. The speech-language pathologist and the team lead used the same intervention fidelity checklist as Ms. Baker. Intervention fidelity was calculated by dividing the number intervention steps completed by the total number of steps on the fidelity checklist. This number was then multiplied by 100. Intervention fidelity for Ms. Baker was 91%. Inter-observer agreement for the speech pathologist and the team lead was calculated by dividing the number of agreements between each observer by the number of disagreements plus agreements. This number was then multiplied by 100. Inter-observer agreement was 93%.

Intervention Outcome Data

Continuous progress monitoring of students' performance revealed that most students demonstrated an increase in their performance from baseline to the end of the intervention as measured by the progress monitoring probes for rhyming and alliteration. For example, the highest number of correct items for each probe was eight. During baseline, most students were only able to correctly answer two items; however, by the end of the intervention, most students answered six items correctly, with some students occasionally answering all eight items correctly. Additionally, most students were able to maintain their performance once the intervention concluded.

The school-based problem-solving team also analyzed students' performance on the Spring administration of the myIGDIs Rhyming, Alliteration, and Sound ID subtests. Data revealed that only 10% of students in Ms. Baker's class had scores in the Tier 2/3 range which means that 90% of students were now performing in the Tier 1 range. The team agreed that students performing in the Tier 2/3 range would now be recommended for additional early literacy support in a small group setting. The school psychologist also reviewed the results of students' performance on the Print Knowledge and Phonological Awareness subtests of the TOEL. Overall, although there was some increase in standard scores from the Fall to the Spring, this increase was not statistically significant, which was expected given the lack of sensitivity in norm-referenced measures administered within the same academic year. During the Fall administration, the mean standard score on the Print Knowledge subtest was 91 and during the spring the mean standard score was 95. On the Phonological Awareness subtest, the mean standard score in the Fall was 85 and the mean standard score in the Spring was 90. Since there were students in Ms. Baker's class who continued to perform in the Tier 2/3 range on the myIGDIs, the team conducted a closer review of their performance on the TOPEL subtests. This review indicated that these students also demonstrated difficulty on the Phonological Awareness subtest with standard scores in the below average range further suggesting the need for additional early literacy support.

Intervention Acceptability

The school-based problem-solving team discussed the importance of measuring the acceptability of RIA to assess its long-term feasibility as an intervention to improve students' overall phonological awareness skills, specifically in the areas of rhyming and alliteration, but also later foundational skills such as blending and segmenting phonemes. The team selected the Intervention Rating Profile (IRP-15; Martens et al., 1985) to measure Ms. Baker's perceptions of the acceptability and effectiveness of RIA for the students in her classroom. The IRP-15 is a 15-item measure and items are arranged on a 6-point Likert scale, with 1 indicating strongly disagree and 6 indicating strongly agree. Internal consistency for the IRP-15 is .98. Ms. Baker completed the IRP-15 prior to implementing the RIA curriculum and after the intervention period concluded. Pre-intervention ratings on the IRP-15 was 92.29 and post-intervention ratings were 105. Scores within the range of 84–126 suggest moderate to high levels of acceptability. Therefore, these numbers indicated that Ms. Baker had positive perceptions of the RIA curriculum prior to implementation and those perceptions remained consistent after the implementation of the intervention. Ms. Baker also provided qualitative feedback to the school-based problem-solving team regarding her perceptions of the RIA intervention. Ms. Baker noted the following, "I am really surprised by how easy it was to implement the RIA curriculum. It was extremely helpful to have all teachers attend the training prior to the beginning of the school year. I also appreciated that I could consult with members of the school-based problem-solving team if I had any specific questions related to a lesson. I think the students also found the intervention to be very fun and engaging."

Intervention Considerations

Although the availability of early literacy interventions has slightly increased over the last decade, selecting an intervention may still pose several challenges for preschool programs. Therefore, there are several important items to consider. First, it is critical that the selected intervention is targeting the skill area that has been identified as an area of need. In this particular case study, the targeted skill areas were onset sounds, rhyming, and alliteration. When the school-based problem-solving team selected RIA as the intervention, they conducted a thorough review of the materials to confirm that these skill areas would be the focus of the lessons provided to students. Next, it is important to consider the extent to which the intervention has been used with students who have the same and/or similar racial, ethnic, cultural, linguistic, and socioeconomic backgrounds. One of the many reasons that RIA was selected was due to research indicating its use with students from an array of diverse backgrounds. Finally, it is important to consider the cost of the program and feasibility of use. RIA is freely available to the public, is supported by training for those implementing the lessons, and contains several fidelity measures. It is vital for early childhood programs to ensure they are utilizing evidence-based programs that have a strong record of impacting academic outcomes.

Conclusion

The preschool timeframe is a prime opportunity to provide young children with the skills and knowledge needed to enter kindergarten with a strong early literacy foundation so that they may become successful readers in their later academic years. Ensuring that young children have the appropriate skills and knowledge to become successful readers requires collaboration among all school personnel, specifically teachers, speech pathologists, and school psychologists, since each individual holds unique expertise. Phonological awareness has been shown to be a strong predictor of later reading success. It is not just a single skill, but an umbrella term that describes the skills needed at the word, syllable, onset-rime, and phoneme level. This case study illustrated the use of a free and evidence-based class-wide intervention designed to improve young children's early language and literacy development. Within the case study, the teacher was able to implement lessons that specifically targeted students' rhyming and alliteration, which is a precursor to later developing phonological awareness skills, like phoneme segmenting (breaking words into smaller sound units) and blending (putting sounds together). Findings from the National Reading Panel (2000) informed us that segmenting and blending phonemes are the most critical skills needed when learning to read and spell. Utilizing developmentally appropriate tools like RIA and myIGDIs allow early childhood teams to lay the foundation for later reading success.

Appendix A: Intervention Fidelity Checklist Example

Lesson 1
Teacher Name: ______________________________
Date of Lesson: ______________________________
IOA: Yes No 2nd Observer: ______________________

Lesson Components	*Completed (1)*	*Did not complete (0)*
Teacher introduces activity (For example, teacher says "**Today we are going to listen to the first sound in a word. Most words are made up of many sounds. See if you can hear the first sound in these words.**")		
Teacher shows picture card for fan and tells children: **fffan. Fan begins with the sound ffff. Listen, did you hear the sound ffff in the beginning of fan?**		
Teacher shows picture card for five and tells children: **fffive. Five begins with the sound ffff. Listen, did you hear the sound ffff in the beginning of five?**		
Teacher shows picture card for phone and tells children: **ffffone. Phone begins with the sound ffff. Listen, did you hear the sound ffff in the beginning of phone?**		

Lesson Components	*Completed (1)*	*Did not complete (0)*
Teacher introduces words that begin the with the /mmm/ sound. For example, teacher says: **Now we are going to listen to words that begin with the mmmm sound.**		
Teacher shows picture card for mess and tells children:		
mmmess. Mess begins with the sound mmmm. Listen, did you hear the sound mmm in the beginning of mess?		
Teacher shows picture card for mouse and tells children:		
mmmouse. Mess begins with the sound mmmm. Listen, did you hear the sound mmm in the beginning of mouse?		
Teacher shows picture card for moon and tells children:		
mmmoon. Moon begins with the sound mmmm. Listen, did you hear the sound mmm in the beginning of moon?		
Teacher holds all of the picture cards in hand. Teacher gives each student an opportunity to pick a card and say the word.		
Teacher then repeats the word and asks students "**What sound does _____ start with?** If children are unable to identify the first sound, teacher models the correct answer. For example, **mmmooon starts with mmmm.**		
Teaching Practices	Observed (1)	Did not observe (0)
Teacher engages students in discussion (makes eye contact, responds to students' questions and answer)		
Students respond to questions and contribute to discussion.		
Teacher is well-prepared (has all materials or appropriate alternatives).		
Lesson pace is appropriate.		

Total Points Earned________/Total Points Possible_______=_______*100 =
____

Appendix B: Intervention Fidelity Checklist Example

Lesson 12
Teacher Name: ________________________________
Date of Lesson: ________________________________
IOA: Yes No 2nd Observer: ________________________

Lesson Components	*Completed (1)*	*Did not complete (0)*
Teacher reminds students that words are made up of many parts (For example, teacher says "**Remember, words are made up of many sounds. You can try to listen for the sounds in words. Like the word fffan. Do you hear the first sound in fffan? What do you hear? That's right! Fffan starts with the fff sound.**		
Teacher tells the children: **Let's play a game. Let's see if you can think of words that start with the same sound as your name.**		
Teacher allows student to say a word that the starts with the same sound as his or her name. Teacher may have to help children identify the first sound of their names. (**Ex. Raymond, your name starts with the rrrr sound. Tell me another word that starts with the rrr sound. That's right! Red and Raymond share the same first sound.**)		
Teacher allows student to say a word that the starts with the same sound as his or her name. Teacher may have to help children identify the first sound of their names. (**Ex. Raymond, your name starts with the rrrr sound. Tell me another word that starts with the rrr sound. That's right! Red and Raymond share the same first sound.**)		
Teacher allows student to say a word that the starts with the same sound as his or her name. Teacher may have to help children identify the first sound of their names. (**Ex. Raymond, your name starts with the rrrr sound. Tell me another word that starts with the rrr sound. That's right! Red and Raymond share the same first sound.**)		

Lesson Components	*Completed (1)*	*Did not complete (0)*
Teacher allows student to say a word that the starts with the same sound as his or her name. Teacher may have to help children identify the first sound of their names. **(Ex. Raymond, your name starts with the rrrr sound. Tell me another word that starts with the rrr sound. That's right! Red and Raymond share the same first sound.)**		
Teaching Practices	Observed (1)	Did not observe (0)
Teacher engages students in discussion (makes eye contact, responds to students' questions and answer)		
Students respond to questions and contribute to discussion.		
Teacher is well-prepared (has all materials or appropriate alternatives).		
Lesson pace is appropriate.		

Total Points Earned________/Total Points Possible_______=_______*100 = ____________________________

References

Albritton, K., Patton Terry, N., & Truscott, S. D. (2018). Examining the effects of performance feedback on preschool teachers' fidelity of implementation of a small-group phonological awareness intervention. *Reading & Writing Quarterly*, *34*, 361–378. doi:10.1080/10573569.2018.1456990

Bleses, D., Højen, A., Justice, L. M., Dale, P. S., Dybdal, L., Piasta, S. B., ... & Haghish, E. F. (2018). The effectiveness of a large-scale language and preliteracy intervention: The spell randomized controlled trial in Denmark. *Child Development*, *89*, 342–363. doi:10.1111/cdev.12859

Florida Atlantic University Center for Autism and Related Disabilities (n.d.). *Fact sheet – Incidental teaching*. Retrieved December 1, 2022 from https://www.fau.edu/education/centersandprograms/card/documents/incidentalteaching.pdf

Honig, B., Diamond, L., & Gutlohn, L. (2018). *Teaching reading sourcebook*. Oakland, CA; Core & Novato, CA: Arena Press.

Justice, L. M., McGinty, A. S., Cabell, S. Q., Kilday, C. R., Knighton, K., & Huffman, G. (2010). Language and literacy curriculum supplement for preschoolers who are academically at risk: A feasibility study. *Language, Speech, and Hearing Services in Schools*, *41*, 161–178.

Justice, L., & McGinty, A. (2008). *Read It Again–PreK!*. Preschool Language and Literacy Lab. Columbus, OH: Ohio State University.

Koutsoftas, A., Harmon, M., & Gray, S. (2009). The effect of tier 2 intervention for phonemic awareness in a response-to-intervention model in low-income preschool classrooms. *Language, Speech & Hearing Services in Schools*, *40*, 116–130. doi:10.1044/0161-1461(2008/07-0101)

Lonigan, C. J., Wagner, D. A., & Torgesen, J. K. (2007). *Test of Preschool Early Literacy (TOPEL)*. Austin, TX: Pro-Ed.

Mashburn, A. J., Justice, L. M., McGinty, A., & Slocum, L. (2016). The impacts of a scalable intervention on the language and literacy development of rural pre-kindergartners. *Applied Developmental Science*, *20*, 61–78. doi:10.1080/10888691.2015.1051622

Martens, B. K., Witt, J. C., Elliott, S., & Darveaux, D. (1985). Teacher judgments concerning the acceptability of school based interventions. *Professional Psychology: Research and Practice*, *16*, 191–198.

McConnell, S., Bradfeld, T., Wackerle-Hollman, A., & Rodriguez, M. (2013). *myIGDIs early literacy*. Minneapolis, MN: University of Minnesota: Center for Response to Intervention in Early Childhood.

McGee, G. G., Morrier, M. J., & Daly, T. (1999). An incidental teaching approach to early intervention for toddlers with autism. *Journal of the Association for Persons with Severe Handicaps*, *24*(3), 133–146.

Moats, L., & Tolman, C. (2009). *Excerpted from Language Essentials for Teachers of Reading and Spelling (LETRS): The Speech Sounds of English: Phonetics, Phonology, and Phoneme Awareness (Module 2)*. Boston, MA: Sopris West. Retrieved December 1, 2022 from https://www.readingrockets.org/article/development-phonological-skills

National Early Literacy Panel. (2009). *Developing early literacy: Report of the National Early Literacy Panel*. Jessup, MD: National Center for Family Literacy, the National Institute for Literacy, U.S. Department of Health and Human Services.

National Reading Panel. (2000). *Report of the National Reading Panel. Teaching Children to Read: An Evidence-based Assessment of the Scientific Research Literature on Reading and its Implications for Reading Instruction*. Washington, DC: US Department of Health and Human Services.

Newman, D. S., & Rosenfield, S. A. (2019). *Building competence in school consultation: A developmental approach*. Milton Park, Abingdon, Oxon; New York: Routledge.

Notari-Syverson, A., O'Connor, R. E., & Vadasy, P. F. (2007). *Ladders to literacy: A preschool activity book*. Baltimore, MD: Brookes Publishing.

Piasta, S. B., Sawyer, B., Justice, L. M., O'Connell, A. A., Jian, H., Dogucu, M., & Khan, K. S. (2020). Effects of Read It Again! In early childhood special education classrooms as compared to regular shared book reading. *Journal of Early Intervention*, *42*(3), 224–243. doi:10.1177/1053815119883410

Reading Rockets. (2022). *Onset-Rime Games*. Retrieved December 1, 2022 from https://www.readingrockets.org/strategies/onset_rime

Whitehurst, G. J., & Lonigan, C. J. (1998). Child development and emergent literacy. *Child Development*, *69*(3), 848–872. doi:10.1111/j.1467-8624.1998.tb06247.x

3

WORD BOXES

Laurice M. Joseph

The Ohio State University, Columbus, OH, USA

Introduction

Word boxes is a strategy which helps students connect the phonological properties of words to their orthographic features (i.e., spelling patterns) by having them touch boxes or move counters or letters into boxes corresponding to individual sounds or word parts. A word boxes intervention to improve word reading fluency and accuracy will be described for a first-grade student with an intellectual disability.

According to the simple view of reading, word decoding plus linguistic knowledge yields reading comprehension (Gough & Tunmer, 1986). This view which is consistent with the science of reading emphasizes the importance of explicitly teaching word decoding skills to students who have not acquired those skills so efforts can be put toward gaining meaning from text (Petscher et al., 2020).Word decoding skills can be acquired with ease if children with and without disabilities have acquired phonemic awareness skills (i.e., attending to and manipulating individual sounds in spoken words; Burns et al., 2018; Dessemontet & de Chambrier, 2015).

Despite having received literacy instruction in the classroom, some students continue to experience challenges acquiring foundational literacy skills of phoneme awareness, making letter-sound correspondences and decoding words. This is especially the case for students with intellectual disabilities as they do not acquire literacy skills at a rate comparable to their peers without disabilities as measured by benchmark standards on curriculum-based measures (Lemons et al., 2013). Students with intellectual disabilities are typically taught how to read words using sight word

DOI: 10.4324/9781003275749-3

and vocabulary methods rather than word decoding strategies (Dessemontet et al., 2022). These individuals need intensive high-quality reading instruction (Dessemontet et al., 2019). Dimensions of intensifying instruction include aligning the instruction to students' learning goals, providing sufficient amounts of opportunities to learn and practice skills, scaffolding, giving corrective feedback, prompting in least to most intrusive ways, and incorporating cumulative review (Dessemontet et al., 2019; Fuchs et al., 2017) One method that incorporates many of those dimensions of instructional intensity for helping students acquire phonemic awareness skills is Elkonin/word boxes.

Elkonin boxes, sometimes referred to as sound boxes, word boxes, and say-it-move-it activities is a phonological awareness technique that was originally conceived by a Russian psychologist, D. B Elkonin (Elkonin, 1973). For the remainder of this chapter, the term that will be used to describe this technique is word boxes, a term coined by Marie Clay (1993) to describe extensions of Elkonin boxes. Word boxes not only involves segmenting sounds of spoken words but also involves mapping the phonological (sounds) onto the orthographic (letters) features of words. Word boxes are best used as a supplemental (i.e., tiers 2 and 3 within multi-tiered systems of support) instructional technique for students with severe reading problems who are not responding as well as desired to tier 1 general education phonics instruction. In other words, it is recommended that word boxes be used in addition to the explicit systematic phonics instruction that students are receiving in the general education classroom. This technique is designed to help children acquire small segmentation skills and attend to the smallest elements of a word (i.e., phonemes). In particular, students attend to letter-sound sequences and become aware of the beginning, middle and ending sounds in words when they are using word boxes to decode words.

Visual supports are incorporated within the word boxes technique for the purpose of assisting young children in identifying, segmenting, and blending sounds in words (i.e., phoneme awareness) as well as helping children make letter-sound associations (reading decoding) and detect orthographic patterns (spelling) in words (e.g., Keesey et al., 2015). Essentially, word boxes are created by drawing a rectangle on a piece of paper, cardboard, or dry erase board. Vertical lines are drawn on the rectangle to create connected boxes. The number of boxes may vary as they are designed to correspond to the number of sounds in a word. Plastic or tile letters are placed below the boxes. Each letter is placed below its respective box. A picture of the word or the printed word may be placed above the rectangle consisting of connected boxes. Figure 3.1 is an illustration of the word boxes technique.

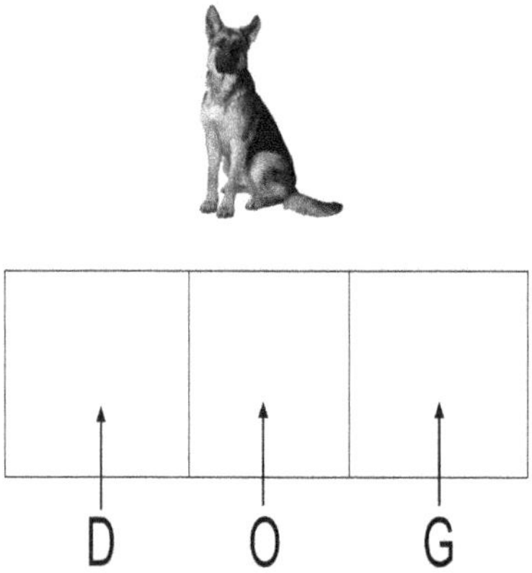

FIGURE 3.1 Illustration of word boxes activity

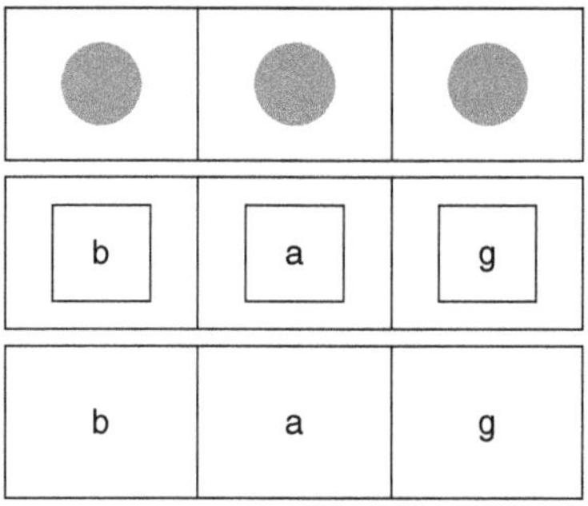

FIGURE 3.2 The three phases of the word box intervention

Word boxes may be taught in three phases. Figure 3.2 depicts an illustration of the three phases for the CVC word, "bag." The first phase is used to help students acquire phoneme awareness and consists of teaching students to segment phonemes (sounds) in words. In this phase, a drawn rectangle is divided into sections (i.e., boxes) according to the number of sounds (phonemes) in a word. For instance, the word "bag" has three distinct sounds (phonemes) /b/ /a/, and /g/ and so three connected boxes are created for this word by dividing the rectangle into three sections. The words "cake" and "boat" would also be represented by three connected boxes as these words contain three distinct sounds. The "e" is silent in the word "cake," and the "a" is silent in the word "boat." Four connected boxes would be represented for a word such as "left." A token (e.g., small plastic round disc) is placed below each box, and children are instructed to slide the tokens into the respective boxes as they slowly articulate (stretch out) each distinct sound (phoneme) in a word. Children identify the beginning, middle, and ending sounds in words (i.e., positional analysis). Sounds are initially stretched out and then blended together faster and faster. Stretching out the sounds has helped children with intellectual disabilities attend to the individual sounds in a word (Dessemontet et al., 2021). In this phase, one syllable words that are phonemically regular are first introduced to help children identify beginning, middle, and ending sounds in words.

The next phase of the word boxes technique involves linking sounds to letters, and this phase helps students gain knowledge about the alphabetic principle such as learning to link sound to print which enhances their phoneme awareness. In this phase, the tokens are replaced with letters such as plastic or tile letters using the same procedures that were implemented in the first phase. In the third (final) phase, the plastic letters are removed, and students are asked to write the letters in the boxes as they slowly articulate the sounds in a word. Some words contain more letters than phonemes and so it is important to make sure that the number of boxes matches the number of sounds in a word rather than the number of letters in a word. For example, the word, "boat" would have three divided boxes with the letter "b" written in the first box, the letters "oa" written in the middle box, and the letter "t" written in the last box.

Incorporating all phases may be particularly helpful for students who have not acquired phonological decoding skills, as phonemic awareness training coupled with letter-sound correspondence instruction had an even greater effect on reading performance than phoneme awareness training alone (National Reading Panel, 2000). Having stated that, the implementation of each phase depends upon the learning needs of the student. For instance, the sound box phase of the word boxes may be omitted and the instructor can begin with the word box phase if the student has mastered phoneme segmentation skills but still needs instruction on making letter-sound correspondences.

According to a recent review of studies that examined the effects of word boxes, this technique was found to be effective for helping young students with reading problems improve on their phoneme segmentation, word identification, and spelling skills (Ross & Joseph, 2019). The word boxes technique was also effective for helping students across a range of disability categories. For instance, word boxes helped students with specific learning disabilities (Joseph, 1998), young children at risk of reading problems (Keesey et al., 2015); students with intellectual disabilities (Joseph, 2002), and children with autism (Joseph, 2018) improve their literacy skills. Moreover, an electronic application (app) version of the word boxes (i.e., *Build a Word-Easy Spelling with Phonics*; AtReks, 2013) helped learners of English as an additional language improve their performance on linking sounds to letters (Ross & Joseph, 2021). In the aforementioned studies that examined the effects of word boxes, it should be noted that evidence-based components of explicit instruction such as modeling, guided practice, corrective feedback, and independent practice were used when implementing the word boxes. The use of these components likely played a large role in producing positive outcomes in students' reading performance (Ross & Joseph, 2019).

Case Study

Background Information

Steven is a first-grader with intellectual disabilities and attends a public school in a rural geographic region of the United States. He currently receives individualized educational services in a special education classroom for students with intellectual disabilities. According to his pediatrician, Steven does not have any apparent physical illnesses. His parents reported that Steven was delayed in meeting some developmental language milestones such as talking, labeling objects in his environment, and following simple directions. The school nurse conducted a vision and hearing screening and found that both his vision and hearing were in the normal range. Steven's first-grade general education teacher, Ms. Tate, implements structured and systematic phonics instruction in her first-grade classroom. She also administers the Dynamic Indicators of Basic Early Literacy Skills (DIBELS) benchmark measures at the beginning, middle, and end of the school year to identify which students are and are not meeting performance-based standards. Steven's beginning of the year and middle of the year benchmark scores on DIBELS Phoneme Segmentation Fluency (PSF) and Nonsense Word Fluency (NSF) were classified in the at-risk range. On this measure, Steven was only able to segment a few phonemes and correctly read two basic consonant-vowel-consonant (CVC) nonsense words. Based on Steven's performance on the DIBELS, he, along with a small group of students with similar reading skill problems, were provided additional instructional support (tier 2) in the general education classroom. An instructional classroom aid provided Steven and the small group of students with additional opportunities to practice the reading skills learned in class. Steven's progress was monitored using DIBELS middle of the school year PSF and NSF progress monitoring measures. Steven made slight improvements on these measures over six weeks; however, his rate of improvement remained low and his scores were still classified as at-risk.

After consulting with his parents, Ms. Tate referred Steven for an evaluation for suspected disabilities. Steven was evaluated by a team of professionals, including the school psychologist, speech and language therapist, and an intervention specialist at his school. The school psychologist administered the latest edition of the Wechsler Intelligence Test for Children (WIISC), and Steven obtained an overall intellectual functioning (i.e., Full Scale) standard score of 68 which is considered Well Below Average compared to peers his age. His verbal and nonverbal abilities were both well below the intellectual functioning level of his same age peers. On a norm-referenced adaptive behavior scale, Steven exhibited deficits in the areas of communication and social skills. On a norm-referenced standardized achievement test, Steven obtained a standard score of 65 on Word Identification subtest and a standard score of 55 on a Nonsense Word Identification subtest, both of which were classified as well below average compared to his same age peers. The speech and language therapist administered the latest edition of the Comprehensive Test of Phonological Awareness (CTOPP) to assess Steven's phonological processing skills. Steven obtained a score classified in the Well Below Average range on Phoneme Segmentation and Phoneme Blending subtests. The intervention specialist administered a criterion-referenced test to determine specifically which phonological decoding skills Steven has mastered and which skills need further instruction. Steven's performance on this measure indicated that Steven was able to say the following correct sounds of letters when presented in isolation: the consonant sounds for c, d, f, g, h, j, k, l, m, n, p, q, r, s, t, u, v, w, x, y, and z and only the long and short vowel sound for the letter "a." According to his performance on the measure, Steven was only able to read the following words as a whole correctly: "cat," "bat," "sit," "hop," "pop," "sip," and "not." He was not able to read other words with consonant-vowel-consonant spelling patterns.

Problem Identification

Steven has not acquired phoneme awareness skills of segmenting and blending sounds in words and has not acquired making letter-sound correspondences for most words that consist of consonant-vowel-consonant (CVC) spelling patterns.

Problem Analysis

Despite receiving structured systematic phonics and small-group supplemental instruction in the general education classroom, Steven continues to struggle to make sufficient progress on making letter-sound correspondences. Although the supplemental instruction consisted of providing Steven with several opportunities to practice sounding out words, it became clear that Steven needed additional instructional supports to achieve his learning goals.

Intervention Goals

Based on Steven's current levels of reading performance, acquisition, maintenance and generalization intervention goals have been identified for Steven. With regards to his acquisition goal, Steven is expected to make letter-sound correspondences at 100% accuracy for the following sets of words: Set A: cat, bat, sat, mat, hat; Set B sit, kit, lit, fit, bit; Set C: mop, top, cop, hop, Set D: pet, net, bet, get; Set E: cot, not, hot, pot, lot, and Set F: lip, dip, sip, hip, rip. After Steven demonstrates mastery on reading the sets of words, Steven is expected to demonstrate maintenance over time on reading those sets of words. His generalization goal consists of Steven being able to read the target words correctly in a sentence, which is a different context than the context in which they were directly taught.

Measurement of Target Reading Skill, Data Collection Strategies, and Progress Monitoring

The target reading skill for Steven was reading decodable words containing consonant-vowel-consonant (CVC) spelling patterns. His performance was measured using daily probes containing a set of five different words consisting of CVC spelling patterns. Appendix A is a sample of a recording form for word identification probes. Steven was presented with a word on a flashcard and asked to read the word as a whole word. If the whole word was read correctly, he obtained a point for every letter-sound sequence in the word. For instance, if he read the word "sit" correctly then he obtained a score of 3. If he only made one correct letter-sound sequence in a word, he would obtain a score of 1, if he made two correct letter-sound sequences, he would obtain a score of 2, and so forth, and if he said part of the word correct such as "it" in the word "sit," he obtained a score of 2. The probes were administered daily until he achieved mastery on a set of words. Criteria for achieving mastery was obtaining a score of 100% accuracy on the administration of three consecutive probes containing the same set of words. Once the criterion for mastery was obtained, probes containing a different set of five CVC words were administered, and so forth. Maintenance probes were administered two days after criterion levels were met on a given set or sets of words. Maintenance probes consisted of a random selection of 5 to 10 words from each set that were mastered during word box instructional sessions. Generalization probes were administered to Steven after mastery criterion was achieved for a given set of words. These probes consisted of five short sentences each containing a target word from a set that was mastered. The sentences were presented on a worksheet, and Steven was asked to read each sentence. The item was counted as correct if the target word in the sentence was read correctly. If the other words with the exception of the target word in the sentence are read incorrectly. the item is still marked as correct.

Intervention Plan

The following sets of words contain mostly words that Steven has not yet mastered, and these words were taught during the instructional lessons using the word boxes: Set A: cat, bat, sat, mat, hat; Set B: sit, kit, lit, fit, bit; Set C: mop, top, cop, hop, Set D: pet, net, bet, get; Set E: cot, not, hot, pot, lot, and Set F: lip, dip, sip, hip, rip. Set A words were taught first until mastered, and then set B, and so forth. There is at least one word in each set that Steven was able to read accurately on the aforementioned criterion-referenced measure. Having included at least one word in each set that Steven was able to read accurately may serve as a reinforcer for Steven to gain some momentum for learning to read the other words in the set. that are "unknown" to him. Moreover, each set contains words with similar sound and spelling patterns which may also help Steven read the words accurately and quickly, thereby possibly obtaining mastery criterion levels in a small number of trials.

In each lesson, the word boxes technique was presented in three phases for Steven so that he acquires and understands the connections among phoneme segmentation, letter-sound correspondence, and spelling skills. The first phase of each lesson focusses on helping Steven segment the sounds in the words of a given set. In this phase, a cardboard rectangle divided into three vertical sections (creating three connected boxes) and three tokens placed below each divided section are placed on a table in front of Steven. The rectangle is divided into three sections because the words that are taught contain three distinct sounds (i.e., phonemes). Once these materials are in view, the instructor introduces the word box intervention and explains the purpose of using the word boxes to Steven. For instance, the instructor may state:

> These materials that you see on this table are there to help you identify the sounds you hear in words. I am going to show you how you can use these materials to help you sound out words. First, look at these three boxes that are connected. Each box has a token placed below it, and I am going to say a word and then show you how to use the boxes and the tokens when sounding out the word.

After the instructor introduces the task to Steven, the instructor models using the word boxes through the following steps. Step 1 consists of the instructor saying one of the words that Steven is already able to read from the set of words. Next, the instructor slowly articulates the sounds of the word and places each token in its corresponding section as each sound is slowly articulated (stretched out). For instance, for the word "bat," the instructor says the word "bat" and then slides the token (placed below the first box) into that first box while the /b/ sound is slowly articulated. Next, the instructor slides the token (placed below the second box) into that second box while the short vowel /a/ sound is slowly articulated. This is followed by the instructor sliding the token (placed below the last box) into the last box while the sound /t/ is slowly articulated. Step 2 involves the instructor and Steven, together, saying the same word (e.g., /bat/) that the instructor modeled in Step 1 and placing the tokens in their respective boxes as they articulate each sound in that word. Next, the instructor and the student blend all the sounds together to say the word. Step 3 involves having Steven complete the task on his own with instructor feedback using the same word presented in steps 1 and 2. The instructor provides verbal praise for correct responses. Corrective feedback is provided when Steven makes errors. Errors are first corrected using verbal prompts. Verbal prompts may consist of asking Steven to place his finger on the token and asking him to say the sound as he slides the token in the box. If Steven cannot correct his error with verbal prompts, the instructor models accurate responding and asks Steven to repeat the task again. Steven is asked to repeat the task until he is able to complete it correctly without instructor guidance. Step 4 involves the instructor removing the tokens and replacing them with plastic or tile letters (i.e., replacing the three tokens with the letters "b," "a," and "t.") Steven is asked to say the sound of each letter and place it in its respective box. Feedback is provided to Steven using the same prompts as in Step 3 with the exception of having him place his finger on the letter instead of the token. To facilitate Steven blending all the sounds together to say the word as a whole, he is asked to say all the sounds faster and faster as he slides his finger from left to right in a sweeping fashion back and forth below the boxes that contain the letters in them. Step 5 consists of the instructor removing the plastic letters and asking Steven to write the letters (e.g., "b," "a," and "t") in their respective boxes as he articulates their sounds. The same type of feedback as in Steps 3 and 4 is provided to Steven. The five-step process is repeated for the remaining words in the set. Modeling and guided practice steps are faded/removed as Steven is able to use the materials and complete the tasks independently with instructor feedback.

At the end of a daily lesson, Steven is administered a five-item probe that contains the set of words that were taught in that lesson. As described in a prior section, words are placed on flashcards and presented to Steven.

When the instructor presents a flashcard with a word printed on it, Steven is asked to read the whole word. Once Steven achieves 100% accuracy on reading words as a whole on three consecutive probes containing the same set of words, a new set of words is introduced and taught to Steven using the same procedures as stated above. After Steven demonstrates mastery criterion on sets of words, those sets of words are judiciously reviewed during subsequent sessions. As sessions progress, the instructor can remove instructional supports such as modeling and guided practice when Steven performs the word boxes independently using a set of words.

Maintenance and Generalization

Maintenance probes containing a random selection of words from each set are administered about two days after Steven demonstrates mastery on a given set of words. Maintenance probes contained mastered words printed on flashcards and are administered and scored following the same procedures as the probes that are administered daily. In order to determine if Steven is able to generalize reading words in isolation to reading words in context, Steven is presented with a generalization probe once he achieves mastery criterion on a set of words. The generalization probes consist of a total of five items in which each mastered word in a set is placed in a simple sentence on a worksheet. For example, the target word "sat" may be used in the following sentence: "The dog sat on the rug." An item on the generalization probe is scored as correct as long as Steven reads the target word accurately. If the other words with the exception of the target word in the sentence are read incorrectly, the item is still marked as correct. There is a total of six generalization probes, each pertaining to a set of words.

Intervention Fidelity and Interobserver Agreement Plans

Professional staff such as a school psychologist can provide support to the instructor by periodically observing the instructor implement the word boxes and administer the probes to ensure that procedures are implemented with fidelity. It is recommended that independent observations of the procedures should occur for at least 30% of all the instructional sessions. Procedural integrity can be achieved by recording on a checklist whether procedures were followed as planned. The checklist can consist of the specific steps involved in implementing the word boxes as well as for administering the progress monitoring probes. Appendix B is a sample of a word box intervention integrity checklist that can be used to verify that all intervention procedures and administration of probes were implemented with fidelity. Training can be provided as needed on observing and recording adherence to procedures. To calculate a percentage of procedural integrity, the number of steps completed correctly were divided by the total number of applicable steps, and then this number was multiplied by 100%.

Word identification probes can be independently scored for interobserver agreement by having a professional staff member, an instructor aid, a paraprofessional, or an older student periodically observe administering the probes to Steven and score them using an unscored sheet containing the items. The independent observer receives training on how to score the probes and is provided with practice on scoring the probes until the independent observer feels comfortable in completing the scoring on their own. After the scoring is complete, the independent observer and the instructor compare their scores item by item to determine if there is agreement between their scores. If there is disagreement, the independent observer and the instructor discuss possible reasons for the disagreement. To calculate IOA, the point-by-point agreement method will be used, which is the percentage of probes in which the two raters record the same ratings for the same items (Gast & Ledford, 2014). The formula is the number of agreements divided by the total number of agreements plus disagreements, and then this number is multiplied by 100% (Gast & Ledford, 2014). IOA that is 80% to 90% agreement is considered acceptable (Kratochwill et al., 2010).

Intervention Outcome Data

Table 3.1 presents Steven's correct letter-sound sequence performance on daily probes during intervention sessions. On daily probes during intervention sessions, Steven's mean scores on correct letter sequences range from 12 to 14 across sets of words. Table 3.2 presents Steven's correct whole-word identification performance on daily probes each containing a set of word. Steven's mean scores on whole-word identification probes range from 4 to 5 on daily probes containing sets of words. It took three sessions for Steven to obtain mastery criteria on Sets A, B and E. It took five sessions for Steven to obtain mastery (i.e., total score of 5 (100%) on three consecutive probes) on Sets C and D. It took Steven three and two sessions, respectively, to obtain mastery for sets E and F. Table 3.3 presents Steven's scores on maintenance probes. His scores on maintenance probes ranged from 13 to 15 with a mean of 14 on correct letter sequences and ranged from 4 to 5 with a mean of 4 correct on whole-word identification probes. Table 3.4 presents Steven's scores on generalization probes. Steven's scores ranged from 4 to 5 with a mean of 5 on reading target words correctly within the context of a sentence.

TABLE 3.1 Steven's Scores on Correct Letter-Sound Sequences (CLS) on Word Identification Probes (Total Correct CLS on each Probe = 15)

Probes	*Set A*	*Set B*	*Set C*	*Set D*	*Set E*	*Set F*
Baseline	3	3	3	3	3	3
WB 1	9	9	11	9	12	13
WB 2	12	9	11	9	12	14
WB 3	12	11	12	11	13	15
WB 4	15	15	13	12	15	15
WB 5	15	15	12	12	15	15
WB 6	15	15	15	15	15	
WB 7			15	15		
WB 8			15	15		
Mean	13	12	13	12	14	14

TABLE 3.2 Steven's Scores on Whole Word (WW) on Word Identification Probes (Total Correct on each WW probe = 5)

Probes	*Set A*	*Set B*	*Set C*	*Set D*	*Set E*	*Set F*
Baseline	1	1	1	1	1	1
WB 1	3	3	3	3	4	4
WB 2	3	3	3	3	4	4
WB 3	4	3	4	3	4	5
WB 4	5	5	4	4	5	5
WB 5	5	5	4	4	5	5
WB 6	5	5	5	5	5	
WB 7			5	5		
WB 8			5	5		
Mean	4	4	4	4	4	5

TABLE 3.3 Steven's Performance on Maintenance Probes

Probes	Correct Letter-Sound Sequences *Total Correct = 15*	Correct Whole Words *Total Correct = 5*
1	13	4
2	14	4
3	15	4
4	15	5
5	14	4
6	15	4
Mean	14	4

TABLE 3.4 Steven's Performance on Generalization Probes

Sets of Words	Generalization Probe. *Total Correct = 5*
A	5
B	5
C	5
D	4
E	5
F	5
Mean	5

Summary of Intervention Effects

The word boxes appeared to have immediate positive effects (with little variability in performance) on helping Steven improve on making letter-sound correspondences and reading CVC words among all sets of words that were taught to him. Before word boxes was implemented, he was only able to read one word correctly from each set of words. Mastery on all the sets of words was achieved. The overall mean trials it took Steven to achieve mastery across sets of words was 4 trials with a range between 2 and 5 trials. It took Steven fewer and fewer trials to meet mastery criterion as he progressed through the sets of words. Thus, it took relatively few trials for Steven, when using the word boxes, to achieve mastery levels on reading words correctly. Steven was able to maintain making correct letter-sound correspondences and reading words over time as demonstrated in his performance on maintenance probes. These results were important as the words from each mastered set were randomly selected to be placed on the maintenance probes. This means that on each probe, Steven was able to correctly read words that consisted of different spelling patterns (i.e., words from different word families). Steven was able to generalize reading the trained words correctly when they were presented in a sentence. He demonstrated that he could read the words correctly when they were presented in a different context than the context in which they were directly taught.

Intervention Acceptability

Intervention acceptability may be assessed using questionnaires that can be administered to Steven's teacher and to Steven after several intervention sessions using the word boxes took place. Appendix C is an example of a questionnaire that may be administered to Steven. This particular questionnaire is designed to primarily ask Steven questions about how felt the word boxes helped him read words. A simple modified Likert-type scale is placed below each question on the questionnaire. The scale consisted of the following multiple choice response types: no, maybe, and yes. Each response type is accompanied with a depiction of a facial expression. The "no" response choice is printed below a face with a frown. The "maybe" response is presented with a face depicting a neutral expression, and the "yes" response is depicted below a smiley face. Appendix D is a sample of the teacher intervention acceptability questionnaire. The teacher questionnaire is designed to primarily ask the teacher how he/she felt about the effectiveness of the word boxes for helping Steven improve his reading skills. The multiple-choice scale responses range from strongly disagree to strongly agree.

Intervention Considerations

Materials may vary when implementing the word boxes. For instance, dry erase boards with a drawn rectangle with divided sections can be used to represent the connected boxes and magnets, and magnetic letters can be used to represent tokens and letters of the alphabet. Alternative materials such as square-shaped tiles with letters printed on them can also be used and arranged to form a word as the sound of each letter is articulated. In addition to the letters that match the sound of a targeted word, other letters can be placed below the divided rectangle and used as distractors to determine if the student can discriminate among letters that do correspond and letters that do not correspond to the sounds. The instructor can remove all the letters and ask children to engage in positional analysis by asking them to point to which box they hear a certain sound in a target word. For example, the instructor can say the word, "hat" and ask the students to point to the box where they hear the /a/ sound followed by asking them to point to the box where they hear the /h/ sound and then where they hear the /t/ sound. The materials used in word boxes are likely to be appealing to young children, particularly those in the primary grades. Despite its potential effectiveness for older students with disabilities, it may not be acceptable to students who are in the intermediate and higher grade levels.

An electronic application (app) version of the word boxes called *Build a Word-Easy Spelling with Phonics* (AtReks, 2013) may be an alternative for children and some older students who may find this tool appealing, game-like and easier to manipulate than the materials typically used in this activity. Indeed, this app version has been effective for helping English language learners make letter-sound associations (Ross & Joseph, 2021) as well as helping students who struggle with reading remain on task (Larabee et al., 2014). This app version contains a pool of over 800 words that can be targeted for instruction. A target word is voiced in the app, and question marks are displayed on a screen according to the number of letter-sound correspondences in word. For example, three question marks are displayed for the word, "bag." Below the question marks are empty boxes that represented each letter-sound correspondence (e.g., three boxes for the word *bag*). Below the boxes are six letters (e.g., *b, a, o, p, g,* and *t*). Each letter is placed in a box. Three boxes contain the correct letters, and three boxes contain the distractor letters (i.e., letter-sound correspondences not found within the CVC words). Each time a target word is voiced, the app displays the letters that comprise the target word and three distractor letters, all of which are displayed in a random order on the screen that comprise that word and randomly generates three distractor letters. A stylus is used to drag a letter into its respective box on the screen. The sound of that letter is voiced as the letter is selected to be placed in its respective box. Vowel letters were colored red and consonants were colored blue on the app. When the correct letter is dragged into its corresponding box, the box is highlighted in blue as visual feedback that the correct response was made. Errorless learning is embedded within the app as a selected incorrect letter (distractor) does not move (drag) into an empty box. This electronic version with embedded feedback may be particularly useful during independent work time in and outside of the classroom when students are practicing skills without direct instructor assistance.

Not only are word boxes used to teach children small segmentation skills; they may also be used to help children learn large segmentation skills such as compound and other multisyllabic words (e.g., affixes and inflectional endings). For instance, the words that involve inflectional endings such as "camping" may involve a rectangle divided into two sections with index cards, one card with the word "camp" and the other card with the ending "ing" printed on them. The student is instructed to place the cards in their respective sections of the divided rectangle.

Modeling, guided practice, and the visual supports of the boxes can be faded as students achieve mastery with making letter-sound correspondences and reading words. With regards to fading the visual supports, the divided sections (vertical lines) of the rectangle can be removed as students achieve mastery on making sequential one to one letter-sound correspondences in the words. This may be followed by removing the entire rectangle. The plastic letters can then be replaced with the printed word on a worksheet or flashcard to resemble how the word is presented in an authentic context.

Word boxes may not be the most time-efficient method for teaching decoding skills to all children. Not all students need the level of supports that are inherent in this technique. Moreover, it may be challenging to teach some words using the word boxes method. Not all words have regular spelling patterns and can be sequentially decoded. Some words have irregular spellings and are hierarchically decoded. For example, in the word, "brought," the "ght" prompts reading the vowel "o" as a short sound and saying the /t/ sound and not the /g/ and /h/ sounds as the "g" and "h" are silent. Other techniques may be better suited for learning those types of words.

Word boxes instruction should supplement rather than replace systematic and explicit comprehensive phonics instruction in the classroom. Word boxes can be used with other supplemental word identification intervention strategies. After children learn to decode words using the word boxes activity, the words can be placed in a mixed-up order on flashcards and children can sort them according to similar sound and spelling patterns (e.g., Joseph, 2002). In addition, children can continue to practice, review, and increase their fluency by reading those words using constant time delay flashcard or electronic drill methods (e.g., Bradley & Noell, 2018). Word boxes may also be incorporated as a decoding error correction procedure during oral reading passage instruction. For instance, if a student reads a word incorrectly in the passage, boxes can be drawn around parts of the word and students are prompted to put their finger below each box and sound out those parts of the word and then blend them together to read the word as a whole.

Conclusion

Word boxes is a relatively low-cost, easy-to-implement technique that helps children segment sounds and make sequential letter-sound correspondences in words. Word boxes can be implemented in a large-group, small-group, and one-to-one instructional format. It has been incorporated as one of the activities within published comprehensive early literacy programs such as the Kindergarten Peer Assisted Learning Strategies (KPALS; Fuchs et al., 2001) program. The technique is most effective when modeling, guided practice, corrective feedback, and cumulative review are incorporated as components of instruction. The visual and manipulative materials serve as scaffolds (support structures) to assist children in identifying the position of sounds and letters in words and map those sounds onto the letters. These types of supports are especially helpful for children who struggle with acquiring fundamental literacy skills and can be gradually removed as children master the skills.

Appendix A: Word Identification Probe

Appendix A
Word Identification Probe

Student Name____________________ Date__________

Word	CLS	Score	Whole Word	Score
	_____ _____ _____			
	_____ _____ _____			
	_____ _____ _____			
	_____ _____ _____			
	_____ _____ _____			
	_____ _____ _____			

Word	CLS	Score	Whole Word	Score
	_____ _____ _____			
	_____ _____ _____			
	_____ _____ _____			
	_____ _____ _____			
	_____ _____ _____			
	_____ _____ _____			

Word	CLS	Score	Whole Word	Score
	_____ _____ _____			
	_____ _____ _____			
	_____ _____ _____			
	_____ _____ _____			
	_____ _____ _____			
	_____ _____ _____			

Word	CLS	Score	Whole Word	Score
	_____ _____ _____			
	_____ _____ _____			
	_____ _____ _____			
	_____ _____ _____			
	_____ _____ _____			
	_____ _____ _____			

FIGURE 3.A.1

Appendix B: Intervention Session Protocol and Procedural Integrity Checklist

Student: Observer Initials:
Date: Session:

Instructions for the observer: Place a check in corresponding column for each step. Only place a check in the *Yes* column if the entire step was completed correctly. Content in bold should be said aloud. N/A stands for Not Applicable.

Steps for Modeling Phase	Yes	No	N/A
1. Instructor states, **today you will use the word boxes to learn the sounds that letters make and to practice reading words.**			
2. Instructor places on the table the cardboard containing the drawn word boxes with a token placed below each box.			
3. **The instructor says, the word is [states the target word].**			
4. The instructor places his/her finger on the first token or letter and slides the token or letter into the box as he/she says the first sound in the word. **The instructor states, The first sound in [state the target word] is [state the first sound] and so I will place this first token or letter [states the name of the letter] in the first box.**			
5. The instructor places his/her finger on the second token or letter and slides the token or letter into the box as he/she says the first sound in the word. The instructor states, **the second sound in the word [state the target word] is [state the second sound] and so I will place this first token or letter [states the name of the letter] in the second box.**			
6. The instructor places his/her finger on the third token or letter and slides the token or letter into the box as he/she says the first sound in the word. The instructor states, **the third sound in the word [state the target word] is [state the third sound] and so I will place this first token or letter [states the name of the letter] in the box.**			
Steps for Guided Practice Phase			
7. Instructor states, **We will practice together this time with the same word [state the target word].**			
8. Instructor states, **Together, let's say the word**			
9. Instructor prompts the student to place his/her finger on the first token or letter and asks the student to say its sound and slide the token or letter into the first box.			
10. Instructor prompts the student to place his/her finger on the second token or letter and asks the student to say its sound and slide the token or letter into the second box.			

11. Instructor prompts the student to place his/her finger on third token or letter and asks the student to say its sound and slide the token or letter into the third box.
12. Instructor provides verbal praise (e.g., **Good!** or **Good job!**) if the student does the task correctly.

    If the student completes the task incorrectly, explains the error and allows the student to try the task again.

    If the student completes the task incorrectly again, instructor re-models the task and allows the student to keep trying the task until it is correct

Steps for Independent Practice Phase

13. The instructor states, **you will practice this time on your own with the same word [state the target word]. The instructor watches as the student completes the task on his/her own.**
14. The instructor provides verbal praise (e.g., **Good!** Or **Good job!**) if the student does the task correctly.

    If the student completes the task incorrectly, the instructor verbally prompts the student without providing the correct answer. If the student cannot complete the task correctly after the verbal prompt, the instructor explains the error and allows the student to try the task again. If the student completes the task incorrectly again, the instructor re-models the task and allows the student to keep trying the task until it is correct.
15. All steps are repeated as needed for each target word. Steps in modeling and guided practice phases can be omitted if the student is able to complete the task on his/her own.

Steps for Daily and Maintenance Probe Administration

17. The instructor removes all the instructional materials (word boxes, tokens, letters). Instructor states, **I am going to show you some words on flashcards and ask you to read each word.**
18. When each flashcard with a target word printed on it is presented, the instructor asks the student to read the word.
19. Student is given 5 seconds to read the word. The instructor records words read correctly and words read incorrectly.
20. If the student reads the word correctly, the instructor provides verbal praise.
21. If the student reads the word incorrectly or cannot read the word, the instructor provides error correction by stating the word.

Steps for Generalization Probes

22. After the administration of a daily probe, the instructor states, **I am going to present some sentences on a worksheet for you to read.**
23. The instructor presents the worksheet containing five sentences with each sentence containing a target word that was taught using the word boxes during the daily session. The instructor points to the first sentence and asks the student to read the sentence. The instructor records if the target word was read correctly or incorrectly.
24. The instructor provides verbal praise for words read correctly and provides error correction by stating the word for words read incorrectly.
25. The procedures are repeated for the remaining four sentences.

Appendix C: Student Acceptability Questionnaire

1. Do you like the word boxes activity?

 No

 Maybe

 Yes

2. Do you think the word boxes activity helps you become a better reader?

 No

 Maybe

 Yes

3. Would you tell your classmates about the word box activity to become better readers?

No

Maybe

Yes

4. Would you use the word boxes again?

No

Maybe

Yes

Appendix D: Teacher Acceptability Questionnaire

Please answer the following questions about the intervention used for this study.

1. The intervention was effective at improving my student's reading skills.
   1. = strongly disagree
   2. = disagree
   3. = neutral
   4. = agree
   5. = strongly agree

2. I am pleased with my student's progress in learning the sounds that letters make using the word boxes.
   1. = strongly disagree
   2. = disagree

   3. = neutral
   4. = agree
   5. = strongly agree

3. I am pleased with my student's progress in learning to read common CVC words using the word boxes.
   1. = strongly disagree
   2. = disagree
   3. = neutral
   4. = agree
   5. = strongly agree

4. I would recommend this intervention to other students who are learning to read.
   1. = strongly disagree
   2. = disagree
   3. = neutral
   4. = agree
   5. = strongly agree

5. What was beneficial about the word boxes intervention?

6. What was not beneficial about the word boxes intervention?

References

AtReks. (2013). *Build a word-easy spelling with phonics: Version 3.0* [mobile application software]. Available at: http://www.atreks.com/build-a-word-phonics. Retrieved September 2018.

Bradley, R. L., & Noell, G. H. (2018). The effectiveness of supplemental phonics instruction employing constant time delay instruction for struggling readers. *Psychology in the Schools*, *55*(7), 880–892. doi:10.1002/pits.22148

Burns, M. K., Young, H., Maki, K. E., Helman, L., & McComas, J. J. (2018). Contributions of the components of phonemic awareness to letter-sound knowledge with kindergarten students in high-poverty urban elementary schools. *Reading & Writing Quarterly*, *34*(5), 409–418. doi:10.1080/10573569.2018.1468835; doi:10.1007/s10864-012-9160-2

Clay, M. (1993). *Reading recovery: A guidebook for teachers in training*. Portsmouth, NH: Heinemann.

Dessemontet, R. S., & de Chambrier, A.-F. (2015). The role of phonological awareness and letter-sound knowledge in the reading development of children with intellectual disabilities. *Research in Developmental Disabilities*, *41*, 1–12. doi:10.1016/j.ridd.2015.04.001

Dessemontet, R. S., de Chambrier, A. F., Martinet, C., Meuli, N., & Linder, A.-L. (2021). Effects of a phonics-based intervention on the reading skills of students with intellectual disability. *Research in Developmental Disabilities*, *111*, N.PAG. doi:10.1016/j.ridd.2021.103883

Dessemontet, R. S., Linder, A.-L., Martinet, C., & Martini-Willemin, B.-M. (2022). A descriptive study on reading instruction provided to students with intellectual disability. *Journal of Intellectual Disabilities*, *26*(3), 575–593. doi:10.1177/17446295211016170

Dessemontet, R. S., Martinet, C., de Chambrier, A.F., Martini-Willemin, B.-M., & Audrin, C. (2019). A meta-analysis on the effectiveness of phonics instruction for teaching decoding skills to students with intellectual disability. *Educational Research Review*, *26*, 52–70. doi:10.1016/j.edurev.2019.01.001

Elkonin, D. B. (1973). U.S.S.R. In J. Downing (Ed.), *Comparative reading: Cross-national studies of behavior and processes in reading and writing* (pp. 551–579). New York, NY: Macmillan.

Fuchs, D., Fuchs, L. S., Al Otaiba, S., Thompson, A., Yen, L., McMaster, K., Svenson, E., & Yang, N. J. (2001). KPALS helping kindergartners with reading readiness: Teachers and researchers in partnerships. *Teaching Exceptional Children*, *33*, 76–80.

Fuchs, L. S., Fuchs, D., & Malone, A. S. (2017). The taxonomy of intervention intensity. *Teaching Exceptional Children*, *50*(1), 35–43. doi:10.1177/0040059917703962

Gast, D. L., & Ledford, J. R. (2014). *Single case research methodology: Applications in special education and behavioral sciences*. New York, NY: Taylor & Francis.

Gough, P. B., & Tunmer, W. E. (1986). Decoding, reading, and reading disability. *Remedial and Special Education*, *7*, 6–10. doi:10.1177/074193258600700104

Joseph, L. M. (1998). Word boxes help children with learning disabilities identify and spell words. *Reading Teacher*, *52*(4), 348–356.

Joseph, L. M. (2002). Facilitating word recognition and spelling using word boxes and word sort phonic procedures. *School Psychology Review*, *31*, 122–129.

Joseph, L. M. (2018). Effects of word boxes on phoneme segmentation, word recognition, and spelling for a sample of children with autism. *Child Language Teaching and Therapy*, *34*, 303–317.

Keesey, S., Konrad, M., & Joseph, L. M. (2015). Word boxes improve phonemic awareness, letter-sound correspondences, and spelling skills of at-risk kindergartners. *Remedial and Special Education*, *36*, 166–180.

Kratochwill, T. R., Hitchcock, J., Horner, R. H., Levin, J. R., Odom, S. L., Rindskopf, D. M. & Shadish, W. R. (2010). *Single-case design technical documentation*. Retrieved from https://ies.ed.gov/ncee/wwc/Docs/ReferenceResources/wwc_scd.pdf

Larabee, K., Burns, M., & McComas, J. (2014). Effects of an iPad-supported phonics intervention on decoding performance and time on-task. *Journal of Behavioral Education*, *23*(4), 449–469. doi:10.1007/s10864-014-9214-8

Lemons, C. J., Zigmond, N., Kloo, A. M., Hill, D. R., Mrachko, A. A., Paterra, M. F., Bost, T. J., & Davis, S. M. (2013). Performance of students with significant cognitive disabilities on early-grade curriculum-based measures of word and passage reading fluency. *Exceptional Children*, *79*(4), 408–426. doi:10.1177/001440291307900402

National Reading Panel (NRP). (2000). *Report of the National Reading Panel. Teaching children to read: An evidence-based assessment of the scientific research literature on reading and its implications for reading instruction*. Washington, DC: U.S. Department of Health and Human Services.

Petscher, Y., Cabell, S. Q., Catts, H. W., Compton, D. L., Foorman, B. R., Hart, S. A., Lonigan, C. J., Phillips, B. M., Schatschneider, C., Steacy, L. M., Terry, N. P., & Wagner, R. K. (2020). How the science of reading informs 21st-century education. *Reading Research Quarterly*, *55*, S267–S282. doi:10.1002/rrq.35

Ross, K. M., & Joseph, L. M. (2019). Effects of word boxes on improving students' basic literacy skills: A literature review. *Preventing School Failure*, *63*(1), 43–51. doi:10.1080/1045988X.2018.1480006

Ross, K. M. & Joseph, L. M. (2021). Effects of a word boxes electronic app on improving letter-sound correspondences of learners of English as an additional language. *Journal of Applied School Psychology*. doi:10.1080/15377903.2020.1848953

4

KINDERGARTEN PEER ASSISTED LEARNING STRATEGIES

Cheryl P. Lyon

University of Connecticut, Mansfield, CT, USA

Douglas Fuchs

American Institutes for Research and Vanderbilt University, Nashville, TN, USA

Melissa V. Stalega and Devin M. Kearns

University of Connecticut, Mansfield, CT, USA

Introduction

Many children do not begin kindergarten with extensive early literacy skills. Some children may not have had practice reciting nursery rhymes and engaging in different forms of sound play, for example. Other children may not have had an opportunity to learn other early literacy skills like name and letter recognition. Some will not be familiar with concepts of print like the direction of a book, the functions of author and illustrator, and the idea that the words match spoken language. Other children will come to school with a great deal of early literacy knowledge. How do we address the varied needs of children in kindergarten classrooms?

Kindergarten Peer-Assisted Learning Strategies for Reading (K-PALS) is one way to support students' diverse needs. K-PALS is a supplemental program for improving reading outcomes for all students within a kindergarten classroom. K-PALS activities are designed to improve students' phonological awareness skills, increase their letter-sound and high-frequency word knowledge, and develop their decoding skills.

DOI: 10.4324/9781003275749-4

Supporting Research

K-PALS is an evidence-based practice supported by data from multiple studies. K-PALS was designed for and was tested in general education classrooms, and the studies all included students from the entire range of reading abilities present in such classrooms. The version of K-PALS described in this chapter had effects on phonological awareness tasks in multiple studies (e.g., identifying sounds in spoken words) ranging from 0.46 to 1.30 in one study (Fuchs et al., 2001; Fuchs et al., 2002) and 0.20 to 0.55 in another (Fuchs et al., 2001) in effect size terms. (For early literacy, effect sizes are sometimes interpreted as representing a percentage of instructional time across a year. On this basis, an effect size of 0.20 represents about 20% more instructional time, about the equivalent of two additional months compared with students who did not participate in K-PALS.) For early reading and spelling measures (e.g., letter-sound identification; pronunciation of printed nonsense words), effect sizes ranged from 0.08 to 1.96 in the first study to 0.98 to 1.25 in the second (Fuchs & Fuchs, 2005).

The positive K-PALS effects have been reported so consistently that K-PALS has been identified as a highly cost-efficient practice, providing a greater benefit for dollar spent on implementation than many other programs designed for students with and without disabilities (Hollands et al., 2013). Other versions of PALS have shown similarly positive effects using the same peer-mediated approach described here (Fuchs, Fuchs, & Burish, 2000; Fuchs, Fuchs, Mathes, & Martinez, 2002; Lee, 2014; Lemons, Fuchs, Gilbert, & Fuchs, 2014; Mattatall, 2017; McMaster, Fuchs, & Fuchs, 2006).

Summary of K-PALS Activities

K-PALS lessons are designed to be completed 3 times per week for about 30 minutes. K-PALS lessons have two components: teacher-directed whole-group lessons and partner activities. The names and purposes of the activities are described in Table 4.1. The teacher-directed whole-group component serves two purposes: (a) students build phonological awareness (PA) skills and (b) students have a model of the K-PALS lesson they will complete in pairs. The partner activity component is designed to maximize the amount of time students practice reading.

Within the teacher-led whole-group lessons, the teacher first leads the PA activity, Sound Play. This activity helps students practice detecting (identifying in words) and manipulating (combining) sounds in spoken words. The Sound Play lessons last only 3–5 minutes, in alignment with

FIGURE 4.1 K-PALS Partners Completing What Sound Activity

recommendations about the amount of PA practice needed by beginning readers. The teacher then models how the students will complete their partner activities to assure they know how to do the jobs (described next) correctly.

During partner activities, students receive a one-page partner lesson sheet that they will read together (see the example in Figure 4.1). They take turns serving as Coach and Reader. As Reader, the student practices (a) letter-sounds (i.e., giving the pronunciation for a letter), (b) reading high-frequency words, (c) sounding out words using letter-sounds students have already learned, and (d) reading sentences that contain words and high-frequency words students have already learned.

These procedures are modeled and practiced during the whole-group component to assure Coaches follow the procedures correctly. A final component is added to K-PALS around the 39th lesson, after about 13 weeks of K-PALS implementation. This component, Partner Reading, allows partners to apply their developing reading skills to interesting level-appropriate books outside the controlled partner activity context.

An important feature of K-PALS is the partner assignment system. Students do not work with partners at their exact reading level. Rather, the students with the greatest reading needs are paired with some students at about grade level and some students at grade level are paired with students above grade level. The pairs are changed frequently to maximize the benefits of working with peers at different levels, the strongest reading skills are paired with their peers who have the greatest reading needs.

The final important feature of K-PALS is that teachers have time to monitor individual students closely. As described at the beginning of the chapter, one challenge in teaching Kindergarten is that students vary dramatically in their preparation for beginning to read at school. Some students have had little exposure to school-like experiences and no knowledge of basic reading concepts. Other children will already have learned their alphabet letters and know some alphabet sounds. Some students may have learned some sight words and can read short simple books even on the first day.

The opportunity to monitor during K-PALS supports teachers in addressing these very diverse needs. Because students are working with a partner and have tasks that fill the entire instructional period (however long it is; K-PALS lessons last 20–30 minutes), the teacher can listen to a single student read. The teacher can take notes about student needs to identify instructional foci for small-group instruction. The teacher can also briefly review routines or pronunciations for pairs as needed. In short, the opportunity to monitor provides teachers with time to examine the needs of specific students without worrying about what else the other students are doing—even when the teacher is not leading small group instruction. K-PALS activities are summarized in Table 4.1.

Case Study

Background Information

Ms. Ursa is a third-year Kindergarten teacher at Sterling Elementary School. The school is in a low-middle-class suburban town with a high population of Spanish-speaking families. About 31% of families have income below the poverty level and 39% receive food stamps/SNAP benefits. As a third-year teacher, Ms. Ursa entered the school year feeling confident about her teaching and prepared to support her students; however, this was an exceptional school year. There were 26 students in Ms. Ursa's class, an increase from previous years, and the school district in general was understaffed and low in resources. About 30% of her class (8 students total) were multilingual with only 5 of those students meeting English proficiency standards on WIDA, a common assessment used to evaluate language

TABLE 4.1 K-PALS Activities

Activity	*Purpose*	*Modeled and practiced in teacher-directed whole group lesson*		
		Teacher as coach	*Student as coach*	*Practiced in partner activities*
Sound Play	Develop phonological awareness skills to support decoding words with phonics.	Yes	Yes	No
What Sound	Build knowledge of sound-spellings	Yes	Yes	Yes
Sight Words	Build knowledge of high-frequency words	Yes	Yes	Yes
Sound Boxes	Practice phonics blending with already-taught sound-spellings	Yes	Yes	Yes
Sentence Reading	Practice transferring word-level skills to larger text units	Yes	Yes	Yes
Partner Reading	Practice transferring word and sentence skills to reading texts (after Lesson 39)	No	No	Yes

knowledge. In addition, one student received special education services for a speech/language delay.

At the beginning of the year, Ms. Ursa believed many of her students were behind in reading-related skills. Unlike prior years, many students had started the school year unable to name the letters of the alphabet and the concept of story reading was a new experience for them. When Ms. Ursa had her students create their own name cards, some wrote down letters resembling their names while others scribbled or drew abstract pictures. The wide range of abilities was of concern as she began to plan out her reading instruction. She was particularly struck by how far behind many of her students appeared to be, seeming to have no experience with words or letters, and she worried the Tier 1 curriculum in place at Sterling would not be sufficient to meet all their needs. How was she to provide class-wide instruction with such a large group of students of various skill levels? Ms. Ursa had anecdotal evidence to support her suspicions about her students' reading skills, but she needed assessment data to determine an adequate instructional plan.

Problem Identification

To assess students' readiness for literacy instruction, fall universal screening for kindergarten classes in Sterling Elementary included measures of phonological segmentation, phonics, and letter naming. Students who spoke Spanish at home were also tested using the Spanish versions of measures, where applicable (see Tables 4.2 and 4.3). Results of one universal screening measure, a phonics survey (CORE, 2018) which measures students' knowledge of letter-sound correspondences, for Ms. Ursa's class are described in Table 4.2.

Typically, students who scored at the strategic and intensive levels on screening measures would be identified for further testing using several diagnostic assessments, e.g., letter sound fluency, letter naming fluency, and sight word knowledge. For this class, since most students scored at the strategic and benchmark levels, Ms. Ursa decided to assess all students in the class for letter naming fluency and phoneme segmentation (Spanish version where appropriate) using DIBELS benchmark measures (University of Oregon, 2021). These scores would also serve as a baseline performance measure in each area. Scores for individual students on these assessments are shown in Table 4.3.

Overall, Ms. Ursa noticed that students' skills in each of these areas varied widely but were skewed toward the most intensive needs. These results were not unanticipated: kindergarten screening before school began included an assessment of students' concepts of print knowledge, and kindergarten teachers in all classes at Sterling Elementary saw a great deal of variability in the skills associated with these literacy conventions. Ms. Ursa could see from the data that she had collected that she would need a supplemental intervention which would target a wide variety of literacy skills, and which would be feasible within her full and diverse classroom.

TABLE 4.2 CORE Phonics Survey: Kindergarten Fall Scores

	Benchmark	*Strategic*	*Intensive*
English	5	8	10
Spanish	1	1	1

Note: Columns show the number of students in the class who scored at Benchmark, Strategic, and Intensive levels (CORE, 2018)

TABLE 4.3 DIBELS Benchmarks: Kindergarten Fall Scores

Student	*MLL?*	*Letter Naming Fluency (LNF)* 25/16	*Fluidez en Nombrar Letras (FNL)* 6/3	*Phoneme Segmentation Fluency (PSF)* 5/1	*Fluidez en la Segmentacion de Fonemas (FSF-TLP)* 15/5
Alejandra	Y	23		10	
Beatriz	Y	27		14	
Jaime	Y	16		4	
Luis	Y	14		3	
Gabriela	Y	28		8	
Miguel	Y		7		16
Javier	Y		2		14
Isabel	Y		5		4
Jordan		19		0	
Ava		25		2	
Wesley		30		6	
Nicholas		27		4	
Brooklyn		27		7	
Jacob		13		0	
Chloe		25		7	
Kai		26		5	
Ang		19		4	
Hiram		21		3	
Nora		20		3	
Deandre		16		2	
Jadalyn		25		4	
Shannon		10		3	
Martin		26		7	
Cari		25		4	
Olivia		6		0	
Brian		9		0	
	Benchmark	11 (48%)	1 (33%)	8 (35%)	1 (33%)
	Strategic	7 (30%)	1 (33%)	11 (48%)	1 (33%)
	Intensive	5 (22%)	1 (33%)	4 (17%)	1 (33%)

Note. Scores listed under each measure (e.g., 25/16) represent benchmark and risk point scores, respectively. Scores for individual students are listed under the appropriate benchmark assessment (DIBELS 8th Edition; University of Oregon, 2021). Total number of students and percentages for the class falling into each category are noted at the bottom of the table.

Problem Analysis

Ms. Ursa was an early-career teacher, but she had knowledge of several reading programs from her graduate studies and from colleagues who worked in other districts. Many programs, however, required intensive preparation and relied on small-group instruction; Ms. Ursa knew that with a large class she did not have the time for this type of instruction. Ms. Ursa also relied on instructional assistants to support the small-group instruction she already incorporated her lessons, but she did not think she would have the resources to provide an additional segment of explicit small group instruction to the students who really needed it.

Faced with these challenges, Ms. Ursa decided to reach out to fellow kindergarten teachers as well as the school psychologist, Ms. Stansbury, and the school's speech-language pathologist, Mr. Kendall, for suggestions about an instructional program that might feasibly fit along with the regular kindergarten curriculum Ms. Ursa needed to follow. Ms. Ursa presented the data she had collected as she explained to her colleagues that they had to consider the diversity of this class. She felt it would be a challenge to find a program that would be a good fit for all her students, who clearly presented with a wide range of skills and areas in need of support. She worried that her students who were behind in their acquisition of these literacy skills would fall further behind as the year went on.

As members of the school data team, Ms. Stansbury and Mr. Kendall understood the challenges faced by teachers in remediating reading difficulty, and they were interested in working with Ms. Ursa to search for an appropriate program. They also knew that other teachers would benefit from Ms. Ursa's experience because they were faced with many of the same challenges. Analyzing the problem, the team decided they needed a program that was a good fit for this population. The program would need to meet several criteria: (1) it would need to work for a large classroom such as Ms. Ursa's; (2) it must be appropriate for students from diverse backgrounds and home languages; and (3) it must address those foundational skills most in need of support in Ms. Ursa's kindergarten classroom: phonemic awareness, letter naming and letter sound fluency, letter-sound correspondence, high-frequency word knowledge, and fluency.

The team decided K-PALS fit this description because it met these criteria. As described previously, K-PALS includes activities for the entire class to complete. The built-in routines ensure that every student engages in practice at every moment during the lesson. K-PALS is not just a convenient way to manage whole-class activities; rather, it works because peer-mediated routines support student success and because research data show the effectiveness of K-PALS.

K-PALS addresses the needs of diverse students in two ways. First, the pair assignment system engages students in cross-level instruction that will increase the needs of below-level students and reinforce the skills of both on-level and above-level students. Second, the opportunity to monitor allows teachers to support students at every level. During K-PALS, teachers strategically decide which pairs they will visit—to evaluate the needs of students with the most persistent and severe academic difficulties and to check whether students who made slow growth earlier in the year are showing accelerated growth during K-PALS implementation.

K-PALS addresses the critical needs of all Kindergarten students at Sterling Elementary School. It includes (a) phonological awareness, (b) letter-sound, (c) high-frequency word, (d) decoding, and (e) fluency instruction and practice. These five foci align exactly with kindergarten students' needs: they must acquire foundational word-recognition skills because these skills will support their reading comprehension skills and will increase the likelihood that they will show long-term reading success. For the multilingual students in the classroom, K-PALS offers this foundational instruction as well as the additional benefit of providing multiple opportunities for cooperative learning, connecting content to students' background and experiences, and promoting language development (e.g., Cárdenas-Hagan, 2020).

Intervention Goals

According to the Common Core State Standards (CCSS) for English Language Arts (National Governors Association Center for Best Practices & Council of Chief State School Officers, 2010), Kindergarten students are expected to master some criteria in the following foundational reading skills: (1) print concepts, (2) phonological awareness and (3) phonics (see Table 4.4). These standards are also common to state standards in other states that do not follow the CCSS (e.g., Texas Essential Knowledge and Skills in reading; Texas Educational Agency, 2017). The ability to identify and produce the sounds in spoken words serves as a foundation for the acquisition of word-reading skill early on (Snowling & Hulme, 1994) and linking those sounds to common spellings is integral to reading. The universal screening data had revealed that over 75% of the students in Ms. Ursa's class were below benchmark in phonological awareness, sight word reading, and letter-sound knowledge. The areas of skill instruction listed in Table 4.4 reflect the areas of need identified by the screening and those critical for early literacy skill.

If Ms. Ursa and the other kindergarten teachers wanted their students to meet CCSS and be prepared for first-grade reading instruction, they needed

TABLE 4.4 Common Core State Standards ELA

Foundational Skill	*Grade-Level Expectations*	*K-PALS Connection*
Print Concepts	Domain: Demonstrate understanding of the organization and basic features of print. Specific Standards: • Follow words from left to right, top to bottom, and page by page. • Recognize that spoken words are represented in written language by specific sequences of letters. • Understand that words are separated by spaces in print. • Recognize and name all upper- and lowercase letters of the alphabet.	K-PALS includes instruction on all 26 letters and their names and pronunciations a. *Saying Sounds*
Phonological Awareness	Domain: Demonstrate understanding of spoken words, syllables and sounds (phonemes) • Recognize and produce rhyming words. • Count, pronounce, blend, and segment syllables in spoken words. • Blend and segment onsets and rimes of single-syllable spoken words. • Isolate and pronounce initial, medial vowel, and final sounds (phonemes) in three-phoneme (consonant-vowel-consonant, or CVC) words* (This does not include CVCs ending with /l/, /r/ or /x/.) • Add or substitute individual sounds (phonemes) in simple, one-syllable words to make new words.	K-PALS includes a teacher-led activity that includes extensive practice identifying sounds at the beginning of words, in the middle, and at the end and practice segmenting and blending phonemes to pronounce words in addition to practice with rhyming. b. *Sound Play*

(*Continued*)

TABLE 4.4 (Continued)

Foundational Skill	*Grade-Level Expectations*	*K-PALS Connection*
Phonics and Word Recognition	Domain: Know and apply grade-level phonics and word analysis skills in decoding words. a. Demonstrate basic knowledge of one-to-one letter-sound correspondences by producing the primary or many of the most frequent sound for each consonant. b. Associate the long and short sounds with common spellings (graphemes) for the five major vowels. c. Read common high-frequency words by sight (e.g., *the, of, to, you, she, my, is, are, do, does*). d. Distinguish between similarly spelled words by identifying the sounds of the letters that differ.	K-PALS includes extensive practice pronouncing the sounds for individual letters. c. *Saying Sounds* K-PALS includes practice reading common high-frequency words d. *Sight Words* e. *Sentences* f. *Partner Reading* K-PALS includes practice looking at the letters in printed words and linking them to their sounds and blending the sounds together to pronounce words. g. *Sound Boxes* h. *Sentences* i. *Partner Reading*

National Governors Association Center for Best Practices & Council of Chief State School Officers (2010). *Common Core State Standards for English language arts and literacy in history/social studies, science, and technical subjects*. Washington, DC: Authors.

a supplemental reading program that included: 1) sound awareness at the syllable and phoneme level, 2) one-to-one letter-sound correspondence and 3) sight word reading (high-frequency words). Ideally, their students would also be able to decode some simple CVC words, making the link between sounds and spellings.

Measurement of Target Reading Skill, Data Collection Strategies, and Progress Monitoring

The kindergarten team met to decide on the best way to measure student trajectory toward grade-level standards. They devised a monthly progress monitoring plan with all students who were identified as being below benchmark at the beginning of the year. Tracking phonological awareness and letter-sound naming was the priority given the expectations students were to meet in preparation for first grade. They decided on DIBELS 8 Phoneme Segmentation Fluency (PSF; University of Oregon, 2021) for monthly progress monitoring and CORE Phonics Survey (Consonant & Vowel Sounds; CORE, 2018) for benchmark assessment at the beginning, middle and end of the year. Each assessment takes about 1 minute to administer and would be able to give a clear picture of whether students are responding to the instruction.

Sight words would be introduced throughout the supplemental reading program, gradually. The team decided that mastery of each sight word could be tracked by the classroom teacher and that monthly assessment would not be necessary. For example, the CORE Grade High Frequency Word Survey (2018) might be used to informally track sight word reading progress.

An end of the year assessment would provide the team with an adequate picture of student reading skill. Besides re-administering the beginning-of-year benchmarks, the DIBELS 8 Nonsense Word Reading Fluency (NWF; University of Oregon, 2021) would be administered at the end of kindergarten to identify those students who may need continued additional support at the start of first grade.

Intervention Plan

K-PALS is only part of the intervention plan, but it is the focus of this chapter because it will help students at the benchmark, strategic, and intensive levels of need improve their reading outcomes. The team decided that they would implement K-PALS as the manual recommended: 3 times a week for 30 minutes, each time using the scope and sequence provided in the manual, knowing they could adjust this plan if they determined students were not progressing as they had hoped. Ms. Stansbury and Mr. Kendall would each observe and possibly implement some of the K-PALS lessons in the kindergarten classrooms so they could become familiar with the routine and get a better understanding of its feasibility.

Intervention Fidelity and Interobserver Agreement Plans

Ms. Ursa knew that the key to students' K-PALS success was a strong implementation of K-PALS. As a result, she made sure she completed the K-PALS lessons with fidelity. Fidelity means that Ms. Ursa reviewed the procedures for each part of a K-PALS lesson and assured that she was completing every activity the way it was designed. Ms. Ursa knew that fidelity focuses primarily on (a) using the language of the K-PALS routines and (b) completing all the K-PALS activities. She also knew that K-PALS must be integrated into her existing practice, meaning that students still followed her general classroom procedures and that she included her other external reinforcement systems (e.g., stickers for high levels of effort during activities) throughout the lessons. Figure 4.2 includes a part of the fidelity checklist Ms. Ursa used to check her own fidelity; Ms. Stansbury and Mr. Kendall also assisted in tracking fidelity on the days that they observed her lessons. Ms. Ursa and the other Kindergarten teachers also talked about K-PALS as part of their professional learning community activities every month or so to discuss their successes and address any needs that were making it hard for them to implement the program with fidelity.

Intervention Outcome Data

Ms. Ursa did not expect every student would experience dramatic success as a result of K-PALS. The kindergarten team estimated that the program addressed the needs of about 80% of their students. In Ms. Ursa's class, all students showed adequate progress after the first month; however, several students were not performing as she hoped. She addressed this need in two ways. First, her schedule included time for small-group instruction 3 days per week, and she used this time to address the specific needs of these students (identified when she was monitoring students during K-PALS). Second, she collaborated with other members of the school team to support these students. The administrators at Sterling were beginning to implement a systematic supplemental instructional program for students who needed additional support. Ms. Ursa also collaborated with the teacher who provided first-language instruction to multilingual students to make connections where they existed and to identify needs that might arise during K-PALS (e.g., students pronouncing sounds in unexpected ways that

Peer-Mediated What Sound Checklist	
Pair One	
Coach:	Reader:
The Coach prompts the Reader to say each sound by saying, "What Sound?"	
The Coach watches while the Reader is saying each sound.	
The Reader says each sound.	
The Coach praises the Reader at each star.	
Coach corrects the Reader when needed (receives a '+' value if the Coach does correct, a '–' if the Coach misses 2 or more mistakes.) Must complete components from steps a, c & e to receive "+."	
The Coach tells the sound (e.g., "Stop. That sound is _____.")	
The Coach tells the Reader to repeat the sound (e.g., "What sound?")	
The Reader repeats the sound.	
The Coach asks the Reader to repeat the line (e.g., "Good. Go back and read that line again.")	
The Reader reads the line again.	
When they have completed the activity one time: mark one happy face.	
Student or teacher marks 1 point on the point sheet. If the teacher marks the points, check back with the pair later.	
The students switch roles. Coach:	Reader:
The Coach prompts the Reader to say each sound by saying, "What Sound?"	
The Coach watches while the Reader is saying each sound.	
The Reader says the sounds.	
The Coach praises the Reader at each star.	

FIGURE 4.2 K-PALS Fidelity Checklist

should be considered correct). She did the same with the speech-language pathologist to assure that her instruction would help her student with a developmental language disorder.

By January, Ms. Ursa was pleased at the overall progress her students had made. After administering the same benchmark measures she used in September, she could see that students had made the most progress in Letter Naming Fluency and considerable progress in Phoneme Segmentation. As described earlier, Ms. Ursa and the kindergarten team also used other benchmark measures at mid-year, but those repeated measures are described in Table 4.5.

Based on mid-year progress, Ms. Ursa expected most students to meet grade-level expectations by the end of the year—despite their low initial screening data. In addition, by January, the K-PALS routine was so familiar in Ms. Ursa's classroom that students followed it independently, allowing her to spend even more time listening to and supporting her most struggling students. Ms. Ursa's expectations were borne out by end-of-year benchmarks which showed the progress students had made (see Table 4.6 for students' progress on the repeated measures and the Nonsense Word Fluency benchmark the team had decided to add as part of its progress monitoring plan). Most students moved up at least one proficiency level by

TABLE 4.5 January Benchmark Scores

	Letter Naming Fluency (LNF) 25/16	*Fluidez en Nombrar Letras (FNL)* 6/3	*Phoneme Segmentation Fluency (PSF)* 5/1	*Fluidez en la Segmentacion de Fonemas (FSF-TLP)* 15/5
Benchmark	17	2	12	2
Strategic	3	1	9	1
Intensive	3	0	2	0
Benchmark	74%	67%	52%	67%
Strategic	13%	33%	39%	33%
Intensive	13%	0%	9%	0%

TABLE 4.6 May Benchmark Scores

	Letter Naming Fluency (LNF) 25/16	*Fluidez en Nombrar Letras (FNL)* 6/3	*Phoneme Segmentation Fluency (PSF)* 5/1	*Fluidez en la Segmentacion de Fonemas (FSF-TLP)* 15/5	*Nonsense Word Fluency (NWF-CLS)* 31/24
Benchmark	20	3	16	2	17
Strategic	2	0	5	1	7
Intensive	1	0	3	0	3
Benchmark (%)	87	100	70	67	65
Strategic (%)	8	0	22	33	27
Intensive (%)	5	0	8	0	6

Note: Only scores for Correct Letter Sounds (CLS) are represented for the DIBELS Nonsense Word Fluency subtest (University of Oregon, 2021).

the January screening, suggesting they were on track for success by the end of the year. Ms. Ursa could see that the students needed the most work in phoneme segmentation fluency. She expected that the implementation of K-PALS with Sound Play and the other sound-spelling routines, in addition to other individualized supports would result in grade-level performance for all or most of her students at the end of the year.

Intervention Acceptability

Ms. Ursa and the other Kindergarten teachers enjoyed K-PALS; that is, they found it very acceptable. They shared with teachers in other grades that they thought the program was helpful. They highlighted that K-PALS gave students extensive practice, gave them an opportunity to work with peers at different levels, and provided a consistent routine that was not difficult to teach and could be used the entire year.

Important to note is that Ms. Ursa and her colleagues implemented K-PALS without immediate support from an instructional coach or a member of the K-PALS research team that designed the program. The researchers previously found that teachers were more likely to sustain implementation of K-PALS if they did it without immediate guidance (Kearns et al., 2010). The researchers theorized that implementation without immediate supervision allowed teachers greater flexibility in the use of the program and therefore could more easily implement it on their own terms. Ms. Ursa and her colleagues implemented K-PALS on their own terms—meaning that they made a few changes to the program not included in its design (e.g., breaking lessons by into parts to complete across two days). Implementation of individualized changes meant their fidelity was not as high as possible, but it also may be associated with her commitment to ongoing implementation.

Intervention Considerations

As part of their evaluation of the success of K-PALS in Ms. Ursa's classroom, the team considered whether the program had been as culturally responsive as they anticipated when they chose it early in the year. The team knew that the dimensions of culturally responsive teaching included engaging and validating students' cultural knowledge and experiences while setting high expectations for students' success (e.g., Aronson & Laughter, 2016), and they worked to be comprehensive in this way in their classrooms. Because of the flexibility of the K-PALS program, teachers were able to incorporate culturally responsive texts at the correct levels for the students in the class after the first thirteen weeks of lessons, and they were able to create cross-leveled pairs so multilingual students were supported by Spanish- and English-speaking peers.

For example, Ms. Ursa considered what she knew about the students' interests and how cultural diversity is represented in texts, working to align books with students' interests and choosing those books that show affirming and authentic representations of varied cultures—including those shared by students in the classroom.

Teachers appreciated that K-PALS allowed them to individualize instruction in this way, and they also liked that K-PALS allowed for flexible grouping, which Ms. Ursa felt had contributed to the development of a cooperative and positive classroom culture. Ms. Ursa also appreciated that the flexible nature of implementing the K-PALS routine allowed her to make those adjustments (e.g., collaborating with specialists and incorporating supplemental instruction for students who needed it) that she considered key to some of her students' success at meeting grade-level benchmarks by the end of the year.

Conclusion

Because of the ease with which teachers and their students could incorporate K-PALS into their instructional routines, the flexibility and adaptability of the program in allowing for culturally and instructionally responsive text choice and teacher autonomy, and the clear improvement in students' foundational skills by year-end, the kindergarten teachers at Sterling Elementary decided to continue to use K-PALS as part of their curriculum the following year. First-grade teachers also appreciated that they could reintroduce K-PALS to their students in the fall, knowing that drawing on a routine familiar to students would ease students' transition to a new classroom. The routine would also be valuable for those students who needed more intensive foundational support in first grade. In short, K-PALS worked well for teachers at Sterling Elementary in several ways: it filled an instructional gap for kindergarten teachers who were initially faced with the daunting challenge of meeting the needs of large and diverse classrooms of students, and it proved to be valuable to teachers across the early grades who needed an easily adopted and effective routine for foundational reading skill instruction.

References

Aronson, B., & Laughter, J. (2016). The theory and practice of culturally relevant education: A synthesis of research across content areas. *Review of Educational Research*, *86*(1), 163–206. doi:10.3102/0034654315582066

Cárdenas-Hagan, E. (Ed.). (2020). *Literacy foundations for English learners: A comprehensive guide to evidence-based instruction*. Baltimore, MD: Paul H.Brookes Publishing Co.

Continuum on Reading Excellence in Education, Inc. (CORE). (2018). *Assessing reading: Multiple measures*. L. Diamond & B. J. Thorsnes (Eds.). Novato, CA: Arena Press.

Fuchs, D., & Fuchs, L. S. (2005). Peer-assisted learning strategies: Promoting word recognition, fluency, and reading comprehension in young children. *The Journal of Special Education*, *39*(1), 34–44. doi:10.1177/00224669050390010401

Fuchs, D., Fuchs, L. S., & Burish, P. (2000). Peer-assisted learning strategies: An evidence-based practice to promote reading achievement. *Learning Disabilities Research & Practice*, *15*(2), 85–91. doi:10.1207/sldrp1502_4

Fuchs, D., Fuchs, L. S., Mathes, P. G., & Martinez, E. A. (2002). Preliminary evidence on the social standing of students with learning disabilities in PALS and No–PALS classrooms. *Learning Disabilities Research & Practice*, *17*(4), 205–215. doi:10.1111/1540-5826.00046

Fuchs, D., Fuchs, L. S., Otaiba, S. A., Thompson, A., Yen, L., Mcmaster, K. N., Yen, L., Svensen, E., & Yang, N. J. (2001). K-PALS helping kindergartners with reading readiness: Teachers and researchers in partnerships. *Teaching Exceptional Children*, *33*(4), 76–80. doi:10.1177/004005990103300411

Hollands, F., Pan, Y., Shand, R., Cheng, H., Levin, H. M., Belfield, C. R., ... & Hanisch-Cerda, B. (2013). Improving early literacy: Cost-effectiveness analysis of effective reading programs. doi:10.3102/0162373713511850

Kearns, D. M., Fuchs, D., Meyers, C., Berends, M., McMaster, K., Sáenz, L. S., Fuchs, L. S., Yen, L., Meyers, C., Stein, M., Compton, D., Berends, M., & Smith, T. M. (2010). Factors contributing to teachers' sustained use of kindergarten peer-assisted learning atrategies. *Journal of Research on Educational Effectiveness*, *3*(4), 315–342. doi:10.1080/19345747.2010.491151

Lee, Y. (2014). Promise for enhancing children's reading attitudes through peer reading: A mixed method approach. *The Journal of Educational Research*, 107(6), 482–492. doi:10.1080/00220671.2013.836469

Lemons, C. J., Fuchs, D., Gilbert, J. K., & Fuchs, L. S. (2014). Evidence-based practices in a changing world: Reconsidering the counterfactual in education research. *Educational Researcher*, 43(5), 242–252. doi:10.3102/0013189x14539189

Mattatall, C. A. (2017). Using peer assisted learning strategies for boys, aboriginal learners, and at-risk populations. *Reading & Writing Quarterly*, 33(2), 155–170. doi:10.1080/10573569.2016.1142914

McMaster, K. L., Fuchs, D., & Fuchs, L. S. (2006). Research on peer-assisted learning strategies: The promise and limitations of peer-mediated instruction. *Reading & Writing Quarterly*, 22(1), 5–25. doi:10.1080/10573560500203491

National Governors Association Center for Best Practices & Council of Chief State School Officers. (2010). *Common core state standards for English language arts and literacy in history/social studies, science, and technical subjects*. Washington, DC: Author.

Snowling, M., & Hulme, C. (1994). The development of phonological skills. *Philosophical Transactions of the Royal Society of London Series B: Biological Sciences*, *346*(1315), 21–27. doi:10.1098/rstb.1994.0124

Texas Education Agency. (2017). *19 TAC Chapter 110. Texas essential knowledge and skills for English language arts and reading*. Austin, TX: Author. Retrieved from https://tea.texas.gov/sites/default/files/ch110toc.pdf

University of Oregon. (2021). *8th Edition of Dynamic Indicators of Basic Early Literacy Skills (DIBELS ®)*. Eugene, OR: University of Oregon. Retrieved from https://dibels.uoregon.edu/

5

SOUND PARTNERS

Patricia F. Vadasy

Oregon Research Institute, Eugene, OR, USA

Introduction

In kindergarten and first-grade classrooms across the country, teachers notice with concern students who struggle to learn basic reading skills. District-wide screening assessments help to identify the students with limited letter-name and letter-sound knowledge, phoneme segmenting and blending, decoding, and spelling. Schools that use Multi-tiered Systems of Support (MTSS) and Response-to-Intervention (RTI) models develop plans to guide instruction for these struggling students. Classroom teachers often try to add practice for these students during their Tier I reading instruction, and to carefully monitor student rate of growth. When a student does not respond adequately to a scientifically based classroom reading program, a team of teachers often meets to consider a more intensive small group or one-to-one intervention.

Beginning in the late 1990s our research team set out to develop a one-to-one tutoring intervention, *Sound Partners* (Vadasy, Wayne, et al., 2005), to supplement classroom instruction in early word-reading skills for kindergarten and first-grade students. We wanted to develop a scalable intervention that the Title I schools we worked with at that time could use to help students overcome the most common hurdles beginning readers encounter to acquire accurate decoding and word-reading skills. For these schools, a costly program like Reading Recovery implemented by trained specialist teachers was beyond their reach (see Iversen & Tunmer, 1993; University of Delaware, 2022). The schools needed an intervention that was cost-effective, feasible to implement in schools serving

DOI: 10.4324/9781003275749-5

large numbers of underperforming students, and based on scientific research on reading acquisition. Children with early reading difficulties most often have limited phonological skills and alphabet knowledge. We designed lessons that incorporated explicit and systematic instruction in phonemic awareness and phonics that is informed by the Science of Reading (Castles et al., 2018; Piasta & Hudson, 2022). Explicit instruction is characterized by instructional routines to support student learning (Gunn et al., 2021), and in *Sound Partners* this includes modeling how to segment or blend phonemes, and providing frequent practice and clear corrections and feedback.

Sound Partners is a systematic and explicit phonics intervention. It uses a synthetic approach (explicitly teaching letter-sound correspondences and how to blend sounds to read words) to introduce children to phonemic awareness skills and letter-sound correspondences prerequisite for decoding (see Piasta & Hudson, 2022). Letter-sound knowledge, for example, is a difficult learning task for many children (Roberts et al., 2018). Many children require more intensive support and practice to learn alphabet knowledge and phonological recoding than classroom teachers can provide. Therefore, we set out to design a phonics intervention that non-teachers, primarily paraeducators and other trained adult tutors, could deliver effectively. We conducted a series of randomized control trials to evaluate the intervention implemented by these tutors in typical urban school settings (Vadasy & Sanders, 2010, 2011, 2012, 2013). We initially tested the instruction with first-graders, and later developed a version for kindergarteners (Vadasy, 2013). Development was iterative, incorporating observations and feedback from users in a series of implementations and revisions. During the period of our research on the program, the school enrollments of English learners increased (U.S. Department of Education, 2022). In the later intervention studies, we compared intervention outcomes for kindergarten and first-graders, for Dual Language Learners (DLLs) and native English speakers, for 1:1 and 2:1 implementation, and examined intervention outcomes at posttest and two-year follow up. Later research added further support for the program's phonics content and sequence (Vadasy & Sanders, 2021).

Both kindergarten and first-grade levels of *Sound Partners* were designed for one-to-one tutoring (a highly effective means of helping struggling readers). One goal was to design the intervention so that it could be delivered by paraeducator staff we had observed working in schools. Paraeducators serve in many roles, and there are an estimated 730,000 paraeducators employed in U.S. public schools (U.S. Department of Education, 2014). Many paraeducators have the knowledge and experience to effectively extend classroom reading instruction if they are provided with clearly designed instructional scripts and training (Vadasy & Sanders, 2011).

The kindergarten and upper levels of *Sound Partners* target: alphabetics, phonemic awareness, phonics, fluency, and application of word-level skills in decodable storybook reading. Components and features of the programs are outlined in Table 5.1.

The later lessons in the upper-level program also include instruction in silent-e words, multisyllable words (Heggie & Wade-Wooley, 2017), and

TABLE 5.1 Sound Partners Program Components and Features

Alphabetics—Letter–sound relationships (single-letter grapheme-phoneme correspondences progressing to digraphs, diphthongs, and affixes) are introduced at a recommended and tested rate and sequence, with extensive opportunities for practice and feedback (Vadasy & Sanders, 2021).
Decoding—Practice decoding individual words made up of new and previously introduced letter sounds. Tutors learn to model and teach stretched or continuous blending of the phonemes in words (Gonzalez-Frey & Ehri, 2021). Beginning decoders often have difficulty applying their new decoding strategies to read words in context. Individual lesson components offer many opportunities for word identification in context-free text (e.g., word lists) and in sentence and storybook reading.
Segmenting and spelling—Practice segmenting two–four phoneme words, and spelling both decodable and irregular words being learned in the lessons (Ehri, 2000). Suggestions for scaffolding spelling with sound boxes.
Storybook reading practice—Students practice accurate and fluent reading in decodable storybooks that feature the letters and sounds they are learning (Carnine et al., 1997). Storybooks are matched to the phonics content to provide decoding practice and build motivation and confidence.
Strategic integration—Individual instructional components are linked to help students make connections between skills. For example, letter–sound correspondence that have been introduced are used to teach phonemic blending and segmenting, decoding, and spelling practice, and are featured in the decodable storybook reading. Words that are used for decoding practice are also used for spelling.
Opportunities to respond—Lesson design for each skill features clear tutor models and scaffolds. Students have multiple opportunities to respond to support student engagement, reinforce student learning, and provide tutors with opportunities to reinforce or correct (Cuticelli, Collier-Meek, & Coyne, 2016; Gunn et al., 2021).
Judicious review—Less experienced tutors may have difficulty determining how much review to provide. Lessons have been extensively tested with numerous cohorts of students who were identified in the lowest quartile in reading skills and are designed to provide adequate review for most students who need more intensive instruction.

common affixes. It is helpful to compare the content for the kindergarten and upper levels of *Sound Partners*. We will refer to the original version as the "upper level" because while we evaluated that version with first-graders, many schools use that level with students in grades 2–3 with limited word-reading skills. The kindergarten level includes added practice to develop phonemic awareness and alphabet knowledge, and introduces skills at a slower rate than the upper level (see Appendix A).

Figures 5.1 and 5.2 feature Lesson 10 from each level of the program. By Lesson 10 in the kindergarten level, the student has been introduced to five letters, and continues to practice syllable segmenting. The lesson directs the tutor to explicitly model stretched out blending of words. By Lesson 10 in the upper level, the student has been introduced to six letters, and begins to practice reading decodable sentences and storybooks. A direct comparison of the scope and sequence for each level details the differences between the programs in teaching activities and rates for introducing and practicing new skills.

	Remember to find one thing to praise each student for today. Give specific praise to point out how your student is improving in one skill.
d D dog	**Say/Write the Sounds** Trace new letter with finger. "Now you trace the letter. Say the sound. Say the name."
d a s c apple sun cat	"Point to each letter. Say the sound."
t d s m table moon	(Paper) ____ "Write the letter that makes the sound. Write it three times." Choose three or more sounds to practice.
a d t m	"Circle your best letter."

FIGURE 5.1 Kindergarten Lesson 10

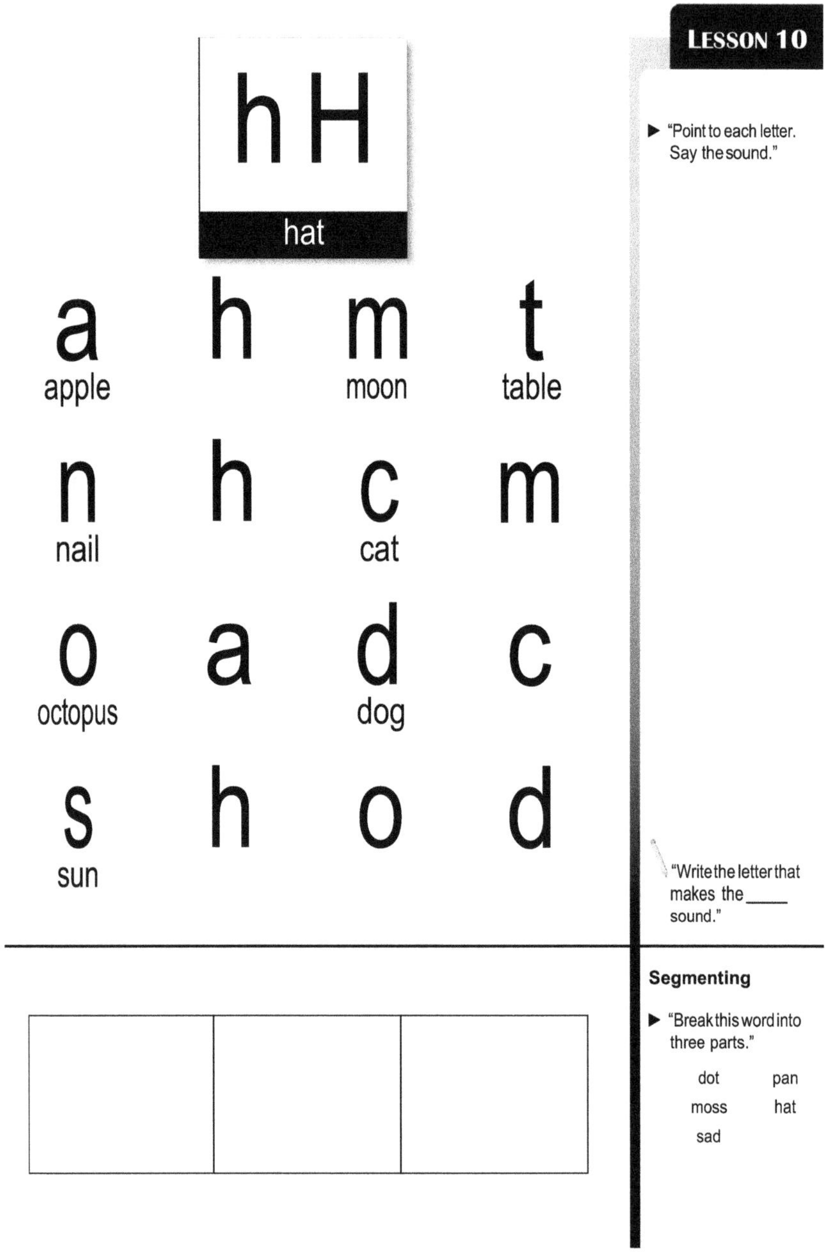

FIGURE 5.2 Upper Level Lesson 10

hot		
hot	Mac	dot
mad	and	cat
hat	cod	cot
not	ham	and
had	mat	at

Mac had a cat. Mac and cat sat on a cot.

Lesson 10 cont'd

Word Reading

▶ "Sound these out and say them fast."

"What sound does ____ **start** with?"

"What sound does ____ **end** with?"

"Now you spell____."

Choose three words for student to spell and read.

Tutor Notes Always have student repeat/say the word before spelling. Always have student read all words after spelling them.

▶ "Read these sentences. Point to each word."

Tutor Notes Supply the sight word a.

Book Reading

▶ Read Sam.

FIGURE 5.2 (Continued)

Below we summarize the research supporting the program (both the original and the kindergarten versions) and its components. Following this review, we describe the process of implementing *Sound Partners* with two students at a hypothetical elementary school in a large urban school district similar to the sites in which the program was evaluated.

Establishing Intervention Efficacy

Our research team investigated the implementation of *Sound Partners* in typical urban public school settings in a series of studies with 10 cohorts of students between 1998 and 2011, funded by the U.S. Department of Education's Institute of Education Sciences. Most students enrolled in these studies were nonwhite, often attending Title I schools, and eligible for free- or reduced-cost meals. Reflecting trends in school enrollments, in the later years the studies included larger numbers of English language learners. In the later studies, we employed the most rigorous research designs to compare the efficacy of *Sound Partners* tutoring with kindergarten and first-grade students, and with DLLs and native English-speaking students. We also examined long-term effects of tutoring at two years post-intervention, at the end of grade 2 and 3, respectively. Table 5.2 summarizes the intensity of the interventions in these studies.

The published studies summarize in detail these research procedures, measures, fidelity, and student outcomes. While rigorously designed research is necessary to determine program effectiveness, individual students are often lost in the detailed aggregate data of these studies. Many schools begin to use *Sound Partners* with their first-graders and older students with

TABLE 5.2 Intensity of Sound Partner Interventions

Sound Partners *intervention intensity in published studies*

Study year and journal	*Grade level*	*Average total weeks of intervention*	*Average total lessons completed*	*Average lessons per week completed*
2004, *SSR*	1	25	76	3.04
2006, *JEP*	K	18	47	2.6
2010, *JEP*	K	18	64	3.5
2011, *SSR*	1	20	66	3.3
		Average 20 total weeks of intervention	Average 51 total lessons completed	Average 3.11 lessons completed per week

SSR: Scientific Studies of Reading; JEP: Journal of Educational Psychology.

Sound Partners 2007–08 Efficacy Trial Results (in Brief)

Immediate and Long-Term Benefits for English Learners (ELL) and non-ELLs in Grades K-1

Kindergarten Intervention[1,2]

In 2007–2008, kindergarten students in the lower half of their classroom in reading skills were randomly assigned to *Sound Partners* tutoring ($n = 67$, 38 ELLs), or classroom control ($n = 81$, 46 ELLs). Students averaged in the 22nd percentile in receptive vocabulary and 32nd percentile in word reading at pretest.

Findings: Across both ELL and non-ELL students, tutored students were significantly higher at kindergarten posttest in word reading, spelling, fluency, and comprehension.

Follow up: Two years after intervention (end of grade 2), non-ELL tutored students maintained a significant advantage over non-ELL controls across all outcomes: word reading, spelling, fluency, and comprehension. ELL tutored students maintained a significant advantage over ELL controls in word reading and spelling.

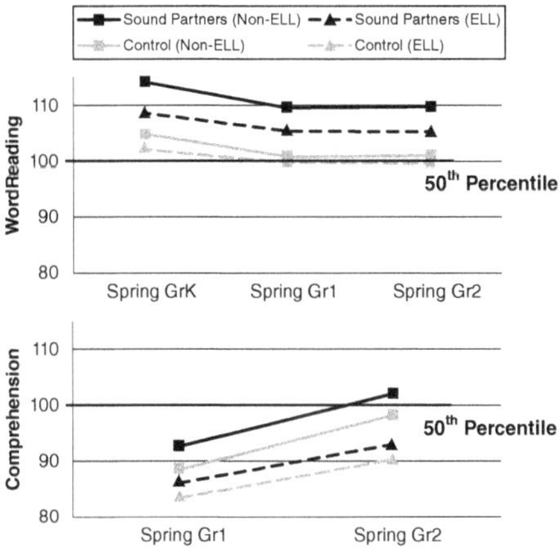

First-Grade Intervention[3,4]

Also in 2007–2008, first-grade students in the lower half of their classroom in reading skills were randomly assigned to *Sound Partners* tutoring ($n = 93$, 48 ELLs), or classroom control ($n = 94$, 50 ELLs).

Findings: Tutored students were significantly higher than controls at first grade posttest in word reading, spelling, fluency and comprehension. ELL students who received tutoring were also significantly higher than controls in word reading and spelling.

Follow up: Two years after intervention (end of grade 3), non-ELL tutored students maintained a significant advantage over non-ELL controls in word reading and spelling. ELL tutored students maintained a significant advantage over ELL controls in word reading and comprehension.

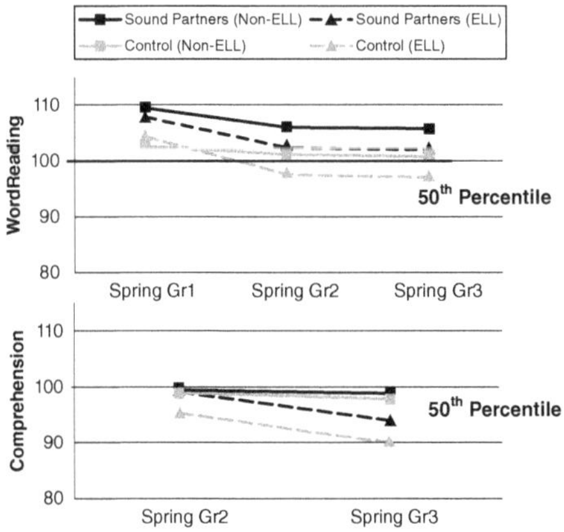

[1]GradeKdata from analyses in Vadasy &Sanders (2010) *Journal of Educational Psychology*.
[2]Grade 1-2data from analysesinVadasy&Sanders (2012) *Journalof Educational Psychology*
[3]Grade 1data fromanalyses in Vadasy &Sanders (2011) *Scientific Studiesof Reading*.
[4]Grade 2-3data from analysesinVadasy&Sanders (2013) *Readingand Writing: An InterdisciplinaryJournal*.

FIGURE 5.3 Kindergarten and First-Grade Findings

word-reading difficulty. Later in our work, as kindergarten literacy objectives increased, schools began to provide early supplemental interventions for these younger students. Our findings (see Figure 5.3) comparing student outcomes for kindergarten and first-grade students supported the benefits of the kindergarten intervention.

Student Selection

In our research studies, the screening procedure for students included three measures. The first two were measures of alphabetic knowledge, the number of letter sounds and letter names produced correctly out of 52 randomly ordered upper-case English letters (Fuchs et al., 2001). The third was a test of phonological awareness (Sound Matching subtest from the Comprehensive Test of Phonological Processing (CTOPP; Wagner et al., 1999)). Both alphabetic knowledge (Chall, 1967; Share et al., 1984; Tunmer, Herriman, & Nesdale, 1988) and phonological awareness (Adams, 1990; Bus & van IJzendoorn, 1999; Shankweiler & Liberman, 1989; Share, 1995; Snowling, 1991a; Stanovich, 2000) are well-established early predictors of reading outcomes in monolingual English speakers. Phonological awareness and alphabetic skills are related to English word reading in language-minority children (Chiappe et al., 2002; Lesaux et al., 2006; Lipka & Siegel, 2007). Teachers also shared with us their recommendations for students in need of Tier 2 intervention. Screening measures for the later kindergarten studies included alphabet knowledge and Dynamic Indicators of Basic Early Literacy Skills (DIBELS) subtests (see Appendix B). At the time of this writing, many schools use Acadience assessments to help identify students for instructional modifications (Good & Kaminski, 2020; Kaminski et al., 2019). Acadience is a screener used to identify early reading problems in elementary students. It includes standardized, brief, individual assessments that help teachers identify core early literacy skills (e.g., first sound fluency, nonsense word fluency) they can target for instruction.

Tutor Training

Research staff trained the tutors in the research studies, providing 4–6 hours of initial training, and follow-up coaching during on-site observations. Trainers provided an overview of phonemic awareness skills that were taught in the lessons. To insure that tutors modeled the letter-sound correspondences correctly, trainers modeled and tutors practiced the accurate pronunciation for each letter. During the initial training, the researchers introduced the lesson components, and modeled how to implement each of the lesson activities. Trainers reviewed effective organization and strategies to support student-learning behaviors, including positive behavior supports to support their instruction (Lindstrom et al., 2022). The tutors then paired up to practice delivering instruction, with researchers observing and providing feedback. Schools that adopt *Sound Partners* may train tutors in several ways. A reading coach or reading specialist may use the published implementation guide to offer tutor training similar to that provided in the research sites. This often works well when the tutors (i.e., paraeducators, experienced tutors) have had experience using other explicit reading programs and have previous experience working with students. More recently, a research team at the University of North Carolina Charlotte (UNCC) led by Drs. Kristen Beach, Samantha Gesel, and Erin Washburn developed a virtual implementation of *Sound Partners* (Beach et al., 2021), as well as virtual asynchronous training and consultation. COVID-19 accelerated the transition from in-person to online instruction in schools, and our collective knowledge of what makes virtual instruction feasible and effective is growing. Virtual training and tutoring formats for *Sound Partners* such as the materials prepared by the UNCC team and others have expanded options for tutoring students (Beach et al., 2021; Haggerty, 2022). For example, the Literacy Trust group offers virtual *Sound Partners* training to schools in the New York City area and beyond (https://literacytrust.org/literacy-intervention). Future research on variations in implementing programs like *Sound Partners* will inform effective modifications that maintain fidelity (McMaster et al., 2014).

Intervention Fidelity

Our team of research staff observed instruction for all students served in the research studies. We recorded fidelity and notes using the Tutor Observation Form included in the program. To establish inter-rater reliability, after tutor training but prior to field observations, researchers viewed six videotaped tutoring sessions of paraeducators implementing instruction with students. We calculated internal consistency of the observers' mean implementation ratings for the videotaped sessions to insure they were adequate. Research staff provided regular feedback on lesson implementation and general instruction recommendations for: organizing materials and seating arrangements to minimize distractions; maintaining a brisk pace for instruction; being receptive to coach feedback. Fidelity observations were scored on a 5-point rating scale, ranging from 1 (*never implements correctly*) to 5 (*always implements correctly*), for each of the instructional components. Researchers conducted an average of 7–9 observations per tutor. Fidelity ratings across our studies averaged $M = 4.41$ ($SD = 0.57$). We recommend that schools establish inter-rater or within-rater reliability for their coaches or observers before they begin to implement the program in their sites. Both levels of the program include fidelity checklists that local supervisors and coaches can use and adapt to maintain high levels of implementation.

Summary of Intervention Effects

We conducted an extended series of studies to test the effectiveness of *Sound Partners* on target literacy skills, primarily alphabet knowledge, decoding, word reading, and spelling. In several studies, we also examined fluency and reading comprehension outcomes. The earlier studies conducted published between 1997 and 2005 compared tutored students to classroom-matched controls, with sample sizes averaging 20 students in each group. In the later studies published between 2006 and 2013 we employed more rigorous research designs with larger sample sizes, with random assignment to groups within classrooms allowing us to control for student pretest levels, language status, and the influence of classroom instruction. In the early studies, we also compared the benefits of individual versus dyad tutoring, and the influence of tutoring intensity and book reading practice, including use of decodable storybooks. (Jenkins et al., 2004; Vadasy, Sanders, Jenkins, & Peyton, 2002; Vadasy, Sanders, & Peyton, 2005). In several of the later studies we were able to follow up kindergarten and first-grade students, including English learners, through grades 2 or 3 (Vadasy et al., 2002; Vadasy, Sanders, & Peyton, 2006; Vadasy, Sanders, & Abbott, 2008; Vadasy & Sanders, 2012, 2013).

The overall impact of the program has also been examined by panels of external experts (i.e., What Works Clearinghouse, National Center on Intensive Interventions), and in syntheses of research on reading interventions. These reviews are included in the references.

Intervention Acceptability

Classroom teachers often find it challenging to schedule the logistics for supplemental interventions like *Sound Partners* during the school day. The tutor coordinator and the classroom teachers often need to carefully work out schedules for tutors to work with students who also receive bilingual or speech services. In the school-based intervention studies, researchers worked closely with classroom teachers to accommodate their scheduling preferences, help teachers protect their literacy and math blocks, and identify times of day when students can receive tutoring without missing core instruction (or recess). This can be more difficult when there are fewer tutors in the building to work around teacher scheduling preferences. In the larger studies, we found that teacher acceptability for this tutoring increased when they began to observe student progress, review growth on the mastery tests, and notice increased student confidence and participation in the classroom. Building coordinators should plan time to collaborate with teachers to create workable tutoring schedules.

The program was designed and informed by tutor acceptability and scalability. While classroom teachers may be constrained by scripted programs, the paraeducators tutors we worked with welcomed the scripted approach. We collected tutor feedback to shape the instructions for each activity as well as the instructional content. *Sound Partners* tutors often work with students who most need skilled instruction. The research helped us to identify the critical skills that non-teachers could teach effectively to support all students below benchmarks.

Finally, intervention acceptability is supported by the typical gains students experience in a well-implemented *Sound Partners* intervention. Figure 5.3 illustrates average growth that kindergarten and first-grade students made toward grade-level foundation skills at end of intervention. In typical (non-research) implementation of *Sound Partners*, schools can adjust the length of tutoring for individual students based on school resources and district and school assessments. Students who acquire the target skills, based on school assessments, can be "graduated" allowing the tutor to serve another student.

Case Studies

The remainder of the chapter describes *Sound Partners* tutoring for two students at a hypothetical elementary school in a large urban school district. The case studies below are hybrids drawn from the test scores and data from two students in research conducted between 2008–2011 (Vadasy & Sanders, 2010, 2011). One is a kindergarten student who is an English learner, and one is a first-grader. The case study data are composites drawn from students who participated in our research studies and attended schools with a high enrollment of Black and language-minority students with family incomes below the federal poverty level. Students from over 40 language groups were enrolled in the district. We have drawn on our research data and extensive observations of students in our intervention studies to create these two student profiles. Because most schools now use a universal screening and progress monitoring assessment to track growth in reading skills, we add data from Acadience screening (Good & Kaminski, 2020) and fall scores that schools today might use to identify students for supplemental tutoring. The case studies describe progress that was typical for participants in the studies.

Intervention Plan for Kindergarten Student

Haji was very excited to begin kindergarten in the fall. He had not previously attended preschool, and he looked forward to meeting other students and learning to read. Although Oromo was the language spoken at home, his teacher noticed that Haji was rapidly gaining English language skills. During the fall, she also noticed that Haji was falling behind his classmates in gaining alphabet and phonemic skills. Haji was becoming less enthusiastic when it came time for literacy instruction. His teacher included Haji's name on her list of students she recommended for participation in our research. When we pretested Haji in late November, his alphabet knowledge was limited, and his raw scores for word reading and decoding were zero. Today schools that use the Acadience Reading K-6 assessment for screening might identify kindergarten students for tutoring based on a fall assessment for First Sound Fluency (FSF) that is below or well below benchmark (below 10), and with Nonword Fluency-Correct Letter Sounds Fluency (NWF-CLS) scores below 17. Table 5.3 indicates the scores that we might expect Haji to have on these fall screenings. Haji met the screening criteria for inclusion in our intervention study, and he began tutoring on January 6 after the winter break.

Haji was a little nervous when he first met his tutor who explained that they would work together to build his reading skills. The tutor used one of the program's mastery tests to place Haji in the kindergarten lessons, and

TABLE 5.3 Haji's Kindergarten Pre- and Post-Test Scores

Measure	*Pretest*	*Posttest*	*Follow up end of Grade 2*
Letter Names (LN) (correct per minute)	0	49	
Letter Sounds (LS) (correct per minute)	10	52	
CTOPP PA	75	89	
WRMT-R WAT	94	114	127
WRMT-R WID	87	116	126
WRAT Spelling	103	99	101
WRMT-R Passage Comp	—	103	101
All standard scores except for LN and LS			
Tutor mean fidelity rating: 5.0 (of total 5)			
Student average attendance: 47 days			
Tutoring average intensity: 70 lessons			
Pretest 12/3/07			
Instruction starts 1/6/08			
Posttest 5/28/08			
Acadience initial fall assessment:			
Phoneme Segmenting Fluency (PSF)	5	—	
Nonword Fluency-Correct Letter Sounds (NWF-CLS)	7	—	
Nonword Fluency-WWR	0	—	

they began working on Lesson 1. Haji quickly picked up the directions for each lesson activity, and the pattern of the daily lessons.

Phoneme segmenting was initially difficult for Haji. The initial training provided tutors with suggestions for how to scaffold the phoneme-segmenting task with sound boxes. Haji's tutor scaffolded the task by sounding out the word slowly herself, saying each individual sound while pointing to each box. Next, the tutor isolated and spoke each sound and asked Haji to point to each box for each sound. They switched roles, Haji said the word, and the tutor said each sound and pointed to each box. When Haji was able to segment with these supports, they returned to the unassisted segmenting task in the lessons.

Teaching children to decode accurately is the primary goal of *Sound Partners*. When children first learn to decode it is often challenging to coordinate their newly acquired knowledge of letter-sound correspondences and phonemic awareness, and apply this knowledge to blend sounds to pronounce or read a word. This requires paying attention to each letter form in a word, retrieving the sound from memory, repeating the process for each letter, remembering all of the sounds, and pushing the remembered sounds together. Many children discover this relationship between phonemic awareness and the alphabetic principle with classroom phonics instruction, but many struggling beginners need explicit demonstration and added practice to apply this knowledge to decoding. Lessons are designed to help students gradually develop accuracy and efficiency in their knowledge and memory for these representations until they are able to blend sounds together. This is a complex and challenging learning task for many beginning readers. Haji needed support sounding out words before he could efficiently retrieve the blended pronunciations to decode. In the early kindergarten lessons, Haji's tutor modeled stretched-out blending (e.g., blending the sounds in the word man like "mmmaaannn" without stopping between the sounds, so that the sounds stay connected). When students try to sound out a word by stopping between each sound, it is often difficult for them to remember each of the phonemes when blending the sounds. When they stop between the sounds they will often add a "schwa" vowel, which makes it difficult for them to recognize and pronounce the word (see Gonzalez-Frey & Ehri, 2021). Together Haji and his tutor practiced applying this strategy to read lists of decodable words. At first, it was very difficult for Haji to transfer his alphabet knowledge to decoding words.

The kindergarten-level lessons provide added modeling and practice in decoding. The dynamic process of phoneme blending also requires children to co-articulate the sounds to obtain word-like pronunciations. Children draw upon their prior word exposures, written and spoken, and their semantic knowledge to help them recognize and pronounce the words (Harm & Seidenberg, 1999; Muter et al., 2004). To acquire decoding skill, children must discover how sounds are co-articulated when assembled. This can be more challenging for DLL children like Haji with more limited English vocabulary knowledge to help recognize the blended word. Word recognition is not surprisingly the most common obstacle for beginning readers.

When the coach observed Haji and his tutor, she suggested scaffolding to make the task easier.

- "First, practice and build Haji's success blending words in the lists that begin with continuous sounds like /m/ and /s/." These continuous sounds are easier to stretch out unlike the stop consonants (e.g., /b/ or /t/).
- "If Haji drops the *first* sound when blending (e.g., says /aaat/ for /mmmaaat/)—ask him to blend the first two sounds (mmmaaa), keep saying those sounds (mmmaaa) while you point to and add the last sound. Immediately sweep your finger under the word and say the whole word together. Do this together until Haji can do it alone. Remember, timing is important. Don't wait too long before you go back and blend all the sounds!"
- "Now if Haji drops the *last* sound, cover the first sound, point and ask him to blend the last two sounds (be sure he knows the sounds), then try again. Help him stretch blend the last two sounds (e.g., /aaammm/) and while he continues to say those two sounds, uncover and point to the first sound, have Haji add that sound, then say the word (e.g., /sssaaammm/). Again, do this together until Haji can do it alone. Timing is very important."

During the initial tutor training, the researchers discussed common obstacles students encounter, and ways in which tutors can scaffold tasks. However, for many new tutors, this information is quite abstract until they begin to work with individual students. For this reason, schools should plan to provide strong initial training for all tutors who will be implementing *Sound Partners*. Reading specialists, teachers, or school psychologists familiar with the program may be able to provide this training. As we noted, virtual training and consultation options are available from the University of North Carolina Charlotte (Beach et al., 2021; Washburn et al., 2021) and from the Literacy Trust (https://literacytrust.org/literacy-intervention). Initial training should then be followed by regular observations and coaching visits, especially for new tutors, and for tutors who request support for helping individual students.

Progress Monitoring for Haji

Haji's tutor administered brief lesson progress tests every 10 lessons, and by midtest in the study he was able to identify 43 letter sounds and 45 letter names correctly in a random array of letters; he could also decode 8 words featuring taught letters. His tutor shared copies of the progress tests with Haji's teacher. The tests provided added detail on his progress in gaining alphabet knowledge, and word decoding.

Haji worked with his tutors 4 days a week for 16 weeks. When Haji's tutor arrived at his classroom to escort him for tutoring, Haji was eager and happy, and many of his classmates also wanted to go with the tutor. In these early grades, students value this individual time and attention with an adult. Haji performed at about 94% accuracy on each progress test, and the tutor's coach agreed that the pace of the lessons was a good fit. Haji's classroom teacher shared that Haji was more confident in the classroom. He raised his hand to respond more often to read or spell words, and proudly read aloud one of the decodable *Bob* books he practiced with his tutor.

When his tutor reviewed Haji's errors on progress tests, they revealed that that, like many students, Haji had some confusion accurately identifying and pronouncing vowel sounds (i.e., /e/ and /i/ sounds). The coach encouraged his tutor to model the sounds and add more incidental practice opportunities for these letters, while continuing progress through the lessons. An important point for schools to keep in mind is that the lessons have been carefully designed and fine-tuned over the years to feature practice opportunities and cumulative review that are adequate for most students. Further, lesson progress and completion has been a strong predictor of student outcomes. In Haji's cohort of students, treatment students received M = 55.36 tutoring sessions (or M = 27.68 hrs. of tutoring, SD = 2.74 hrs.), completed M = 64.99 lessons (SD = 13.69), and had a lesson coverage rate of M = 1.18 lessons per session (SD = 0.25). Average cohort attendance was 47 days, and Haji's attendance was 50 days, another factor contributing to strong student outcomes.

Finally, Haji's cohort of students were followed up at the end of grade 2 on reading and spelling outcomes. Based on normed measures of word attack, word identification, spelling, and passage comprehension, Haji maintained grade level scores on these measures at follow up.

Intervention Plan for First-Grade Student

Lamonte was identified in October of first grade with pretesting on alphabet knowledge and normed word reading and spelling measures. As seen in Table 5.4, his alphabet knowledge was limited, and his word attack, word

TABLE 5.4 Lamonte's First Grade Pre- and Post-Test Scores

Measure	*Pretest*	*Posttest*	*Follow up end of Grade 3*
Letter Names (LN) (correct per min)	14	57	
Letter Sounds (LS) (correct per min)	5	47	
WRMT-R WAT	81	104	91
WRMT-R WID	85	99	96
WRAT Spelling	89	89	81
WRMT-R Passage Comp	—	93	91
All standard scores except for LN and LS			
Tutor fidelity rating: 4.86 (of total 5.0)			
Student attendance: 79 days			
Tutoring intensity: 60 lessons			
Pretest: 10/3/07			
Posttest: 5/13/08			
Acadience initial fall assessment			
Phoneme Segmenting Fluency (PSF)	30	—	
Nonword Fluency-CLS	7	—	
Nonword Fluency-WWR	2	—	

identification, and spelling scores were below grade level. Lamonte began working his tutor in late October, starting with Lesson 1. His tutor administered a mastery test every 10 lessons, and for most of these mastery checks Lamonte scored between 85–90% correct on sounds, word reading, and spelling. His tutor shared these tests with Lamonte's classroom teacher, and reviewed them to target skills for additional incidental practice. For example, when the /i/ sound was introduced, Lamonte confused the /e/ and /i/ sounds on the mastery test. His tutor continued to model these sounds and add practice on these sounds during the lessons – just a few more repetitions each day to discriminate between the two letter sounds (Burns et al., 2022).

Both mastery tests and feedback from Lamonte's classroom teacher indicated that Lamonte needed more support in spelling. His tutor's coach suggested that they use grid paper for spelling tasks. While many students are able to spell dictated works on lined paper, the grid paper makes the phonemes more concrete for students. His tutor would scaffold by dictating one of the words and have Lamonte repeat the word. The tutor would point to each box and ask, "What sound in this box?" Lamonte quickly learned to use the grid paper without his tutor's prompts. After a few weeks of spelling with grid paper, his accuracy improved, and they transitioned back to lined paper.

Progress Monitoring for Lamonte

The mastery tests a few weeks later indicated that Lamonte had difficulty remembering taught sight words. The tutor made flashcards to add review on these words. Lamonte and his tutor sometimes practiced with these word cards on their way to or from the tutoring session.

Like many students who are first gaining word-reading skills, Lamonte had difficulty transferring these skills to reading connected text in the *Bob Books*. Words he could identify correctly in the word lists were more challenging to identify in the story contexts. His tutor helped slowly build his confidence in storybook reading, requiring Lamonte to point to each word as he sounded it out, and covering sentences so that Lamonte could focus on one line at a time. It was a big day when Lamonte could read one of the *Bob Books* without any support. The school had extra sets of the books so that when a student could read a *Bob Book* independently, the student could take the book home to read it to a parent or another adult. Once Lamonte was reading accurately in the storybooks, his tutor would suggest, "Now let's try reading the next page really smooth" to help build fluency. In their training tutors learn that the priority is for the student to read words accurately before trying to develop fluency.

Schools today that use the Acadience Reading K-6 assessment might identify a first-grade student for tutoring based on: fall assessment scores for Phoneme Segmenting Fluency (PSF) below 40, and Nonword Fluency (NWF) Correct Letter Sounds/Whole Word Reading scores that are below 27 and 0, respectively. Lamonte's fall PSF was 30, and his NWF scores for Correct Letter Sounds and Whole Word Reading were 6 and 0.

Students in Lamonte's cohort were also followed up in the study at the end of grade three. While Lamonte did not maintain his posttest levels on normed measures of word attack and spelling at follow up, his word identification skills maintained at about grade level. His teacher might consider continued explicit phonics instruction in more complex phoneme-grapheme correspondences and syllable types, integrating instruction in both reading and spelling words.

Intervention Considerations

Schools frequently have two questions when considering a supplemental reading intervention. First, will the intervention align with their adopted literacy curriculum? Second, does the intervention address the key elements of literacy instruction? During two decades of research on the *Sound Partners*, we studied its implementation in schools using many different early literacy curricula. We accounted for school or classroom membership in most of our growth model studies.

We offer a final caveat to address the second question. *Sound Partners* has an intentionally narrow focus, on alphabetic and word-reading skills. It does not address fluency, vocabulary, or comprehension. We designed *Sound Partners* specifically to address critical foundation skills that are the most common obstacles for beginning readers. Moreover, research findings demonstrate that the program enables paraeducators and other adult tutors to effectively supplement classrooms instruction for students who most often struggle with these skills.

Conclusion

Decoding is the most common obstacle that kindergarten and first-grade children encounter in learning to read. Many children struggle to acquire decoding skills, even with strong core reading instruction. They simply need more explicit and systematic phonics instruction than teachers can provide in classroom instruction. Supplemental phonics tutoring is one means to help these students acquire accurate decoding skills. *Sound Partners* provides one tool for the large numbers of paraeducators who work in U.S. schools to help close the gap in these skills for underachieving and at-risk students. With early screening tools, schools can intervene in a timely manner, target students for more intensive and explicit instruction to accelerate decoding development, and monitor students' progress with both criterion-referenced and screening assessments. Validated early-reading interventions and assessments that reflect the science of how children learn to read help struggling readers acquire basic word reading skills when they most need it, in the initial stages of learning to become readers.

Appendix A: Comparing the Two Levels of *Sound Partners*

***Sound Partners* Original (Vadasy, Wayne, et al., 2005)** was designed for first-graders and older students identified in the lower quartile in word-reading skills. The scope and sequence includes a broad range of advanced word-reading skills, including digraphs, diphthongs, inflections, high frequency affixes, and a large corpus of sight words.

***Sound Partners Kindergarten* (Vadasy, 2013)** has a strong focus on helping students learn initial basic decoding and spelling skills. It was designed for kindergarten students identified with limited letter-name and letter-sound knowledge, initial sound identification, and phoneme segmenting. The lessons target prerequisite word-reading skills, including phoneme segmenting instruction and practice, and blending modeling to prepare students to learn a decoding strategy. The lessons include instruction in all single-letter names and sounds and a handful of consonant digraphs. The rate of introducing letter-sound correspondences is slower than in the Original version, including added review and practice. The rate and cumulative review cycles were tested and adjusted based on our observations of kindergarten and first grade students in our research studies.

The following outlines the major differences between the original *Sound Partners* (*SP*) program and the kindergarten version (*SPK*) in terms of a slower pace of introducing new concepts and skills, and extended practice to consolidate new concepts.

Say the Sounds—*SPK* includes instructions for the child to trace the letter sound prior to writing. The task is more scaffolded for these younger children. The pace of introducing new letter-sound correspondences in *SPK* is extended and slower. For example:

Grade 1 *SP* – introduces 9 letters in lessons 1–10
SPK – introduces 6 letters in lessons 1–10
Grade 1 *SP* – introduces 7 letters in lessons 11–20
SPK – introduces 5 letters in lessons 11–20

First Sound Identification—Practice in this task was added to *SPK* to scaffold initial phoneme identification prior to introducing phoneme segmenting in lesson 10

Segmenting—First-grade *Sound Partners* begins with phoneme segmenting. *SPK* begins with segmenting compound words, then two-syllable words, and finally moves into phoneme segmenting (after first introducing students to First Sound Identification activity, above)

Guess the Word—Practice in this task was added to *SPK*. The tutor models stretched phoneme blending (orally, without print) and asks the student to listen carefully and say the word fast ("guess the word"). This prepares the student forstretched phoneme blending instruction (with print) in the Word Reading tasks.

Alphabet naming—Because many kindergarten students in our studies had limited or partial knowledge of alphabet names, we added practice in *SPK* in letter naming through Lesson 42, with suggestions for how to individualize this practice.

Appendix B: How Students Were Selected in the Research on *Sound Partners Kindergarten* Tutoring

Students selected for participation in the research studies on the kindergarten level of *Sound Partners* (Vadasy, 2013) were chosen based on measures that predict risk of reading difficulties.

- In Vadasy, Sanders, and Peyton (2006) children were eligible for tutoring if they: could identify 13 or fewer individual letter sounds; scored in the "deficit" range on the Dynamic Indicators of Basic Early Literacy Skills (DIBELS: Good & Kaminski, 2002) Initial Sound Fluency subtest (less than 10 per min); and, scored in the "at-risk" range on two of the following three DIBELS subtests (and scored "at some risk" on the remaining subtest): Letter Naming Fluency (less than 27 per min), Phoneme Segmentation Fluency (less than 18 per min), and Nonsense Word Fluency (less than 13 per min). These scores were based on the 2002 version of the DIBELS and cut points for risk.
- In Vadasy and Sanders (2010), students were screened on three measures: letter sounds, letter names, and phonological awareness (the Sound Matching subtest of the Comprehensive Test of Phonological Processing (CTOPP-2: Wagner, Torgesen, Rashotte, & Pearson, 2013). A composite score was computed based on the mean z score of each of these three measures. Students scoring in the lower half of their classroom on this composite score were eligible for participation in the study. Students who participated in the studies on *Sound Partners Kindergarten* that were reviewed by the What Works Clearinghouse were selected based on these criteria: at risk based on measures of their alphabet knowledge and phoneme awareness skills in October-December of kindergarten.

Schools that offer *Sound Partners* tutoring for their kindergarten or older students often use several criteria to select students. In most cases, these schools begin to identify and serve kindergarten students in late fall or winter of the school year:

- Teacher identification of students who are struggling in the classroom with alphabet and decoding skills
- School or district kindergarten screening measures of alphabet and/or phoneme awareness
- School or district universal screening assessments (e.g., Acadience Learning)

Finally, schools with a Multi-Tiered Systems of Support (MTSS) or Response to Intervention (RTI) model plan in place may choose to assign students based on their process for implementing the plan in their building. The National Center on Intensive Intervention (NCII) features reviews of *Sound Partners Kindergarten* and *Sound Partners* for grades 1–2 to help intervention teams consider "evidence of efficacy for improving academic outcomes for students whose performance is unsatisfactory in the core program."

References

Adams, M. J. (1990). *Beginning to read.* Cambridge, MA: MIT Press.

Beach, K. D., McIntyre, E., Philippakos, Z., Mraz, M., Pilonieta, P., & Vintinner, J. (2018). Effects of a summer reading clinic on reading skills for low-income Black and Hispanic students in elementary school. *Reading & Writing Quarterly, 34*(3), 263–280. doi:10.1080/10573569.2018.1446859

Beach, K. D., Washburn, E. K., Gesel, S. A., & Williams, P. (2021). Pivoting an elementary summer reading intervention to a virtual context in response to COVID-19: An examination of program transformation and outcomes. *Journal of Education for Students Placed at Risk, 26*, 112–134. doi:10.1080/10824669.2021.1906250

Burns, M. K., Young, H., McCollom, E. M., Stevens, M. A., & Izumi, J. T. (2022). Predicting intervention effects with pre-intervention measures of decoding: Evidence for a skill-by-treatment interaction with kindergarten and first-grade students. *Learning Disability Quarterly, 45*, 320–330. doi:10.1177/07319487221113026

Bus, A. G., & van IJzendoorn, M. H. (1999). Phonological awareness and early reading: Meta-analysis of experimental training studies. *Journal of Educational Psychology, 91*, 403–414.

Carnine, D. W., Silbert, J., & Kame'enui, E. J. (1997). *Direct instruction reading.* Upper Saddle River, NJ: Prentice Hall.

Castles, A., Rastle, K., & Nation, K. (2018). Ending the reading wars: Reading acquisition from novice to expert. *Psychological Science in the Public Interest, 19*(1), 5–51. doi:10.1177/1529100618772271

Chall, J. S. (1967). *Learning to read: The great debate.* New York: McGraw-Hill.

Chiappe, P., Siegel, L. S., & Wade-Wooley, L. (2002). Linguistic diversity and development of reading skills: A longitudinal study. *Scientific Studies of Reading, 6*, 369–400.

Cuticelli, M., Collier-Meek, M., & Coyne, M. (2016). Increasing the quality of Tier 1 reading instruction: Using performance feedback to increase opportunities to respond during implementation of a core reading program. *Psychology in the Schools, 52*, 2016. doi:10.1002/pits.21884

Ehri, L. C. (2000). Learning to read and learning to spell: Two sides of a coin. *Topics in Language Disorders, 20*, 191–236.

Fuchs, D., Fuchs, L. S., Thompson, A., Al Otaiba, S., Yen, L., Yang, N. J., Braun, M., & O'Connor, R. E. (2001). Is reading important in reading-readiness programs? A randomized field trial with teachers as program implementers. *Journal of Educational Psychology, 93*, 251–267.

Gonzalez-Frey, S. M., & Ehri, L. C. (2021). Connected phonation is more effective than segmented phonation for teaching beginning readers to decode unfamiliar words. *Scientific Studies of Reading, 25*, 272–285. doi:10.1080/10888438.2020.1776290

Good, R. H., & Kaminski, R. A. (2002). *Dynamic Indicators of Basic Early Literacy Skills* (*DIBELS*) (6th ed.) Eugene, OR: Institute for the Development of Educational Achievement.

Good, R. H., & Kaminski, R. A. (2020). *Acadience reading K-6 assessment manual.* www.acadiencelearning.org

Gunn, B., Smolkowski, K., Stryker, L. A., & Dennis, C. (2021). Measuring explicit instruction using classroom observations of student–teacher interactions (COSTI). *Perspectives on Behavior Science*, *44*, 267–283.

Haggerty, N. K. (2022). *Examining the online implementation of the evidence-based Sound Partners reading intervention on a measure of phonics skills of kindergarten and first-grade students with reading difficulties*. [Unpublished doctoral dissertation]. University of Hawai'i at Manoa.

Harm, M., & Seidenberg, M. S. (1999). Reading acquisition, phonology, and dyslexia: Insights from a connectionist model. *Psychological Review*, *106*, 491–528.

Heggie, L., & Wade-Wooley, L. (2017). Reading longer words: Insights into multi-syllable word reading. *Perspectives of the ASHA Special Interest Group*, *2*, Part 2. Retrieved from http://perspectives.pubs.asha.org/pdfaccess.ashx?url=/data/journals/persp/935966/

Iversen, S., & Tunmer, W. E. (1993). Phonological processing skills and the Reading Recovery Program. *Journal of Educational Psychology*, *85*, 112–126.

Jenkins, J. R., Peyton, J. A., Sanders, E. A., & Vadasy, P. F. (2004). Effects of reading decodable texts in supplemental first-grade tutoring. *Scientific Studies of Reading*, *8*(1), 53–86.

Kaminski, R. A., Good, R. H., Powell-Smith, K. A., Stollar, S., Wallin, J., Abbott, M., & Wheeler, C. E. (2019). *Position paper on use of Acadience™ Reading K–6 for student-level accountability decisions* (Revised January, 2019). Dynamic Measurement Group. Retrieved from https://acadiencelearning.org/wp-content/uploads/2020/01/Student_Level_Accountability_2019.pdf

Lesaux, N. K., Koda, K., Siegel, L. S., & Shanahan, T. (2006). Development of literacy. In D. August & T. Shanahan (Eds.), *Developing literacy in second-language learners: Report of the National Literacy Panel on language-minority children and youth* (pp. 75–122). Mahwah, NJ: Lawrence Erlbaum Associates.

Lindstrom, E. R., & Roberts, G. J. (2022). Preparing teachers to facilitate engagement in reading intervention through embedded behavioral supports. *Intervention in School and Clinic*. doi:10.1177/10534512221130067

Lipka, O., & Siegel, L. S. (2007). The development of reading skills in children with English as a second language. *Scientific Studies of Reading*, *11*, 105–131.

McMaster, K. L., Jung, P. G., Brandes, D., Pinto, V., Fuchs, D., Kearns, D., Saenz, L., & Yen, L. (2014). Customizing a research-based reading practice: Balancing the importance of implementation fidelity with professional judgment. *Reading Teacher*, *68*, 173–183. doi:10.1002/trtr.1301

Muter, V., Hulme, C., Snowling, M. J., & Stevenson, J. (2004). Phonemes, rimes, vocabulary, and grammatical skills as foundations of early reading development: Evidence from a longitudinal study. *Developmental Psychology*, *40*(5), 665–681. doi:10.1037/0012-1649.40.5.665

Piasta, S. B., & Hudson, A. K. (2022). Key knowledge to support phonological awareness and phonics instruction. *The Reading Teacher*, *76*, 201–210. doi:10.1002/trtr2093

Roberts, T. A., Vadasy, P. F., & Sanders, E. A. (2018). Preschoolers' alphabet learning: Letter name and sound instruction, cognitive processes, and English proficiency. *Early Childhood Research Quarterly*, *44*, 257–274.

Shankweiler, D., & Liberman, I. Y. (1989). *Phonology and reading disability: Solving the reading puzzle.* Ann Arbor, MI: University of Michigan Press.
Share, D. L. (1995). Phonological recoding and self-teaching: Sine qua non of reading acquisition. *Cognition, 55*, 151–218.
Share, D. L., Jorm, A. F., Maclean, R., & Matthews, R. (1984). Sources of individual differences in reading acquisition. *Journal of Educational Psychology, 76*, 1309–1324.
Snowling, M. J. (1991a). Developmental reading disorders. *Child Psychology & Psychiatry & Allied Disciplines, 32*(1), 49–77.
Stanovich, K. E. (2000). *Progress in understanding reading: Scientific foundations and new frontiers.* New York, NY: Guilford Press.
Tunmer, W. E., Herriman, M. L., & Nesdale, A. B. (1988). Metalinguistic abilities and beginning reading. *Reading Research Quarterly, 23*, 134–158.
U.S. Department of Education. (2014). *Common core of data: State nonfiscal survey of public elementary/secondary education.* Washington, DC: National Center for Education Statistics.
U.S. Department of Education. (2022). *Our nation's English learners: What are their characteristics?* Retrieved from https://www2.ed.gov/datastory/el-characteristics/index.html#four
University of Delaware. (2022) *An efficacy follow-up study of the long-term effects of Reading Recovery under the 13 scale-up.* Center for Research in Education and Social Policy. Retrieved from https://www.cresp.udel.edu/research-project/efficacy-follow-study-long-term-effects-reading-recovery-i3-scale/
Vadasy, P. F. (2013). *Sound Partners Kindergarten: A tutoring program in phonics-based early reading skills.* Dallas, TX: Sopris Voyager Learning.
Vadasy, P. F., & Sanders, E. A. (2010). Efficacy of supplemental phonics-based instruction for low-skilled kindergarteners in the context of language minority status and classroom phonics instruction. *Journal of Educational Psychology, 102*(4), 786–803.
Vadasy, P. F., & Sanders, E. A. (2011). Efficacy of supplemental phonics-based instruction for low-skilled first graders: How language minority status and pretest characteristics moderate treatment response. *Scientific Studies of Reading, 15*, 471–497. doi:10.1080/10888438.2010.501091
Vadasy, P. F., & Sanders, E. A. (2012). Two-year follow-up of a kindergarten phonics intervention for English learners and native English speakers: Contextualizing treatment impacts by classroom literacy instruction. *Journal of Educational Psychology, 104*, 987–1005. doi:1037/a0028163
Vadasy, P. F., & Sanders, E. A. (2013). Two-year follow-up of a code-oriented intervention for lower-skilled first-graders: The influence of language status and word reading skills on third-grade literacy outcomes. *Reading and Writing: An Interdisciplinary Journal, 26*, 821–843.
Vadasy, P. F., & Sanders, E. A. (2021). Introducing grapheme-phoneme correspondences (GPCs): Exploring rate and complexity in phonics instruction for kindergarteners with limited literacy skills. *Reading and Writing: An Interdisciplinary Journal, 34*, 109–138. doi:10.1007/s11145-020-10064-y
Vadasy, P. F., Sanders, E. A., Jenkins, J. R., & Peyton, J. A. (2002). Timing and intensity of tutoring: A closer look at the conditions for effective literacy tutoring. *Learning Disabilities Research and Practice, 17*(4), 227–241.

Vadasy, P. F., Sanders, E. A., & Peyton, J. A. (2005). Relative effectiveness of reading practice or word-level instruction in supplemental tutoring: How text matters. *Journal of Learning Disabilities*, *38*(4), 364–380.
Vadasy, P. F., Wayne, S., O'Connor, R., Jenkins, J. R., Pool, K., Firebaugh, M., & Peyton, J. (2005). *Sound Partners: A tutoring program in phonics-based early reading*. Dallas, TX: Sopris Voyager Learning.
Vadasy, P. F., Sanders, E. A., & Peyton, J. A. (2006). Code-oriented instruction for kindergarten students at risk for reading difficulties: A randomized field trial with paraeducator implementers. *Journal of Educational Psychology*, *98*(3), 508–528.
Vadasy, P. F., Sanders, E. A., & Abbott, R. D. (2008). Effects of supplemental early reading intervention at 2-year follow up: Reading skill growth patterns and predictors. *Scientific Studies of Reading*, *12*(1), 51–89.
Wagner, R., Torgesen, J. K., & Rashotte, C. A. (1999). *Comprehensive test of phonological processing*. Austin, TX: Pro-Ed.
Wagner, R. K., Torgesen, J. K., Rashotte, C. A., Pearson, N. A., (2013). *Comprehensive Test of Phonological Processing-2nd ed. (CTOPP-2)*. Austin, TX: Pro-Ed.
Washburn, E. K., Beach, K. D., Gesel, S. A., Billingsley, M., Howard, C., King, B., & Vintinner, J. P. (2021). Zooming into summer: Key takeaways from a virtual summer reading intervention. *The Reading Teacher*, *74*, 812–818. doi:10.1002/trtr.2000

External Reviews of Sound Partners *and Research Syntheses and Meta-Analyses Including* Sound Partners

American Institutes for Research, National Center on Intensive Intervention (NCII). (n.d.). Retrieved from https://intensiveintervention.org/sites/default/files/Sound-Partners-Brief-2021.pdf; https://charts.intensiveintervention.org/aintervention
Denton, C. A., Hall, C., Cho, E., Cannon, G., Scammacca, N., & Wanzek, J. (2022). A meta-analysis of the effects of foundational skills and multicomponent reading interventions on reading comprehension for primary-grade students. *Learning and Individual Differences*, *93*. doi:10.1016/j.lindif.2021.102062
Elbaum, B., Vaughn, S., Hughes, M. T., & Moody, S. W. (2000). How effective are one-to-one tutoring programs in reading for elementary students at risk for reading failure? A meta-analysis of the intervention research. *Journal of Educational Psychology*, *92*, 605–619. doi:10.1037//0022-0663.92.4.605
Gersten, R., Haymond, K., Newman-Gonchar, R., Dimino, J., & Jayanthi, M. (2020). Meta-analysis of the impact of reading interventions for students in the primary grades. *Journal of Research on Educational Effectiveness*, *13*, 401–427. doi:10.1080/19345747.2019.1689591
Ludwig, C., Guo, K., & Georgiou, G. K. (2019). Are reading interventions for English learners effective? A meta-analysis. *Journal of Learning Disabilities*, *52*, 220–231.
Nickrow, A., Oreopoulos, P., & Quan, V. (2020). *The impressive effects of tutoring on prek-12 learning: A systematic review and meta-analysis of the experimental evidence*. National Bureau of Economic Research Working Paper No. 27476. July.

Richards-Tutor, C., Baker, D. L., Gersten, R., Baker, S. K., & Smith, J. M. (2016). The effectiveness of reading interventions for English learners: A research synthesis. *Exceptional Children*, *82*, 144–169.

Roberts, G. J., Dumas, D. G., McNeish, D., & Cote, B. (2021). Understanding the dynamics of dosage response: A nonlinear meta-analysis of recent reading interventions. *Review of Educational Research*, *92*, 209–248. doi:10.3102/00346543211051423

Roberts, G. J., Hall, C., Cho, E., Cote, B., Lee, J., Qi, B., & Van Ooyik, J. (2022). The state of current reading intervention research for English learners in Grades K-2: A best-evidence synthesis. *Educational Psychology Review*, *34*, 335–361. doi:10.1007/s10648-021-09629-2

Snowling, M. J. (1991b). Developmental reading disorders. *Journal of Child Psychology and Psychiatry*, *32*, 49–77.

Solari, E. J., Kehoe, K. E., Cho, E., Hall, C., Vargas, I., Dahl-Leonard, K., Richmond, C. L., Henry, A. R., Cook, L., Hayes, L., & Conner, C. (2022). Effectiveness of interventions for English learners with word reading difficulties: A research synthesis. *Learning Disabilities Research & Practice*, *37*, 158–174. doi:10.1111/ldrp.12286

What Works Clearinghouse, Institute of Education Sciences, U.S. Department of Education (report issued 2010, September). Retrieved from https://ies.ed.gov/ncee/wwc/Docs/InterventionReports/wwc_soundpartners_092110.pdf

6

HELPING EARLY LITERACY WITH PRACTICE STRATEGIES (HELPS) PROGRAM

John C. Begeny and Natasha K. Newson

North Carolina State University, Raleigh, NC, USA

Felicia L. Davidson

Helps Education Fund, Raleigh, NC, USA

C. Shannon O'Neal and Jesslyn M. Durling

North Carolina State University, Raleigh, NC, USA

Introduction

There is a general consensus among researchers and educators that text-reading fluency (often referred to more simply and interchangeably as *reading fluency*) is one of only a handful of essential components that should be taught and firmly developed by all students during early-reading instruction, usually starting during first grade and continuing through third or fourth grade. This has been highlighted, for example, more than 20 years ago by the U.S. National Reading Panel (National Reading Panel, 2000) and by countless reading researchers since then (e.g., Daane et al., 2005; Lee & Yoon, 2017; Stevens et al., 2017; White et al., 2021). Yet, despite the substantial amount of research that has emerged about the importance of reading fluency and strategies to strengthen students' reading fluency, a significant percentage of students across the U.S. are not proficient in this foundational literacy skill. For example, the two most recent nationally representative reading assessments in the U.S. prior to the COVID pandemic revealed that 65–66% of fourth-graders lack proficiency in reading (NCES, 2019; White et al., 2021). Furthermore, over half of those non-proficient readers—totaling about 1.3 million U.S. public school fourth-graders—performed below the *Basic* achievement level and

DOI: 10.4324/9781003275749-6

demonstrated particular difficulty with fluent reading of connected text, defined as "sufficiently fast and accurate reading of sentences and passages" (White et al., 2021). Unfortunately, this overall pattern of student performance in reading and reading fluency has remained relatively stable for over a decade (Daane et al., 2005; NCES, 2019; White et al., 2021) and has only been exacerbated by the COVID pandemic (NCES, 2022).

It is important to know that reading fluency is a core component of early-reading instruction and that many students still need support with this critical skill, but it also important to highlight some reasons why fluency is so essential to overall reading proficiency. One reason is that reading fluency impacts several areas of academic development and is a strong predictor of reading comprehension, end-of-grade test scores, and motivation (Good et al., 2001; Hintze et al., 2003; McGlinchey & Hixson, 2004). Poor reading fluency requires an individual to exert more cognitive effort in decoding and understanding words, which ultimately has a negative impact on reading comprehension (LaBerge & Sameuls, 1974). In other words, the lack of automaticity with text reading can hinder a student's ability to process information and, in turn, efficiently comprehend text (Perfetti, 1977, 1985). Additionally, studies have shown that motivation to read is closely related to a student's level of reading fluency. Strong readers are more likely to choose to read compared to students with lower fluency (e.g., Daly et al. 2015; Kaskaya, 2016). Taken together, this evidence base highlights both the importance of reading fluency as well as the need to support many students in improving their reading fluency.

Overview of Empirical Literature Related to Fluency-based Interventions

Using evidence-based instructional practices to improve reading fluency means using the most well-supported and effective techniques found in the research literature. Several meta-analyses on reading interventions have shown that one of the most effective strategies to improve reading fluency is repeated reading (RR), usually with a prescribed number of reading repetitions with a passage of ability-appropriate text until an appropriate level of fluency is reached (Lee & Yoon, 2017; Stevens et al., 2017; Therrien, 2004). Past studies and meta-analyses have also shown that RR on its own can increase oral reading fluency and comprehension with students of varying skill levels and characteristics (e.g., students with and without learning disabilities, English language learners), but that combining RR with other evidence-based strategies to support fluency is most beneficial for students (e.g., Alber-Morgan et al., 2007; Cho et al., 2021; Strickland et al., 2013; Therrien, 2004). For example, using model reading (e.g., having a skilled reader read a passage of text aloud to "model" proper speed, accuracy, and expression while the learner follows along) and systematic error-correction procedures (to assist students with words or phrases previously read incorrectly or less fluently) both help to strengthen students' reading fluency skills (Alber-Morgan et al., 2007; Begeny et al., 2006; Martens et al., 2007). Another way to strengthen the application of RR is to provide students with clear verbal cues (i.e., directions) to read with fluency and comprehension (e.g., O'Shea et al., 1987; Therrien, 2004).

In addition to using evidence-based instructional strategies that directly target students' reading fluency, motivational strategies should be combined with instruction, especially when targeting improvements in fluency (Haring et al., 1978). There are at least a few key strategies that past studies and meta-analyses highlight as particularly effective for supporting skills such as reading fluency. Namely, using goal-setting procedures, performance feedback combined with graphical displays of student progress, and systematic praise embedded within a structured reward system have all been shown to increase student motivation (McBreen & Savage, 2022) as well as reading fluency and comprehension skills (Alber-Morgan et al., 2007; Begeny et al., 2011; Martens et al., 2007; Morgan & Sideridis, 2006).

Overview of the Helping Early Literacy with Practice Strategies (HELPS) Program

The research on overall literacy development, reading fluency, and fluency-building strategies specific to reading—as well as learning more generally (e.g., Haring et al., 1978)—served as a foundation for developing the Helping Early Literacy with Practice Strategies (HELPS) program (Begeny, 2009). The main goals of HELPS are to strengthen a student's text reading fluency and confidence as a reader. As noted earlier, as a student improves reading fluency, they are better able to focus on and improve other important reading skills, including comprehension. This "overview" section provides a brief summary of HELPS because our case study will summarize school-wide implementation of that program. Those interested in receiving more detailed information about HELPS should contact the first author of this chapter.

Strategies integrated within HELPS. HELPS combines each of the instructional and motivational strategies most associated with improved outcomes for text-reading fluency and, as a result, reading comprehension. Specifically, the following teaching and learning strategies are strategically integrated into every HELPS instructional session: repeated reading of ability-appropriate text; having students listen to a more skilled reader read a passage aloud (model reading); systematic error-correction procedures; goal-setting (i.e., practicing a passage of text until meeting a predetermined performance criterion); performance feedback (e.g., using verbal feedback and occasional graphical displays for students to understand their progress and improvements); systematic praise and a structured reward system to highlights students' accomplishments and enhance their motivation during HELPS sessions; and verbal reminders for students to read with fluency and for comprehension. The HELPS Instructor's Manual (Begeny, 2009) provides additional details and research summaries for users to better understand the evidence base for these strategies and how to specifically use them as part of the structured HELPS program. The manual (available for free) also provides users with all instructional materials needed to fully implement HELPS and use it with fidelity.

Using HELPS. HELPS instructional sessions last approximately 15–25 minutes, depending on whether it is used in the one-on-one format or small-group format, and whether it is used in-person or virtually with platforms such as Zoom or Google Meet. Regardless of implementation format, it is recommended that students receive at least three sessions per week. As shown through years of research and practice, HELPS can be used effectively and with fidelity by a wide range of individuals, including but not limited to professionally credentialed educators (e.g., classroom teachers, school psychologists, intervention teachers, reading specialists), teaching assistants, university students training to be teachers, and even parents or community volunteer tutors (Begeny et al., 2011; Mitchell & Begeny, 2014; Richardson, 2019; Vess et al., 2018). As discussed by Begeny (2009), ensuring broad usability of HELPS was intentional as part of its research, development, instructional design—and this is reflected in its recommended implementation materials and training activities. Ensuring broader usability was also intentional as one of several inter-connected development and dissemination factors that can be used to improve educational equity nationally and internationally.

Because nearly all students must develop text-reading fluency to become proficient readers (NRP, 2000), HELPS can be used with learners of all ages as long as they have at least some proficiency in basic decoding and phonics skills. Within the U.S. and globally, HELPS is most often used with students in grades 1 through 5. However, several years of research and practice have also shown how HELPS can be highly effective with learners who are in grades 6 and above if they are still working to develop proficiency with text reading fluency (Musti-Rao et al., 2023; Vess et al., 2018). As noted above, HELPS can be implemented effectively both in-person (which is how it was originally developed) or virtually (Musti-Rao et al., 2023); and it can be implemented one-on-one (adult-student; see

Begeny, 2009) or with a small group of 2–5 students (see Begeny, 2018b). Later we summarize how both the one-on-one and small-group HELPS programs can be easily used within instructional problem-solving models such as Response to Intervention (RTI), Multi-tiered Systems of Support (MTSS), or others.

Since its development, HELPS has positively supported students in the U.S. (where it was originally developed and researched) and globally. As of early 2022, estimates suggest HELPS has been used with hundreds of thousands of students ranging from grade 1 to adults. It is being used in all 50 U.S. states and has been used in more than 60 countries. Using principles and practices of internationalization in school and educational psychology (see Begeny, 2018a), formal HELPS implementation and partnership work has supported teachers and students in several countries (e.g., Australia, Brazil, Costa Rica, Spain, Tanzania, Uzbekistan, and others). HELPS is currently available in English, Spanish, and Portuguese, with ongoing work being conducted to offer the program in additional languages. The benefits of using HELPS have been well-documented in both formal research studies (see next section) and several comprehensive program evaluations that occur every year as part of schools', school districts', and education nonprofits' systematic use of HELPS.

Research on HELPS. More than a dozen studies to date have evidenced the benefits of HELPS for a broad and diverse group of students, including but not limited to students in elementary and middle school, students with and without disabilities, students for whom English is or is not the student's first language, and students eligible for free or reduced-price lunch (e.g., Begeny, 2011; Begeny et al., 2011, 2012a; Malouf et al., 2014; Vess et al., 2018). In addition to studies evidencing the program's effectiveness, HELPS is also summarized in the most recent "Educator's Practice Guide" for early reading instruction (Foorman et al., 2016). Published by the U.S. Department of Education's What Works Clearinghouse, this guide highlights HELPS as one of only a small number of reading programs that significantly improved children's word reading, oral reading fluency, and reading comprehension.

Accessing HELPS materials and training. The program is made freely available from the author and Helps Education Fund, a U.S. 501(c)(3) non-profit organization that disseminates several research-validated programs and services for free or low cost. Educators who wish to access all the free HELPS materials simply need to download them from the Helps Education Fund website (see link provided in the Begeny [2009] reference). Prior research suggests that many educators can self-learn the program and use it with fidelity after accessing the freely available instructor's manual and 90-minute training video (e.g., Begeny et al., 2013). For educators and school administrators who prefer to receive training and/or research-validated coaching from a certified HELPS trainer (or prefer to receive pre-assembled HELPS materials instead of freely downloading, printing, and assembling them), these options are also available from Helps Education Fund for free or low cost.

Case Study

As an overview, our case study will summarize one elementary school's use of HELPS programming as part of a school-wide intervention to support students' text-reading fluency. Like most schools and districts we have worked with, both the one-on-one (Begeny, 2009) and small-group (Begeny, 2018b) versions of HELPS are used to support students' text-reading fluency and reading confidence. Henceforth, we will simply use *HELPS* to refer to the one-on-one program and *HELPS-SG* to refer to the small-group program.

In our case study, the school uses both HELPS-SG and HELPS. This approach to supporting students' text-reading fluency can be used in any school (or outside-of-school program), regardless of whether a formal model for instructional problem-solving is used. However, because many schools and districts are adopting tiered approaches to intervention (such as RTI or MTSS models), we note that HELPS and HELPS-SG can easily be used in a tiered intervention model. A full description of RTI and MTSS is beyond the scope of this chapter, but those familiar with such models are aware that they often involve providing core instruction at Tier 1 and, for students in need, intervention support is offered at Tier 2 and then—if still needed with a respective student—more intensive intervention is provided at Tier 3. With HELPS programming, schools most often use HELPS-SG at Tiers 1 or 2 (depending on how many students could benefit) and use HELPS at Tier 2, Tier 3, and/or with students who qualify for even more intensive intervention services in reading (e.g., students with a formal IEP).

Most germane to our chapter, the school we describe uses HELPS-SG at Tier 2 and uses HELPS at Tier 3, as well as an occasional Tier 2 supplement when needed. Begeny (2018b) describes in detail how this approach to using both HELPS and HELPS-SG can be used effectively. Similarly, Field et al. (2019) summarize a study where 78 students began the school year by getting HELPS-SG as a Tier 2 intervention and then, for students who performed below the "at-risk" cut-point during the school's winter benchmark assessment, those students received HELPS to increase the intervention intensity. The space limitations of a single book chapter prohibit us from describing a comprehensive case study of both HELPS-SG and HELPS, so we focus our chapter on one school's use of HELPS and mention HELPS-SG when necessary.

Finally, it is important to highlight that our case study is based on more than a dozen projects in recent years where HELPS and/or HELPS-SG was being implemented in a school-wide or district-wide capacity. In such projects, we had the opportunity to support schools and districts with implementation components such as training and coaching, monitoring of intervention fidelity, recruitment of volunteer interventionists, program evaluation, and more. Our work in this regard was largely connected to the programming and services provided by the Helps Education Fund non-profit organization mentioned previously, as HELPS is currently one of 11 educational programs offered by that organization. Our case study therefore represents an amalgam of the many projects we have supported and it therefore serves as a fictional synthesis of common characteristics and aspects across those different projects. Nearly all details of our case summary come from real-life scenarios we have experienced in our HELPS-related work, but details or events from one project are blended with those of others. There were a few reasons we decided to present a synthesized, hypothetical case rather than give details about one specific "case" or project, and we hope our summary is one that readers can easily imagine and connect to their school-based training and/or practice.

Background Information

The fictional name of our school is Oakland Elementary School, or simply *Oakland* for short. Oakland is one of 46 K-5 elementary schools in a mid-size U.S. school district that uses HELPS-SG and HELPS as part of their standard treatment protocol to support students who perform below expectations during *Dynamic Indicators of Basic Early Literacy Skills* (DIBELS) Oral Reading Fluency (DORF) assessments (University of Oregon, 2020) that are administered with all students at the beginning, middle, and end of the school year (BOY, MOY, and EOY, respectively). Oakland is a racially and ethnically diverse Title 1 school, and 71% of students receive free or reduced-price lunch. In recent years, approximately 35% of the students were eligible for English language services and 12% were identified as having a disability. Using the state's end-of-grade test, approximately 40% of Oakland's students meet proficiency standards in reading. Classroom sizes range from 18–22 students per class, there are 2–3 classrooms per grade, and 88% of classroom teachers have at least three years of experience.

Three years ago, all schools in the district began using the same core reading curriculum, and although the curriculum's publishers describe how several aspects of the curriculum align with the science of reading, curriculum specialists in Oakland's school district acknowledge that the curriculum is similar to many core reading curricula in that there is insufficient attention given to text reading fluency—a common scenario of core curricula for many years (Daly et al., 2015). The school district is also in their third year of having a formal Standard Treatment Protocol (STP) for academic interventions and they are continuing to identify and formally select targeted reading and math interventions. Implementation of HELPS and HELPS-SG began as a pilot two years ago, within five elementary schools within the district. Pilot data were encouraging, and the programs were adopted as part of the district's STP for text reading fluency at the end of the pilot year. Oakland was not part of the pilot and, as part of a phased roll-out, HELPS and HELPS-SG were planned for implementation in Oakland across three years: last year, it began for identified students in grades 2–3; in the current school year, it will be used with all eligible students in grades 2–5; and in the next school year, first-grade students identified as needed reading fluency support at the middle of the school year will be eligible for HELPS-SG.

Based on Oakland's DORF scores from the past couple years, it is estimated that the BOY assessment will identify approximately 40% of students in grades 2–3 (roughly 42 total students) and approximately 30% of students in grade 4–5 (roughly 31 total students) who would be eligible for and benefit from a text-reading fluency intervention. Of those roughly 70–75 students, approximately 50–55 would begin the school year receiving HELPS-SG and 20–25 would begin getting HELPS. Determinations about whether to start students with HELPS or HELPS-SG are guided by data-based decision-making processes described in the next section. HELPS-SG interventionists are usually classroom teachers who provide that intervention with one or two small-groups of 3–5 students during the small-group instructional break-out times that the school requires within the daily, 100-minute English and Language Arts block. HELPS interventionists include the school's fulltime reading specialist, one intervention teacher who covers all grade K-2 classrooms, an intervention teacher for grade 3–5 classrooms, two of the school's five part-time paraprofessionals, and six community volunteers who volunteer 1–3 hours per week. Volunteers include three local college students (two of whom receive Federal Work Study for the work), two parents of students in the school, and one volunteer connected with a local nonprofit organization.

School-level and Student-level Problem Identification and Analysis

The "problem" in our specific case study is a discrepancy between the student's grade-level expectations (based on state standards and associated national norms of the DORF) and the student's DORF score. As discussed earlier, such discrepancies can be analyzed during BOY, MOY, or EOY assessments; but for simplicity, we situate the timing of our case study as starting at the beginning of the school year; thus, for the initial "problem identification phase," we are interested in identifying students who perform in a DIBELS classification/category of likely needing intervention in order to perform proficiently on more comprehensive assessments of reading (e.g., during end-of-grade tests). Later we explain specific DIBELS classifications.

There could be several reasons why a student may perform below expectations (e.g., presence of a learning disability in reading, chronic absenteeism, undetected vision or hearing difficulties), but the most common reason (generally speaking) is that, for a multitude of reasons, the student has not yet obtained sufficient reading instruction that is most likely to meet the student's learning needs (e.g., lack of exposure to evidence-based instruction and/or intervention).

Following the school-wide BOY assessment, we complete an analysis of all students' data to identify students who are not meeting grade-level expectations. This can be efficiently done with a data spreadsheet of all students and "sorting" the DORF scores from highest to lowest per grade and then identifying students who (for this case study) perform below grade-level expectations. DORF is just one example of a commonly used, commercially published assessment tool that utilizes an assessment of oral reading fluency (ORF) along with assessments of phonics-based reading skills, such as Nonsense Word Fluency (NWF) and Word Reading Fluency (WRF). Our case study specifically discusses use of the DIBELS 8th Edition assessment system (University of Oregon, 2020) because Oakland, like 100% of public schools in the respective state, use DIBELS assessments for students in grade K-5. However, the same logic of our problem identification and analysis could be used with other reading assessments, especially those that occur at BOY, MOY, and EOY.

To elaborate on this important step of school-wide identification of students in need of reading intervention, it is important to highlight that DIBELS specifies four categories of performance (each with a corresponding color-code) for each of their reading measures (e.g., DORF, NWF, WRF, etc.). The categories aim to specify the level of support each student likely needs based on performance during the assessment process. Students can be categorized as needing (a) core support (blue, reflecting the highest performing students), (b) core support (green), (c) strategic support (yellow), and (d) intensive support (red). Students needing "core support" do not likely need intervention and instead should continue to get core instruction unless there is competing evidence to suggest otherwise. In contrast, students needing *strategic* or *intensive* support would likely benefit from targeted, evidence-based intervention. The specific scores associated with each DIBELS assessment and performance range by grade can be found at the following link: https://dibels.uoregon.edu/sites/dibels1.uoregon.edu/files/2021-06/DIBELS8thEditionGoals.pdf. It is with this guide that we identify students at Oakland who are likely to need and benefit from HELPS or HELPS-SG.

To elaborate on the steps for identifying students most likely to need and benefit from HELPS, we created Figure 6.1 as a systems-level (in this case, school-level) decision-making flow chart, inclusive of relevant tables and notes to best understand the flow chart. The flow chart in Figure 6.1 specifically assists educators in making clear, data-based decisions regarding a grade 2–5 student's fit with HELPS.[1] Decisions are based on DIBELS scores, but the notes in Figure 6.1 also indicate where educators' input is also very important to consider in light of the assessment data. For example, different decisions for a student may need to be made if there is compelling evidence suggesting the BOY assessment was invalid or there are other contextual factors to consider.[2]

The decision-making guidance represented in Figure 6.1 follows a sensible logic, but we recognize that it could reflect "aspirational decision-making" compared to realities of many school settings. We recognize the often-competing responsibilities educators must juggle when attempting to use uniform, school-wide systems for instructional problem-solving. However, the goal of presenting this framework for decision-making guidance is to describe a logical approach for problem identification and analysis that is consistent with structured *systems of instructional problem solving* (e.g., the Systems-Oriented Plan for Academic Achievement [SOPAA]; Begeny et al., 2012b) but not always fully described or used within *models of instructional problem solving*, such as RTI or MTSS.

Using Figure 6.1 to analyze BOY data in the present school year for grade 2–5 students at Oakland, 73 students were determined as eligible and needing targeted support in text reading fluency. The data and processes also indicated that 51 students would begin the school year getting HELPS-SG (3–7 students per classroom) and 22 would begin by getting HELPS (2–3 students per classroom). From here, the sole focus of our case study will be on the 22 students who were identified to receive HELPS.

Intervention Setting and Materials

HELPS sessions can be easily facilitated in a wide range of settings—pretty much anywhere that an adult and student can sit near each other without significant distractions and where the student feels comfortable receiving one-on-one reading support. In Oakland, HELPS is implemented with the

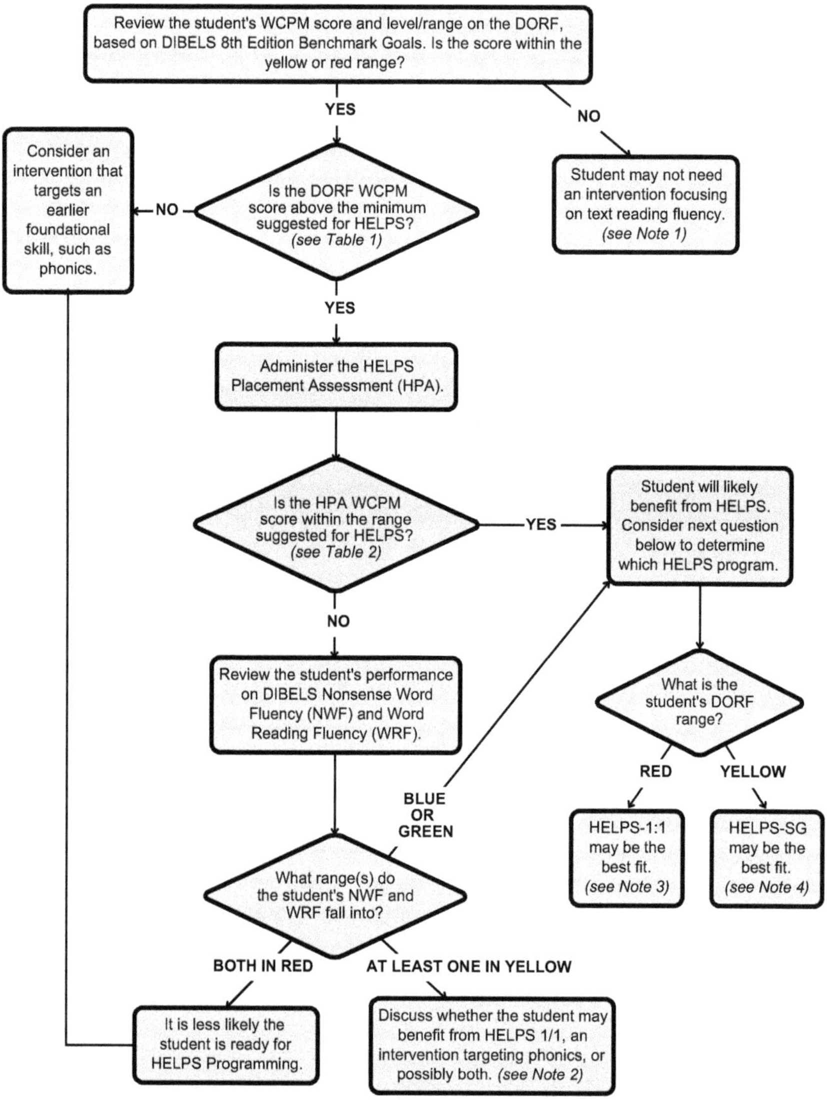

FIGURE 6.1 Decision-making Recommendations for Identifying Students in Grades 2–5 Who Would Likely Benefit from HELPS as a Targeted Text Reading Fluency Program

identified 22 students in either the intervention classroom, a small space in the library, or at a desk in the hallway just outside of students' classrooms. Primary HELPS materials include a curriculum of 100 systematically sequenced passages (Begeny et al., 2009) as well as some implementation

Table 1. *Minimum Suggested DORF WCPM Score for HELPS (Begeny, 2009).*

Student's Grade Level	Minimum WCPM at Fall Benchmark	Minimum WCPM at Winter Benchmark
Second	25	40
Third	20	35
Fourth	35	50
Fifth	50	50

Table 2. *Suggested HPA WCPM Score Range on Highest Administred Level.*

Student's Grade Level	WCPM Score Range
Second	35-80
Third	55-100
Fourth	70-115
Fifth	80-135

Note 1. Some students scoring the green range, especially those scoring at the bottom of that range and those in grades 1-4, may still benefit from HELPS as a program that will strengthen text reading fluency. Additionally, a student who received HELPS in the beginning of the school year based on definite need may still benefit from strengthening text reading fluency in the second part of the school year even if their MOY DORF score is in the green range. In both cases, educators who work with the student should decide what is best for the individual student.

Note 2. Students who score in the yellow range on NWF, WRF, or both, especially those scoring at the top of that range, likely have some of the necessary skills to benefit from HELPS. On the other hand, students who score at the bottom of the yellow range on one or both of the measures may require an intervention targeted more specifically at an earlier foundational skill than fluency, such as phonics. Educators who work with the student should consider performance on these measures along with with a targeted skills observation in order to determine what intervention(s) might be the best fit for the individual student. Additionally, regardless of NWF and WRF scores, students in any grade who score fewer than 35 WCPM on the HPA likely require an intervention targeted at an earlier foundational skill, as 35 WCPM is viewed as a standard minimum for elementary school students to be eligible for HELPS.

Note 3. ORF scores in the red range indicate the need for intensive support in fluency HELPS-1:1, because it is a one-on-one intervention, is relatively more intensive than HELPS-SG. However, there may be scenarios in which these students would benefit equally from HELPS-SG. Educators may want to consider using HELPS-SG with a student in the red range when there are 2-4 additional students with similar abilities and when time and resources are limited, making a small group intervention more efficient. Additionally, for a student who scored in the red range on their BOY DORF and subsequently received HELPS-1:1, if their MOY DORF demonstrates good progress (e.g., they score in the yellow range), they may transition to HELPS-SG in the middle of the year. See the HELPS for Small Instructional Groups Teacher's Manual for more information (Begeny, 2018).

Note 4. DORF scores in the yellow range indicate the need for strategic support. HELPS-SG, as a small group intervention, is considered more resource and time efficient than HELPS-1:1, and can therefore be a good starting point for students requiring strategic support. However, educators may want to consider using HELPS-1:1 with a student in the yellow range if there are no other students with similar abilities to create a small group and/or if time and resources allow for one-on-one intervention support. Additionally, a student in the yellow range on DORF, who is also in the red or yellow range on NWF and/or WRF may benefit from one-on-one support that can more directly target their specific profile of strengths and weaknesses. Finally, for a student who scored in the yellow range on their BOY DORF and subsequently received HELPS-SG, if their MOY DORF does not demonstrate adequate progress (e.g., they score in the red range), they may benefit from transitioning to HELPS-1:1 in the middle of the year.

FIGURE 6.1 (Continued)

materials that are available within the instructor's manual (Begeny, 2009). The HELPS Curriculum of passages (also available for free download) has a book for students and a book for the instructor. The passage content is exactly the same, but the book for the instructor has word counts at the end of every line of text and a space to record students' total words read, words read correctly per minute (WCPM), and words read incorrectly per minute (WIPM). Implementation materials for the instructor include a flow chart summarizing the implementation steps, directions for the instructor to give the student so they know what to expect for each implementation step, a Progress Tracking Form, a Star Chart, and a Student Graph used to show the student achievement and progress. These materials are described in detail by Begeny (2009), including descriptions of what they are, how to use them, and why they are important for implementation. HELPS materials are also available in digital form (see Musti-Rao et al., 2023) so an instructor could use the program virtually or benefit from some efficiencies that can come with a virtual "folder" of materials while implementing in-person. At Oakland, interventionists use the virtual folder on a school laptop while implementing in-person.

Intervention Plan

As part of Oakland's STP and evolving system for instructional problem-solving, they use an Intervention Planning Form (IPF) to document the intervention plan and details for each student identified as needing intervention. Figure 6.2 shows an example IPF for one third-grade student who will receive HELPS. This IPF was adapted from a form provided by Begeny et al. (2012a) in their comprehensive description of systems-level instructional problem-solving and from Appendix B-4 in the HELPS-SG Instructor's Manual (Begeny, 2018b). As shown, the IPF example shows key details that should be determined for intervention delivery and monitoring.

Intervention Goals

There are both short-term and longer-term goals associated with HELPS implementation. As part of the program, short-term goals are assessed in every single session (through *embedded assessments*, discussed later) and if a student meets the goal, they move to a new passage in the HELPS Curriculum. If the student does not meet the Reading Goal in the session, they continue to practice the passage for up to three total sessions with a respective passage. The Reading Goal includes a grade-specific WCPM goal, as well as a WIPM goal and a "retell check" to ensure the student has sufficient comprehension of the content they read. Specific details about the session Reading Goal are described in the HELPS Instructor's Manual (Begeny, 2009) and the associated HELPS training materials. In short, by using specific decision rules for a student to read each respective passage at a pre-determined fluency level, this systematic reading of passages within the HELPS Curriculum ultimately allows students to build their text reading fluency. Research evaluating HELPS shows not only that

Classroom Teacher's Name:	Ms. Castro (3rd grade classroom teacher)	**HELPS Intervention Teacher(s):**	Ms. Pryor (school volunteer) and Mr. Elrom (grade 3-5 intervention teacher)
Student's Name:	Jasmine Smith	**Date of completing this IPF:**	September 13, 2023

1. Who will implement HELPS? Ms. Pryor, the university student volunteer (twice per week); and Mr. Elrom, the grade 3-5 intervention teacher (once per week).

2. Will HELPS be modified in any way, and if so, how and why? No planned modifications. Implementation will be consistent with the recommendations in the HELPS Instructor's Manual.

3. How will HELPS interventionists get trained (if not already trained)? Ms. Pryor and Mr. Elrom were trained in the prior school year and, after training, were observed by a certified HELPS Coach to implement with 100% fidelity three separate times in the past school year.

4. Where and when will the HELPS be implemented? HELPS sessions will occur every Mon, Wed, and Thurs between 11-11:30am, which is the designated intervention block for 3rd graders. HELPS will be provided in hallway immediately outside of the students' classroom.

5. How many sessions of HELPS will occur each week? At least three sessions per week. A fourth session (or as needed, a makeup session) will be implemented on Fridays, if needed.

6. On what date will HELPS sessions begin, and when will the HELPS Placement Assessment occur? HELPS sessions will begin the week of Sept 18th. The Placement Assessment will occur on Sept 15th (completed by Mr. Elrom).

7. How will intervention fidelity be evaluated, by whom, and when? One of the school district's certified HELPS Coaches will virtually (with Zoom) observe Ms. Pryor and later Mr. Elrom for intervention fidelity. Both observations will happen no later than Oct 9. Because each interventionist demonstrated perfect fidelity 3 times last year, only one observation is planned for each person in this school year (unless further observation/support is needed or requested).

8. How will student progress be monitored (e.g., with what form of assessment, how often, by whom)? Students' progress will be monitored with the HELPS individual ORF assessments that occur at the beginning of each session. Every two weeks those assessments will be compared to existing HELPS norms for immediate ORF gains to ensure student falls within or above the expected range. DORF BOY and MOY benchmarks assessments will also be used.

FIGURE 6.2 Intervention Planning Form (IPF) for HELPS One-on-One program: An example showing how data can be recorded for one student receiving HELPS at Oakland Elementary

students develop better text-reading fluency for brand-new reading content, but they are also better able to comprehend the new content. Research publications on HELPS (e.g., Begeny, 2011; Begeny et al., 2010, 2011; Vess et al., 2018) illuminate these relationships between short-term goals and longer-term goals (e.g., generalized improvements in word reading, text fluency, and comprehension), but for the purposes of this chapter and practice-based focus of our case study, we will explain one type of

9. Who will contact the student's caregiver(s) to inform them about the intervention plan, seek caregiver input, and seek possible support? Ms. Castro will talk to a parent of the student. This will be done by phone or in person when she sees the parent at the end-of-day student pick-up.

10. When will the caregivers(s) be contacted? ***(Also report here if a caregiver offers objections, input, or support that prompts a change in the intervention plan).*** Sept 14th or 15th.

11. What objective goals should the students achieve, presumably as a result of receiving intervention? On average, the student should meet the individual Reading Goal within at least 2 sessions of a particular passage at least 80% of the time. Also, compared to the student's BOY DORF score, the MOY DORF score should increase by 20 or more WCPM.

12. By what date will the intervention teacher(s) do an *initial,* informal review of how intervention is going (e.g., intervention fidelity, consistency, effectiveness)? Ms. Castro and Mr. Elrom will complete this initial review no later than the week of Oct 30th.

13. How will periodic "follow-ups" of intervention success occur (e.g., who will initiate them, approximately how often, and where will follow-up notes be recorded)? Brief (5 min) follow-up meetings between Ms. Castro & Mr. Elrom will occur every 2-3 weeks. Ms. Castro will initiate these, and notes from those meetings will be recorded on the back of the student's HELPS Progress Tracking Form. As needed, challenges observed during intervention will be discussed during bi-weekly 3rd grade teacher and intervention team meetings.

14. How many weeks of HELPS will occur before completing a more comprehensive review of intervention effectiveness? A more comprehensive review of intervention effectiveness will occur after student takes the MOY DORF benchmark assessment. Considering school holidays and field trips, this will allow for at least 12-13 weeks of HELPS intervention and at least 35 HELPS sessions.

FIGURE 6.2 (Continued)

longer-term goal that school-based educators can evaluate as a type of generalized reading gain.

The longer-term goal that is relatively easy for educators to examine is the growth in WCPM between a student's BOY, MOY, and EOY score on a measure such as the DORF. This is not the only long-term goal worth considering, but for the purposes of this case study, Oakland Elementary School educators wanted to see if students exceed expected rates of DORF growth based on each student's level of performance. Within school psychology and other disciplines, there are numerous ways to formulaically determine goals and goal lines, and each has its merits and disadvantages. For Oakland, educators are interested in a relatively straightforward and uniform way to analyze the growth of each student receiving HELPS—and this can be done by (a) looking at each student's BOY, MOY, and EOY scores; and (b) comparing those scores to school district, state-level, and/or national norms for expected rates of improvement (ROI).

Simply for explanatory purposes, Figure 6.3 shows a small sample of available DORF ROI norms from their 7th edition (i.e., *DIBELS Next*)

Grade level	Percentile	Fall (BOY) WCPM	Winter (MOY) WCPM	Spring (EOY) WCPM
3rd grade	40th	68	86	96
	39th	67	85	95
	38th	66	84	94
	37th	65	84	93
	36th	64	83	92
	35th	63	82	90
	34th	62	81	89
	33rd	61	80	88
	32nd	60	78	87
	31st	59	77	86
	30th	58	76	85

FIGURE 6.3 Small sample of DIBELS Oral Reading Fluency (DORF) Rate of Improvement (ROI) norms from their 7th edition (i.e., DIBELS Next) materials

materials, which were based on approximately 15,000 students from across the United States. As an illustration, Figure 6.3 shows what WCPM scores would be expected of third-grade students performing between the 30th to 40th percentile, with each percentile corresponding to a specific WCPM score. For Oakland's educators to examine, for example, the relative growth for each student who receives HELPS throughout the fall season of the school year (roughly 18 weeks between the BOY and EOY assessment), they could assess the student's BOY "WCPM starting point," determine how much growth (i.e., the ROI) would be anticipated based on DORF national norms, and then examine whether the student's MOY score is below, at, or above the expected ROI. For example, if a third-grade student scores 60 WCPM at BOY (corresponding to a score at the 32nd percentile), the DORF norms suggest that (on average) such a student in the US would likely improve 18 WCPM between the BOY and MOY assessment (i.e., from 60 to 78 WCPM during that time). With this logic, Oakland's educators can examine whether a third-grade student who scored 60 WCPM at BOY met or exceeded 78 WCPM at MOY, and exceeding that score would be an indicator of promising growth for the student and likely influenced by intervention received during that time. As shown in Figure 6.3, expected ROI between MOY to EOY is generally less than expected ROI between BOY to MOY assessments.

Unfortunately, it is beyond the scope of this chapter to describe the various strategies and considerations that could be used in evaluating student growth with DORF benchmark assessment scores (or of similar commercially available measures of oral reading fluency). The aim here was to offer one brief illustration of how Oakland's educators can use available data for expected ROI in WCPM to assess reading gains between benchmark assessment periods. Also, strategies to assess student improvement relative to expected ROI continue to evolve and, at times, their use is influenced by the available ROI data. For example, the DIBELS 8th edition offers built-in formulaic methods to examine expected ROI for each individual student through their web-based data management software, so educators with access to that software have a relatively simple way of analyzing whether students are improving at desired rates. Those without such software can use publicly available DIBELS technical reports to use data analyses strategies that are similar to those described in this section.

Measurement of Target Reading Skill, Data Collection Strategies, and Progress Monitoring

The previous section describes one way to assess intervention impact at a student- and school-wide level—that is, through assessing ROI between BOY, MOY, and EOY assessment periods. However, more immediate and ongoing progress monitoring are essential to intervention delivery and can be accomplished in multiple ways. Chapter 6 of Begeny et al. (2012b) describes numerous ways—and more than a dozen corresponding assessment resources—to monitor student progress during academic intervention; and it describes methods that are not intervention-specific. In our case study, Oakland's educators do not have the time or resources to facilitate ongoing (e.g., weekly or bi-weekly) "outside" assessments to monitor each student's progress, especially when considering more than 100 students receiving some form of intervention within the school). Instead, Oakland educators opted to use the progress monitoring assessments that are directly embedded within the HELPS intervention (for more detail, see Begeny et al., 2015) to regularly monitor progress of the 22 students getting HELPS.[3]

Embedded assessments occur as part of intervention delivery and offer educators a logical and time-efficient method to regularly monitoring student progress during intervention (Begeny et al., 2012b, 2015; Oslund et al., 2012). There are at least four main types of embedded assessments for progress monitoring within HELPS. Along with preliminary research (e.g., Begeny et al., 2015), additional research is underway to further understand each of the different embedded assessments in HELPS; however, in our case study, Oakland's educators are considering student performance across three of the embedded assessments. Specifically, they are examining (a) a student's average immediate gain score; (b) a student's average retention gain score; and (c) the percentage of time the student meets the HELPS Reading Goal within 1–2 HELPS sessions with a respective passage. Table 6.1 explains more about these embedded assessments and provides data from a small but representative sample of students who recently received HELPS during a school year.

In practice, each of the scores shown in Table 6.1 serve as a "proxy" or indicator of whether the student appears to be responding well to the HELPS intervention. For example, if students are averaging an immediate gain score of at least 15–25 WCPM and are frequently meeting their Reading Goal per passage within 1–2 HELPS sessions (ideally with a frequency of 80% or higher), these are good indicators that students are responding well and similarly to the many students who, over past years, make generalized reading gains with that type of session-by-session performance. Additionally, monitoring students with these "proxy" measures assists educators with identifying whether a student's intervention plan may need to be slightly adjusted (e.g., slightly decreasing a student's WCPM criterion for the Reading Goal, enhancing an element of the motivation system, adding one additional session per week if possible). The HELPS Instructor's Manual provides detailed guidance for educators to follow in cases where the standard HELPS intervention plan should be adjusted to best support the student, and such guidance is specifically connected to the embedded assessment discussed above.

Intervention Fidelity and Inter-scorer Agreement Plans

Intervention fidelity of HELPS has always been central to program development, research, training, and dissemination. The instructor's manual (Begeny, 2009) and associated training materials detail exactly what intervention fidelity should look like with HELPS. As noted previously, several HELPS interventionists at Oakland had already received training (inclusive of coaching), and in this section we summarize some key aspects of training to ensure all of Oakland's HELPS interventionists use the program with fidelity.

The most optimal level of intervention fidelity with HELPS means that the interventionist is routinely implementing the 13 core procedures with 100% fidelity and using the 31 quality implementation indicators with at

TABLE 6.1 Illustrative Sample of HELPS One-on-One Data Showing Students' Mean Growth per Session and Frequency of Meeting the Reading Goal

		Mean Growth in WCPM and (SD) per Session[1]		*Mean Percentage of Time Student Met the Reading Goal*[2]			
Grade	*n*	*Immediate Gain*	*Retention Gain*	*After 1–2 Sessions*	*After 3 Sessions*	*Did Not Meet Goal*	*Decision Error*[3]
Second	108	22.1 (8.4)	1.6 (5.4)	86.0%	7.1%	5.6%	1.3%
Third	105	22.4 (7.4)	0.8 (4.7)	81.6%	9.6%	5.5%	3.2%
Fourth	75	19.0 (8.9)	−1.0 (4.1)	78.9%	11.1%	4.7%	5.5%
Fifth	35	18.8 (6.2)	−1.9 (4.5)	80.0%	9.1%	4.4%	6.5%
Total	323	21.1 (8.1)	0.4 (4.9)	82.3%	9.0%	5.2%	3.5%

Notes: WCPM = words read correctly per minute. SD = standard deviation. This tables presents an example set of data that would be applicable in our case study with Oakland Elementary School. The data do not reflect the full body of HELPS data for the measures shown in the table; they are instead a recent representative sample of data presented here for the purpose of this case study.

1 Immediate growth is measured by calculating the difference between the student's WCPM during the first and last (i.e., third) Timed Reading of that same passage during one HELPS session (i.e., Timed Reading 3 of the session – Timed Reading 1 of the session = Immediate Gain score). Retention growth is measured by subtracting the difference between the student's WCPM of a passage at the beginning of a new HELPS session and the third (last) reading of that same passage in the most recent HELPS session.

2 The HELPS Reading Goal is grade-specific (e.g., the WCPM criterion for second and third grade students is 100 and 120 WCPM, respectively; and other grade levels have a different WCPM criterion). With each HELPS session, the student has one opportunity at the beginning of the session to meet the respective Reading Goal. This portion of the table indicates, on average, how many sessions a student read a passage in the HELPS Curriculum before meeting the Reading Goal. See Begeny (2009) and related HELPS training materials for more details.

3 Occasionally, HELPS interventionists make a decision-error on whether the student did or did not meet the Reading Goal (e.g., the student did not truly meet the Goal criteria according to the intervention procedures, but the interventionist made a mistake in interpreting the data and incorrectly moved the student to the next passage). The data in this column therefore reflects the percentage of time a decision-error occurred among the sample of data shown in this table. Such errors are not common, but sometimes happen during the initial weeks an intervention is using HELPS and is still receiving coaching to ensure 100% intervention fidelity.

least 90–100% fidelity. In recent years, Certified HELPS Trainers refer to this level of fidelity as "gold standard" fidelity. The 13 core procedures of HELPS are summarized in the Instructor's Manual (Begeny, 2009) and Appendix K of that manual summarizes each step within a one-page "flow chart" that the interventionist always has during implementation so the steps can be sequentially followed and it is less likely that steps get missed. Although having 31 important quality indicators to implement (see Appendix M of the Instructor's Manual) may seem intimidating on the surface, those indicators are the "fine-tuned" quality characteristics that must be used to implement the 13 core steps most effectively. Many of those 31 quality characteristics are things a seasoned educator may do without specific training (e.g., using enthusiastic and specific praise statement versus general statements, such as "good job;" or reading at a pace just slightly faster than the student's pace during the model reading procedure). Other quality indicators, however, are more specific to HELPS implementation steps (e.g., recording all the correct information on the student's graph). Collectively, those 31 quality indicators are also referred to as HELPS implementation "Tips and Reminders" because interventionists often just need a tip about the 'how and why' for the implementation characteristic or a reminder to do it consistently. Although the goal of HELPS training and coaching is always gold standard fidelity, program evaluation data suggests that consistent implementation with *high fidelity* (defined as 90–100% implementation of core procedures and 80–100% of the quality characteristics) still seems to benefit a large percentage of students receiving HELPS.

Along with core procedures and quality characteristics, proper implementation dosage is also a critical aspect of intervention fidelity. Research has not yet systematically analyzed all the various permutations of HELPS dosage, but research (e.g., Begeny, 2011; Begeny et al., 2010) and practice for the past decade continues to suggest that dosage should include (on average) three HELPS sessions per week for a total of at least 30 sessions. However, recent data also suggests that providing students with more than 30 sessions has a meaningful, value-added impact on student performance for HELPS specifically (e.g., Richardson, 2019) and academic interventions more generally (e.g., Roberts et al., 2022). With this in mind, Oakland educators plan to get students 30–50 HELPS sessions during the current school year, as long as the data throughout the school year continue to suggest that students continue to benefit (also see next section on Intervention Outcome Data). The approach of planning to get students 30–50 HELPS sessions is consistent with ongoing program evaluation findings (e.g., see Richardson, 2019).

Training in HELPS involves some form of "didactic" training, structured practice opportunities combined with feedback from an expert interventionist, as well as coaching from a Certified HELPS Coach. Didactic training can be accomplished in a do-it-yourself (DIY) way, whereby the interventionist accesses the freely available Instructor's Manual and 90-minute online training video and then follows each step of the training specified in Chapter 3 of the Manual. Depending on the interventionist's prior familiarity with HELPS and/or reading fluency intervention strategies, this DIY training generally takes between 5 and 9.5 hours. However, we have learned over the years that many educators prefer and benefit most from opportunities to learn directly from a HELPS Certified Trainer. This was true of the plan for Oakland's school district, and Certified Trainers ultimately provided one 3.5- to 4-hour workshop for each HELPS interventionist, generally in groups of 15–30 educators per workshop. At the district's request for two workshop format options, some workshops were provided virtually and some in-person.

This workshop allowed all interventionists to get a brief overview of reading fluency and then to learn, practice, and get immediate feedback about each of the core implementation steps for HELPS. Following the workshop, Oakland educators were also given the option to do a separate 30-minute practice/verification session, where a Certified HELPS Coach pretended to be an elementary-aged student while the newly training interventionist practiced the implement HELPS while getting feedback from the coach. In the next school year, some of the not-yet-trained HELPS interventionists in Oakland's school district will have a third option for the didactic training: participating a newly developed, asynchronous online training module that covers the same content as the aforementioned virtual (synchronous) or in-person workshop.

Coaching is critical to the HELPS training process and it is essential for getting all interventionists implementing the program with strong fidelity. Oakland followed the recommended model of each interventionist receiving at least three coaching sessions (all completed virtually, via Zoom) for cost and time efficiency. Each coaching session involves the interventionist implementing HELPS with a student while a Certified HELPS Coach observes. Corrective feedback on core implementation steps is provided (as needed) during the HELPS session and then additional feedback and time for answering interventionist questions occurs immediately after the session (requiring, on average, 6–8 minutes). Coaching follows a specific evidence-based approach that has been used effectively with HELPS (e.g., Begeny et al., 2013, 2023; Wang et al., in press) and several other academic interventions. Because of the school-wide and district-wide implementation of HELPS, there are now also district-level staff who have become Certified HELPS Coaches and over the current school year, Oakland's intervention teacher for grades 3–5 will complete the process of becoming a

Certified Coach (and eventually a Certified HELPS Trainer for the district). In addition to systematic training and coaching connected to HELPS, the program's core implementation steps also include a step for the interventionist to self-review all core steps implemented in the session and then systematically reporting any steps missed on a student tracking form used each session. The self-monitoring and reporting of fidelity is the last step of each session and past research suggests the process captures intervention fidelity with strong reliability (Begeny et al., 2013, 2023).

As part of HELPS training and coaching, the interventionists also learn how to score the one-minute timed readings that are completed during DORF assessments and during HELPS sessions (as discussed as part of embedded assessments in the previous section, *Measurement of Target Reading Skill*). There are several guides for accurate scoring of these timed readings, and Begeny (2009) provides such guidance along with DIY practice exercises and training videos. That resource also explains the rationale and steps (along with practice exercises) for completing inter-scorer agreement (i.e., the process of having two independent scorers occasionally score the same timed reading to determine if scoring is consistent among the two individuals). Fortunately, this process for assessing inter-scorer agreement is embedded within the HELPS coaching sessions described previously; so at Oakland, the plan to monitor and ensure accurate scoring of timed readings (and also relevant for DORF assessments) is built into that coaching process.

Intervention Outcome Data

The content of previous sections on Intervention Goals, Assessment, and Progress Monitoring provides the main details by which Oakland staff evaluated learning gains for the 22 students receiving HELPS at the start of this school year. In addition to evaluating ROI between BOY and MOY DORF scores, they also looked to see how many students moved into the blue or green DIBELS classifications suggesting a student does not likely need intervention. In practice, it is fairly uncommon that 10–12 weeks of intervention will move a student (especially students in grades 3 and up) from the red (in need of *intensive support*) classification to green because this far exceeds typical ROI, even with intensive intervention. However, over the course of a school year, some students are able to move from red to green and relatively more students from yellow to green. At Oakland, 16 (73%) of students receiving HELPS exceeded expected growth and more than half of those students moved from the red to yellow DIBELS classification range. Given those students' learning needs and initial positive responsiveness to HELPS, they continued to receive the program into the winter months (with five of the students moving into HELPS-SG instead of HELPS) and each of those students again exceeded expected growth from MOY to EOY—with some moving into the green range by end of year. Of the six (27%) of students who did not exceed expected growth from BOY to MOY, Oakland staff assessed their data to determine next steps. Four of those students were showing positive responsiveness to HELPS, including growth in self-confidence, but it was determined they should receive at least 4–5 sessions per week during the winter. This plan was implemented and those 4 students exceeded expected growth from MOY to EOY. Two students (both in second grade) were not responding as positively during the fall and it was determined that one of those students would only receive an intensive phonics-based intervention starting in January while the other would receive a phonics-based intervention 2–3 times per week and HELPS twice per week.

Intervention Acceptability

Student and interventionist acceptability was assessed using adapted forms provided by Begeny et al. (2012) and those offered by Helps Education Fund. Formal student acceptability was evaluated with surveys at the middle and end of the school year, whereas interventionist acceptability was formally evaluated at the end of the school year. Consistent with past years and other schools in Oakland's school district, 90–100% of the students and interventionists responded favorably to the survey items, as indicated with Agree or Strongly Agree ratings on key items (e.g., for students: "this reading program helped me feel more confident as a reader;" for interventionists: "overall, I am satisfied with using the HELPS program"). That said, formal surveys and other sources of feedback during the school year identified some important opportunities that could allow Oakland educators to improve HELPS implementation (see next section); as such, this information was used in continuous improvement cycles at the school and district level. In the coming school year, Oakland and other schools in the district also plan to survey classroom teachers and parents about their impressions of student improvements in reading. Helps Education Fund will share commonly used survey items for that purpose.

Intervention Considerations and Conclusions

School-wide implementation of any intervention program takes significant time, planning, collaboration, communication, and iterative cycles of improvement. This case study summarized Oakland Elementary School's second year of using HELPS and HELPS-SG as part of their school-wide STP.

Although many sources of data suggested the roll-out of HELPS had several successes (e.g., improved student learning, interventionist acceptability), both survey data and school leaders' observations revealed additional needs and considerations. For example, (a) to support overall student learning, some classroom teachers requested more quality communication between them and HELPS interventionists, especially if the interventionist was not an Oakland staff member; (b) some newer volunteer interventionists did not get a sufficient number of coaching sessions, and technology (e.g., internet and/or computer) issues in the school were barriers to this that need to be resolved by the district's Instructional Technology Department; (c) many staff in the school highlighted the ease of access to HELPS training and materials, as well as its versatility allowing for one-on-one or small-group intervention and the ability to involve school-volunteer interventionists—but the school now recognizes that at least one staff person should have at least 10 hours per week to further cultivate the relationships and communication necessary for a strong volunteer base of interventionists; (d) school administrators see added benefit of getting some students more than three HELPS or HELPS-SG sessions per week and for the coming school year they are seeking to work with a local afterschool program to get two of the afterschool staff trained to use HELPS for that purpose; and (e) in preparation for roll-out of HELPS with first-grade classrooms in the coming school year, administrators in the school recognize that some first grade teachers will need additional support in understanding the purpose of HELPS and the types of first grade students who can benefit from it most.

The aforementioned considerations present opportunities to strengthen school-wide systems for implementation and impact of HELPS and HELPS-SG. Such work is worth the intentionality, collaboration, and effort, as the programming has potential to improve the literacy and lifelong opportunities for hundreds of Oakland Elementary students in the coming years.

Notes

1 A similar decision tree could be used for students in Grade 1 (but not until a MOY DORF assessment) and for students in grades 6 and up (but not without consideration of age-appropriate adaptations of HELPS for students in grade 6 or older). These topics fall outside of the scope of this chapter, but Begeny (2018b) is one resource for related information.

2 The decision-making guidance in Figure 6.1 is usually applicable for the vast majority of students, but we also recognize that some decisions may require additional problem-solving amongst educator(s) who work directly with the student. For instance, educators may want to consider contextual variables such as: how long the reading difficulty (e.g., oral reading fluency) has been present; how prevalent this concern is among other classmates; the student's

strengths; what strategies (if any) have been tried previously and which strategies were successful; are there other concerns (e.g., difficulty with decoding, student behavior) that may be related to the primary concern? These contextual variables, taken together with data on present levels of performance and targeted skills observations, will best inform appropriate intervention selection. See Begeny et al. (2012) for detailed discussion on these topics as part of student-level and systems-level instructional problem-solving.

Student motivation is also important to consider, as many students have difficulties with engagement and motivation during academic interventions. Thankfully, when school-level screening procedures are utilized, identified skill deficits are generally well-detected and it would be uncommon for the deficit to be driven solely by a lack of motivation or engagement. Specific to this case study and knowing that motivation can sometimes be a challenge for struggling readers, HELPS uniquely addresses both skill deficits and motivation by specifically integrating evidence-based instructional and motivational strategies.

3 This section describes embedded assessments for HELPS. The HELPS-SG program has conceptually similar embedded assessments within that program, but they do not function in the exact same ways as the HELPS embedded assessments.

References

Alber-Morgan, S. Ramp, E. Anderson, L. & Martin, C. (2007). Effects of repeated readings, error correction, and performance feedback on the fluency and comprehension of middle school students with behavior problems. *The Journal of Special Education*, *41*, 17–30.

Begeny, J. C. (2009). *Helping Early Literacy with Practice Strategies (HELPS): A one-on-one program designed to improve students' reading fluency*. Helps Education Fund. Retrieved from https://www.helpseducationfund.org/programs-services/helps-one-on-one/

Begeny, J. C. (2011). Effects of the Helping Early Literacy with Practice Strategies (HELPS) reading fluency program when implemented at different frequencies. *School Psychology Review*, *40*, 149–157.

Begeny, J. C. (2018a). A working definition and conceptual model of internationalization for school and educational psychology. *Psychology in the Schools*, *55*, 924–940.

Begeny, J. C. (2018b). *Helping Early Literacy with Practice Strategies for small instructional groups (HELPS-SG): A small-group program designed to improve students' reading fluency*. Raleigh, NC: Helps Education Fund.

Begeny, J. C., Daly, E. J., & Vallely, R. J. (2006). Improving oral reading fluency through response opportunities: A comparison of phrase drill error correction with repeated readings. *Journal of Behavioral Education*, *15*, 229–235.

Begeny, J. C., Mann, C. M., Cunningham, M. D., & Tsuen, H. Y. (2009). *The Helping Early Literacy with Practice Strategies (HELPS) curriculum: Instructional passages developed for use with the HELPS program*. Raleigh, NC: Helps Education Fund.

Begeny, J. C., Mitchell, R. C., Whitehouse, M. H., Harris, C. F., & Stage, S. A. (2011). Effects of the HELPS reading fluency program when implemented by classroom teachers with low-performing second-grade students. *Learning Disabilities Research & Practice*, *26*, 122–133.

Begeny, J. C., Ross, S. G., Greene, D. J., Mitchell, R. C., & Whitehouse, M. H. (2012a). Effects of the Helping Early Literacy with Practice Strategies (HELPS) Reading Fluency Program with Latino English language learners: A preliminary evaluation. *Journal of Behavioral Education*, *21*, 134–149.

Begeny, J. C., Schulte, A. C., & Johnson, K. (2012b). *Enhancing instructional problem solving: An efficient system for assisting struggling learners*. New York, NY: Guilford Press.

Begeny, J. C., Upright, J. J., Easton, J. E., Ehrenbock, C. A., & Tunstall, K. R. (2013). Validity estimates and functionality of materials and procedures used to monitor the implementation integrity of a reading intervention. *Journal of Applied School Psychology*, *29*, 284–304.

Begeny, J. C., Whitehouse, M. H., Methe, S. A., Codding, R. S., Stage, S. A., & Neupert, S. (2015). Do intervention-embedded assessment procedures successfully measure student growth in reading? *Psychology in the Schools*, *52*, 578–593.

Begeny, J. C., Wang, J., Levy, R. A., Sanetti, L. M., Loehman, J., & Rodriguez, K. (2023). Considering the implementation research-to-practice gap: An experimental evaluation of intervention-general methods for assessing and supporting intervention fidelity through coaching. *Journal of School Psychology*, *97*, 152–170.

Cho, Y., Kim, D., Jeong, S. (2021). Evidence-based reading interventions for English language learners: A multilevel meta-analysis. *Heliyon*, *7*, e07985.

Daane, M. C., Campbell, J. R., Grigg, W. S., Goodman, M. J., & Oranje, A. (2005). *Fourth-grade students reading aloud: NAEP 2002 special study of oral reading*. U.S. Department of Education, Institute of Education Sciences, National Center for Education Statistics. https://files.eric.ed.gov/fulltext/ED488962.pdf

Daly, E. J., Neugebauer, S., Chafouleas, S., & Skinner, C. H. (2015). *Interventions for reading problems: Designing and evaluating effective strategies* (2nd ed.). New York, NY: Guilford Press.

Field, S. A., Begeny, J. C., & Kim, E. K. (2019). Exploring the relationship between cognitive characteristics and responsiveness to a Tier 3 reading fluency intervention. *Reading and Writing Quarterly: Overcoming Learning Difficulties*, *35*, 374–391.

Foorman, B., Beyler, N., Borradaile, K., Coyne, M., Denton, C., ... & Wissel, S. (2016, 2019). *Foundational skills to support reading for understanding in kindergarten through 3rd grade* (NCEE 2016-4008). Washington, DC: National Center for Education Evaluation and Regional Assistance (NCEE), Institute of Education Sciences, U.S. Department of Education. Retrieved from https://ies.ed.gov/ncee/wwc/Docs/PracticeGuide/wwc_foundationalreading_040717.pdf

Good, R. H., Simmons, D., & Kame'enui, E. (2001). The importance and decision-making utility of a continuum of fluency-based indicators of foundational reading skills for third-grade high-stakes outcomes. *Scientific Studies of Reading*, *5*, 257–288.

Haring, N. G., Lovitt, T. C., Eaton, M. D., & Hansen, C. L. (1978). *The fourth R: Research in the classroom*. Columbus, OH: Charles E. Merrill.

Hintze, J. M., Ryan, A. L., & Stoner, G. (2003). Concurrent validity and diagnostic accuracy of the Dynamic Indicators of Basic Early Literacy Skills and the Comprehensive Test of Phonological Processing. *School Psychology Review*, *32*, 541–556.

Kaskaya, A. (2016). Improving reading fluency and reading comprehension with NIM-assisted teaching: An activity research. *Education and Science*, *41*, 281–297.

LaBerge, D., & Sameuls, S. J. (1974). Toward a theory of automatic information processing in reading. *Cognitive Psychology*, *6*, 293–323.

Lee, J. & Yoon, S. Y. (2017). The effects of repeated reading on reading fluency for students with reading disabilities: A meta-analysis. *Journal of Learning Disabilities*, *50*, 213–224.

Malouf, R. C., Reisener, C. D., Gadke, D. L., Wimbish, S. W., & Frankel, A. C. (2014). The effect of Helping Early Literacy with Practice Strategies on reading fluency for children with severe reading impairments. *Reading Improvement*, *51*, 269–279.

Martens, B. K., Eckert, T. L., Begeny, J. C., Lewandowski, L. J., DiGennaro, F. D., Montarello, S. A., … & Fiese, B. H. (2007). Effects of a fluency-building program on the reading performance of low-achieving second and third grade students. *Journal of Behavioral Education*, *16*, 39–54.

McBreen, M., & Savage, R. (2022). The impact of a cognitive and motivational reading intervention on the reading achievement and motivation of students at-risk for reading difficulties. *Learning Disability Quarterly*, *45*(3), 199–211.

McGlinchey, M. T., & Hixson, M. D. (2004). Using curriculum-based measurement to predict performance on state assessments in reading. *School Psychology Review*, *33*, 193–203.

Mitchell, C. & Begeny, J. C. (2014). Improving student reading through parents' implementation of a structured reading program. *School Psychology Review*, *43*, 41–58.

Morgan, P. L., & Sideridis, P. D. (2006). Contrasting the effectiveness of fluency interventions for students with or at risk for learning disabilities: A multilevel random coefficient modeling meta-analysis. *Learning Disabilities Research & Practice*, *21*, 191–210.

Musti-Rao, S., Smith, J. M., & Begeny, J. C. (2023). A virtual tutoring program to increase students' text reading fluency. *Intervention in School and Clinic*. https://doi.org/10.1177/10534512221140474

National Center for Education Statistics. (2019, 2022). *The nation's report card: Reading*. U.S. Department of Education, Institute of Education Sciences. https://www.nationsreportcard.gov/highlights/reading/2019/; https://www.nationsreportcard.gov/highlights/reading/2022/

National Reading Panel (2000). *Report of the National Reading Panel. Teaching children to read: An evidence-based assessment of the scientific research literature on reading and its implications for reading instruction*. Washington, DC: US Department of Health and Human Services.

O'Shea, L. J., Sindelar, P. T., & O'Shea, D. J. (1987). The effects of repeated reading and attentional cues on the reading fluency and comprehension of learning disabled readers. *Learning Disabilities Research*, *2*, 103–109.

Oslund, E. L., Hagan-Burke, S., Taylor, A. B., Simmons, D. C., Simmons, L., Kwok, O. M., … Coyne, M. D. (2012). Predicting kindergarteners' response to early reading intervention: An examination of progress-monitoring measures. *Reading Psychology*, *33*, 78–103.

Perfetti, C. A. (1977). Language comprehension and fast decoding: Some psycholinguistic prerequisites for skilled reading comprehension. In J. T. Guthrie (Ed.), *Cognition, curriculum, and comprehension* (pp. 20–41). Newark, DE: International Reading Association.

Perfetti, C. A. (1985). *Reading ability*. Oxford, England: Oxford University Press.

Richardson, M. (2019). Perspective: We can close the reading achievement gap in North Carolina. *EducationNC*. https://www.ednc.org/perspective-north-carolina-reading-fluency-achievement-gaps/

Roberts, G. J., Dumas, D. G., McNeish, D., & Coté, B. (2022). Understanding the dynamics of dosage response: A nonlinear meta-analysis of recent reading interventions. *Review of Educational Research*, *92*, 209–248.

Stevens, E. A., Walker, M. A., & Vaughn, S. (2017). The effects of reading fluency interventions on the reading fluency and reading comprehension performance of elementary students with learning disabilities: A synthesis of the research from 2001 to 2014. *Journal of Learning Disabilities*, *50*, 576–590.

Strickland, W. D., Boon, R. T., & Spencer, V. G. (2013). The effects of repeated reading on the fluency and comprehension skills of elementary-age students with learning disabilities (LD), 2001–2011: A review of study and practice. *Learning Disabilities: A Contemporary Journal*, *11*(1), 1–33.

Therrien, W. J. (2004). Fluency and comprehension gains as a result of repeated reading: A meta- analysis. *Remedial and Special Education*, *25*, 252–261.

University of Oregon (2020). *8th Edition of Dynamic Indicators of Basic Early Literacy Skills (DIBELS®): Technical Manual*. https://dibels.uoregon.edu/sites/dibels1.uoregon.edu/files/DIBELS8-TechnicalManual_04152020.pdf

Vess, S. F., Begeny, J. C., Norwalk, K. A., & Ankney, R. (2018). Tier 2 reading fluency interventions with middle school students: A comparison of the HELPS-SG Program and a teacher-directed evidence-based intervention. *Journal of Applied School Psychology*, *34*, 316–337.

Wang, J., Begeny, J. C., Smith, J. M., & Newson, N. K. (in press). Adapting school-based implementation support from in-person to virtual: An experimental evaluation of a virtual coaching program to improve intervention fidelity. *Manuscript in review*.

White, S., Sabatini, J., Park, Bl. J., Chen, J., Bernstein, J., and Li, M. (2021). *Highlights of the 2018 NAEP Oral Reading Fluency Study* (NCES 2021-026). U.S. Department of Education, Institute of Education Sciences, National Center for Education Statistics. https://nces.ed.gov/nationsreportcard/subject/studies/pdf/2021026_2018_orf_highlights.pdf

7

MULTISYLLABIC WORD DECODING WITH CONTINUOUS READING

Stephanie Hammerschmidt-Snidarich and Kathrin E. Maki

University of Florida, Gainesville, FL, USA

Introduction

It is almost magical to watch a fluent reader translate letters on a page into the many forms that written language can take. Words and sentences long and short are read automatically—quickly, easily, accurately, and with expression. Most of the words are processed so rapidly that they can be considered "sight words"—words that the reader can read immediately on sight. Through the act of fluent reading, the reader gains access to an infinite world of ideas, experiences, and information.

Students who are learning to read move through a series of phases that require increasingly sophisticated and automated integration of foundational reading subskills before they can process and comprehend written text automatically. Those phases are: (1) pre-alphabetic, (2) partial alphabetic, (3) full alphabetic, (4) consolidated alphabetic, and (5) automatic (Ehri, 2005). In the pre-alphabetic phase, students use visual cues to "read," essentially mimicking the act of reading by looking at text and saying words. These students have not yet begun to develop letter-sound correspondence. In the partial alphabetic phase, students are beginning to use grapho-phonemic information to process text because they have developed partial letter-sound correspondence. However, they may only be able to guess at a word based on its first letter or decode very short words that contain the letter sounds they already know. In the full alphabetic phase, students have developed letter-sound correspondence knowledge that they leverage to decode entire words, although decoding is mostly letter-by-letter and somewhat laborious. In the consolidated alphabetic phase,

DOI: 10.4324/9781003275749-7

students have more advanced decoding skills, having acquired an increasing repertoire of word chunks and patterns that they can use to decode longer, multisyllabic words. An important aspect of this phase is that students develop the ability to read word chunks and letter combinations "on sight," which helps to facilitate their automaticity with reading whole words, even difficult unknown or multisyllabic words. With explicit instruction and plenty of practice, students advance to the final automatic phase and become a fluent reader who reads most words from memory quickly, easily, accurately, and with expression.

Yet we know that many students stall in their reading progress before reaching the final automatic phase, as evidenced by the persistently low reading performance of millions of students across the nation (National Center for Education Statistics, National Assessment of Educational Progress, 2019). Struggling readers in the early elementary grades often have underdeveloped decoding skills (Leach et al., 2003), which do not spontaneously develop and must be taught explicitly. While skilled readers use decoding strategies when encountering unfamiliar words, readers with fewer skills tend to use less reliable strategies such as contextual clues and pictures to guess words (Archer et al., 2003; Bhattachary & Ehri, 2004). This lack of decoding skill and automaticity in word reading can create a bottleneck that inhibits reading progress in later grades (Roembke et al., 2021). Thus, struggling readers will likely continue to have difficulty with all school activities that require reading unless they receive appropriately targeted intervention (Scammacca et al., 2015).

Developing Fluent Word Reading

Researchers have made strides in parsing out how fluent word reading occurs (see Ehri, 2020), and there is convergence around the notion that it is a multilinguistic process. A reader must process sounds (phonology) at the same time as they process letters and letter patterns (orthography), what they know about phonics, and the meanings of words and word parts (morphology). This integration of multiple skills requires a multilinguistic instructional approach (Collins et al., 2020; Ehri, 2014).

The word reading task first requires knowledge of the alphabetic principle, which includes letters, their sounds, and how those sounds correspond to accurate word reading and pronunciation. Students remember words (or word parts) when they link graphemes, or how a word is represented by letters in written text (i.e., its spelling), to phonemes (i.e., its sound; how a word is pronounced). For example, the word *lead* in the sentence, "*The dog will lead the pack*" has three grapheme-phoneme correspondences. To read the word, a student must know the letters l, e, a, d, the sounds of those letters, and that e and a together make a long -e sound. They must also be able to blend each sound together smoothly to say the whole word. The correct reading of such a word or word part, is secured in a student's memory when they engage in this process. Once decoded, a student may use semantic and syntactic properties of the word to confirm the pronunciation. In the case of the sentence above, the word *lead* can actually be pronounced as "leed" or "led." Given its use in the sentence, *lead* (pronounced with a long-e sound) makes the most sense semantically and syntactically, which rules out the alternative pronunciation.

We cannot overstate the importance of the alphabetic principle to the word reading process. As stated, ensuring that students develop mastery of the alphabetic principle includes teaching individual sounds of letters, but also the sounds that certain letter combinations make. For example, letter combinations such as consonant digraphs (e.g., sh, ch, th, ck, ng) and trigraphs, (e.g., tch, dge), vowel teams (e.g., ee, oo, ea, igh) and diphthongs (e.g., oy in *toy*, oi in *oil*, ow in *town*), as well as affixes and base words (Archer et al., 2003; Ehri, 2002). Mastery also includes developing familiarity with, and automatic recognition of, common letter patterns and word parts that recur frequently (Moats, 2019), making it easier to read words that contain those patterns and parts (Bowey & Hansen, 1994). Research has consistently confirmed that a student without firm grounding in the alphabetic principle lacks fundamental knowledge and skills necessary to decode and is forced to guess at words (Ehri, 1976, 2020; Ehri & Wilce, 1979a, 1979b), a practice that has negative effects on reading accuracy and comprehension.

When a student has developed a base-level knowledge of, and fluency with, the alphabetic principle, its application to decoding must be explicitly taught and practiced. Part of that instruction includes developing knowledge of the morphological structure of words, which builds understanding and awareness of word parts that a student can leverage to break multisyllabic words into smaller, more easily decodable chunks. For example, an early important skill is knowing the basics of syllabication—that each syllable has a vowel sound—and applying that skill to divide multisyllabic words into parts (Collins, et al., 2020). Knowing the basic syllable types and being able to quickly recognize them within words is also helpful as part of that process (Bhattacharya & Ehri, 2004; Collins et al., 2020; Diliberto et al., 2008; McKenna, 2008; Shefelbine & Calhoun, 1991; Shefelbine et al., 1989). Open and closed syllables, which can be found in nearly 75% of the most common words (Stanbeck, 1992), are typically taught first (Blevins, 2001; McKenna, 2008).

Through repeated exposure to the grapheme–phoneme correspondences in words and word parts via decoding instruction and reading of connected text, students move from laboriously decoding each letter sound-by-sound to *unitization*. Unitization is the ability to read whole words or word chunks as single visual spelling units as soon as they are seen (i.e., "on sight"). It is regarded as the final phase of word recognition, wherein students have stored spellings of particular words in memory and bonded them to their pronunciations as well as their meanings (Ehri & Wilce, 1983). You have probably experienced the phenomenon of unitization when you encounter a stop sign. Most likely, you could not keep from reading the word *stop* even if you wanted to—it is *that* automatic. Unitization is necessary to provide immediate access to a word as soon as it is perceived and to enable increasingly fluent reading of written text.

It is important to note that word familiarity also contributes to automatic word reading (Ehri & Wilce, 1983) and, by extension, fluent reading of connected text. Students can better read words that are already part of their oral vocabulary—words they know and whose meanings are familiar. This connection between familiar words and fluent reading underscores the importance of continuously striving to develop students' oral vocabulary in conjunction with word decoding and connected text reading.

As students get older, literacy instruction typically transitions from learning to read to reading to learn (Chall, 1983). In addition, texts become more demanding to read as students advance to higher grades. There are fewer pictorial cues, sentences are longer with more complex structures, and they contain more multisyllabic words—many of which are new to the student. In fact, students in fifth grade and higher may encounter as many 10,000 novel words per year, the majority of which are likely to be multisyllabic (Nagy & Anderson, 1984). For students with reading difficulties, it is imperative that literacy instruction maintain a dual focus on building students' reading skills in conjunction with using those reading skills to learn information across various contexts. A student must continue building both decoding and reading fluency skills to independently read increasingly complex texts, which can be done by providing instruction that combines multisyllabic word decoding instruction with reading fluency practice.

Brief Intervention Description

Multisyllabic word decoding with continuous reading is a two-part intervention that targets beginning multisyllabic word reading and reading fluency. The intervention is typically implemented with readers in mid- to late elementary or middle school because students should have developed proficient early decoding skills incorporating basic letter-sound patterns (e.g., CVC, blends, digraphs, vowel teams) before working on applying those skills to multisyllabic word decoding and fluency building. Note that, for students who are English Learners (ELs), it is not necessary to wait to begin these reading interventions until students develop proficiency in their second language (L2; i.e., English) because EL and monolingual students have both been shown to benefit from early reading intervention (Burns et al., 2017).

The two intervention components, multisyllable word decoding and continuous reading, use explicit instruction with modeling, guided practice, and independent student practice with feedback. In the first part of the intervention, students learn basic strategies for approaching multisyllabic word decoding that leverage fundamental syllable division skills and knowledge of two of the most common syllable types, open and closed syllables (Stanbeck, 1992). Each syllable has a vowel. An open syllable is a syllable that ends in a long vowel sound. Examples of open syllables include *she*, the ō in *open* (o | pen), and rē in *return* (re | turn). A closed syllable is a syllable that has a short vowel sound and ends with one or more consonants. Examples of closed syllables include *fan*, *brass*, *catch*, răb in *rabbit* (rab | bit), and tĕm in *tempo* (tem | po). Students learn the definition of a syllable, how to identify the vowels and consonants in a multisyllabic word, and a basic strategy for dividing the word into chunks. The student then uses what they know about open and closed syllable types in a flexible way to decode each chunk, and finally the entire word. Students are provided with sufficient practice in the targeted syllable types to establish fluency in applying the strategy to connected text. It is important to note that after fluency has been established in the targeted syllable type(s), teaching additional syllable types helps to further expand students' strategies for multisyllabic word decoding.

In the second part of the intervention, students complete fluency practice by engaging in continuous reading of several passages of text, which provides multiple opportunities to apply their developing multisyllabic word decoding skills and assess generalization of the skill to connected text. Continuous reading is similar to the commonly implemented repeated reading intervention except that instead of reading the same passage of text multiple times, students read a new text passage for each reading.[1] Thus, during each intervention session, a student may read three or four different text passages, which provides practice with, and exposure to, a greater number of words and vocabulary than in repeated reading. Continuous reading intervention protocols differ, with some prescribing a set number of readings (e.g., 3 or 4) for a certain amount of time (e.g., 1 or 2 mins) or having students read each passage in its entirety (e.g., read an entire 200-word passage). The intervention protocol we outline in this chapter requires students to complete four readings in their entirety in an effort to ensure that students receive adequate and equitable dosage in the form of the total number of words read. This requirement to read each assigned passage in its entirety (rather than reading each for 1–2 minutes) is an essential and intentional aspect of this protocol given that student reading rates can vary significantly (see Maki & Hammerschmidt-Snidarich, 2022 for more information). The intervention protocol is outlined in detail below.

Case Study

Background Information

To illustrate implementation of beginning multisyllabic word decoding with continuous reading, we present a case study of a student who participated in the intervention. The student, Maya (pseudonym), was a 12-year-old white and Latinx girl who recently completed the sixth grade and was attending summer school prior to entering seventh grade. She attended a public Kindergarten through 12th-grade University laboratory school. During summer school and her sixth-grade English Language Arts (ELA) class, instruction primarily focused on meaning making, text structure, and analysis of text arguments in line with state ELA standards.

Maya's sixth-grade high-stakes ELA test score fell in the level 2 range, which is considered unsatisfactory. Her ELA teacher also administered Dynamic Indicators of Basic Early Literacy Skills (DIBELS) MAZE passages seasonally, and Maya received a fall score of 9 correct words (at-risk), a winter score of 15 correct words (some risk), and a spring score of 18 correct words (at-risk). During elementary school, Maya received tier 2 and tier 3 reading intervention focusing on phonics and fluency. However, she did not receive targeted interventions once she entered sixth-grade.

Problem Identification

Multisyllabic word decoding with continuous reading targets two primary areas of reading: decoding accuracy of multisyllabic words and reading fluency. Prior to intervention implementation, we collected baseline data on Maya's phonics and oral reading fluency (ORF) skills. These measures served as diagnostic data to ensure that this intervention would appropriately target Maya's needs. The data also served as baseline data to compare Maya's skills before and after intervention to evaluate intervention effectiveness. To assess Maya's phonics skills, we administered the CORE Phonics Survey, which is a diagnostic measure of decoding skills with separate sections that assess different groupings of letter patterns. The results can be

TABLE 7.1 Maya's Baseline CORE Phonics Survey Data

CORE Phonics Survey Section	*Score*	*Mastery Level*
CVC	15/15	Benchmark
Blends	15/15	Benchmark
Digraphs	15/15	Benchmark
R-Controlled Vowels	15/15	Benchmark
Long Vowels	15/15	Benchmark
Variant Vowels	14/15	Benchmark
Low Frequency Vowel and Consonant Spellings	15/15	Benchmark
Multisyllabic Words	16/24	Strategic

TABLE 7.2 Maya's ORF Baseline Data

	WRCM	*Accuracy (%)*	*Grade Level WRCM*	*Grade Level Accuracy (%)*
Passage 1	118	91	141	96
Passage 2	97	88	141	96
Passage 3	114	90	141	96
Median	114	90	141	96

Note: WRCM = words read correctly per minute.

used to determine the types of words a student has difficulty decoding and to determine where to begin intervention. We also administered three DIBELS ORF (i.e., CBM-R) sixth-grade spring benchmark passages to assess Maya's ORF skills. Maya's baseline data (pre-intervention) on the CORE Phonics Survey and DIBELS ORF are presented in Tables 7.1 and 7.2.

Problem Analysis

Although the proposed intervention targets multisyllabic words, we administered all sections of the CORE Phonics Survey (except letter names and letter sounds) because we wanted to ensure that Maya had mastered basic decoding skills before intervening with multisyllabic word decoding. The CORE Phonics Survey is a criterion measure, and it is expected that students eventually demonstrate 100% accuracy on all sections. The survey provides mastery levels that indicate whether the student demonstrates mastery of the skill (i.e., benchmark level), or needs strategic or intensive levels of intervention support. Maya's data showed that she was at the benchmark level for all skills except for multisyllabic words, where her score fell at the strategic level. In sum, Maya demonstrated mastery of most letter-sound patterns and did not need intervention in those areas, but she demonstrated need for intervention with multisyllabic words. In addition, Maya's median baseline ORF score of 114 WRCM was significantly lower than the end-of-sixth-grade benchmark of 141 WRCM and fell in the at-risk range. According to DIBELS norms, an at-risk ORF score indicates that Maya exhibited below grade-level ORF skills and was thus in need of intensive fluency intervention.

Other Considerations

Can't do vs. won't do. Although not necessary for Maya's problem analysis prior to or during intervention implementation, there may be other factors for interventionists to consider when analyzing student data and determining how best to intervene. One consideration is whether the student is exhibiting a "can't do" or "won't do" problem (VanDerHeyden, 2014). In other words, is the student exhibiting difficulty with the reading task because they do not have the skills to complete it *or* because they do not want to do it *or*, in some cases, both? To analyze for these problems, interventionists can assess the student's skills through the process described in the problem identification phase both with and without a reinforcer. If the student is unable to increase their performance, even with a reinforcer, it is likely a "can't do" problem that requires skill building. If the student's reading performance increases with a reinforcer, "won't do" is at least a component of the problem. This does not mean the student does not also need to build skills, but reinforcers are needed to enhance performance—at least temporarily. This phenomenon can be due to various reasons; one of which may be a history of negative associations with reading tasks. It is important to keep in mind that a reinforcer must be rewarding to the student so it is best to ask the student what *they* find rewarding.

Dosage issues. When analyzing the data of a student who is not making enough progress, it is helpful to examine whether the student has received adequate intervention dosage. One question to consider is whether the student's behavior or motivation during intervention sessions interferes with their participation. Another question to consider is whether the student has been absent from intervention frequently or altogether. If the answer to either question is yes, it may not be necessary to change the intervention. Rather, modifications to the intervention may suffice, such as adding reinforcers for completing intervention activities.

Habitual use of ineffective strategies. A student may have learned ineffective approaches to unknown words that need to be **un**learned and replaced with effective decoding strategies. For example, rather than first leveraging decoding strategies, students who have been taught a three-cueing system may use semantic (meaning), syntactic (structure), or graphic (visual) cues to guess at words based on whether they make sense, sound right, or look right. Students may have also been reinforced for appealing for help from a teacher, interventionist, or a more proficient student rather than attempting to decode unknown words. Such habits may be deeply ingrained, in which case the student will need to be explicitly taught and reinforced for using their newly acquired (and more effective!) decoding strategies. Interventionists may also want to work with other educators who provide reading instruction to the student and ensure that they do not continue to be taught and reinforced for ineffective strategies.

Intervention Goals

We set several intervention goals for Maya that aligned with the intervention purpose, targets, and procedures. The goals were to (1) increase multisyllabic word reading accuracy to 100% on the CORE Phonics Survey, (2) increase ORF reading rate to 130 WRCM, and (3) increase decoding accuracy to 90% independence on a subskill mastery measure (SSMM).

Prior to intervention, Maya's multisyllabic word reading accuracy was 66.67%. Maya's ORF score was 114 WRCM compared to the sixth-grade spring benchmark score of 141 WRCM. We set the second goal to increase her ORF score to 130 WRCM by the end of the intervention period during summer school, which was six weeks. Thus, Maya's goal was ambitious at 2.67 words gained per week for six weeks. Maya's third goal was to decode with 90% accuracy because Maya demonstrated difficulties with applying decoding strategies when encountering multisyllabic words.

Measurement of Target Reading Skill, Data Collection Strategies, and Progress Monitoring

Frequent monitoring of student progress is imperative to support data-based decision-making during intervention implementation. Frequent progress monitoring should be used to determine if (1) the intervention is effective for the individual student and should be continued, (2) intervention modifications are necessary, or (3) the intervention should be discontinued because the student met their intervention goals. Intervention modifications may include changing the intervention entirely, intensifying the intervention (e.g., increasing dosage), or incorporating reinforcers.

Because multisyllabic word decoding with continuous reading targets both decoding and fluency, it is necessary to administer multiple assessments that measure both components. Thus, for Maya, we administered a curriculum-based measure-reading (CBM-R) ORF probe three times per week during baseline and then once per week during intervention. CBM-R directly measures oral reading rate and serves as a general outcome measure (i.e., broad indicator) that has been shown to predict reading comprehension skills (Shin & McMaster, 2019). Moreover, when older students participate in interventions that directly target non-fluency skills such as multisyllabic words, they can also be used to monitor student progress toward grade-level benchmarks.

In addition to monitoring Maya's progress toward her ORF goal using CBM-R as a general outcome measure, we also monitored Maya's progress using a SSMM. We developed the SSMM, which consisted of alternate forms of multisyllabic word lists containing 20 words (2-syllable, open/closed pattern) per form. The SSMMs were administered three times per week during baseline and once per week during intervention. The SSMMs provided a direct measure of Maya's progress on multisyllabic word reading accuracy directly related to the skills she was learning.

Following six weeks of intervention, we also re-administered the Multisyllabic Words section of the CORE Phonics Survey. This administration served as a post-intervention measure to monitor student responsiveness to intervention on a standardized measure of multisyllabic words. Although the CORE Phonics Survey can be administered more than once, it is not sensitive enough to be administered weekly to monitor student progress throughout the intervention. However, in non-experimental examinations of student progress, such as in typical school interventions, administering a pre-post assessment such as the CORE can provide useful information on student growth over the course of an intervention.

Other Considerations

We used commercially produced CBM-R probes to monitor Maya's fluency progress and created multisyllabic word lists as an SSMM that were similar to, but not the same as the words practiced during the intervention. However, doing so may not always be feasible within school settings due to limited resources (e.g., money, time). Teachers, interventionists, and others providing reading intervention can alternatively use intervention materials to also monitor student progress, if needed. For example, interventionists can create a word list that the student will practice during the intervention session and use the same list (arranged in a different order) as an SSMM. Thus, interventionists only need to develop one set of words that will serve as both the intervention and assessment materials rather than two sets of words (one for the intervention and one for the SSMM assessment). Interventionists can also access some commercially produced CBM materials for free such as Acadience Reading (i.e., DIBELS; Good et al., 2019) and easyCBM (Anderson et al., 2011).

Intervention Plan

The intervention was implemented three days per week over the course of six weeks while Maya was attending summer school, but continuous reading with multisyllabic word work can be implemented for longer periods of time based on student needs. A graduate student in school psychology implemented the intervention after the second author trained her in the intervention and assessment procedures. Although a graduate student implemented the intervention for the purposes of the case study illustration, the intervention procedures can easily be adapted to the classroom setting and implemented by a classroom teacher or school-based interventionist. The interventionist employed explicit instruction and followed a scripted protocol that we developed based on Hammerschmidt-Snidarich et al. (2019) and modified to include multisyllabic word work components. The intervention protocol included the steps outlined below. The detailed scripted protocol is included in the Appendix. Note that we provide examples of multisyllabic decoding strategy scripts focusing on open and closed syllables for two-syllable words, but as students progress in their decoding skills, it is appropriate to guide students in applying the strategy to words with three or more syllables. After students have mastered applying their knowledge of open and closed syllable types to decoding multisyllabic words, additional syllable types can be introduced and practiced (Archer et al., 2003; McKenna, 2008). Such intervention strategies can follow a format similar to those provided here.

1. **Gather materials**
   a. Whiteboard, marker, sticky notes, four instructional-level passages with targeted multisyllabic word types [approximately 150–200 words per passage], timer
2. **Prepare to support vocabulary development**
   a. Anticipate words the student may not know. Prepare brief, student-friendly explanations of unfamiliar words to provide when words are encountered during the multisyllabic word decoding or continuous reading components of the intervention.
3. **Multisyllabic Word Decoding**
   a. Introduce purpose of multisyllabic word decoding.
   b. Provide brief explicit instruction on syllable type (e.g., open, closed) and how to read them, using description and examples.
   c. Model syllable division to break multisyllabic words into smaller, more manageable chunks and using knowledge of the targeted syllable type(s) flexibly to read the word.

   d. Provide guided practice, coaching and prompting the student using a gradual release model; provide explicit corrective feedback as needed.
   e. Provide independent practice on additional words containing the target syllable type when the student is ready for the challenge; provide explicit corrective feedback as needed.
   f. Summarize and review the day's target syllable type. Encourage the student to independently use the strategy they practiced when they encounter unknown words during other reading activities.
4. **Continuous Reading**
   a. Describe/review purpose of continuous reading
   b. Provide explicit directions on continuous reading intervention
   c. Student completes reading #1, reading the entire passage. Interventionist starts timer when student starts reading and stops timer when student reads last word in passage.
   d. Provide corrective feedback on errors made in passage.
   e. Student completes reading #2, reading the entire passage. Interventionist starts timer when student starts reading and stops timer when student reads last word in passage.
   f. Provide corrective feedback on errors made in passage.
   g. Student completes reading #3, reading the entire passage. Interventionist starts timer when student starts reading and stops timer when student reads last word in passage.
   h. Provide corrective feedback on errors made in passage.
   i. Student completes reading #4, reading the entire passage. Interventionist starts timer when student starts reading and stops timer when student reads last word in passage.
   j. Provide corrective feedback on errors made in passage.
   k. Student graphs WRCM on first and fourth readings.

Intervention Fidelity and Interobserver Agreement Plans

Measuring implementation fidelity and interobserver agreement is imperative to ensure that intervention outcomes were measured as intended and that the data are reliable. Without such information, drawing conclusions about the effectiveness of the intervention, even for an individual student, may be challenging. Moreover, the conclusions may be inaccurate.

To ensure that the intervention was implemented with fidelity, we developed an implementation fidelity checklist composed of the steps of the intervention (see Appendix). Implementation fidelity was monitored for one intervention session per week (33% of all intervention sessions) by a second graduate student in school psychology who was trained in the intervention and assessment procedures. Implementation fidelity was computed by dividing the total number of correctly implemented steps by the total number of correctly implemented plus incorrectly implemented steps. Implementation fidelity across the intervention sessions ranged from 90.91% to 100%, with the average being 99.78% for all sessions.

Interobserver agreement (IOA) was also assessed for one intervention session per week, or 33% of all sessions. The same second graduate student who assessed implemented fidelity assessed interobserver agreement after being trained in the assessment procedures by the second author. IOA data were collected on both the CBM-R and multisyllabic word list progress monitoring data. To assess IOA, the second graduate student also used an assessment scoring sheet and scored the student's responses during administration. Following the assessment session, the graduate students compared their scoring. Agreements were words that both scorers marked as correct or incorrect, and disagreements were those that one scorer marked as correct and the other marked as incorrect. IOA was computed by dividing the total agreements by the total agreements plus disagreements. Mean IOA across the intervention sessions was 98.54% (range = 95.23–100%).

Other Considerations

To promote intervention implementation fidelity, it is also important to consider text selection. When working on reading fluency, the text should be at a level that the student can read with relative accuracy (e.g., 93%–97% accuracy; Gickling & Armstrong, 1978) to promote automaticity and reading at an adequate rate. If the passage is too difficult and the student cannot read it with accuracy, they will likely get stuck on individual words, which will hinder development of overall reading fluency. When selecting texts, interventionists should also try to select texts that are culturally relevant and match student interests. Although there are challenges with doing so given that texts and literacy instruction have typically reflected white, middle-class cultures (Ciampa & Reisboard, 2021), options are expanding, and interventionists can seek out texts that are in line with topics and subjects in which students are interested. Finally, it can be useful to use content area (e.g., science, social studies) text passages when engaging in multisyllabic word decoding with continuous reading. Students receiving intervention may have trouble accessing subject matter due to their reading difficulties. Using content area reading passages provides opportunities for students to develop their reading fluency and provides them with access to the content they are working on in class, but with interventionist support.

Intervention Outcome Data

Improvements in Multisyllabic Word Reading

As noted above, Maya's progress was monitored weekly with two measures, multisyllabic word lists, which served as an SSMM, and CBM-R ORF, which served as a general outcome measure. Maya's multisyllabic SSMM progress monitoring and CBM-R ORF data are presented in Figures 7.1 and 7.2. Maya's multisyllabic word reading improved over the course of the six-week intervention period. At week 1, she read 70% of the words on the SSMM word list correctly, and at week 6, she read 90% of the multisyllabic words correctly. Although mastery criteria and benchmarks for SSMM are not as well-defined as they are for CBM-R, 90% skill mastery has been shown to be an effective mastery level for discrete skills (Burns, 2004). Thus, we set the goal of 90% accuracy of multisyllabic word reading for Maya, and she met this goal, achieving 90% accuracy on the SSMM multisyllabic word reading list. Maya's post-intervention scores on the CORE Phonics Survey also showed improvements in multisyllabic word reading skills, increasing her score from 16/24 (66.67%) words read correctly to 21/24 (87.50%) words read correctly.

Improvements in Oral Reading Fluency

Over the course of six weeks, Maya's ORF improved from 114 WRCM during baseline and 119 WRCM during week 1 of intervention to 128

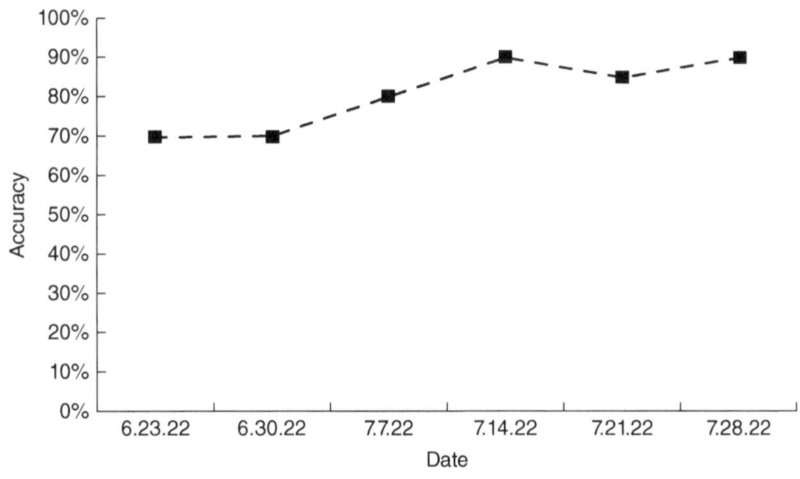

FIGURE 7.1 Maya's Progress on Multisyllabic Word Reading

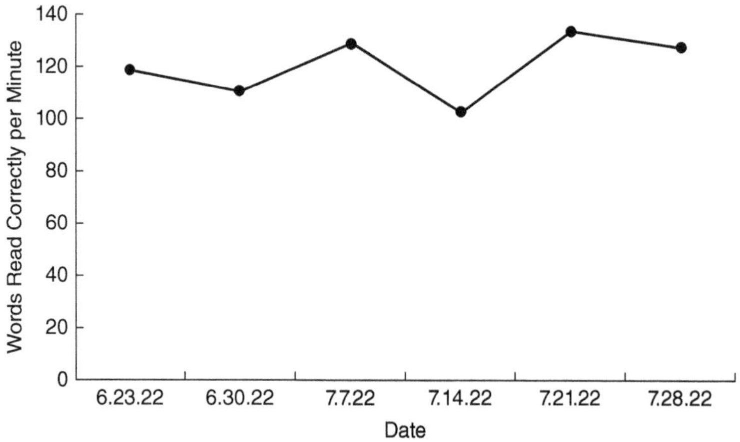

FIGURE 7.2 Maya's Progress on Oral Reading Fluency

TABLE 7.3 Maya's Pre- and Post-Intervention CORE Phonics Survey Data

	Pre-Intervention		*Post-Intervention*	
CORE Phonics Survey Section	*Score*	*Mastery Level*	*Score*	*Mastery Level*
Multisyllabic Words	16/24	Strategic	21/24	Strategic

WRCM at week 6 and 134 at post-intervention. Although there is variability in Maya's ORF data from week to week, such variability is typical given the standard error of measurement within CBM-R passages. Further, Maya's growth rate was 2.5 words gained per week, which exceeds typical growth rates for sixth- and seventh-grade students (e.g., Anderson et al., 2011; Good et al., 2019) and neared her goal of 2.67 words gained per week. Maya's reading accuracy also significantly improved during the intervention, from 90% accuracy at pre-intervention to 95% accuracy at post-intervention. This improvement in connected text reading accuracy also suggests that Maya's decoding skills improved as a result of the multisyllabic word decoding with continuous reading intervention. See Figure 7.2, and Tables 7.3 and 7.4 for intervention results.

Next Steps for Maya

Maya made considerable progress in both multisyllabic word decoding and reading fluency; however, she demonstrated some continuing reading needs after the six weeks of intervention. Maya's score on the SSMM

TABLE 7.4 Maya's Pre- and Post-Intervention CBM-R Data

	Pre-Intervention		*Post-Intervention*			
	Maya's WRCM	Maya's Accuracy (%)	Maya's WRCM	Maya's Accuracy (%)	Grade Level WRCM	Grade Level Accuracy (%)
Passage 1	118	91	121	95	141	96
Passage 2	97	88	134	95	141	96
Passage 3	114	90	139	97	141	96
Median	114	90	134	95	141	96

exceeded the 90% goal, but her score on the multisyllabic portion of the CORE assessment at post-intervention still fell into the strategic range, indicating that she should continue to receive targeted intervention in multisyllabic word reading because she had not yet mastered this skill according to the CORE diagnostic criteria. Moreover, Maya did not reach her goal of 100% accuracy on the CORE Phonics Survey at post-intervention. Maya also made notable reading fluency growth during the six weeks of intervention, but the CBM-R data suggested that the intervention should be continued because she did not meet the sixth-grade WRCM benchmark of 141 based on her progress monitoring data or post-intervention data (median WRCM = 134). Thus, Maya would likely benefit from continuing to receive the continuous reading intervention during her seventh-grade year with progress monitoring with seventh grade CBM-R ORF passages.

Other Considerations

There are also other factors educators should consider when examining student outcome data. Progress monitoring data and post-intervention measures are needed to make inferences about student responsiveness to intervention. However, educators will also want to look for skill generalization across reading passages and individual word reading. For example, if a student has demonstrated fluency with decoding multisyllabic words during intervention sessions and on progress monitoring measures, they should also begin to accurately decode these words when they encounter them reading other passages or in other classes. Additionally, if a student has met their intervention goals and therefore is no longer receiving intervention, educators will likely want to monitor student reading performance, sometimes formally with progress monitoring measures and sometimes informally through periodic observation of student reading. If the student's skills do not maintain, they may require review or booster sessions in which they practice decoding multisyllabic words and reading fluency through continuous reading.

Technology tools for progress monitoring. As we illustrated with Maya's data, examining intervention progress monitoring and outcome data can easily be implemented using technology readily accessible in a school setting. For the purposes of this illustration, we used Microsoft Excel to record Maya's data, create the graphs of Maya's progress, and to calculate her CBM-R growth rate using the "slope" function. School psychologists and other interventionists in school settings can use such programs to easily store student data and to share data with other stakeholders such as teachers and parents.

Intervention Acceptability

At the end of the intervention period, Maya completed an intervention acceptability rating scale, adapted from the Children's Intervention Rating Profile (Elliott, 1986). The intervention acceptability scale included five Likert-type items in which Maya selected the extent to which she agreed with the statement included in the item, which asked about Maya's enjoyment of the reading intervention in which she participated. The scale was from 0 to 3 and included a picture of a thumb to provide further description of 0, 1, 2, and 3 ratings, with 0 (thumbs down) representing "strongly disagree," 1 (thumb sideways to the left) representing "somewhat disagree," 2 (thumb sideways to the right) representing "somewhat agree," and 3 (thumbs up) representing "agree." After Maya completed the scale, item 2 was reverse-coded for interpretation.

Maya completed the scale with her teacher rather than with the interventionist in an effort to minimize perceived pressure to rate the intervention favorably. However, it should be noted that Maya still completed the rating scale with a teacher and knew that the interventionist would eventually see her ratings. Thus, although Maya was informed that we wanted her honest feedback and no one would be upset if she did not like the intervention, it is possible that Maya's ratings were influenced by wanting to please the adults at school. Maya rated each item on the scale a 3, indicating that she strongly agreed with the statement except for the item, "Other ways to practice reading are better than this way," which she rated a 2, and we reverse-coded as a 1. Thus, overall, Maya appeared to rate the intervention favorably.

Intervention Considerations

As students advance in grade, they are expected to generalize more advanced decoding skills in the context of reading increasingly challenging text (and doing so independently and for the purpose of learning the content). Because of this, we advise ensuring that students are able to leverage one decoding strategy with a high level of ease and accuracy (ideally, 90% or higher) before teaching them another, more advanced decoding strategy. In the case of this student, Maya, it might have been beneficial to intensify her instruction to 4–5 days per week. During a typical school year, Maya would have had many opportunities throughout the day to apply her newly developed decoding skills while the context of summer school likely afforded her fewer of those opportunities. Practitioners are encouraged to monitor both accuracy and rate of progress and use those data to determine whether an intervention should be intensified. For example, interventions may be intensified by adding more time per session, more sessions per week, or more practice opportunities within the existing intervention.

Conclusion

Multisyllabic word decoding with continuous reading is a two-part intervention appropriate to implement with students who have developed proficient early decoding skills incorporating basic letter-sound patterns (e.g., CVC, blends, digraphs, vowel teams), but are struggling to apply those skills to multisyllabic word decoding and demonstrate below-grade level oral reading fluency. Students learn basic syllable division strategies that leverage knowledge of two of the most common syllable types (open and closed) to flexibly divide and read multisyllabic words. They then apply those strategies directly during the continuous reading portion of the intervention. Previous research supports the effectiveness of both intervention components, and the positive results of our case study student, Maya, illustrate the promise of the procedure if implemented with students who have similar needs.

Appendix

Students need a variety of decoding strategies to leverage when reading unknown words. The ability to detect and divide words into syllables, combined with knowledge of syllable types and phonic patterns, can help support students in these efforts.

The example scripts below teach students to decode multisyllabic words by first identifying vowels and consonants, then dividing the word into syllables, and flexibly using knowledge of open and closed syllables to read the word. After fluency has been established in the targeted syllable type(s), additional syllable types can be taught to further expand students' strategies for multisyllabic word decoding.

Other strategies for decoding multisyllabic words may also be helpful to teach students. For example, even before providing instruction on open and closed syllable types, students typically learn the high-utility practice of dividing two syllable words with a VCCV pattern between the two middle consonants (e.g., *muffin* → muf | fin; *submit* → sub | mit), unless the two consonants are a digraph, in which case the syllable is divided after the digraph (e.g., *racket* ➔ rack | et). Students may also benefit from a variation of syllable division known as graphosyllabic training. Students are told the unknown word (e.g., *habit*), orally divide it into syllables (hab | it), and study the spoken syllable's correspondence to its written form (see Bhattacharya & Ehri, 2004).

Open and Closed Syllables Intervention Protocol - Introduction

Purpose/Rationale

Today we're going to learn about syllable types. Remember that syllables are parts of words. For instance, the word veto has two parts—two syllables. Ve-to (clap to illustrate). Each syllable has at least one vowel.

Many of the words you are reading now that you're older have more than one syllable, or word part. It's important to know how to decode those longer words so you can read any words you come across! Learning syllable types will help you to decode those longer words.

Teaching Open and Closed Syllables

Let's start with open and closed syllables. These are some of the most common syllable types you will see when you read.

An open syllable ends in one vowel. The vowel sound is long. Examples of open syllables include words like me, she, or both syllables in the word veto, ve, to.

A closed syllable ends with one or more consonants. They have a short vowel sound. Examples of closed syllables include words like hat, bun, sit… or the second syllable in robot–bot.

Let's take a closer look at how open and closed syllables work. I can take a strip of paper and fold over one end to make a door. When I open the door so the paper is flat, you can see here's an open syllable word, "we". Remember that an open syllable ends in one vowel and the vowel sound is long. Write "we" on the left hand side of a piece of paper and show the student.

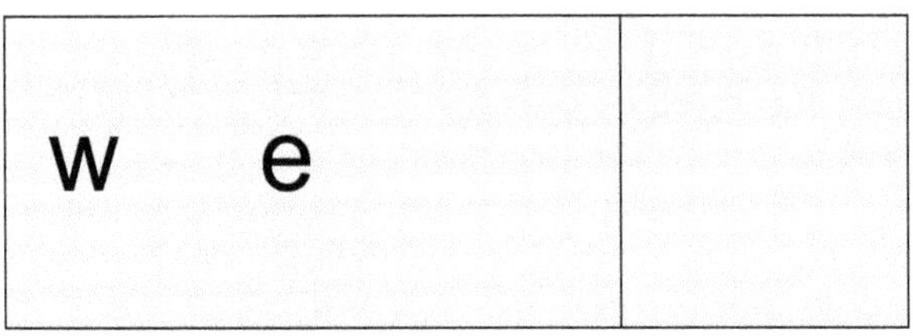

Next, I'll close the door. You can see that now there's a consonant at the end. This is a closed syllable. Remember that a closed syllable ends with one or more consonants. The vowel makes a short sound. This word is wet.

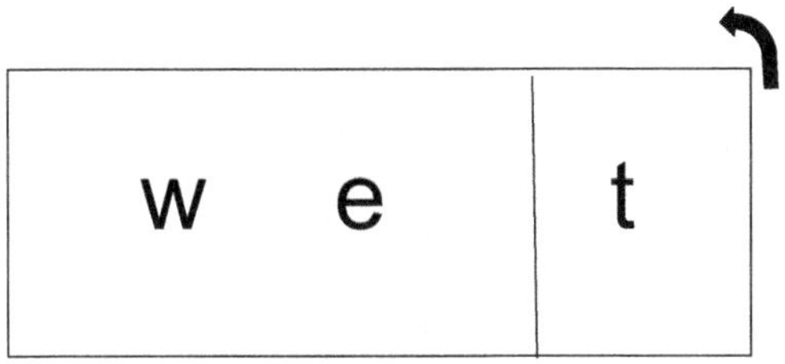

Now you try. **[Practice several words with the student - words like a-and, so-sod, me-met, me-mend, be-best]**

Open and Closed Syllables Intervention Protocol - 2-Syllable Words

This protocol provides basic instructions for teaching students to decode 2-syllable words, leveraging what they know about syllable division and open and closed syllables.

- First, the protocol provides a brief review of open and closed syllable types.
- Next, the protocol provides instructions for helping students identify the syllables in 2-syllable words and divide them into smaller, decodable chunks.
- Finally, the protocol provides instructions for helping students use what they know about open and closed syllables in a flexible way to decode and read the entire word.

Purpose/Rationale

Remember that we learned about open and closed syllables? Can you tell me what you remember about open syllables? [give time for the student to respond]

[Student should provide an answer similar to the one below; if not, read the definition.]

An open syllable ends in a vowel sound. The vowel sound is long. Examples of open syllables include words like so, be, or the first syllable in robot—ro.

Can you tell me what you remember about closed syllables? [give time for the student to respond]

[Student should provide an answer similar to the one below; if not, read the definition.]

A closed syllable ends with one or more consonants. They have a short vowel sound. Examples of closed syllables include words like dog, pin... or the second syllable in robot–bot.

Today we're going to use what we know about open and closed syllables to read words with more than one syllable. Learning to decode words with multiple syllables will help you when you're reading!

Teaching Syllable Division of Two-Syllable Words Using Knowledge of Open and Closed Syllables

I'll demonstrate with this word. [write the word *begin* on a whiteboard].

The first step is to identify the vowels. Remember that each syllable has one vowel sound. How many vowels do you see in this word? [student should answer, 2]. *Yes! Two vowels. So, how many syllables?* [student should answer, 2]. *Yes! Two vowels, two vowel sounds, two syllables.* **If student does not answer correctly, provide feedback and review from the previous lesson.**

Now, I'm going to mark each of these vowels by making them a different color. I see the vowel e and the vowel i. I'm going to make them a different color and then write a v underneath each one [write over the e and the i with a red marker; make a v underneath each vowel].

Next, I'm going to draw a bridge between the vowels. [draw a bridge between the e and i]

Then, I'm going to mark the consonant between the vowels. What is the consonant you see between the e and i? [student should say, g]. *That's right! It's a g. I'm going to write a c under the g to label it as a consonant* [write a c under the g].

As I'm looking at this word, I see a VCV pattern. Vowel, consonant, vowel. [point out to the student].

When we see this kind of pattern in a word, we will start by dividing the word after the first vowel, like this. [draw a vertical line between the e and the g]

be |gin

Now let's use what we know about open and closed syllables to decode this word. Let's start with the first syllable. I see that it ends in a vowel. What kind of syllable is that? [student should say, open]. *Yes! It's an open syllable. I know that an open syllable ends with a vowel and has a long vowel sound. Be.*

Now let's decode the second syllable, gin. I see that it ends in a consonant. What kind of syllable is that? [student should say, closed]. *Yes! It's a closed syllable. I know that a closed syllable ends with one more more consonants and it has a short vowel sound. Gin.*

Let's put the two parts together—be, gin—begin. Does that sound like a word you know? [student should say yes].

Great! Do you see how we used what we know about open and closed syllables to break apart and decode this word? Let's try another one!

Let's try another word. [write the word *closet* on a whiteboard].[2]

Start by identifying the vowels. Remember that each syllable has one vowel sound. How many vowels do you see in this word? [student should answer, 2]. *Yes! Two vowels. So, how many syllables?* [student should answer, 2]. *Yes! Two vowels, two vowel sounds, two syllables.* **If student does not answer correctly, provide feedback and review from the previous lesson.**

Now, I'm going to mark each of these vowels by making them a different color. I see the vowel o *and the vowel* e. *I'm going to make them a different color and then write a v underneath each one.* [write over the e and the i with a red marker; make a v underneath each vowel].

Next, I'm going to draw a bridge between the vowels. [draw a bridge between the o and e]

Then, I'm going to mark the consonant between the vowels. What is the consonant you see between the o *and e?* [student should say, s]. *That's right! It's an s. I'm going to write a c under the s to label it as a consonant* [write a c under the s].

I see another VCV pattern. Vowel, consonant, vowel. [point out to the student].

When we see this kind of pattern in a word, we will start by dividing the word after the first vowel, like this. [draw a vertical line between the o and the s]

clo |set

Now let's use what we know about open and closed syllables to decode this word. Let's start with the first syllable. I see that it ends in a vowel. What kind of syllable is that? [student should say, open]. *Yes! It's an open syllable. I know that an open syllable ends in a vowel and makes a long vowel sound. /c/, /l/, /o/ — clo* [say long vowel o].

Now let's decode the second syllable, set. I see that it ends in a consonant. What kind of syllable is that? [student should say, closed]. *Yes! It's a closed syllable. I know that a closed syllable ends with one more more consonants and it makes a short vowel sound. /s/, /e/, /t/–set.*

Let's put the two parts together—clo, set—closet [pronounce like cloe-set]. *Does that sound like a word you know?* [student should say no].

Okay—let's try moving the line to after the consonant. [move the vertical line after the s]

clos let

The first syllable now ends with a consonant. What type of syllable is that? [student should say, closed]. *Yes! It's a closed syllable, so the vowel sound will be short.*

/c/, /l/, /o/, /s/ — clos

/e/, /t/ — et. closet.

Continuous Reading Intervention Protocol

Materials

Student Folder(s)
4 passages
Session Timer
Markers
Stopwatch
Stickers

1. ARTICULATE OBJECTIVE
   Explain that students will read several passages. "*Today, we'll read some stories to work on increasing our fluency. Fluency is the rate, accuracy, and expression that we read—not just how fast we can read. Each time you read, you'll start with a new story. If you come to words you don't know, be sure to use your decoding strategies.*"
2. EXPLAIN GAME OR ACTIVITY
   Explain to the students that they will be reading passages together or separately. "*You will read four stories. Each time that you read, you'll try to read more quickly than the last time. I will be here to monitor the reading and help correct any mistakes.*"
3. STUDENT COLD READ (READ #1)
   "*You will read this story. I'll keep track of your time. Do your best reading. Begin.*" Start stopwatch. Stop timing at the last word read by the students.Record the amount of time the student took to complete the passage.
4. CORRECTIVE FEEDBACK
   Provide corrective feedback for any words student missed. "*This word is ___. What word is this? Yes, that word is ___. Please re-read from here*" Indicate a starting point so the student reads a short phrase that includes the word missed. Collect passage from student.
5. REPEAT STEPS 3 AND 4 FOR THE ADDITIONAL STUDENTS

6. **READINGS #2 and #3.**
   Complete reads #2 and #3. "*Now you will read two more stories. I'll keep track of your time. For this (second/third) reading, (Name of student) will read aloud, starting at the beginning of the story. Do your best reading. (pause) Begin.*" Start stopwatch. Stop timing at the last word read by the students.Record the amount of time the student took to complete the passage.
7. **CORRECTIVE FEEDBACK**
   Provide corrective feedback for any words student missed. "*This word is ___. What word is this? Yes, that word is ___.Please re-read from here*" Indicate a starting point so the student reads a short phrase that includes the word missed. Collect passage from student.
8. **REPEAT STEPS 6 AND 7 FOR THE ADDITIONAL STUDENTS**
9. **READ #4**
   Complete read #4. "*Now you will read one more story. When you are finished, you will answer some questions about the story. I'll keep track of your time. Do your best reading. Begin.*" Start stopwatch. Stop timing at the last word read by the students.Record the amount of time the student took to complete the passage.
10. **CORRECTIVE FEEDBACK**
    Provide corrective feedback for any words student missed. "*This word is ___. What word is this? Yes, that word is ___.Please re-read from here*" Indicate a starting point so the student reads a short phrase that includes the word missed. Collect passage from student.
11. **REPEAT STEPS 9 AND 10 FOR THE ADDITIONAL STUDENTS**
12. **GRAPH STUDENT PROGRESS**
    Graph students' reading time for first and last read. Show graphs to students.
13. **PROGRESS MONITOR**
    Once weekly, administer progress monitoring measures.

Continuous Reading with Multisyllabic Word Work Fidelity Checklist

Intervention Procedure	*Item Weight*
MULTISYLLABIC WORD WORK	
1. Introduced purpose	2
2. Reviewed previous day's syllable type (after the first day)	2
3. Provided explicit instruction on syllable type	3
4. Modeled how to determine syllable types within words.	3

Intervention Procedure	Item Weight
5. Provided guided practice on target syllable type.	3
6. Provided independent practice on target syllable type.	3
7. Provided summary and review of day's target syllable type.	1
CONTINUOUS READING	
8. Articulated objective	2
9. Explained game or activity	1
10. Student cold read (read #1)	3
11. Started/stopped timer at start/end of cold read	2
12. Gave specific feedback	3
13. Provided guided practice (read #2) with new passage	3
14. Started/stopped timer at start/end of read #2	2
15. Gave specific feedback	3
16. Provided practice (read #3) with new passage	3
17. Started/stopped timer at start/end of read #3	2
18. Gave specific feedback	3
19. Provided practice (read #4) with new passage	3
20. Started/stopped timer at start/end of read #4	2
21. Gave specific feedback	3
22. Student behavior did not interfere with intervention	1
/53	Total Points: 53

Notes

1 Continuous reading (sometimes referred to a wide reading [Ardoin et al., 2016]) or sustained reading (Mathes & Fuchs, 1993) is a reading-fluency practice strategy where students read multiple text passages or pages of a book a single time (Wexler et al., 2010). Repeated reading is also a reading fluency practice strategy, but the difference is that students read a single text passage or page of a book multiple times (Therrien, 2004).

Both practices have been shown to be effective for improving students' reading fluency (Hammerschmidt-Snidarich et al., 2019). However, reading researchers and practitioners have raised concerns about whether repeated reading is an authentic reflection of the way fluent readers typically read. Moreover, they have questioned whether students should be reading the same passage over and over, even for the purposes of fluency practice.

Arguments in favor of repeated reading include that repeated exposure to new words in texts can help move words and word meanings into long-term memory and thereby build students' vocabulary along with their reading fluency. In addition, there is research that suggests students might demonstrate better comprehension after reading a text multiple times (Therrien, 2004). Arguments in favor of continuous reading include that reading a broader range of unique texts exposes students to a greater number of new vocabulary words.

What do the students have to say? Some students favor repeated reading. They like to see the increase in their reading rate increase with each reading of the passage. Other students dislike having to read repeatedly, and may show resistance to the task. Many students favor continuous reading over repeated reading. Anecdotally, they have expressed that they like to keep going in the story and/or find it boring to read the same thing over and over.

The good news is that both practices are effective strategies for increasing reading fluency. Educators may choose to implement either practice with a student, depending on the context—perhaps even allowing students some autonomy to choose between the two.

2 Notice that two example words with a VCV pattern (begin, closet) are used to demonstrate how to divide a multisyllabic word, and then to apply the concept of using open and closed syllable types to arrive at the correct pronunciation of each syllable.

In this intervention, we teach students to first divide words with a VCV pattern after the vowel and try pronouncing the first syllable as an open syllable with a long vowel sound. If the word does not sound right, remind the student to be flexible and try dividing the syllable after the consonant, and try pronouncing the first syllable as a closed syllable with a short vowel sound. The selected words help students to see an example of each case: when a syllable is open and the long vowel sound is correct AND when the syllable is closed and the short vowel sound is correct.

References

Anderson, D., Alonzo, J., & Tindal, G. (2011). *easyCBM reading criterion related validity evidence: Oregon state test 2009–2010 (technical report #1103)*. Eugene, OR: Behavioral Research and Teaching.

Archer, A. L., Gleason, M. M., & Vachon, V. L. (2003). Decoding and fluency: Foundation skills for struggling older students. *Learning Disability Quarterly*, *26*, 89–101.

Ardoin, S. P., Binder, K. S., Foster, T. E., & Zawoyski, A. M. (2016). Repeated versus wide reading: A randomized control design examining the impact of fluency interventions on underlying reading behavior. *Journal of School Psychology*, *59*, 13–38.

Bhattachary, A., & Ehri, L. C. (2004). Graphosyllabic analysis helps adolescent struggling readers read and spell words. *Journal of Learning Disabilities*, *37*, 331–348.

Blevins, W. (2001). *Teaching phonics & word study in the intermediate grades: A complete sourcebook*. New York, NY: Scholastic.

Bowey, J., & Hansen, J. (1994). The development of orthographic rimes as units of word recognition. *Journal of Experimental Child Psychology*, *58*, 465–488.

Burns, M. K. (2004). Empirical analysis of drill ratio research: Refining the instructional level for drill tasks. *Remedial and Special Education*, *25*, 167–173. doi:10.1177/07419325040250030401.

Burns, M. K., Frederick, A., Helman, L., Pulles, S. M., Mccomas, J. J., & Aguilar, L. (2017). Relationship between language proficiency and growth during reading interventions. *Journal of Educational Research*, *110*(6), 581–588. doi:10.1080/00220671.2016.1158689

Chall, J. S. (1983). *Stages of reading development*. New York, NY: McGraw-Hill.

Ciampa, K., & Reisboard, D. M. (2021) Books like me: An investigation of urban elementary teachers' journey towards more culturally relevant pedagogy. *Multicultural Education Review*, *13*(2), 128–147, doi:10.1080/2005615X.2021.1919960

Collins, G., Wolter, J. A., Meaux, A. B., & Alonzo, C. N. (2020). Integrating morphological awareness in a multilinguistic structured literacy approach to improve literacy in adolescents with reading and/or language disorders. *Language, Speech, and Hearing Services in Schools*, *51*(3), 531–543.

Diliberto, J. A., Beattie, J. R., Flowers, C. P., & Algozzine, R. F. (2008). Effects of teaching syllable skills instruction on reading achievement in struggling middle school readers. *Literacy Research and Instruction*, *48*(1), 14–27.

Ehri, L. C. (1976). Word learning in beginning readers and prereaders: Effects of form class and defining contexts. *Journal of Educational Psychology*, *68*(6), 832–842. doi:10.1037/0022-0663.68. 6.832

Ehri, L. C. (2002). Reading processes, acquisition, and implications instructional. *Dyslexia and Literacy: Theory and Practice*, *1*, 167.

Ehri, L. C. (2005). Development of sight word reading: Phases and findings. In M. J. Snowling & C. Hulme (Eds.), *The science of reading: A handbook* (pp. 135–154). Blackwell Publishing. doi:10.1002/9780470757642.ch8

Ehri, L. C. (2014). Orthographic mapping in the acquisition of sight word reading, spelling memory, and vocabulary learning. *Scientific Studies of Reading*, *18*(1), 5–21. doi:10.1080/10888438.2013.819356

Ehri, L. C. (2020). The science of learning to read words: A case for systematic phonics instruction. *Reading Research Quarterly*, *55*, S45–S60.

Ehri, L. C., & Wilce, L. S. (1979a). Does word training increase or decrease interference in a Stroop task? *Journal of Experimental Child Psychology*, *27*(2), 352–364. doi:10.1016/0022-0965(79) 90055-9

Ehri, L. C., & Wilce, L.S. (1979b). The mnemonic value of orthography among beginning readers. *Journal of Educational Psychology*, *71*(1), 26–40. doi:10.1037/0022-0663.71.1.26

Ehri, L. C., & Wilce, L. S. (1983). Development of word identification speed in skilled and less skilled beginning readers. *Journal of Educational Psychology*, *75*(1), 3–18. doi:10.1037/0022- 0663.75.1.3

Elliott, S. N. (1986). Children's ratings of the acceptability of classroom interventions for misbehavior: Findings and methodological considerations. *Journal of School Psychology*, *24*(1), 23–35.

Gickling, E. E., & Armstrong, D. L. (1978). Levels of instructional difficulty as related to on-task behavior, task completion, and comprehension. *Journal of Learning Disabilities*, *11*, 559–566. doi:10.1177/002221947801100905

Good III, R. H., Kaminski, R. A., Dewey, E. N., Wallin, J., Powell-Smith, K. W., & Latimer, R. (2019). *Acadience Reading K-6 technical manual.* Retrieved from https://acadiencelearning.org/wp-content/uploads/2020/01/Acadience_Reading_K-6_Technical_Manual.pdf

Hammerschmidt-Snidarich, S. M., Maki, K. E., & Adams, S. R. (2019). Evaluating the effects of repeated reading and continuous reading using a standardized dosage of words read. *Psychology in the Schools*, *56*(5), 635–651.

Leach, J. M., Scarborough, H. S., & Rescorla, L. (2003). Late-emerging reading disabilities. *Journal of Educational Psychology*, *95*(2), 211–224.

Maki, K. E., & Hammerschmidt-Snidarich, S. (2022). Reading fluency intervention dosage: A novel meta-analysis and research synthesis. *Journal of School Psychology*, *92*, 148–165.

Mathes, P. G., & Fuchs, L. S. (1993). Peer-mediated reading instruction in special education resource rooms. *Learning Disabilities Research & Practice*, *8*(4), 223–243.

McKenna, M. (2008). Syllable types: A strategy for reading multisyllabic words. *Teaching Exceptional Children*, *40*(3), 18–24.

Moats, L. (2019, Oct. 18). *How spelling supports reading instruction. [Conference presentation] Dyslexia and literacy: Understanding Executive functions, language, and reading*. Boston, MA: Harvard Medical School.

Nagy, W., & Anderson, R. C. (1984). How many words are there in printed school English? *Reading Research Quarterly*, *19*, 304–330.

National Center for Education Statistics. (2019). *Nation's report card*. National Assessment of Educational Progress. Retrieved from https://nces.ed.gov/nationsreportcard/

National Institute of Child Health and Human Development. (2000). *Report of the National Reading Panel. Teaching children to read: An evidence-based assessment of the scientific research literature on reading and its implications for reading instruction* (NIH Publication No. 00-4769). Washington, DC: U.S. Government Printing Office.

Roembke, T. C., Hazeltine, E., Reed, D. K., & McMurray, B. (2021). Automaticity as an independent trait in predicting reading outcomes in middle-school. *Developmental Psychology*, *57*(3), 361.

Scammacca, N. K., Roberts, G., Vaughn, S., & Stuebing, K. K. (2015). A meta-analysis of interventions for struggling readers in grades 4–12: 1980–2011. *Journal of Learning Disabilities*, *48*(4), 369–390. doi:10.1177/0022219413504995

Shefelbine, J., & Calhoun, J. (1991). Variability in approaches to identifying polysyllabic words: A descriptive study of sixth graders with highly, moderately, and poorly developed syllabication strategies. In J. Zutell & S. McCormick (Eds.), *Learner factors/teacher factors: Issues in literacy research and instruction* (pp. 169–177). Chicago, IL: National Reading Conference.

Shefelbine, J., Lipscomb, L., & Hern, A. (1989). Variables associated with second, fourth, and sixth grade students' ability to identify polysyllabic words. In S. McCormick & J. Zutell (Eds.), *Cognitive and social perspectives for literacy research and instruction* (pp. 145–149). Austin, TX: National Reading Conference.

Shin, J., & McMaster, K. (2019). Relations between CBM (oral reading and maze) and reading comprehension on state achievement tests: A meta-analysis. *Journal of School Psychology*, *73*, 131–149. doi:10.1016/j. Jsp.2019.03.005

Stanback, M. L. (1992). Syllable and rime patterns for teaching reading: Analysis of a frequency-based vocabulary of 17,602 words. *Annals of Dyslexia*, *42*(1), 196–221.

Therrien, W. J. (2004). Fluency and comprehension gains as a result of repeated reading: A meta-analysis. *Remedial and Special Education*, *25*(4), 252–261.

VanDerHeyden, A. M. (2014). Best practices in can't do/won't do academic assessment. In P. Harrison & A. Thomas (Eds.), *Best practices in school psychology: Data-based and collaborative decision making* (pp. 305–316). Bethesda, MD: NASP.

Wexler, J., Vaughn, S., Roberts, G., & Denton, C. A. (2010). The efficacy of repeated reading and wide reading practice for high school students with severe reading disabilities. *Learning Disabilities Research and Practice*, *25*, 2–10. doi:10.1111/j.15405826.2009.00296.x

8

THE TAPED WORDS INTERVENTION

Christopher H. Skinner, Virginia C. Kessler, Tabitha N. Wandell and Chelsea Wilson

The University of Tennessee – Knoxville, Knoxville, TN, USA

Introduction

The taped words intervention requires students to read words from a printed list of words as a recording of the words being read is played. This low-tech intervention requires little student time, typically requiring about 3 minutes to complete. Additionally, it takes little time to train students to implement this simple procedure. Thus, once materials are developed students can apply the procedure independently. Finally, students can work on idiosyncratic lists and at their own pace. Once installed, it is relatively easy to maintain the taped words intervention across contexts (Skinner, 2013; Taylor et al., 2013).

Research on the taped words intervention suggests that it can enhance students' word reading accuracy and word list reading fluency (Bliss et al., 2006; Freeman & McLaughlin, 1984; Shapiro & McCurdy, 1989; Sterling et al., 1997). Freeman and McLaughlin (1984) evaluated the effects of a 1-minute taped words intervention on word list reading using a multiple baseline design across six high school students with a learning disability. Researchers developed a list of 80 words that were selected from the student curricula materials but were above the students' reading level. The 80 words were printed on sheets of paper in random order. To prevent students from learning words based on their order, multiple lists of the 80 words were made with words presented in a different order on each list. For each list, a tape recording was made by having someone read the list of 80 word in 1 minute. Students were then instructed to read the list of words aloud as the tape played the recordings. Results showed all students

DOI: 10.4324/9781003275749-8

increased their word list reading fluency (i.e., words read correctly per minute or WCPM) and reduced their word reading errors.

Subsequent studies found that similar taped words interventions (i.e., words read on tape at 60 to 80 words per minute) were effective for high school students with emotional-behavioral disorders (EBD) and reading skill deficits (Shapiro & McCurdy, 1989; Skinner & Shapiro, 1989). Other researchers working with elementary students with EBD found that the taped words intervention was similarly effective in increasing WCPM when words were presented every second versus every 5 seconds (Skinner et al., 1994, 1995). When working with students with intellectual disability, Sterling et al. (1997) presented the word list four different times per session. Again, results showed the intervention was similarly effective when words were presented every second versus every 5 seconds.

Causal Mechanisms

During studies which compared presentation rates, when rates of presentation were reduced to every 5 seconds, researchers noticed that students began to attempt to read the word before hearing the tape play the word (Bliss et al., 2006; Taylor et al., 2013). Thus, the students were not reading "with the tape." Rather, they had altered the taped words intervention so that it served as a series of stimulus–response–stimulus learning trials. The first stimulus was the written word, then the student had a response interval (i.e., 5 seconds) to respond before they heard the word being read correctly on the tap (second stimulus). Thus, the word being read on the tape served as feedback.

Consequently, Bliss et al. (2006) altered the taped words intervention when teaching words to an English language learning (ELL) elementary student. Rather than instructing the student to read with the tape, the student was instructed to try to read each word before hearing it on the tape (i.e., beat the tape). The word list was repeated three time per session. The first time through the list there was a 1 second response interval between words (1 second to read the word before the student heard it played). The second time through there was 3-second response interval and the final time there was no response interval; therefore, the student was often reading with the tape. This modified version of the taped words intervention caused rapid increases in word reading fluency. Researchers used similar procedures to enhance math fact fluency (McCallum et al., 2004; McCallum et al., 2006; Poncy et al., 2012; Windingstad et al., 2009).

There are several causal mechanisms that have been used to explain why the taped words intervention causes increases in word reading accuracy and fluency. One theory suggested that the intervention models for students both reading accuracy and reading speed (Freeman & McLaughlin, 1984), which explains why early taped words interventions presented words so rapidly. Another theory suggested that prompting rapid reading impressed upon the students' neurological systems a pattern of more rapid responding (Rivers, 1980; Smith, 1979). However, results from numerous studies which showed that presenting words every 5 seconds versus every 1 second failed to support these hypothetical causal mechanisms (Skinner et al., 1989, 1994; Sterling et al., 1997).

Other researchers posited that the increases in words read correctly during baseline phases suggest that the opportunities to read words (i.e., practice opportunities) embedded in the taped words intervention and subsequent assessments may have caused the improved word list reading (Greenwood et al., 1984). Two studies found clear evidence that the opportunities to read words embedded within the intervention and during assessments may account for the effectiveness of the taped words intervention (Shapiro & McCurdy, 1989; Skinner & Shapiro, 1989).

Finally, when word presentation rates were slowed and students began to attempt to read words before the tape, they were essentially applying a series of learning trials (Bliss et al., 2006). In these instances, the increase in learning may have been caused by the increase in stimulus–response–stimulus learning trials, as opposed to the increase in opportunities to respond (Belfiore et al., 1995; Ferkis et al., 1997; Taylor et al., 2013). This application which includes a response interval (e.g., 5 seconds to respond) and importantly feedback, provided by the tape, may be particularly important when students are having difficulty acquiring the ability to read novel words (Daly et al., 2015).

Learning Speed

Researchers have found no difference in increases in words read correctly per minute when words were presented by the tape every second versus every 5 seconds (Skinner et al., 1994; Sterling et al., 1997). However, these findings do not mean the two interventions were equally effective (Skinner et al., 2002). If students are behind, then the goal should be to enhance their skills as rapidly as possible (Skinner, 2008). Therefore, when interventions are equally effective, researchers should apply the intervention that takes the least student time (Cates et al., 2003; Skinner, 2010). Applying such interventions can allow students to learn more in the same amount of time and/or learn the same amount in less time (Solomon et al., 2017). As the taped words intervention with words presented every second takes much less student time than the intervention with words presented every 5 seconds, the one second intervention causes more rapid learning (Yaw et al., 2014). Consequently, these findings of similar effectiveness suggest that educators attempting to remedy deficits should select the more rapid taped words intervention (i.e., words presented every second) as it allows students to learn the same in less time (Skinner et al., 2002).

Case Study

Background Information

Since the passage of the Higher Education Opportunity Act (2008), over 300 universities have begun to offer post-secondary education programs for students with intellectual disability (Think College, 2021). In addition to specialized courses, social programs, and vocational instruction and experiences, students enrolled in these programs often take several inclusive elective courses with the general student body (Grigal et al., 2019). This case was initiated by staff and faculty at one such post-secondary education program.

Problem Identification

One of the elective inclusive courses that was popular with students was an introductory psychology course. The staff in the program noticed that while some students had receptive knowledge (i.e., they could understand the word when they heard it) and/or expressive knowledge (i.e., they could say the words) of terms used in this course, in many instances they could not read these course-specific terms. Program staff thought it would enhance the students' engagement and comfort with their inclusive courses if they could read the course-specific words that are frequently presented during lectures (e.g., PowerPoint slides) and in course materials (e.g., text).

Problem Analysis

One of the post-secondary education staff approached the professor who regularly taught introductory psychology to discuss pre-teaching content-specific words from her class. The psychology professor indicated that she enjoyed having post-secondary education program students in her class and fully supported the program. The professor also indicated that sometimes she struggled to keep some of these students engaged and attending. Finally, the professor indicated that she thought that enhancing student ability to read these content-specific words may allow them to learn more in the class and enhance their engagement and comfort in class.

The professor asked the post-secondary staff if they were planning to teach the meaning of the content-specific words as well. The program staff professional told her it was not their intent to teach meanings of the words. The professor was glad to hear that as she spent a good deal of time explaining these words and the concepts. She further indicated that she does not always define terms and concepts in the same manner as the text. Thus, she thought providing standard definitions would possibly confuse the students.

Intervention Goals

The goal of the program was to enhance the student ability to read content-specific words from an introductory psychology class, both accurately and rapidly, with little effort. The students' post-secondary education program schedules were very full of activities designed to enhance social, emotional, and independent living skills, as well as employment experience and opportunities. Consequently, staff decided that they needed a word reading intervention that was effective but required little student time.

Over the years many students enrolled in the post-secondary education program took this Introductory Psychology course. Therefore, a second goal was to prepare materials that could be used across students and semesters. A graduate student working in the program learned about the taped word intervention and presented the intervention and research supporting the intervention to a committee. After some discussion, the committee decided that they would develop, install, and evaluate the effects of the taped words intervention, focusing first on the introductory psychology course.

Measurement of Target Reading Skill, Data Collection Strategies, and Progress Monitoring

The taped words intervention was selected because it was supported by research, it is efficient, and the intervention materials could be used across students and over semesters. Additionally, the staff felt that the post-secondary student experience in their inclusive classes would be enhanced if they could read content-specific psychology words accurately and rapidly, with little effort. The first step was to collect a list of words that were included in the curriculum. Staff divided the work across four staff with each person reviewing one unit (3 chapters per unit) and a total of 4 units (12 chapters) and selecting content-specific words (i.e., words unique to psychology). During the review, team members were tasked with selecting words that were content-specific (i.e., words unique to psychology) and either important or frequently used. Some important words or terms were highlighted in chapters in various ways (e.g., included words with a definition in text, included in an appendix, glossary, or text box).

Next, each staff person developed a list of words for each unit and put them in order of appearance in the unit. In many cases, the same word was selected across chapters and units. Because words were repeated across chapters and units, the number of target words was higher for the earlier units than later units. Some of these selective words were complex multisyllabic words (e.g., self-actualize) and others were just unusual (e.g., id). After developing their list of words, the post-secondary staff approached the professor and asked if she thought being able to read this set of words would help the post-secondary program students in her class. She agreed that it would and added some additional words to the list for each unit. When these activities were complete, a list of words for each of four units was identified. The first unit contained 55 words, while the second, third, and fourth units contained 45, 40, and 35 words, respectively.

Assessment Procedures. Staff worked with four students (Jane, Sara, Jorge, and Tom) who had elected to take the introductory psychology class as one of their inclusive electives. As the program and staff wanted to encourage students to make choices for themselves, student consent or assent was obtained for all four students. When required, parental consent was also obtained. Because staff thought that they may want to share any findings with other post-secondary education programs, approval was sought and granted from the university IRB board prior to implementing any assessment and intervention procedures.

Table 8.1 provides some data on the four students. Full-scale IQ scores were in a tight range (i.e., 66–71), but reading grade-level equivalents ranged from third to seventh grade. Additionally, two of the students reported taking a high school psychology course.

The students arrived on campus for orientation, a week before school started. Prior to student arrival, staff developed 12 lists of words for each

TABLE 8.1 Participant Characteristics

Participant Characteristics

	Jane	*Sara*	*Jorge*	*Tom*
Age	21	20	21	20
Gender	Female	Female	Male	Male
Approximate Reading Level	6th grade	4th grade	7th grade	3rd grade
Full Scale IQ	71	68	69	66
High School Psychology Course	Yes	Yes	No	No

unit. In each unit, six of the lists were used for intervention and six were used for assessments designed to establish pre-intervention reading levels (e.g., baseline), to determine if the student needed an intervention, and to monitor student progress after the intervention was implemented. Each list consisted of the unit words printed in a different random order by columns.

Assessment procedures were always the same. Sitting across from a program staff person, the student was handed a list of words upside down and given the following instructions:

> On this sheet is a list of words. When I say begin, turn the page over and begin reading down the list. When you are done with one column, move on to the next column. Try your best to read each word as quickly as you can. If you do not know a word, I will instruct you to move on to the next word. Ready, begin.

The student would then turn the page over and the staff member would start a stopwatch. As the student read, the staff scored words for accuracy on a matched word list. If a student spent more than 3 seconds on a word, the staff would instruct her/him to move on to the next word. After the students completed the last word, the staff would record the time the student spent reading.

Following assessment procedures, staff would calculate the number of total words read correctly and the number of words read correctly per minute. Words read correctly per minute was calculated by multiplying the number of words read correctly by 60 seconds and dividing by the number of seconds the student spent reading the word list. Words read correctly per minute provides an indication of the students' ability to read both accurately and rapidly (Shapiro & McCurdy, 1989).

Prior to the intervention implementation (e.g., the baseline phase), word list reading assessments were conducted once per day over the last three days of orientation. During each assessment, students completed one assessment per unit. After the intervention was implemented (e.g., the intervention phase), one assessment was conducted on each day prior to implementing the intervention in the morning.

Table 8.2 provides the highest pre-treatment words correct and words correct per minute scores the four students. These data show all could read some words. Additionally, these data show that two students who had a psychology class in high school (Jane and Sara) read the most words correctly before the taped words intervention was applied. Tom, who had the lowest reading level and who had not previously taken a psychology class, had the lowest scores. Based on these scores, the post-secondary staff decided to proceed with the intervention.

TABLE 8.2 Highest Scores Across the Three Pre-Intervention Assessments

Highest Scores Across the Three Pre-Intervention Assessments								
	Unit A		*Unit B*		*Unit C*		*Unit D*	
	WC	*WC/M*	*WC*	*WC/M*	*WC*	*WC/M*	*WC*	*WC/M*
Jane	19	15.62	16	14.42	16	14.98	12	11.32
Sara	15	10.24	12	9.62	13	10.22	9	9.99
Jorge	11	9.41	10	9.61	11	10.07	9	10.45
Tom	8	5.03	6	5.97	6	6.27	4	4.97

Note: WC = Words Correct. WC/M = Words Correct per Minute.

Intervention Plan

The next step was to develop a recording of each list of words. From the available staff, the person with the clearest diction was selected to read each of the six-word lists for every unit. The staff person reviewed each list of words and then used a metronome to pace their word read at one word per second. Recordings were made on computers and stored on electronic files. It took about 1.5 trials to make a clean recording of each list. After these recordings were finished, staff had six lists of words and a recording of the words being read that matched each list.

After reviewing the students' scores and their schedules, staff decided to run the taped words intervention twice a day for five days during the first week of school: once in the morning when the students arrived and once in the afternoon before they left. Except for the first intervention session that was run on a Monday morning, immediately before each intervention, staff or mentors assessed each student's words-list reading. Thus, assessment of students' learning took place either about 7.5 hours or 16 hours after their last intervention session. This delayed assessment strategy meant that students had to maintain their enhanced word reading after the intervention was applied. These data, along with the baseline data, were plotted on time series graphs which were used to evaluate the intervention effects (e.g., monitor progress).

Each session was run by the staff member in the morning and a student mentor in the afternoon. For each session, students sat at their assigned computer and were given the list of words. Students were told that they would likely come across these words in their psychology class. Thus, they were going to use the computer to enhance their ability to read the psychology words.

Students were then told to open a file labeled unit one, session one. Students were told that when they hit start, the computer would start to play a recording of the list of words and that they were to do their best to read aloud along with the recording. After the list was completed, students were instructed to repeat the procedure two more times with the same word list presented in different order. The staff or mentors monitored the student to ensure that they had the correct list for each recording.

Students had little trouble understanding instructions and appeared to keep up with the tape. If they did fall behind, all students were able to read well enough to catch back up. The first time the tape was played students frequently read known words before the recording and often read unknown words aloud after the tape. By the third session, students were reading more words before they were presented on the tape or with the tape. During intervention sessions, staff or mentors answered questions and praised the student for working hard. At the end of 10 intervention sessions, each student's data was placed on time series graphs and decisions were made regarding each student.

Intervention Fidelity and Interobserver Agreement Plans

The staff recorded each student's assessment during baseline and intervention phases. For one baseline sessions and two intervention phase assessments another staff scored each student's words read correctly and the time required to read each list. Interscorer agreement on word read correctly was calculated on a word-by-word basis. For each word, the number of agreements was divided by the number of agreements plus disagreements and multiplied by 100. Interscorer agreement on words read correctly ranged from 86% to 100% across all assessment. Additionally, for time spent reading, the two scorers always recorded times within 2 second of each other.

The staff or mentor who applied procedures used a treatment protocol to guide their behaviors and record treatment fidelity data. Steps included: 1) handing the student the appropriate word list, 2) instructing the student to open the appropriate file on the computer, 3) monitoring the student opening the appropriate file, 4) providing instruction to the student, and 5) monitoring the student reading words along with the recording. Mentors and staff were also instructed to make a brief note of any prompts they delivered and any other observations they made.

Intervention Outcome Data

The baseline and intervention phase data for the four students in displayed in Figures 8.1–8.4. Figure 8.1 shows that Jane displayed an increase in words read correct and words correct per minute over the three baseline

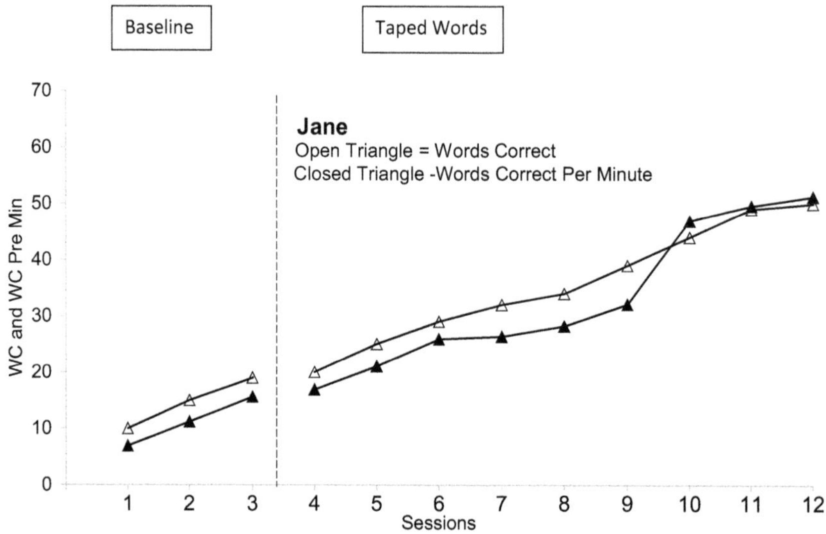

FIGURE 8.1 Jane: Words correct (WC), and words correct per minute across baseline and intervention phases.

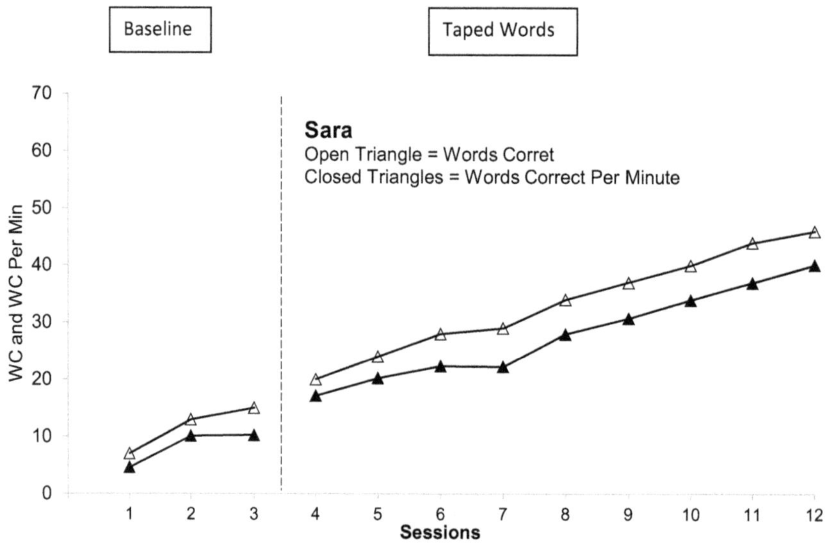

FIGURE 8.2 Sara: Words correct (WC) and words correct per minute across baseline and intervention phases.

assessments. While there were little increases following the first intervention session, Jane displayed a large increase in total words read correct and words read correct per minute following the second intervention session. After this increase, Jane showed rapid increase in both measures until the last three sessions, when Jane only had 9 words left to read accurately. On the final session, Jane read 50 of the 55 words correctly and read 51 words correct per minute.

Figure 8.2 shows that Sara's baseline data were similar to Jane's. During baseline, there was a slight increasing trend across both measures. Immediately after the intervention was applied, there was an immediate increase in total words read correctly and words read correctly per minute. This increase was steady until the final session when Sara read 46 of the 55 words correctly and read 43 words correct per minute.

Figure 8.3 shows Jorge showed less growth in words read correct or words read correctly per minute during baseline than either Jane or Sara. After the intervention was applied, Jorge showed a steady increase in words read correctly and words read correct per minute. By the final session, Jorge read 49 of the 55 words correct and 62 words correct per minute.

Figure 8.4 indicates that Tom showed little increase in words read correct or words read correctly per minute during baseline. After the intervention was applied, Tom did not begin to show clear increases in either measure until after the third treatment. From that point, Tom began to

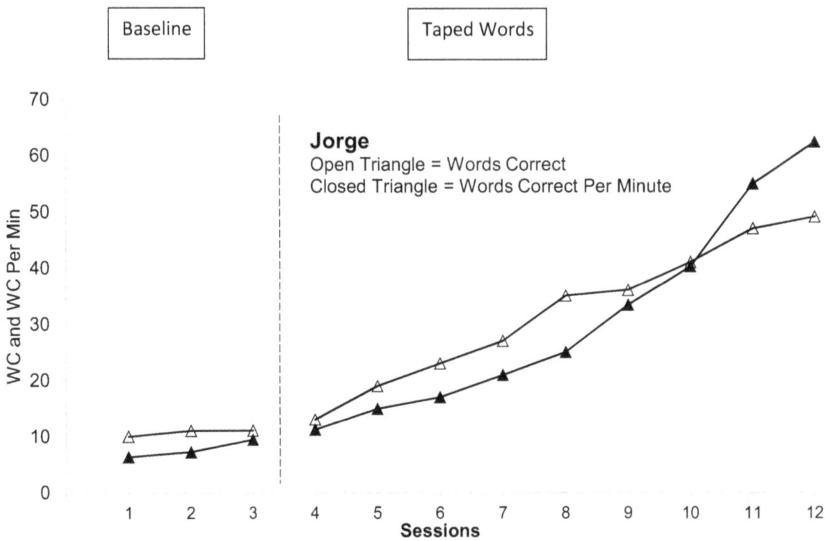

FIGURE 8.3 Jorge: Words correct (WC) and words correct per minute across baseline and intervention phases.

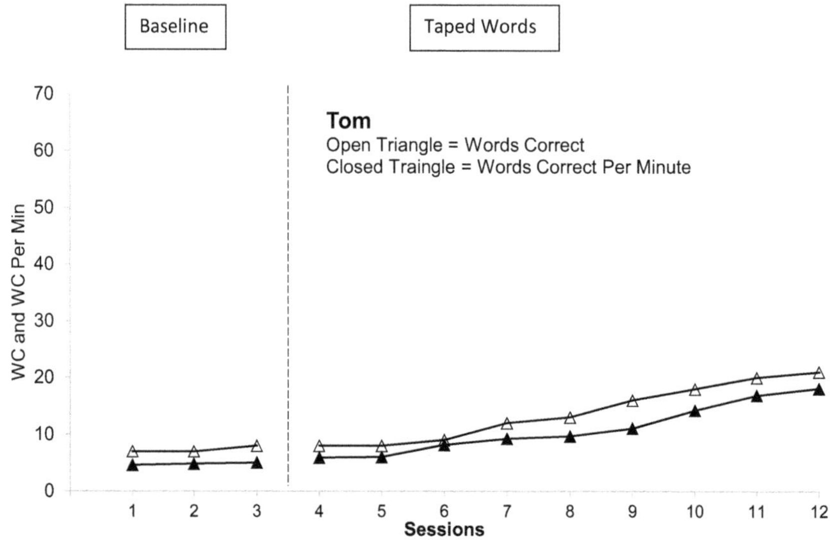

FIGURE 8.4 Tom's: Words correct (WC) and words correct per minute across baseline and intervention phases.

increase his word reading accuracy and fluency, but at a slower rate than the other students. After the final session, Tom read 21 words correct and 29 words correct per minute.

Acceptability Data

After the last day of intervention, students were asked to answer the following questions which their mentor read: 1) Did you like doing the taped words intervention? 2) Did it help you read psychology words? 3) Did it help you read the word list faster? For these questions, all students answered in the affirmative. As the first psychology unit was ending, these three questions were repeated. Additionally, the students were asked if the taped words intervention help them learn psychology and whether they would like to do the intervention with the new words for the next unit. Again, all students answered in the affirmative. However, before Tom answered these questions, he was exposed to another version of the taped words intervention.

Intervention Considerations

Jane, Sara, and Jorge all showed strong growth in total words read correctly and words read correctly per minute. Jane and Sara also showed growth across the three baseline sessions. This growth can possibly be attributed to Jane and Sara taking a psychology course during high school. Thus, they had prior exposure to these words. As both students may have been re-learning some words, an increase in reading accuracy during baseline was expected (Yaw et al., 2014). Although Jorge had not had a psychology class in high school, he did have the strongest reading scores. Additionally, the timing procedure used during the assessment seemed to cause Jorge to focus on reading fast. While all three students were very cooperative, Jorge showed the most enthusiasm for the intervention and especially for the assessments. The staff concluded that the intervention was effective for these three students and would be repeated for the next unit.

After reviewing Tom's progress, the staff met to discuss options. One suggestion was to apply a different computer-based intervention that provided stimulus–response–stimulus–response (S-R-S-R) trials one word at a time. While this intervention had been shown to be effective with post-secondary students with intellectual disability (Cazzell et al., 2016; Wright et al., 2021), staff were concerned that Tom seemed to enjoy the taped words intervention and was proud of the progress he made. Consequently, they decided that they would attempt to strengthen the intervention by decreasing the number of words taught per unit and repeating the list of words four times as opposed to three during the taped words sessions (Poncy et al., 2015; Saecker et al., 2009). After half of the unit words were taught, the other half would be targeted. The changes for Tom appeared to work and after only 4 days he read 18 of his 23 Unit 2A words correctly and then 20 of 22 Unit 2B words correctly.

Moving forward the staff also wanted to make the students more self-sufficient when running the intervention. Staff began by giving students appropriate words lists and having one staff member supervise all the students as they opened their computer files and applied each intervention more independently. All students easily learned how to apply the intervention with minimal staff prompts. Additionally, they wanted to reduce the number of assessments to once per day, in the morning before the first intervention. This time was chosen because it would require students to maintain words over 16 hours as the last intervention was held around 3:30 p.m. on the previous day.

All students seemed to take pride in telling others that they were learning psychology on the computer. Jorge continued to enjoy his assessments where he was constantly trying to read faster and faster. Thus, for the final two units an assessment feedback system was put in place and students were told their best previous words correct and words correct per minute score and encouraged them to try to beat those scores. All students reacted well when told they had beaten their best previous score for that unit. Finally, students continued to rate the intervention favorably as it was applied across the four units.

While the class was covering the fourth unit, one of the post-secondary education staff again interviewed the professor and asked about student engagement. The professor indicated that Jorge was very engaged, but both the professor and staff felt that this was a function of his personality. The professor indicated that all four students appeared to know several more words and seemed to be more engaged in the class than previous students, but she had trouble judging as the class was quite large.

Going forward, the staff decided that they would use the materials and intervention as applied for all students who had a psychology class and wanted to participate in the intervention. They also discussed the need to monitor students' progress during the first session and perhaps alter the intervention for some students when they showed little progress. Thus, they planned to have taped words interventions with all words and only half the words per unit.

Additionally, the staff discussed how motivating it was for students to beat their best score during assessment. Thus, they decided to add this component to all future interventions and considered adding a self-graphing component so students could see their progress (Poncy et al., 2006). Finally, they decided that after one more semester, if the intervention was successful, they would consider making similar interventions for other popular elective courses. One staff member suggested that future research may compare this intervention to another computer-based intervention that taught one word at a time. Another suggested determining if the intervention enhanced comprehension (Taylor et al., 2020).

References

Belfiore, P. J., Skinner, C. H., & Ferkis, M. A. (1995). Effects of response repetition in sight-word training for students with learning disabilities. *Journal of Applied Behavior Analysis*, *28*, 347–348.

Bliss, S., Skinner, C. H., & Adams, R. (2006). Enhancing sight-word reading with a time delay taped word intervention with an English language learning fifth-grade student. *School Psychology Review*, *35*, 663–670.

Cates, G. L., Skinner, C. H., Watson, T. S., Meadows, T., Weaver, A., & Jackson, B. (2003). Instructional effectiveness and instructional efficiency as considerations for data-based decision making: An evaluation of interspersing procedures. *School Psychology Review*, *32*, 601–616.

Cazzell, S. S., Browarnik, B. L., Skinner, A. L., Cihak, D. F., Skinner, C. H., & Forbes, B. (2016). Extending research on a computer-based flashcard reading intervention to post-secondary students with intellectual disabilities. *School Psychology Forum: Research in Practice*, *10*, 191–206.

Daly, E. J., Neugebauer, S., Chafouleas, S., & Skinner, C. H. (2015). *Interventions for reading problems: Designing and evaluating effective strategies* (2nd ed.). New York, NY: The Guilford Press.

Ferkis, M. A., Belfiore, P. J., & Skinner, C. H. (1997). The effects of response repetitions on sight word acquisition for students with mild disabilities. *Journal of Behavioral Education*, *7*, 307–324.

Freeman, T. J., & McLaughlin, T. F. (1984). Effects of a taped word treatment procedure on learning disabled students' sight-word reading. *Learning Disability Quarterly*, 7, 49–54.

Greenwood, C. R., Delquadri, J., & Hall, R. V. (1984). Opportunity to respond and student academic performance. In W. L. Heward, T. E. Heron, J. Trap-Porter, & D. S. Hill (Eds.), *Focus on behavior analysis in education* (pp. 58–88). Columbus, OH: Charles Merrill.

Grigal, M., Hart, D., Papay, C., Smith, F., Domin, D., & Lazo, R. (2019). Year Four Annual Report of the TPSID Model Demonstration Projects (2018–2019). *Think College Reports*. Institute for Community Inclusion.

Higher Education Opportunity Act of 2008, Pub. L. 110-315, 122 Stat. 3078, codified as amended at 20 U.S.C. § 1001.

McCallum, E., Skinner, C. H., & Hutchins, H. (2004). The taped-problems intervention: Increasing division fact fluency using a low-tech self-managed time-delay intervention. *Journal of Applied School Psychology*, *20*, 129–147.

McCallum, E., Skinner, C. H., Turner, H., & Saecker, L. (2006). The taped-problems intervention: Increasing multiplication fact fluency using a low-tech, class-wide, time-delay intervention. *School Psychology Review*, *35*, 419–434.

Poncy, B. C., Skinner, C. H., & McCallum, E. (2012). A comparison of class-wide taped problems and cover, copy, and compare for enhancing mathematic fluency. *Psychology in the Schools*. *49*(8), 744–755.

Poncy, B. C., Skinner, C. H., & O'Mara, T. (2006). Detect, practice, and repair (PPR): The effects of a class-wide intervention on elementary students' math-fact fluency. *Journal of Evidence Based Practices for Schools*, 7, 47–68.

Poncy, B. C., Solomon, G. E., Duhon, G. J., Skinner, C. H., Moore, K., & Simons, S. (2015). An analysis of learning rate and curricular scope: Caution when choosing academic interventions based on aggregated outcomes. *School Psychology Review*, *44*, 289–305.

Rivers, L. E. (1980). Use a tape recorder to teach basic skills. *The Social Studies Teacher*, *71*, 171–174.

Saecker, L., Skinner, C. H., Brown, K. S., & Roberts, A. (2009). Cover, copy, and compare to enhance number-writing accuracy: Linking responsiveness data to intervention modifications. *Journal of Evidence Based Practices in the Schools*, *10*, 171–187.

Shapiro, E. S., & McCurdy, B. L. (1989). Effects of a taped word treatment on reading proficiency. *Exceptional Children*, *55*, 121–125.

Skinner, C. H. (2008). Theoretical and applied implications of precisely measuring learning rates. *School Psychology Review*, *37*, 309–314.

Skinner, C. H. (2010). Applied comparative effectiveness researchers must measure learning rates: A commentary on efficiency articles. *Psychology in the Schools*, *47*, 166–172.
Skinner, C. H. (2013). Contextual validity: Knowing what works is necessary, but not sufficient. *The School Psychologist*, *67*(1), 14–21.
Skinner, C. H., Belfiore, P. B., & Watson, T. S. (2002). Assessing the relative effects of interventions in students with mild disabilities: Assessing instructional time. *Journal of Psychoeducational Assessment*, *20*, 345–356. Reprinted from *Assessment in Rehabilitation and Exceptionality*, *2*, 207–220, (1995).
Skinner, C. H., Johnson, C. W., Larkin, M. J., Lessley, D. J., & Glowacki, M. L. (1995). The influence of rate of presentation during taped word interventions on reading performance. *Journal of Emotional and Behavioral Disorders*, *3*, 214–223.
Skinner, C. H., & Shapiro, E. S. (1989). A comparison of a taped word and drill interventions on reading fluency in adolescents with behavior disorders. *Education and Treatment of Children*, *12*, 123–133.
Skinner, C. H., Smith, E. S., & McLean, J. E. (1994). The effects of intertrial interval duration on sight-word learning during constant time delay. *Behavioral Disorders*, *19*, 98–107.
Skinner, C. H., Williams, J. L., Morrow, J. A., Hale, A. D., Neddenriep, C., & Hawkins, R. O. (2009). The validity of a reading comprehension rate: Reading speed, comprehension, and comprehension rates. *Psychology in the Schools*, *46*, 1036–1047.
Smith, D. D. (1979). The improvement of children's oral reading through the use of teacher-modeling. *Journal of Learning Disabilities*, *12*, 172–175.
Solomon, B. G., Poncy, B. C., Caravello, D. J., & Schweiger, E. M. (2017). Examining learning rates in the evaluation of academic interventions that target reading fluency. *Psychology in the Schools*, *55*, 1–14. doi:10.1002/pits.22100
Sterling, H. E., Robinson, S. L., & Skinner, C. H. (1997). The effects of two taped word interventions on sight-word reading in students with mental retardation. *Journal of Behavior Education*, *7*, 25–32.
Taylor, E. A. P., Skinner, C. H., McCallum, E., Poncy, B. C., & Orsega, M. (2013). Enhancing basic academic skills with audio-recordings. *Educational Research Quarterly*, *27*(2), 22–60.
Taylor, K. L. H., Skinner, C. H., Ciancio, D. J., Daniels, S., Wright, S., Ryan, K., Ruddy, J., Moore, T., McCurdy, M., & Cihak, D. F. (2020). Effects of unfamiliar diverse names on elementary students' passage comprehension. *School Psychology*, *35*(3), 215–225. doi:10.1037/spq0000352
Think College. (2021). *Family resources*. Institute for Community Inclusion at the University of Massachusetts. Retrieved October 8, 2021, from https://thinkcollege.net/family-resources
Windingstad, S., Skinner, C. H., Rowland, E., Cardin, E., & Fearrington, J. (2009). Extending research on a class-wide, math fluency building intervention: Applying taped-problems in a second-grade classroom. *Journal of Applied School Psychology*, *25*, 364–381.
Wright, S., Ryan, K., Taylor, K., Turnbull, S., Skinner, C., Beeson, T., Ciancio, D., & Billington, E. (2021). Computer-based reading interventions with a

post-secondary student with intellectual disability: Self-determined and fixed response intervals. *International Journal on Social and Education Sciences (IJonSES)*, *3*(3), 394–409. doi:10.46328/ijonses.193

Yaw, J., Skinner, C. H., Maurer, K., Skinner, A. L., Cihak, D., Wilhoit, B., Delisle, J., & Booher, J. (2014). Measurement scale influences in the evaluation of sight-word reading interventions. *Journal of Applied Behavior Analysis*, *47*, 360–379.

9

CLASSWIDE PEER TUTORING

Caitlyn C. Chambers, Tai A. Collins, Alexis Blackmon, and Jordan Pollard

University of Cincinnati, Cincinnati, OH, USA

Introduction

Procedures for implementing classwide peer tutoring to improve classwide levels of reading fluency will be described. In classwide peer tutoring, students are paired and take turns assuming the roles of tutor and tutee. To target reading fluency, students take turns reading aloud and providing feedback for reading errors. The chapter will include a case scenario applying classwide peer tutoring to a self-contained class of middle-school students identified with emotional or behavioral disorders.

Emotional and Behavioral Disorders (EBDs)

Emotional and behavioral disorders (EBD) are characterized by a range of behaviors that have an adverse effect on a child's academic performance. Children with EBD often experience lower academic success, occupational, and psychosocial functioning than their peers. Children with EBD often struggle with maintaining successful social relationships. The National Mental Health and Special Education Coalition (Forness & Knitzer, 1992), which is endorsed by the National Association of School Psychologists (NASP), defines emotional and behavioral disorder (EBD) as

> a condition in which behavioral or emotional responses of an individual in school are so different from his/her generally accepted, age appropriate, ethnic, or cultural norms that they adversely affect performance in such areas as self-care, social relationships, personal adjustment, academic progress, classroom behavior, or work adjustment.

DOI: 10.4324/9781003275749-9

EBD, which can co-exist with multiple disabilities, is more than a transient, expected response to stressors in the child's or youth's environment and would persist even with individualized interventions, such as feedback to the individual, consultation with parents or families, and/or modification of the educational environment. The identification of EBD must be based on multiple sources of data about the individual's behavioral or emotional functioning. EBD must be exhibited in at least two different settings, at least one of which is school-related, and can co-exist with other disabilities.

Emotional and behavioral disorders can lead to lower academic performance, as studies on academic performance indicate that students with EBD perform 1 to 2 years below grade level (Trout et al., 2003). These academic difficulties emerge early on in school and can continue throughout most, if not all of schooling (Rosenblatt & Rosenblatt, 1999). Students with EBD often struggle with a range of reading skills, including reading fluently, understanding vocabulary, and comprehending text (Hilsmier et al., 2016; Kauffman, 2001). It is important to have early and intensive reading intervention with these students to minimize the reading gap between them and their peers and improve all areas of reading (McKenna & Bettini, 2018).

Classwide Peer Tutoring (CWPT)

Classwide peer tutoring (CWPT) is a strategy developed to help improve reading instruction and can be particularly beneficial for students with learning and/or behavioral disabilities (Maheady & Gard, 2010). CWPT is a form of peer-mediated intervention, as these interventions provide students with opportunities to lead learning and instruction with their peers (Hoff & Robinson, 2002). In CWPT, the teachers create pairs of students who alternate between being the tutor and tutee. The tutors facilitate the learning by asking questions, recording answers, and offering feedback to the tutees' responses with guidance from the teacher. When errors occur, tutors provide feedback to tutees and often provide opportunities to practice correct responding (e.g., repeat the answer in writing 3 times). CWPT has had fruitful effects on many areas of learning, including reading fluency, specifically for students with EBD (Kamps et al., 1994; Spencer et al., 2009; Sutherland & Snyder, 2007).

Despite CWPT having many positive outcomes (e.g., spelling, reading fluency, vocabulary), it is vital for schools to adapt to the increasing diversity of student populations by implementing culturally relevant practices for curriculum, instruction, assessment, and intervention. Students of color make up more than half the population in 63% of the largest school districts in the nation (Goldenberg, 2014). The growing diversity of the school-age population and the lack of diversity in the teacher population often leads to cultural mismatches that have negative implications for minoritized students. It is essential for schools to adopt culturally relevant interventions for minoritized students to maximize their engagement and decrease the likelihood of negative implications.

There are several ways this can be done, such as implementing interventions built from the ground up for specific populations (e.g., Afrocentric interventions; Aston & Graves, 2016), or adapting evidence-based interventions to be culturally relevant through procedural adaptations, content adaptations, and program delivery adaptations (Brown et al., 2018). Interventions using peer tutors could be culturally responsive when you match the race/ethnicity between the pair. Finding a peer who shares relevant identities with the target student is often more accessible than finding a teacher in schools given the large percentage of racial/ethnic mismatch of the teachers and students. According to social learning theory (Bandura, 1997), individuals learn a variety of behaviors by observing others around them. Evidence suggests that modeling is more effective when the model is similar to the observer in terms of race/ethnicity, gender, age, and ability (Bandura, 1997). Peers can implement interventions with fidelity and cultural relevance if trained appropriately, as Collins and colleagues (2021) argued for the potential cultural relevance of peer-mediated interventions through a Critical Race Theory (CRT) lens. Heidelburg et al. (2022) recently argued for schoolwide implementation of interventions through a critical viewpoint that promotes changes in policies and practices as necessary steps for minoritized students to feel psychologically and physically safe in schools. In addition, Dis/ability Critical Race Theory (DisCrit; Annamma et al., 2013) informs us that individuals experience oppression and marginalization at the intersection of their race, gender, dis/ability, and other identities, which is particularly relevant for minoritized students with EBD. As such, we present the following case study demonstrating attempts to adapt CWPT to be culturally relevant for a group of minoritized students with EBD.

Case Study

Background Information

Mrs. Sola, an African American, female, 6th grade teacher at Calliope Middle School, contacted the school psychologist for academic support. Mrs. Sola's sixth-grade, self-contained classroom included six students (Ethnicity: Black-5, Latinx-1; age range: 11–12) with varying eligibilities under IDEA with emotional/behavioral IEP goals (50% were eligible for Other

TABLE 9.1 DIBELS Oral Reading Fluency (ORF) 6th grade benchmarks

Beginning of year, month 1–3		*Middle of year, month 4–6*		*End of year, month 7–10*	
Scores	*Status*	*Scores*	*Status*	*Scores*	*Status*
ORF ≤ 98	At Risk	ORF ≤ 116	At Risk	ORF ≤ 124	At Risk
99 ≤ ORF ≤ 122	Some Risk	117 ≤ ORF ≤ 132	Some Risk	125 ≤ ORF ≤ 140	Some Risk
123 ≤ ORF ≤ 150	Minimal Risk	133 ≤ ORF ≤ 156	Minimal Risk	141 ≤ ORF ≤ 159	Minimal Risk
ORF ≥ 151	Negligible Risk	ORF ≥ 157	Negligible Risk	ORF ≥ 160	Negligible Risk

Health Impairment, specifically attention-deficit-hyperactivity disorder; 25% were eligible for Emotional Disturbance; 25% were eligible for Autism). All six students experienced reading fluency difficulties, as measured by their sixth grade Beginning of Year (BOY) Dynamic Indicators of Basic and Early Literacy Skills (DIBELS; Good & Kaminski, 2002) ORF-Words Correct benchmark data. Based on the students' reading fluency scores, five students were identified for Tier II reading intervention services. Jeremiah's benchmark scores fell within the "Minimal Risk" category, indicating the need for limited interventions. Mrs. Sola consulted with the school psychologist to explore classwide reading fluency interventions that she could implement, along with a data collection tool to easily track student progress using DIBELS benchmark goals as shown in Table 9.1.

Problem Identification and Analysis

The school psychologist conducted a review of records for Mrs. Sola's class, including a review of the students' IEP goals and their classwide oral reading fluency (ORF)-benchmark data from the beginning of the year, as measured by 6th-grade DIBELS assessment administration data (in Table 9.2). The school psychologist then observed Mrs. Sola's classroom during direct instruction when the students were engaged in reading-aloud activities (i.e., popcorn reading). The school psychologist also observed Mrs. Sola's use of positive reinforcement, physical/visual reminders of classroom expectations, and redirection strategies. The majority of the class exhibited distractibility, at least 25% of the class period observed, in the form of fidgeting, getting out of desk without permission, whispering to peers, and staring into space. One student, Joaquín, was observed with his head on his desk sleeping during the activity. With the combination of reading

TABLE 9.2 Beginning of Year (BOY) Benchmark data per student with Goals for Middle of Year (MOY)

Beginning of year, month 1–3			*Goal for Middle of Year (MOY)*
Student	*Scores*	*Status*	*Scores*
Jaisha	*103*	Some Risk (99 ≤ ORF ≤ 122)	133
Joaquín	*64*	At Risk (ORF ≤ 98)	117
Alexis	*111*	Some Risk (99 ≤ ORF ≤ 122)	133
Jeremiah	*132*	Minimal Risk (123 ≤ ORF ≤ 150)	157
Mark	*105*	Some Risk (99 ≤ ORF ≤ 122)	133
Micah	*83*	At Risk (ORF ≤ 98)	117

fluency benchmark data, direct observations of behavior, classroom expectations, and Mrs. Sola's instruction style, the school psychologist suggested CWPT. To target reading fluency, students take turns reading aloud and providing feedback for reading errors. This was proposed in lieu of Mrs. Sola's popcorn reading activity. Given the students' off-task behavior during popcorn reading, Mrs. Sola and the school psychologist hypothesized that access to appropriate peer attention and increased opportunities to respond would improve students' engagement in peer tutoring relative to popcorn reading.

Intervention Goals

Intervention goals were established for each student by considering the Middle of Year benchmarks from DIBELS. Mrs. Sola reported that she would like all six students' scores to improve such that they reflected reduced risk by one level (i.e., moving from At risk to Some Risk or Some Risk to Minimal Risk, etc). Goals are included in Table 9.2. The school psychologist and Mrs. Sola also established a decision rule that if each student was not making progress toward the goal after 2 progress monitoring assessments and/or if the students expressed negative feedback regarding the intervention during weekly feedback sessions, they would meet to discuss potential modifications to the CWPT procedures.

Measurement of Target Reading Skill, Data Collection Strategies, and Progress Monitoring

The school psychologist decided to train Mrs. Sola on how to assess student progress using 6th-grade DIBELS reading passages. Prior to intervention implementation, students were individually asked to come to Mrs.

Sola's desk during quiet independent reading periods to administer a reading passage probe using a timer and intervention data recording sheet. Throughout the case, data were collected 2–3 times per week. These baseline assessments were conducted over five sessions evenly distributed across a 2-week period and were analyzed using level, trend, and variability to determine students' current level of functioning. Students were not significantly below benchmark, so there was not a need to immediately implement intervention. Each session consisted of each student reading an unpracticed 6th-grade reading passage that Mrs. Sola chose from the DIBELS passages for one minute at her desk.

Follow-up data were collected 3 weeks after the intervention concluded. Follow-up data were collected over 3 sessions, similarly to baseline, where Mrs. Sola assessed students individually at her desk during quiet independent reading periods.

Intervention Plan

Reading passages were selected from the sixth-grade oral reading fluency DIBELS probes. Probes used in intervention were different from probes used for progress monitoring. In addition to reading passages, rewards, small sand/digital timers, student passage booklets, pencils, and recording forms were provided for each student pair.

Prior to implementation, Mrs. Sola was taught the peer-tutoring components as a tutor and tutee (with the school psychologist, switching between both roles). Training included how to operate the timer, implement peer tutoring, and collect DIBELS data with the school psychologist serving as tutee. Once Mrs. Sola was able to correctly use the timer, model the reading of passages, record WCPM and EPM data, and score the probes with accuracy, she was given the tools to train her class the next day.

To train the class on the procedures, Mrs. Sola gave the class materials, and modeled how to read the passages in their respective booklets. The students were then given roles of tutor or tutee and given instructions for each role. Mrs. Sola monitored each group to make sure students were following instructions using a fidelity checklist (Appendix A). Once the students were able to complete a session with 100% accuracy, as recorded by Mrs. Sola's fidelity checklist, the students were ready to begin the intervention. Mrs. Sola then used a fidelity checklist developed for her (Appendix B) to remind her of the steps of the intervention each day.

The intervention was conducted three times a week (Monday, Wednesday, and Friday), during instructional reading time for 6 weeks. Each pair was provided their intervention booklet with (a) fidelity checklist, (b) reading passages, (c) timers, (d) recording sheets, and (e) pencils. The students were randomly paired using popsicle sticks each week. During each session, the students were asked to read and listen to three passages. Mrs. Sola observed each group and collected fidelity checklists for each pair, noting the name of the passage.

To also decrease distractibility and improve engagement, Mrs. Sola got her class excited for the new activity by having them name the activity and come up with a list of one to five activity agreements (i.e., behavioral expectations). These agreements were displayed on a poster as a physical reminder for students. Lastly, the class average reading fluency WCPM scores were posted on the whiteboard in class after each session to physically show student progress. Mrs. Sola also asked the students to identify rewards the students could access during the intervention for following their agreements and the classroom's established PBIS goals (e.g., participating in class activities sitting in chairs appropriately, helping others).

Additionally, we included weekly check-ins with the students to get their real-time feedback about the intervention and inform changes in intervention delivery. Mrs. Sola sought students' input on the intervention during 10-minute sessions, as she asked students guiding questions (Appendix C) and made herself available for both classwide and individual feedback to inform changes in intervention.

Intervention Fidelity and Interscorer Agreement Plans

To measure implementation fidelity across phases, the school psychologist observed at least 30% of sessions in each phase, using a fidelity checklist, to measure teacher fidelity to the procedures. For most sessions, fidelity was above 80%. On occasions when it was lower, the school psychologist reviewed the intervention steps with the teacher. To measure interscorer agreement, Mrs. Sola observed at least 30% (1 out of 3 probe trials) of ORF probes given by each student, during each phase of the intervention. In addition, the school psychologist co-scored 20% of assessment sessions with Mrs. Sola (1 assessment for each phase for each student), with interscorer agreement consistently above 90%.

Modifications

Joaquín, a 12-year-old Latinx male, receiving special education services under the IDEA category of Emotional Disturbance (ED), specifically relating to his difficulty with anxiety, displayed low engagement in the previous popcorn reading activity. Joaquín's parents were fluent in both

Spanish and English and spoke both at home. Based on a review of his IEP, the school psychologist discovered that his anxiety was heightened because, although he can speak both Spanish and English fluently, he has difficulties reading in English. His mother has also reported that she sees similar difficulties at home, and is therefore reading predominantly Spanish language books to him as a child. In anticipation of peer tutoring presenting difficulties for Joaquín, the decision was made to have all of the students develop the behavioral expectations, which included working together and not judging each other. This was expected to contribute to Joaquín's engagement with the peer-tutoring intervention, as well as all of the other students.

Jeremiah, an 11-year-old Black male, told Mrs. Sola, after the training session on day two, that he thought the activity was "boring" and that everyone should be able to read at their age. Jeremiah received special education services under the IDEA category of Autism. Based on a review of his IEP, the school psychologist noted that he was medically diagnosed with high-functioning autism spectrum disorder (ASD) and excelled academically, falling within grade-level expectancy on his reading fluency benchmark tests. To help increase Jeremiah's buy-in to the activity, the school psychologist suggested that Mrs. Sola designate Jeremiah as the peer leader, helping to encourage the class to come up with a name for the activity and develop the rewards list (finalized with teacher approval), as well as being in charge of setting up the intervention each day (e.g., randomizing the pairs using popsicle sticks, handing out materials), before joining in on the intervention with his peers. By designating Jeremiah as a peer leader and engaging him in the activity, he was able to be a positive influence on the rest of his peers by encouraging his peers to participate.

Intervention Outcome Data

Baseline data indicated an Oral Reading Fluency (ORF) classwide average WCPM of 107 (range, 64–143), indicating students fell within the "require strategic and intensive support" range. With the introduction of the intervention, based on visual analysis, the classwide average of WCPM immediately increased to 132 (range: 79–170). This positive trend gradually increased throughout intervention. During the follow-up sessions, the classwide average of 142 WCPM (range, 123–175) sustained with a noted increased level and trend, indicating overall reading fluency growth classwide. Individually, each student met their goal, to reduce risk by one level, within the 6-week intervention period, as shown in Table 9.3 and Figure 9.1.

TABLE 9.3 Students' Middle of Year (MOY) scores

Beginning of Year, month 1–3			*Middle of Year, month 4–6*		
Student	*Scores*	*Status*	*Goal*	*Scores*	*Status*
Jaisha	*103*	Some Risk	133	140	Minimal Risk
Joaquín	*64*	At Risk	117	118	Some Risk
Alexis	*111*	Some Risk	133	139	Minimal Risk
Jeremiah	*132*	Minimal Risk	157	170	Negligible Risk
Mark	*105*	Some Risk	133	142	Minimal Risk
Micah	*83*	At Risk	117	121	Some Risk

Intervention Acceptability

Intervention acceptability was measured using an adapted version of the Children's Intervention Rating Profile (CIRP Witt & Elliott, 1985), a 7-point Likert scale assessing students' satisfaction with the intervention. All students completed this form before and after the intervention phase to assess pre- and post-intervention acceptability (Appendix D). Several questions were modified to assess students' acceptability of the culturally modified intervention materials. Overall, the classwide average was a 5.9, indicating that the students found the intervention acceptable.

Intervention Considerations

This case study demonstrates the application of culturally relevant considerations in the implementation of classwide peer tutoring for students with EBD. In designing this case study, we sought to highlight various decision points in the intervention implementation process and identify methods of developing context-specific and culturally valid interventions. It was particularly relevant for us to consider students' experiences at the intersection of race and ability, as we chose to focus on Black and Latinx students with EBD (Annamma et al., 2013). As such, we made a number of modifications to traditional class-wide peer tutoring to better fit the proposed context.

Each of the culturally relevant modifications were implemented to improve students' receipt and engagement with the intervention. First, we shared power with the students by encouraging them to name their groups and choose their rewards, as allowing choice can increase students' buy-in with interventions (e.g., Morgan, 2006) and it is important to allow students agency in their own educational decision-making. Additionally, we

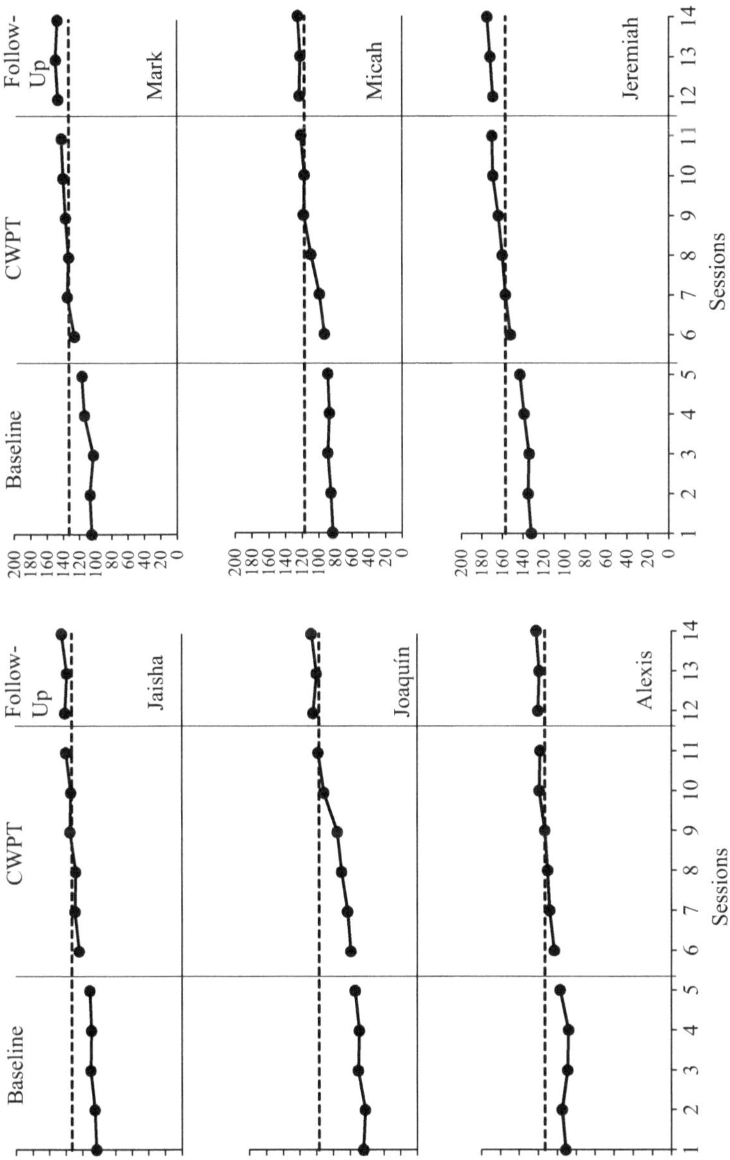

FIGURE 9.1 Individual Student Performance

included weekly check-ins with the students to get their real-time feedback about the intervention and inform changes in intervention delivery. Due to potential concerns with conflict in peer relationships for students with EBD, we chose to randomize the groups each week to keep the combinations fresh and discourage negative interactions. We also chose to include both immediate and delayed rewards for this population of students, tying the intervention into their existing PBIS system. Collins and colleagues (2021) posited that peer-mediated interventions hold promise with regard to cultural relevance due to their collectivist focus, consistent with the lived experiences and values of many minoritized communities. Our goal was to demonstrate how additional modifications can be made to an intervention to maximize its cultural and contextual relevance.

Conclusion

Students with EBD are entitled to an educational experience that allows them access to academic, social, emotional, and behavioral success. Peer-mediated interventions such as peer tutoring can encourage cooperation and support among students. As such, this case study demonstrates some of the culturally and contextually relevant modifications that can be made to interventions to best fit a population of racially and ethnically minoritized students with EBD. Although not exhaustive, the modifications that we highlighted are strong examples of ways to increase students' buy-in with academic interventions and troubleshoot potential pitfalls of interventions. Rather than implementing culture-evasive interventions, it is necessary to center the experiences, values, and preferences of the students and families we are serving. In this manner, we can encourage students to engage with the interventions and benefit most from them.

Appendix A

Procedural Integrity Checklist (Student)

Peer Tutor (Recording)		*Peer (Reading)*	
Step 1	Turn to passage your peer is going to read	Step 1	Turn to passage you are going to read
Step 2	Write down passage name on top of recording sheet	Step 2	Read passage aloud for 1 minute
Step 3	Turn timer on (digital); Flip timer over (sand) for 1 minute	Step 3	Write down your WCPM and EPM after peer provides feedback

Peer Tutor (Recording)		*Peer (Reading)*
Step 4	Mark errors (EPM) on your passage	
Step 5	Record WCPM on your sheet	
Step 6	Give feedback to peer (WCPM/EPM)	

Appendix B

Procedural Integrity Checklist (Teacher)

Step 1	Both students turn to the passage the tutee has chosen to read
Step 2	Students have written down passage name on top of both of their respective recording sheets
Step 3	Student Tutor has either turned timer on (digital) or flipped timer over (sand) for 1 minute
Step 4	Student Tutor has marked errors (EPM) on their passage
Step 5	Student Tutor has recorded WCPM on recording sheet
Step 6	Student Tutor gave feedback to tutee (WCPM/EPM)

Appendix C

Weekly Check In (Teacher)

Weekly Guiding Questions

1. What did you like about the texts you read? Did you like anything about the characters or their stories?

   ____

   ____

2. What is your favorite thing about the intervention so far? What is your least favorite?

   ____

   ____

3. What do you like about the weekly check in? Do you feel like it helps you?

   ____

   ____

4. Is this a good intervention for you? Why or why not?

   ____

   ____

Appendix D

Children's Intervention Rating Profile-Adapted (Pre-Intervention)

	I Agree 				*I Do Not Agree* 
	1	2	3	4	5
1. The program we will use sounds fair.					
2. I think this program may cause problems with my friends/ peer tutors.					
3. This program may help me.					
4. This program may help other kids too.					
5. I think I will like the program we use.					
6. I think I will like learning with my peers.					
7. I think being in this program will help me do better in school.					
8. I think this will be a good intervention for a student like me.					

Questions (Write in Answer)

1. Have you learned to read with a peer before?

 ____

 ____

2. What are you most excited about in the program? Why?

 ____

 ____

Children's Intervention Rating Profile-Adapted (Post-Intervention)

	I Agree 				*I Do Not Agree* 
	1	2	3	4	5
1. The program we used was fair.					
2. Being in this program caused problems with my friends/peer tutors.					
3. This program helped me.					

4. This program could help other kids too.
5. I liked the program we used.
6. I liked learning with my peers.
7. Being in this program helped me do better in school.
8. This intervention is a good intervention for students like me.

Questions (Write in Answer)

What was the most interesting thing you read this week? Why?

____

____

What would you change? Why?

____

____

References

Annamma, S. A., Connor, D., & Ferri, B. (2013). Dis/ability critical race studies (DisCrit): Theorizing at the intersections of race and dis/ability. *Race Ethnicity and Education*, *16*(1), 1–31. doi:10.1080/13613324.2012.730511

Aston, C., & Graves Jr, S. (2016). Challenges and barriers to implementing a school-based Afrocentric intervention in urban schools: A pilot study of the Sisters of Nia cultural program. *School Psychology Forum: Research in Practice*, *10*(2), 165–176.

Bandura, A. (1997). *Self-efficacy: The exercise of control*. New York, NY: W.H. Freeman and Company.

Brown, C., Maggin, D. M., & Buren, M. (2018). Systematic review of cultural adaptations of school-based social, emotional, and behavioral interventions for students of color. *Education and Treatment of Children*, *41*(4), 431–456. doi:10.1353/etc.2018.0024

Collins, T. A., Scott, M. N., Villarreal, J. N., & Endres, B. E. (2021). Peers as culturally relevant change agents. In T. A. Collins & R. O. Hawkins (Eds.), *Peers as change agents: A guide to implementing peer-mediated interventions in schools*. Oxford: Oxford University Press.

Forness, S. R., & Knitzer, J. (1992). A new proposed definition and terminology to replace 'serious emotional disturbance' in individuals with disabilities education act. *School Psychology Review*, *21*, 12–21.

Goldenberg, B. M. (2014). White teachers in urban classrooms: Embracing nonwhite students' cultural capital for better teaching and learning. *Urban Education*, *49*(1), 111–144. doi:10.1177/0042085912472510

Good, R.H. & Kaminski, R.A. (2002). DIBELS oral reading fluency passages for first through third grades. (Technical report no. 10). Eugene, OR: University of Oregon.

Heidelburg, K., Phelps, C., & Collins, T. A. (2022). Reconceptualizing school safety for Black students. *School Psychology International. 43*, 014303432210747.

Hilsmier, A., Wehby, J., & Falk, K. (2016) Reading fluency interventions for middle school students with academic and behavioral disabilities. *Reading Improvement, 53*(2), 53–64.

Hoff, K. E., & Robinson, S. L. (2002). Best practices in peer-mediated interventions. In A. Thomas & J. Grimes (Eds.), *Best practices in school psychology IV* (Vol. 2, pp. 1555–1567). Bethesda, MD: National Association of School Psychologists.

Kamps, D. M., Barbetta, P. M., Leonard, B. R., & Delquadri, J. (1994). Classwide peer tutoring: An integration strategy to improve reading skills and promote peer interactions among students with autism and general education peers. *Journal of Applied Behavior Analysis*, *27*(1), 49–61.

Kauffman, J. M. (2001). *Characteristics of emotional and behavioral disorders in children and youth*. (7th ed.). Hoboken, NJ: Merrill/Prentice Hall.

Maheady, L., & Gard, J. (2010). Classwide peer tutoring: Practice, theory, research, and personal narrative. *Intervention in School and Clinic*, *46*(2), 71–78. doi:10.1177/1053451210376359

McKenna, J. W., & Bettini, E. (2018). Improving reading fluency skills for secondary students with emotional and behavioral disorders. *Beyond Behavior*, *27*, 74–81.

Morgan, P. L. (2006). Increasing task engagement using preference or choice-making. *Remedial and Special Education*, *27*(3), 176–187.

Rosenblatt, J. A., & Rosenblatt, A. (1999). Youth functional status and academic achievement in collaborative mental health and education programs: Two California care systems. *Journal of Emotional and Behavioral Disorders*, 7, 21–30.

Spencer, V. G., Simpson, C. G., & Oatis, T. L. (2009). An update on the use of peer tutoring and students with emotional and behavioral disorders. *Exceptionality Education International*, *19*(1), 2–13.

Sutherland, K. S., & Snyder, A. (2007). Effects of reciprocal peer tutoring and self-graphing on reading fluency and classroom behavior of middle school students with emotional or behavioral disorders. *Journal of Emotional and Behavioral Disorders*, *15*(2), 103–118.

Trout, A. L., Nordness, P. D., Pierce, C. D., & Epstein, M. H. (2003). Research on the academic status of children with emotional and behavioral disorders: A review of the literature from 1961–2000. *Journal of Emotional and Behavioral Disorders*, *11*, 198–210.

Witt, J. C., & Elliott, S. N. (1985). Acceptability of classroom intervention strategies. In T. R. Kratochwill (Ed.), *Advances in school psychology* (Vol. 4, pp. 251–288). Hillsdale, NJ: Erlbaum.

10

REWARDS

Josalyn A. Foster, Kandace W. Mossing, Mary Stepanek and Joseph Wang

University of Cincinnati, Cincinnati, OH, USA

Introduction

According to the National Reading Panel (NRP), phonemic awareness, phonics instruction, reading fluency, vocabulary development, and reading comprehension represent the five critical pillars of effective early reading instruction for young children (NRP, 2000). Although reading fluency is a crucial fundamental reading skill, a significant number of school-aged students in the United States experience challenges with reading grade-appropriate materials fluently (NCES, 2019). Reading fluency comprises three components: rate (i.e., speed), accuracy, and prosody (i.e., expression; Hasbrouck, 2006). Students who are proficient in reading fluency place emphasis on comprehension by focusing on the connection of written ideas and prior knowledge; in contrast, readers who are less fluent dedicate their effort towards decoding words and contribute less to oral expression and comprehension (NRP, 2000). Thus, the interrelationship between word recognition and reading comprehension is established with reading fluency when students are proficient in decoding, automaticity, and precise demonstration of oral expression (i.e., dividing the text into chunks with phrases and clauses; NRP, 2000; Rasinski & Hamman, 2010).

While reading fluency is a key determinant of proficiency and comprehension, explicit instruction in fluency rarely takes place in schools in the United States (Gibson et al., 2011). Explicit instruction is an effective pedagogy in which concepts and skills are unambiguously explained and may

DOI: 10.4324/9781003275749-10

be employed when students have limited prior knowledge of a subject and/or are having difficulty acquiring important skills and strategies (Archer & Hughes, 2010; Carnine, 2006). Specifically, explicit instruction includes an introduction to a novel topic followed by a demonstration or modeling from an instructor, guided practice where the instructor scaffolds learning with a high level of support, and feedback before students work independently without instructor support. When explicit instruction is employed, the instructor (i.e., teacher or paraprofessional) must deliver the lesson in an engaging manner that includes the following facets: (a) recurrently solicits student responses, (b) observes student responses and revises the lesson, if needed, (c) provides immediate feedback (i.e., praise, motivation, corrections), (d) maintains a steady, brisk pace to promote both attention and engagement (Voyager Sopris Learning, 2022). Explicit instruction is an active and introspective process in which the instructor acknowledges that learning is collaborative and that students may be taught to master skills, including reading fluency. Consequently, explicit instruction is a critical component in assisting students who struggle with reading.

Students with reading difficulties can improve their fluency with explicit instruction and several opportunities to read written text at the appropriate instructional level (Kuhn et al., 2006). This may be accomplished using *Reading Excellence: Word Attack and Rate Development Strategies (REWARDS) Intermediate*, a reading program taught by instructors (e.g., teachers, paraprofessionals) to students in Grades 4 to 6. It offers 25 50-minute lessons that may be used as part of individual, small-, or whole-group instruction in many settings, including remedial reading classes, summer school, and after school programs (Archer et al., 2003).

The *REWARDS Intermediate* (Voyager Sopris Learning, 2022) reading program utilizes explicit instruction to achieve its two primary aims: (1) decode words with between two and eight parts and (2) increase oral and silent reading fluency (Archer et al., 2003). In lessons 1–15, students are taught a range of pre-skills, which include the understanding that each part of a word contains a vowel sound and how each vowel is pronounced; whereas lessons 16–25 primarily focus on utilizing flexible decoding strategies (Archer et al., 2003). *REWARDS Intermediate* includes a variety of techniques for accelerating reading performance. Specifically, students are first instructed to decode unfamiliar words and then asked to read a list of successfully decoded words to receive practice with building reading fluency (i.e., speed and accuracy). Finally, students perform repeated reading exercises in which they read a portion of a previously read passage for one minute and identify the number of words read (Archer et al., 2003). The students repeat this practice routine once or twice to increase reading rates

(Archer et al., 2003). Taken together, these strategies are useful at enhancing reading abilities for students across various settings. Research findings indicate that *REWARDS Intermediate* can be implemented as a Tier 1 intervention to benefit students at all reading levels (i.e., intensive, strategic, and benchmark; e.g., Shippen et al., 2005; Zurybida, 2007) and is an effective component of a Tier 2 or Tier 3 RTI (i.e., Response to Intervention) initiative (e.g., Graves et al., 2011). Thus, *REWARDS Intermediate* may be an effective program recognized for enhancing reading fluency through explicit instruction that targets improving students' reading accuracy and speed. The following case study describes the implementation of *REWARDS Intermediate* at the Tier 2 level with four students identified as being below grade level in reading fluency.

Case Study

Background Information and Problem Identification

Ms. Bell, a fifth-grade teacher at Maple Heights Elementary School, sought the assistance of Ms. Wright, the school psychologist, and Mr. Riley, the reading specialist, to provide reading support for four fifth-grade students in her class (Ethnicity: Black—2, Asian—1, White—1; age range 10–11). According to Beginning of Year school-wide benchmarking data, using *Acadience* (Good & Kaminski, 2011), all four students experienced challenges with reading fluency. The benchmarking data revealed that the students demonstrated proficiency in Phoneme Segmentation Fluency (PSF), Nonsense Word Fluency (NWF), and Letter Naming Fluency (LNF); however, results from the Oral Reading Fluency (ORF) subtest indicated that these students were performing at a fourth-grade level. Based on these results, Ms. Bell identified the four students as needing additional Tier 2 reading support targeting reading fluency to meet Grade 5's ORF benchmark.

According to the benchmarks for *Acadience*, students in Grade 5 meeting the benchmark by correctly identifying a minimum of 111 words per minute in the ORF subtest are approximately 80 to 90% more likely to achieve important reading outcomes (Good & Kaminski, 2011). Each of the four target students were identified as "Below Benchmark" and "Likely to Need Strategic Support" when assessed with *Acadience*'s ORF subtest. Liz and Yaya successfully identified 95 words and Leann and Shawn correctly identified 97 and 96 words, respectively (see Table 10.1). Taken together, all four students were identified as meeting *Acadience*'s ORF Beginning of Year benchmark for Grade 4 but not the Beginning of Year Grade 5 ORF benchmark.

TABLE 10.1 Fourth-Grade Fall Benchmarking Probes

	ORF 1 (WC/R)	*ORF 2 (WC/R)*	*ORF 3 (WC/R)*	*PSF (CLS)*	*NWF (CLS/ WWR)*
Liz	90/27	91/28	95/27	60	86/30
Leann	93/27	95/27	100/28	65	74/26
Shawn	103/29	103/30	99/29	66	84/29
Yaya	100/28	94/29	96/27	70	85/29

Note: WC = words correct; R = retell; CLS = correct letter sounds; WWR = whole words read; PSF = phoneme segmentation fluency; NWF = nonsense word fluency; ORF Fourth Grade Beginning of Year benchmark = 90 WC.

TABLE 10.2 Fifth-Grade Fall Benchmarking Probes

	ORF 1 (WC/R)
Liz	95/25
Leann	97/24
Shawn	96/ 23
Yaya	95/22

Note: WC = words correct; R = retell; CLS = correct letter sounds; ORF Fifth Grade Beginning of Year benchmark = 111 WC.

Problem Analysis

The school psychologist, reading specialist, and administrators worked collaboratively to complete beginning of the year benchmarking for all students using *Acadience Learning* CBM probes. After completing benchmarking, the team found that Ms. Bell's 5th-grade classroom had the most student who were not at grade level for ORF given her classroom size (see Tables 10.1 and 10.2). The school psychologist and reading specialist scheduled a meeting with Ms. Bell, who stated that she was experiencing some difficulties with supporting the reading skills of her students after teaching remotely in the previous school year. The school psychologist later observed the classroom during reading instruction, specifically when students were engaged in activities that required them to read aloud. In addition to observing students' skills, she also took direct observation data of academic engagement for the four students identified during benchmarking (i.e., Leann, Yaya, Shawn, and Liz). The school psychologist used momentary time sampling with 15-second intervals over the course of 20 minutes to observe the students across three different days. When observing students reading aloud, she found that the four target students struggled reading aloud more than the other students in the classroom. Additionally, the direct observations showed that these students demonstrated high academic engagement, ranging from 75–90% of intervals. Therefore, the team ruled out academic engagement issues. Based on the benchmarking data and student observations, the team determined that the four target students were not at grade level for ORF because of an instructional mismatch. This means, the instruction they were receiving in the classroom did not appear to align with their skill levels and needs as learners. The team formulated a Tier 2 reading intervention plan to increase reading fluency.

Intervention Goals

The team decided to implement *REWARDS*, a systematic, short-term reading intervention targeting decoding to increase reading fluency. *REWARDS* supports students in the following areas: 1) decoding long, multisyllabic words, 2) identifying prefixes and suffixes, 3) increasing word and passage reading fluency, 4) building academic vocabulary, and 5) building comprehension skills (Voyager Sopris Learning, 2022). The intervention is appropriate for students who have fallen behind but are scoring at least at a 3rd-grade level for reading fluency. Given the teacher consultation, benchmarking data, and observation data, the team hypothesized that supplemental reading instruction would improve reading fluency for the four students. Intervention goals were determined based on students' current performance and the grade-level criterion for 4th grade, end of the year performance on *Acadience* measures. Although an ambitious goal, the team aimed to have all four students approaching grade level for ORF by the end of the 9-week intervention period. The 5th-grade rate of improvement between each ORF benchmark is .63 words correct per minute. Therefore, the team decided to multiply this ROI by three, with a goal for each student to gain two words correct per minute each week.

Measurement of Target Reading Skill, Data Collection Strategies, and Progress Monitoring

Based on the referral and benchmarking scores, reading fluency was identified as the target reading skill to evaluate students' progress over time. The intervention team determined that *Acadience* ORF was an appropriate measure for assessing reading fluency and progress in the intervention. The school psychologist was the primary data collector, as she was not directly providing the intervention to the reading group. The school psychologist administered the ORF probes weekly to collect data on reading fluency data during the baseline and intervention phases for each student in the reading group.

The school psychologist proposed to establish decision rules for modifying the intervention, prior to collecting baseline data. Establishing decision rules allowed the intervention team to make data-based decisions about the intervention's effectiveness while the intervention was occurring. The intervention team determined that the intervention would be modified (i.e., adding or fading intervention components) after 5 consecutive data points above or below a student's goal line. As discussed, the aim line was determined by drawing a trendline connecting each student's average baseline data and their goal. If a decision rule was met, the intervention team agreed to meet and determine an appropriate modification of the intervention to meet the student's need.

Prior to beginning the *REWARDS* intervention, the school psychologist obtained three baseline data points for each student in the reading group. For three consecutive weeks, the school psychologist administered a 1-minute ORF probe to each student during their intervention time. Results from baseline data indicated that Liz, Leann, and Yaya were reading less than 100 words correctly per minute (see Figures 10.1, 10.2, and 10.4). Shawn's baseline data indicated that he was reading slightly above 100 words correctly per minute (see Figure 10.3). Liz and Leann's baseline data showed an increasing trend, while Yaya and Shawn's baseline data showed a decreasing trend.

After starting the *REWARDS* intervention, the school psychologist continued to administer the ORF probes once per week during the classroom's intervention time. The school psychologist pulled out each student individually and administered a 1-minute ORF probe while the reading

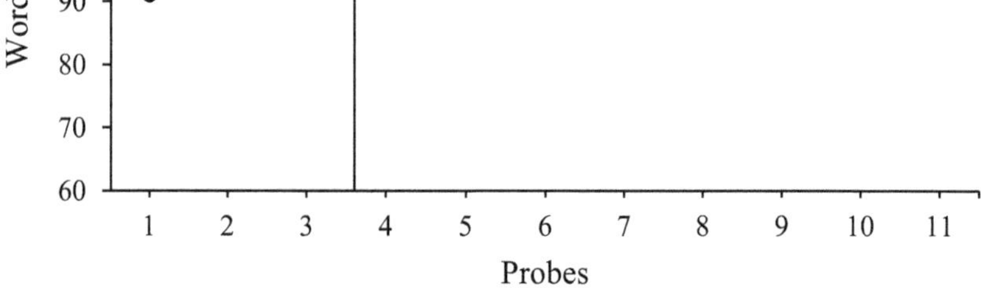

FIGURE 10.1 Liz ORF Words Correct

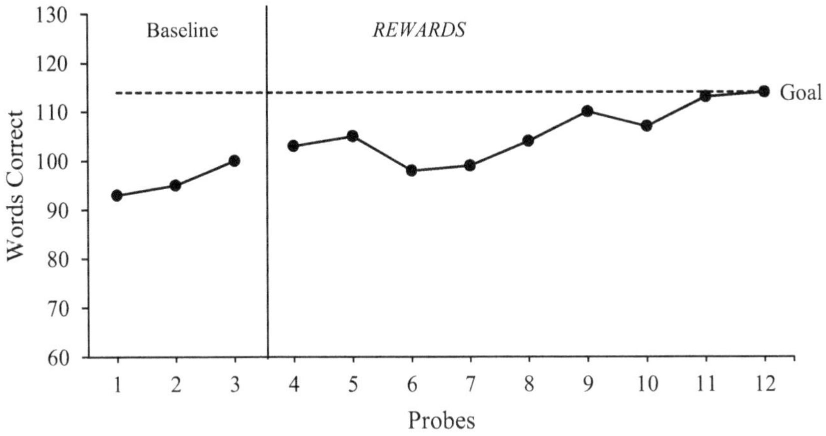

FIGURE 10.2 Leann ORF Words Correct

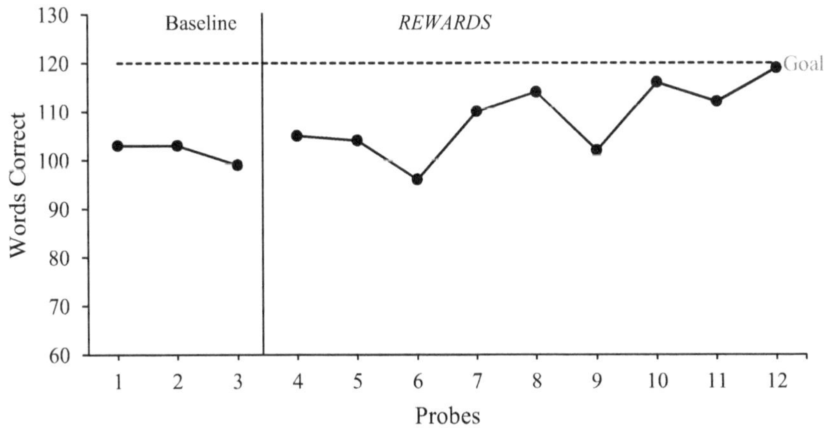

FIGURE 10.3 Shawn ORF Words Correct

specialist worked with the reading group. The intervention team determined that a predictable, consistent schedule for progress monitoring outweighed the brief interruption that was caused during the intervention time. The school psychologist obtained 8–9 intervention data points for each student in the reading group. One student did not have their 9th data point due to an absence. In addition to administering ORF probes, the school psychologist collected data on intervention integrity and social validity. The school psychologist conducted an intervention integrity check each week on a random weekday. The school psychologist collected social validity data at the conclusion of the intervention.

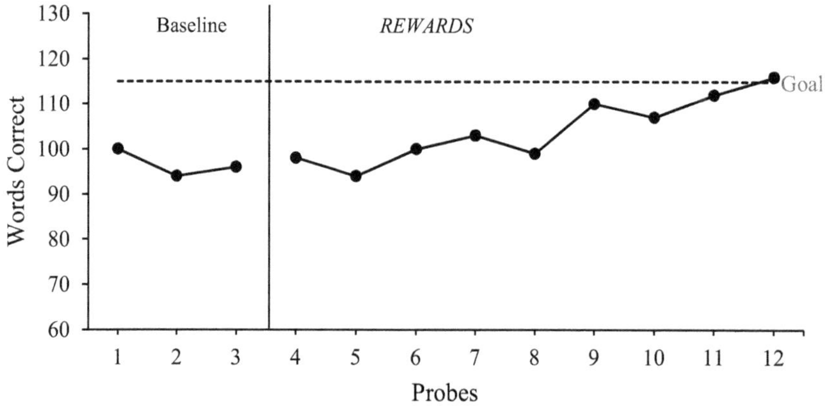

FIGURE 10.4 Yaya ORF Words Correct

REWARDS Overt Decoding Strategy	**REWARDS Covert Decoding Strategy**
1. Circle the prefixes 2. Circle the suffixes 3. Underline the vowels 4. Say the parts of the word 5. Say the whole word 6. Make it a real word	1. Look for prefixes, suffixes, and vowels 2. Say the parts of the word 3. Say the whole word 4. Make it a real word

FIGURE 10.5 REWARDS Overt and Covert Decoding Strategy

Intervention Plan

REWARDS is best suited for students who need to improve their reading fluency but have mastered basic reading skills (Archer et al., 2000). The intervention team determined that *REWARDS* was a good fit for the students who had demonstrated pre-requisite fluency skills but needed increased practice. *REWARDS* teaches students to use an overt and covert strategy to read multisyllabic words (see Figure 10.5). The reading specialist was primarily responsible for delivering the *REWARDS* intervention during the teacher's intervention time. Because the students had demonstrated some multisyllabic word reading skills (e.g., separating multisyllabic words into chunks), the intervention team determined that the reading group would begin with Lesson 16. According to the *REWARDS* manual, advanced students in the program are recommended to receive Lessons 16–25 (see Archer et al., 2000). Each lesson lasted for approximately one hour. The reading specialist delivered *REWARDS Intermediate* two or three times per week, depending on how quickly the students progressed through the lessons. A total of 9 weeks of intervention were planned.

REWARDS Intermediate provided clear intervention steps to implement the reading intervention with integrity. The intervention team delivered *REWARDS* as instructed in the manual. Each lesson was comprised of 9 to 10 activities (i.e., Activity A—I). The first set of activities had the teacher review learned concepts with the students. The second set of activities asked students to practice the skills they learned for decoding multisyllabic words. The third set of activities required students to independently apply their knowledge of strategies to various tasks. Although the content of the activities differs, the activities generally followed a "I do, we do, you do" structure to teach and promote the use of the *REWARDS* strategies (see Archer et al., 2000). The duration of each *REWARDS* session was between 50 and 60 minutes. If a lesson was not completed in a single session, it was reviewed and completed at the start of the next session.

The following describes how the reading specialist delivered Lesson 16 in *REWARDS*:

1. The reading specialist reviewed the previously learned vowel combinations with the students (Activity A).
2. The reading specialist reviewed short and long vowel sounds with the students (Activity B).
3. The students reviewed pronouncing the prefixes and suffixes from Lessons 1–15 (Activity C).
4. The reading specialist guided the students in applying the *REWARDS* decoding strategy to read a list of words (Activity D).
5. The reading specialist asked students to independently apply the strategy to new words (Activity E).
6. The reading specialist introduced students to word families to help students identify the unfamiliar with the familiar (Activity F).
7. The students practiced spelling some of the multisyllabic words they just learned (Activity G).
8. The students applied their knowledge of prefixes and suffixes in new vocabulary (Activity H).
9. The students applied their knowledge of the *REWARDS* strategy to read multisyllabic words in the context of sentences (Activity I).

Intervention Fidelity and Interobserver Agreement Plans

The *REWARDS* intervention was assessed for intervention fidelity using a checklist developed by the intervention team (see Appendix A). The school psychologist collected intervention fidelity data once per week during the baseline and intervention phases. Intervention fidelity was calculated by dividing the actual number of steps completed by the total number of steps on the intervention checklist and multiplying the fraction by 100. During the baseline phase, the REWARDS intervention was not in place, and Ms. Bell provided no additional reading support during her intervention time. During the intervention phase, intervention fidelity was measured at 90% for the 12 sessions that were observed.

Interobserver Agreement (IOA) was collected for 20% of the data collection periods as recommended in the literature (see Cooper et al., 2020). The school psychologist gathered permission from the parent to audio-record each student's oral reading during the ORF probes. IOA was obtained by having a second scorer listen to and score the student's oral reading. The classroom teacher served as the second scorer. The total IOA was calculated by dividing the number of agreements by the total number of agreements and disagreements and multiplying by 100. The total IOA gathered across all students was 85%.

Intervention Outcome Data

Student goals were determined based on the 5th-grade ROI in ORF. This ROI was multiplied by three, indicating that WCPM would increase by 2 words every week of intervention. Although this was a lofty goal, the team believed it was necessary given students' baseline scores and achievable provided the intensity of the intervention. During baseline, Liz read an average of 92 WCPM on ORF (range from 90–95). Figure 10.1 displays an increasing trend with little variability. This positive trend continued throughout the intervention with slightly more variability. Liz's goal was to read 110 WCPM by the end of the intervention. She read 106 WCPM on her last progress monitoring probe, indicating that she did not meet her goal.

During baseline, Leann read an average of 96 WCPM (ranging from 93–100), and her end goal was to read 114 WCPM. Figure 10.2 displays an increasing trend with little variability during baseline. Following the implementation of *REWARDS*, Leann's scores continued to increase steadily, with her final score indicating 114 WCPM; therefore, she did meet her goal.

Shawn's baseline scores ranged from 99 to 103 WCPM, with an average of 102. Using the ROI of 2 words per week, his goal was set at 120 WCPM. Figure 10.3 displays a slightly decreasing trend during baseline. Following the implementation of *REWARDS*, Shawn's data indicates an increasing trend with moderate variability. He read 119 WCPM on his final probe, almost reaching his goal of 120 WCPM.

Finally, Yaya read an average of 97 WCPM during baseline (ranging from 94–100 WCPM), and her goal was set at 115 WCPM using an ROI of 2 words per week. Figure 10.4 displays a slightly variable trend during baseline; however, following the implementation of *REWARDS*, Yaya's data shows a steady increasing trend. Her goal was set at 115 WCPM, and during her final probe, she read 116 WCPM, exceeding her goal.

Intervention Acceptability

Student intervention acceptability was recorded using an adapted social validity survey from Shippen et al. 2005 (See Appendix B). The responses to the survey were delineated on a 5-point Likert-type scale with response choices of strongly agree, agree, neutral, disagree, and strongly disagree for each item. The survey included statements pertaining to the procedures, outcomes, and acceptability of the intervention (Kennedy, 2005). All students in the intervention group completed this form at the conclusion of the intervention to assess intervention acceptability. The classwide average was 4.2, indicating that the students found the intervention acceptable.

Additionally, an adapted version of the Intervention Rating Profile-15 (Witt & Elliot, 1985) was used to determine intervention acceptability for Mr. Riley, the implementer, and Ms. Bell, the students' general education teacher (see Appendix C). Responses to the survey were also delineated on a 5-point Likert-type scale with response choices of strongly agree, agree, neutral, disagree, and strongly disagree for each item. The survey included statements pertaining to the procedures, outcomes, and acceptability of the intervention (Kennedy, 2005), and was completed at the conclusion of the intervention. Mr. Riley scored an average of 4.7, indicating high acceptability, and Ms. Bell scored an average of 3.9 indicating moderate acceptability.

Intervention Considerations

This case study summarizes how the *REWARDS* reading curriculum could be used to increase multisyllabic word reading fluency for 5th-grade students in a public elementary school. Ten *REWARDS* lessons were implemented twice a week for 50–60 minutes a session, and the entire process lasted only 9 weeks. Research recommends that Tier 2 reading interventions be implemented between 3 and 5 times a week for 20–40 minutes (see What Works Clearinghouse, 2009). Considering limited school resources and student and staff absences, this may not always be feasible. It may take multiple days or weeks to complete one *REWARDS* lesson, significantly increasing the overall duration of the intervention. Therefore, the 25 lessons in the *REWARDS* intermediate curriculum could take a significant amount of the school year and may not prove to be a short-term intervention as indicated by the curriculum. Although the timing of the intervention may be disrupted in a school setting, *REWARDS* can easily be implemented by many professionals. Because *REWARDS* is a scripted intervention, teachers, paraprofessionals, and intervention specialists with limited experience in reading instruction can successfully implement the intervention (Voyager Sopris Learning, 2018b).

The students in this case study took part in a Tier 2 reading intervention group; however, *REWARDS* can also be used as part of classwide instruction or individualized instruction (i.e., Tier 3), making it an accessible component of Response to Intervention initiatives. Additionally, *REWARDS* has proven to be an effective intervention for English Learners (EL) and students with learning disabilities (Voyager Sopris Learning, 2018a). *REWARDS*'s focus on teaching language structures, including prefixes, suffixes, and root words, may be beneficial for EL students who are unfamiliar with English language structure, and *REWARDS* includes many elements of explicit instruction (e.g., frequent opportunities to respond, immediate corrective feedback), making the intervention beneficial for all learners, especially students with learning disabilities (Hughes et al., 2017).

The *REWARDS* curriculum includes many components of evidence-based instruction and intervention for decoding and multisyllabic word reading fluency. What Works Clearinghouse's (WWC) first recommends building students' decoding skills so they can accurately and fluently read complex multisyllabic words. WWC provides four steps to carry out this recommendation. First, teach vowel and consonant letter-sounds and combinations as necessary based on students' word-reading skills. *REWARDS* provides this in lessons 1–15, which teach prerequisites to decoding, including pronunciation of vowel sounds, prefixes, and suffixes. Second, WWC recommends teaching students a routine that can be used when decoding multisyllabic words. *REWARDS* uses explicit instruction to teach the following decoding strategies: identify prefixes and suffixes, say vowel sounds, read the word part by part, then read the whole word. Third, WWC recommends concurrently teaching spelling and reading. Each *REWARDS* lesson has students practice saying the word parts as they spell the word, compare their spelling to the correct spelling, and then rewrite the word correctly. The final WWC recommendation involves engaging students in a variety of activities to allow practice in reading multisyllabic words accurately (Vaughn et al., 2022). *REWARDS* lessons include multiple opportunities for practice including guided reading, vocabulary, and sentence reading. In summary, the *REWARDS* curriculum is composed of multiple strategies included in WWC's recommendations for interventions focusing on decoding skills and multisyllabic word reading fluency.

Although *REWARDS* offers a package of evidence-based instructional strategies for developing skills in decoding and multisyllabic reading fluency, individual evidence-based strategies can also be used including affix teaching, peel off reading, and timed reading (Toste et al., 2017). Direct instruction in affixes supports fluency when reading multisyllabic words. This involves teaching high-frequency prefixes and suffixes as well as their multiple corresponding sounds. For example, the suffix -ed makes the sound /ed/ as in planted, the sound /t/ as in brushes, or /d/ as in hugged. Peel off reading focuses on accurate and fluent word reading, not word meaning, by segmenting words into their parts. This involves students reading smaller words or word parts that they already know and then adding the rest. For example, students may cover the affix, read the base word, and then add the affix to the known base word. Finally, the amount of time that students spend reading is a predictor of reading fluency. Therefore, another strategy that supports multisyllabic fluency is repeated practice with corrective feedback targeting multisyllabic words. This can include timed reading of targeted word lists to support reading accuracy and rate (Toste et al., 2017). These strategies, in isolation, are effective in increasing multisyllabic word reading fluency; however, the *REWARDS* curriculum combines multiple evidence-based explicit teaching strategies in reading. In summary, *REWARDS* Intermediate may be a useful choice of reading intervention for students in grade 4–6 who struggle with reading long, multisyllabic words.

Conclusion

REWARDS is an evidence-based intervention for decoding complex words, learning prefixes and suffixes, building vocabulary, and improving reading fluency and comprehension. This case study illustrates the program's effectiveness as a Tier 2 intervention for 5th-grade students of various racial and ethnic backgrounds who have phonemic awareness skills but below grade level reading fluency. After nine weeks of intervention, two of the four target students met their goals as indicated by *Acadience* ORF probes. One student missed their goal by one WCPM, and the other student did not have their final data point due to an absence. The students, teacher, and reading specialist all indicated moderate to high intervention acceptability. While the current case focused on small-group instruction, *REWARDS* can be used at all three Tiers of support. The program may require a large instructional block for implementation and significant resources to obtain the materials and train relevant staff. However, *REWARDS* employs multiple evidence-based strategies and has the potential to be effective for a variety of learners.

Appendix A: Intervention Adherence Checklist

REWARDS Intervention Adherence Checklist

Interventionist:	Oberver:
Lesson:	Date:

Component	**Implementation**	
Students are present and arrived on-time	Yes	No
Instructional materials are present and ready for use (e.g., whiteboard materials, lesson book, pencils/markers)	Yes	No
All activites (A – J) of the lesson are completed during the intervention	Yes	No
A fast pace is maintained throughout the intervention (i.e., each activity takes approximately 6 minutes or less)	Yes	No
Lesson is delivered for 45 – 60 minutes	Yes	No
Positive praise and corrective feedback are delivered throughout the intervention	Yes	No
Students are engaged and participate in the lesson (e.g., students are responding orally or engaging in writing activities)	Yes	No
Total		**/ 7**

Comments:

FIGURE 10.A.1 Intervention Adherence Checklist

Appendix B: Intervention Acceptability Survey - Student

	Strongly Disagree	*Disagree*	*Neutral*	*Agree*	*Strongly Agree*
1 Rewards would be helpful for other middle school students.	1	2	3	4	5
2 Rewards helped me become a better reader.	1	2	3	4	5
3 Rewards helped me read more words correctly.	1	2	3	4	5
4 Rewards helped me with reading in other classes.	1	2	3	4	5
5 I enjoyed timed reading check-ups.	1	2	3	4	5
6 I enjoyed using a workbook.	1	2	3	4	5
7 I hope to continue to use rewards.	1	2	3	4	5
8 I enjoyed participating in Rewards.	1	2	3	4	5

Appendix C: Intervention Acceptability Survey - Teacher

	Strongly Disagree	*Disagree*	*Neutral*	*Agree*	*Strongly Agree*
1 This was an acceptable intervention for the child's needs.	1	2	3	4	5
2 Most teachers would find this intervention appropriate for children with similar needs	1	2	3	4	5
3 This intervention proved effective in supporting the child's needs	1	2	3	4	5
4 I would suggest the use of this intervention to other teachers.	1	2	3	4	5
5 The child's needs were severe enough to warrant use of this intervention.	1	2	3	4	5
6 Most teachers would find this intervention suitable for the needs of this child.	1	2	3	4	5
7 I would be willing to use this intervention in the classroom setting.	1	2	3	4	5

		Strongly Disagree	*Disagree*	*Neutral*	*Agree*	*Strongly Agree*
8	This intervention did not result in negative side effects for the child.	1	2	3	4	5
9	This intervention would be appropriate for a variety of children.	1	2	3	4	5
10	This intervention was consistent with those I have used in classroom settings.	1	2	3	4	5
11	The intervention was a fair way to handle the child's needs.	1	2	3	4	5
12	This intervention was reasonable for the needs of the child.	1	2	3	4	5
13	I liked the procedures used in this intervention.	1	2	3	4	5
14	This intervention was a good way to handle this child's needs.	1	2	3	4	5
15	Overall, this intervention was beneficial for the child.	1	2	3	4	5

References

Archer, A. L., Gleason, M. M., & Vachon, V. L. (2000). *REWARDS, reading excellence: Word attack and rate development strategies*. Longmont, CO: Sopris West.

Archer, A. L., Gleason, M. M., & Vachon, V. L. (2003). Decoding and fluency: Foundation skills for struggling older readers. *Learning Disability Quarterly*, 26, 89–101.

Archer, A. L., & Hughes, C. A. (2010). *Explicit instruction: Effective and efficient teaching*. New York: Guilford Publications.

Carnine, D. (2006). *Teaching struggling and at-risk readers: A direct instruction approach*. Upper Saddle River, NJ: Pearson.

Cooper, J. O., Heron, T. E., & Heward, W. L. (2020). *Applied behavior analysis* (3rd ed.). Upper Saddle River, NJ: Pearson Education.

Gibson, L., Cartledge, G., & Keyes, S. E. (2011). A preliminary investigation of supplemental computer-assisted reading instruction on the oral reading fluency and comprehension of first-grade african american urban students. *Journal of Behavioral Education*, 20(4), 260–282. doi:10.1007/s10864-011-9136-7

Good, R. H., & Kaminski, R. A. (2011). *Acadience reading assessment manual*. Eugene, OR: Dynamic Measurement Group, Inc.

Graves, A. W., Duesbery, L., Pyle, N. B., Brandon, R. R., & McIntosh, A. S. (2011). Two studies of tier II literacy development: Throwing sixth graders a lifeline. *The Elementary School Journal*, *111*(4), 641–661. doi:10.1086/659036

Hasbrouck, J. (2006). For students who are not yet fluent, silent reading is not the best use of classroom time. *American Educator*, Summer 2006, *30*(2).

Hughes, C. A., Morris, J. R., Therrien, W. J., & Benson, S. K. (2017). Explicit instruction: Historical and contemporary contexts. *Learning Disabilities Research and Practice*, *32*(3), 140–148. doi:10.1111/ldrp.12142

Kennedy, C. H. (2005). *Single-case designs for educational research*. Upper Saddle River, NJ: Pearson.

Kuhn, M., Schwanenflugel, P., Morris, R., Morrow, L. M., Woo, D., Meisinger, E., Sevcik, R., Bradley, B., & Stahl, S. (2006). Teaching children to become fluent and automatic readers. *Journal of Literacy Research*, *38*, 357–387

National Center for Education Statistics. (2019). *Nation's report card*. National Assessment of Educational Progress. Retrieved from https://nces.ed.gov/nationsreportcard/

National Reading Panel. (2000). *Report of the National Reading Panel: Teaching children to read: An evidence-based assessment of the scientific research literature on reading and its implications for reading instruction*. National Institute of Child Health and Human Development.

Rasinski, T., & Hamman, P. (2010). Fluency: Why it is "Not Hot". *Reading Today*, *28*, 26.

Shippen, M. E., Houchins, D. E., Steventon, C., & Sartor, D. (2005). A comparison of two direct instruction reading programs for urban middle school students. *Remedial and Special Education*, *26*(3), 175–182. doi:10.1177/07419325050260030501

Toste, J. R., Williams, K. J., & Capin, P. (2017). Reading big words: Instructional practices to promote multisyllabic word reading fluency. *Intervention in School and Clinic*, *52*(5), 270–278.

Vaughn, S., Kieffer, M. J., McKeown, M., Reed, D. K., Sanchez, M., St Martin, K., ... & Yañez, A. (2022). *Providing reading interventions for students in grades 4–9*. Educator's Practice Guide. WWC 2022007. What Works Clearinghouse.

Voyager Sopris Learning. (2018a). *REWARDS grades 4–12* [Brochure]. https://www.voyagersopris.com/docs/default-source/literacy/rewards/rewards_brochure_update_2018_web.pdf

Voyager Sopris Learning. (2018b). *REWARDS: Evidence-based support for REWARDS Intermediate*. https://www.voyagersopris.com/docs/default-source/literacy/rewards/rewards-intermediate-research-base.pdf

Voyager Sopris Learning. (2022). *REWARDS grades 4–12*. Voyager Sopris Learning. https://www.voyagersopris.com/docs/default-source/literacy/rewards/rewards_brochure_update_2018_web.pdf

What Works Clearinghouse (ED). (2009). *Assisting students struggling with reading: Response to intervention (RtI) and multi-tier intervention in the primary grades*. IES Practice Guide. NCEE 2009-4045. What Works Clearinghouse.

Witt, J. C. & Elliott, S. N. (1985). Acceptability of classroom intervention strategies. In T. R. Kratochwill (Ed.), *Advances in school psychology* (Vol. 4, pp. 251–288). Mahwah, NJ: Erlbaum. Reproduced under Fair Use of copyrighted materials for education, scholarship, and research. 17 U.S.C. § 107.

Zurybida, P. M. (2007). *Learning together, but differently: Understanding the impact and implications of a whole group reading intervention.* [Unpublished doctoral dissertation]. University of Washington.

11

SELF-MONITORING

Stacy-Ann A. January, Nicole Wyckoff, Amy Trayers, and Jessica Schloth

University of South Florida, Tampa, FL, USA

Introduction

Self-monitoring is a contingency-based strategy in which an individual learns to observe and record their own behavior(s) and then make changes to their behavior based on what they have recorded. Self-monitoring interventions are based on the behavior learning theory that individuals are influenced by the environment—the act of recording information about the environment results in changes in behavior (Weber et al., 1993). Self-monitoring strategies have been used for a variety of purposes in schools and other settings. For example, self-monitoring interventions have targeted attention, on-task behaviors, pharmaceutical medication adherence, and academic performance (Mathes & Bender, 1997), including for students with disabilities (Vogelgesang et al., 2016). Within the context of schools, students who use self-monitoring strategies can become more aware of their own behavior and can make changes in response to what they observe.

This chapter will detail a self-monitoring intervention for enhancing reading comprehension of a high school student with a medical diagnosis of Attention-Deficit Hyperactivity Disorder (ADHD). Reading comprehension is a complex cognitive process. The reader must actively engage with the text and use vocabulary, their prior knowledge, the context, language, and executive functioning skills to extract meaning (Howell & Nolet, 2000). The skills to decode text accurately and fluently aid in comprehension, as it frees cognitive resources that can be devoted to comprehension (e.g., LaBerge & Samuels, 1974). Readers actively construct

DOI: 10.4324/9781003275749-11

meaning as they read, drawing on their understanding of vocabulary and their prior knowledge. There are several research-based strategies to promote reading comprehension such as activating prior knowledge, making predictions, visualization, questioning, and summarizing (Stevens & Austin, 2022). Reading comprehension monitoring can involve some or all these strategies by providing a structure to help the reader make sense of text, before, during, and after they read. Reading comprehension requires the use of metacognitive skills for learning (e.g., self-assessment, planning and organizing) which are very similar to executive functioning skills. Symptoms of ADHD are often associated with deficits in executive functioning skills (Swanson, 2003), suggesting that many students with ADHD and lower than expected reading comprehension may benefit from a self-monitoring intervention for reading comprehension.

Within school settings, self-monitoring interventions have targeted a range of skills. Often, self-monitoring is used for improving behavioral skills such as academic engagement and on task behavior (Clemons et al., 2016; Rock, 2005; Wills & Mason, 2014) for students in elementary through high school (e.g., Guzman et al., 2018). A robust research base suggests that self-monitoring is effective for improving reading performance. In a systematic review and meta-analysis of the literature, Guzman et al. found that teaching students to self-monitor improved reading comprehension, fluency, and academic engagement, particularly for students in high school. In a review focused on K-12 students with disabilities, Joseph and Eveleigh (2011) concluded that self-monitoring was an effective strategy for increasing the reading performance of students with disabilities.

Self-monitoring interventions have been used with students with ADHD (e.g., Rafferty et al., 2011). Harris et al. (2005) conducted a study with upper elementary students with ADHD who were also receiving special education services. They had students self-monitor their attention and performance during spelling instruction. To self-monitor their attention, students asked themselves if they were paying attention after hearing a tone at variable intervals and recorded a yes or no tally mark. To self-monitor their performance, students counted the number of times they practiced spelling words. In both conditions, they also graphed their data. Results indicated that both self-monitoring of attention and performance had positive impacts of both on-task behavior and the number of times they correctly practiced their spelling words, demonstrating some generalization of the interventions across outcomes. In Crabtree et al. (2010), high school students with ADHD and learning disabilities completed self-monitoring recording sheets while reading. They were asked to identify the main characters, setting, conflicts, the main idea of the story, and how the conflicts were resolved. The goals were for them to increase their comprehension accuracy to at least 80%, as measured by 10 short answer questions. Results of the study indicated an immediate increase in comprehension accuracy after the introduction of the intervention, with all participants meeting the 80% accuracy goal.

Prior to engaging in any intervention work with children, it is important that practitioners understand that learning and behavior is influenced by culture (i.e., the values and practices of members of a group; Beaulieu & Jimenez-Gomez, 2022). Likewise, how practitioners engage with students is influenced by their culture and experiences. To promote social justice, readers are encouraged to practice cultural humility in their work with students and families and engage in culturally inclusive practices. Cultural humility refers to the practice and commitment of self-reflection in which a person is "open to exploring their cultural identity, acknowledging their relationship with power and privilege, and recognizing areas for growth" (Pham et al., 2022; p. 693). Thus, cultural humility is a framework for thinking and engaging in actions to promote equitable outcomes for marginalized youth and families. Although a full review is beyond the scope of this chapter, readers are encouraged to see additional sources (e.g., Pham et al., 2022). Below, we will use a case study to illustrate engaging the problem-solving process to improve the reading comprehension of a high school student with ADHD. Embedded throughout is a focus on promoting culturally and linguistically inclusive pratices.

Case Study

Background Information

Malik is a ninth-grade student with a medical diagnosis of ADHD and who identifies as Black. He is currently being served in both general and special education classrooms. For special education purposes, Malik receives services under the other health impaired (OHI) eligibility, due to his diagnosis of ADHD and his need for specially designed instruction and related services. Malik exhibits inattention and engages in off-task behaviors in both classroom environments. Malik's general education reading teacher, Mrs. Johnson, reported that Malik's inattention and his off-task behaviors impact his comprehension of what he reads. Mrs. Smith, the special education teacher, co-teaches in Ms. Johnson's class, supporting five other students who receive special education services. Mrs. Smith has also reported concerns with Malik's reading comprehension. Both of Malik's teachers utilize explicit instruction strategies and incorporate small-group work into their lessons. They typically aim to place Malik into groups with peers who are likely to model on-task behaviors. The teachers seek the help of the school psychologist to support Malik's reading comprehension skills.

Problem Identification

The first step in the problem-solving process is problem identification. The problem identification step in the problem-solving process involves gathering data to better understand the nature of the problem and objectively defining goals to be obtained from the process. Generally, these goals are determined by examining the expected levels of performance in comparison to the student's current level of performance. The RIOT framework provides a guide for data collection, including Record reviews, Interviews, Observations, and Testing, if appropriate. With Malik, it was determined through his computer-based benchmarking assessment that he is performing at a seventh-grade level for reading, when he should be performing at a ninth-grade level. This demonstrates a discrepancy between how Malik is currently performing in reading and what is expected of his academic performance given his current grade level. Because successful reading requires a basic subset of skills that build on each other, a further analysis was conducted to identify if Malik has academic needs in basic reading skills that are contributing to his inability to perform according to grade-level expectations. In other words, students must be successful in phonological and phonemic awareness, phonics, and oral reading fluency before being able to successfully comprehend passages (National Reading Panel, 2000). The diagnostic determined that Malik is performing according to grade-level expectations in foundational reading skills (e.g., decoding), but is performing below grade level in reading comprehension. Additionally, Malik was presented with reading comprehension questions each day for three days during his small-group reading instruction. These data suggested that Malik could answer questions correctly with 30% accuracy. To achieve grade-level expectations, Malik should be answering reading comprehension questions with at least 80% accuracy.

Although Malik's assessment scores provide valuable insight into the nature of the problem, it is important for school psychologists or other education professionals to seek multiple sources of data to confirm information and rule out potential confounding factors (January, 2023). First, it is important to collect data from the classroom contexts in which the student participates. This can occur through direct observation or an interview with Malik's teachers and with Malik. The purpose of this data gathering is to learn more about the nature of Malik's reading comprehension concerns as well as to understand more about the culturally inclusive practices that are present in the classroom. An interview with Mrs. Johnson and Mrs. Smith was conducted to gain additional insight that would assist in establishing goals. Their reports revealed that Malik has difficulty with reading comprehension tasks, despite demonstrating no difficulties related to reading fluency and decoding. In an interview with Malik, he shared that he has difficulty understanding what he reads. Observation and interview data revealed culturally appropriate and responsive practices in the classroom. However, if this was not the case, then a classwide intervention would have been appropriate. Finally, a record review was conducted to gain information on Malik's previous educational history, including examining report cards, standardized assessment scores, and permanent products (e.g., homework assignments, in-class exams, etc.). During this record review, it was determined that Malik demonstrated consistent below grade level performance in reading since late elementary school.

During the problem identification step, Malik's permanent products, report cards, and test scores were reviewed to determine previous educational history and patterns in Malik's academic performance. Interviews with Malik's teachers were also obtained during the problem identification step, where it was determined that Malik's below-grade level performance is primarily in a skill deficit related to reading comprehension. Observations in the classroom environment provide additional insight into potential ecological or instructional variables that may be impacting Malik's performance. Malik's computer based diagnostic assessment could serve as the testing component of the RIOT framework, as it was determined through this assessment that Malik primarily struggles with reading comprehension skills.

Problem Analysis

The second step of the problem-solving process is problem analysis. During the problem analysis phase, the goal is to gain insight into *why* the problem may be occurring and establish potential hypotheses that can assist in intervention planning. The ICEL (Instruction, Curriculum, Environment, Learner) framework, in addition to RIOT, can be used during this problem analysis phase to collect adequate data to inform hypothesis development, as well as to investigate the reasons why an academic need exists. ICEL is a framework within the problem analysis phase that allows for hypotheses organization within the following areas: Instruction, Curriculum, Environment, and Learner. It is common for teams to attribute a student's academic needs to solely factors within the student (e.g., motivation or skill deficits), rather than address the potential that the student is impacted by instructional, curriculum, or environmental influences. This practice is important to obtain an ecological, socially just perspective into potential reasons for a student's performance.

In the case of Malik, he receives reading instruction from two teachers, Mrs. Johnson, his general education teacher, and Mrs. Smith, his special education teacher. Using the ICEL framework, it was determined that instruction was being delivered at an appropriate pace and utilized evidence-based practices, such as explicit instruction (Archer & Hughes, 2010), frequent opportunities to respond (Harbour et al., 2015), and culturally responsive practices (Paris & Alim, 2017). The curriculum was also determined to be appropriate for grade-level expectations, including having appropriate pacing, rigor, and relevance. An examination of the environment determined that appropriate expectations for classroom behavior were in place, the classroom contained minimal distractions, and Malik's peers were, on average, appropriately engaged with academic content. Learner variables, including attendance, prerequisite skills, organizational habits, etc., revealed that Malik demonstrated inattentive behavior at times during both lessons in general and special education classrooms.

Intervention Goals

As indicated by the data collected (district benchmark tests, diagnostic assessments, classroom assessments), Malik is performing below grade-level expectations in reading, with specific challenges related to reading comprehension skills. Specifically, Malik's comprehension accuracy averaged 30% on the baseline comprehension assessments. One culturally and linguistically appropriate practice is to engage students and families in the development of intervention goals. Consistent with district expectations, the intervention goal is for Malik to demonstrate 80% accuracy in the comprehension of grade-level text.

Measurement and Intervention Plan

Several steps are necessary to implement a self-monitoring intervention for reading comprehension. It is critical that the self-monitoring intervention developed reflects the students' (and family's) strengths, needs, and goals (Rafferty et al., 2011), which is consistent with being culturally and linguistically inclusive. The first step is to identify the academic skill targeted for change. This should be based on the data that were collected in the problem identification step. For Malik, this is his reading comprehension accuracy, as it was significantly lower than grade-level expectations. Next, define the target skills in clear, observable, and unambiguous terms. For Malik, reading comprehension is defined as his ability to demonstrate that his understands what he reads, as evidenced by correctly answering at least 80% accuracy in grade-level text. To increase his comprehension accuracy, Malik would benefit from better organizing his thinking about what he reads. As such, the self-monitoring prompt will have Malik monitor his use of reading comprehension strategies. The third step in implementing this self-monitoring intervention is to determine how data will be collected. The assessment should directly measure the target academic skill. With Malik, this would mean planning to measure his reading comprehension skills at baseline and for progress monitoring. For baseline data, aim to collect 3–5 data points. During intervention condition, progress monitoring should be conducted at least weekly. Malik's progress monitoring will occur twice each week with the same type of assessment used for the baseline condition.

The fourth step is to collect pre-intervention (i.e., baseline) data about the students' current level of performance. Malik received 3 grade-level passages to read; he was then asked to answer 10 comprehension questions about each text. Although data were collecting during the problem identification step, it may not align directly with our intervention data will be collected. If this is the case, baseline data should be collected. The purpose of this baseline data is twofold: (a) confirm that a problem that needs intervention remains, and (b) serve as a comparison for the data that will be collected during intervention. The fifth step in this intervention is to design the self-monitoring materials and procedures. For example, determine exactly which comprehension strategies will be monitored, create the self-monitoring recording sheet, and plan for implementation and fidelity. Additionally, determine how students' self-monitoring behavior will be reinforced and what criteria will allow the student to earn reinforcement. It is always good practice to involve the student in developing potential reinforcers. One could administer an age-appropriate reinforcement questionnaire with potential reinforcers that could be delivered in the school context. Or ask the student what they would like to earn for reinforcement. Reinforcers could be used for both completing the self-monitoring form and improvements on the reading comprehension assessments. Malik completed the high school reinforcement survey in which he rated a list of opportunities, activities, and items that he would most like to earn during the self-monitoring intervention. Ultimately, he chose a homework pass as his preferred reinforcer. As such, during the intervention phase, Malik was able to earn a homework pass for one class period for each time he completed his self-monitoring checklist. Next, the student should be taught how to implement the self-monitoring strategy. Since Malik's target skill is reading comprehension, it would be helpful and important to teach (or reteach) the specific comprehension strategies that he will be monitoring.

After the self-monitoring system has been developed, the next step is to teach the student how to use the system. The teacher/interventionist should explain to the student what they will be working on, teach any necessary prerequisite skills, and explicitly teach the student how to use the self-monitoring sheet. Malik's self-monitoring sheet is provided at the end of this chapter (Appendix). Malik will be engaging in before-reading, during-reading, and after-reading activities. Prior to having Malik attempt to implement the self-monitoring, his teacher should ensure that he knows how to engage in each of the comprehension strategies included in the monitoring sheet. Then, the teacher should have the student practice using the form while the teacher observes and provides feedback. The next step is to implement the intervention and monitor progress. Either Mrs. Johnson or Ms. Smith will closely monitor Malik's implementation of the intervention during the first week, and, if successful, they will gradually reduce the frequency of their monitoring. Once students have been successfully monitoring their performance, reinforcements should be gradually reduced (i.e., faded). After the academic goal has been reached, the intervention can also be gradually faded (Rafferty et al., 2011). However, teachers should occasionally monitor students' performance to ensure maintenance of the skills taught during the intervention. If needed, the self-monitoring intervention can be revisited.

Intervention Fidelity and Inter-scorer Agreement Plans

Prior to implementing the intervention, it is important to plan for supporting high implementation fidelity. Implementation fidelity refers to how well an intervention is delivered as designed (Sanetti et al., 2021). When self-monitoring reading comprehension, a permanent product of the intervention is created when the student accurately completes the self-monitoring form. However, to fully capture the implementation of the intervention, additional steps should be monitored. For example, the designated teacher should check the completion of the self-monitoring checklist, provide the student with feedback, and give them access to the selected reinforcer. To monitor the student's intervention fidelity, the secondary observer (i.e., teacher) can complete the self-monitoring checklist along with the student. Twice during the implementation of the self-monitoring intervention, Mrs. Johnson observed Malik completing his self-monitoring checklist. Results indicated that Malik had 100% fidelity each time.

At the beginning of the intervention and periodically thereafter, it would be useful to collect some inter-scorer agreement data. Inter-scorer agreement refers to the extent to which two people evaluating the same assessment agree on the scoring. Collecting inter-scorer agreement data can help establish the reliability of the data and increase the validity of decisions made based on those data. Across the baseline and intervention phases, Mrs. Johnson and Ms. Smith both independently scored four of Malik's completed reading comprehension assessment probes with 100% inter-scorer agreement on each of the probes.

Intervention Outcome Data

Malik's intervention data are presented in Figure 11.1. Prior to implementing the intervention, baseline data were collected over a period of 3 days. Baseline data, as depicted in the figure ranged from 20–40% accuracy, clearly demonstrating the need for an intervention to increase reading comprehension. When evaluating the self-monitoring intervention data to determine the nature of the student's response, it can be helpful to examine the first few data points immediately after the intervention was implemented as well as whether the student met the intervention goals that were set. After Malik began implementing the intervention, there was an immediate and large increase in his percent accuracy on the 10-item reading comprehension measure. Malik began meeting the intervention goal of 80% accuracy on the fourth day of his implementation of the

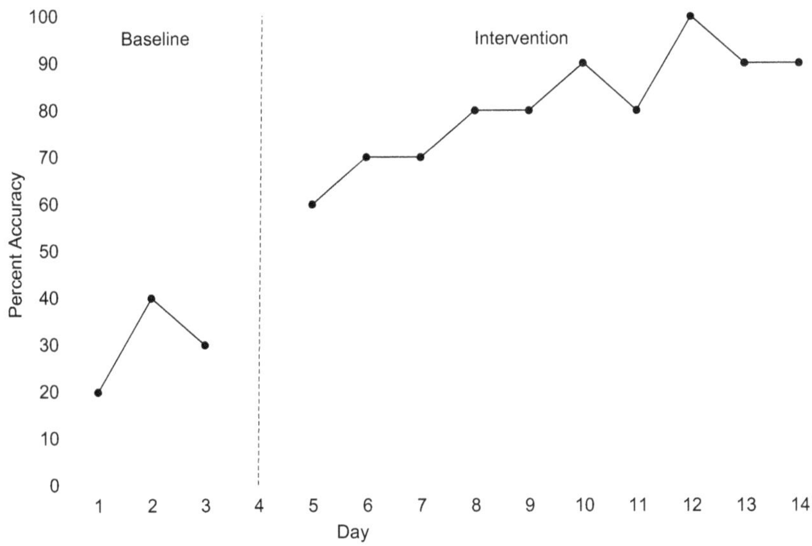

FIGURE 11.1 Malik's Comprehension Accuracy

self-monitoring intervention. Overall, Malik's intervention data ranged from 60–100%, with the final seven data points being at or above 80%. Thus, in comparison to Malik's comprehension accuracy prior to intervention significantly improved and maintained, suggesting that the self-monitoring intervention implemented improved the reading comprehension of this student.

Intervention Acceptability

In addition to choosing an intervention with a high likelihood of being effective for students, it is also important to consider the potential acceptability of the intervention. Intervention acceptability refers to the extent to which users (e.g., teachers, students) of an intervention think it is appropriate for the students' needs and the classroom context and is reasonable in terms of time and effort to implement (Witt & Martens, 1983). There is some research to suggest that acceptability may be related to intervention implementation, and, by extension, the extent to which intervention goals are met (Dart et al., 2012). As such, the degree to which an intervention may be acceptable to users is worthwhile to consider when engaging in the problem-solving process. Interventions that are not time-intensive, that are positive and reinforcement-based, and that fit within the ecology are more likely to be accepted by users (Carter, 2007; Reimers et al., 1987). Self-monitoring interventions generally are not time-intensive and are positive and reinforcement-based. The extent to which they fit within the student's classroom context can be assessed during the problem solving process.

In general, self-monitoring interventions have high levels of acceptability. Across studies targeting social behavior and academic outcomes, evidence indicates students implementing the self-monitoring intervention find it acceptable and that it improved the target behavior or academic skill (e.g., Harris et al., 2005; Rafferty et al., 2011). Further, data can be collected on the intervention's acceptability from the participating student. The Children's Intervention Rating Profile (Witt & Elliott, 1983) is a well-validated measure of students' intervention acceptability (Lane et al., 2015; Turco & Elliott, 1986). The Children's Usage Rating Profile-Actual (CURP; Briesch & Chafouleas, 2009) is another validated option. At the time of this writing, both measures were available for free online. At the end of the intervention, Malik completed the CURP to better understand Malik's perceptions of the self-monitoring intervention. The CURP has 3 factors, personal desirability, feasibility, and understanding, with response options on a Likert-type scale that range from 1 to 4. Malik's average ratings were

3.7, 3.4, and 3.85. These scores indicate that Malik liked participating in the intervention, found it to be feasible, and that he understood why and how to do the self-monitoring intervention.

Intervention Considerations

Self-monitoring can be used across a variety of settings to aid in students' monitoring of their own behaviors or performance. The intervention is practical for teachers to implement in both general and special education classroom settings. It is relatively simple to teach students the self-monitoring strategy and does not take long for students to complete. When implementing self-monitoring interventions in school settings, it is important to describe and specify what is expected of students so that they have clear expectations when self-monitoring (Mathes & Bender, 1997). Initially, it is beneficial to explain to students why they are going to be self-monitoring their behavior or performance, as well as how the strategy may help students to remain on-task. Teachers may provide feedback on students' self-monitoring as they transition into applying the procedure so that students understand how to appropriately rate their behavior.

Another consideration that teachers implementing self-monitoring interventions in school settings must consider the students' schedule and when they will self-monitor their behavior or performance (Rafferty, 2012). Students may self-monitor at either the beginning or end of a class period or school day, depending on the target behavior that is being monitored. Students may also self-monitor either before, during, or after the completion of academic tasks or assignments. For the target behavior of "on-task behavior," it would be beneficial for the student to self-monitor their behavior during the completion of tasks. This may occur at fixed intervals while students are engaging in tasks, such as at the end of a 15-minute time period. If a different target behavior is being used, such as "completion of academic work," it may be appropriate for students to self-monitor once an assignment has been finished. The schedule for which self-monitoring will occur can be altered depending on the setting and target behavior being monitored, and should be determined by the classroom teacher prior to the implementation of the intervention.

One potential pitfall for implementing self-monitoring is that students' productivity may decrease as they attempt to focus more on accuracy when completing academic tasks (Carr & Punzo, 1993). For example, if self-monitoring is being implemented to increase a student's performance in reading, the student may focus more on working to answer individual questions correctly than completing assignments. However, a decrease in total "productivity" in exchange for greater accuracy is a good tradeoff. Another potential problem that may arise in the implementation of self-monitoring is students' exaggeration of self-rating to receive reinforcement (Shapiro et al., 1998). To address this potential concern, it is important to train appropriately, and periodically check the accuracy of the students' recording.

Along with self-monitoring, other evidence-based strategies may be utilized to support students like Malik who have academic needs in the area of reading comprehension. One strategy that may be implemented is self-regulated strategy development (SRSD; Hagaman et al., 2012). SRSD has similarities with self-monitoring; however, it also provides opportunities for students to set goals for themselves while implementing the strategy. The SRSD model consists of six steps: developing background knowledge, discussing the importance of using the strategy, explicit modeling of the strategy, memorizing the strategy, providing support for students using the strategy, and students practicing the strategy on their own (Stewart & Austin, 2020). Another evidence-based strategy that may be implemented to improve students' reading comprehension is TWA, which includes the following steps: Think before reading, think While reading, and think After reading (Sanders et al., 2018; Stewart & Austin, 2020). This strategy may be used in combination with either self-monitoring or SRSD, or it can stand alone to help students develop comprehension skills.

Conclusion

Self-monitoring interventions are an effective approach for targeting a range of academic and behavioral needs for students with and without disabilities (e.g., Guzman et al., 2018; Joseph & Eveleigh, 2011). Using cultural humility as a foundation for practice, this chapter described how to use the problem-solving model and implement a self-monitoring intervention for a high school student with ADHD and challenges with reading comprehension. In this case example, reading comprehension was identified as an area of academic need for Malik; he was performing below grade-level expectations in comparison to peers. Problem analyses identified attention challenges as the function of Malik's reading comprehension difficulties; therefore, self-monitoring of reading comprehension was chosen as the intervention. Intervention outcome data revealed that Malik's reading comprehension skills increased, and he met his intervention goal. Self-monitoring interventions are relatively easy to plan and implement, and have good acceptability, making them a strong choice for students like Malik.

Appendix

Self-Monitoring for Reading Comprehension

Student Recording Sheet

Student Name: ______________________ Date: ____________
Title of Text: ______________________

Before Reading

Predicting

☐ What do I think this text will be about?

During Reading

Main Idea Generation

After each paragraph I read, I briefly summarize the main idea.
☐ First, I identify the main "who" or "what" is this paragraph/section about.
☐ Next, I identify the most important information about that person or thing.
☐ Finally, I combine my answers into one sentence about the paragraph.

After Reading

Summarizing

After reading a text, I summarize what I read.
☐ First, I write a main idea sentence for the whole text.
☐ Next, I write 2–4 supporting details about the text.
☐ Finally, I write a concluding sentence that restates the overall gist of the passage.

Conflict of Interest Statement

The authors have no conflicts of interest to declare.

References

Archer, A. L., & Hughes, C. A. (2010). *Explicit instruction: Effective and efficient teaching*. New York, NY: Guilford Press.

Beaulieu, L., & Jimenez-Gomez, C. (2022). Cultural responsiveness in applied behavior analysis: Self-assessment. *Journal of Applied Behavior Analysis*, *55*(2), 337–356. doi:10.1002/jaba.907

Briesch, A. M., & Chafouleas, S. M. (2009). *Children's usage rating profile (Actual)*. Storrs, CT: University of Connecticut.

Carr, S. C., & Punzo, R. P. (1993). The effects of self-monitoring of academic accuracy and productivity on the performance of students with behavioral disorders. *Behavioral Disorders*, *22*, 241–250. doi:10.1177/019874299301800401

Carter, S. L. (2007). Review of recent treatment acceptability research. *Education and Training in Developmental Disabilities*, *42*(3), 301–316.

Clemons, L. L., Mason, B. A., Garrison-Kane, L., & Wills, H. P. (2016). Self-monitoring for high school students with disabilities: A cross-categorical investigation of I-connect. *Journal of Positive Behavior Interventions*, *18*(3), 145–155. doi:10.1177/1098300715596134

Crabtree, T., Alber-Morgan, S. R., & Konrad, M. (2010). The effects of self-monitoring of story elements on the reading comprehension of high school seniors with learning disabilities. *Education & Treatment of Children*, *33*(2), 187–203. doi:10.1353/etc.0.0090

Dart, E. H., Cook, C. R., Collins, T. A., Gresham, F. M., & Chenier, J. S. (2012). Test driving interventions to increase treatment integrity and student outcomes. *School Psychology Review*, 41, 467–481. doi:10.1080/02796015.2012.12087500

Guzman, G., Goldberg, T. S., & Swanson, H. L. (2018). A meta-analysis of self-monitoring on reading performance of K-12 students. *School Psychology Quarterly*, *33*(1), 160–168. doi:10.1037/spq0000199

Hagaman, J. L., Casey, K. J., & Reid, R. (2012). The effects of the paraphrasing strategy on the reading comprehension of young students. *Remedial and Special Education*, *33*(2), 110–123. doi:10.1037/spq0000199

Harbour, K. E., Evanovich, L. L., Sweigart, C. A., & Hughes, L. E. (2015). A brief review of effective teaching practices that maximize student engagement. *Preventing School Failure: Alternative Education for Children and Youth*, *59*(1), 5–13.

Harris, K. R., Friedlander, B. D., Saddler, B., Frizzelle, R., & Graham, S. (2005). Self-monitoring of attention versus self-monitoring of academic performance: Effects among students with ADHD in the general education classroom. *The Journal of Special Education*, *39*(3), 145–156. doi:10.1177/00224669050390030201

Howell, K. W., & Nolet, V. (2000). *Curriculum-based evaluation: Teaching and decision making* (3rd ed.). Belmont, CA: Wadsworth.

January, S.-A. A. (2023). Best practices in improving data-based decision making in schools. In P. L. Harrison, S. L. Proctor, & A. Thomas (Eds.), *Best practices in school psychology: Vol. 1. Data-based and collaborative decision making* (7th ed.). National Association of School Psychologists.

Joseph, L. M., & Eveleigh, E. L. (2011). A review of the effects of self-monitoring on reading performance of students with disabilities. *The Journal of Special Education*, *45*(1), 43–53. doi:10.1177/0022466909349145

LaBerge, D., & Samuels, S. J. (1974). Toward a theory of automatic information processing in reading. *Cognitive Psychology*, *6*(2), 293–323. doi:10.1016/0010-0285(74)90015-2

Lane, K.L., Oakes, W. P., Powers, L., Diebold, T., Germer, K., Common, E. A., & Brunsting, N. (2015). Improving teachers' knowledge of functional assessment-based interventions: Outcomes of a professional development series. *Education and Treatment of Children*, *38*, 93–120.

Mathes, M. Y., & Bender, W. N. (1997). The effects of self-monitoring on children with attention deficit/hyperactivity disorder who are receiving pharmacological interventions. *Remedial and Special Education*, *18*(2), 121–128. doi:10.1177/074193259701800206

National Reading Panel. (2000). *Report of the National Reading Panel. Teaching children to read: An evidence-based assessment of the scientific research literature on reading and its implications for reading instruction.* Washington, DC: US Department of Health and Human Services.

Paris, D., & Alim, H. S. (Eds.). (2017). *Culturally sustaining pedagogies: Teaching and learning for justice in a changing world.* New York, NY: Teachers College.

Pham, A. V., Goforth, A. N. Aguilar, L. N., Burt, I., Bastian, R., & Diaków, D. M. (2022). Dismantling systemic inequities in school psychology: Cultural humility as a foundational approach to social justice. *School Psychology Review*. *51*(6), 692–709. doi:10.1080/2372966X.2021.1941245

Rafferty, L. A. (2012). Self-monitoring during whole group reading instruction: Effects among students with emotional and behavioral disabilities during summer school intervention sessions. *Emotional & Behavioural Difficulties*, *17*(2), 157–173. doi:10.1080/13632752.2012.672866

Rafferty, L. A., Arroyo, J., Ginnane, S., & Wilczynski, K. (2011). Self-monitoring during spelling practice: Effects on spelling accuracy and on-task behavior of three students diagnosed with attention deficit hyperactivity disorder. *Behavior Analysis in Practice*, *4*(1), 37–45. doi:10.1007/BF03391773

Reimers, T. M., Wacker, D. P., & Koeppl, G. (1987). Acceptability of behavioral interventions: A review of the literature. *School Psychology Review*, *16*(2), 212–227. doi:10.1080/02796015.1987.12085286

Rock, M. L. (2005). Use of strategic self-monitoring to enhance academic engagement, productivity, and accuracy of students with and without exceptionalities. *Journal of Positive Behavior Interventions*, *7*(1), 3–17. doi:10.1177/10983007050070010201

Sanders, S., Ennis, R. P., & Losinski, M. (2018). Effects of TWA on science text comprehension of students with emotional and behavior disorders in a special day school. *Education & Treatment of Children*, *41*(4), 483–505. doi:10.1353/etc.2018.0026

Sanetti, L. M., Cook, B. G., & Cook, L. (2021). Treatment fidelity: What it is and why it matters. *Learning Disabilities Research & Practice*, *36*(1), 5–11. doi:10.1111/ldrp.12238

Shapiro, S. L., Schwartz, G. E., & Bonner, G. (1998). Effects of mindfulness-based stress reduction on medical and premedical students. *Journal of Behavioral Medicine*, *21*, 581–599.

Stevens, E. A., & Austin, C. R. (2022). Structured reading comprehension intervention for students with reading difficulties. In L. Spear-Swerling (Ed.), *Structured literacy interventions: Teaching students with reading difficulties, grades K-6* (pp. 162–188). New York, NY: Guilford Press.

Stewart, A. A., & Austin, C. R. (2020). Reading interventions for students with or at risk of attention-deficit/hyperactivity disorder: A systematic review. *Remedial and Special Education*, *41*(6), 352–367. doi:10.1177/0741932519849660

Swanson, J. M. (2003). Role of executive function in ADHD. *Journal of Clinical Psychiatry*, *64*(Suppl 14), 35–39.

Turco, T. L., & Elliott, S. N. (1986). Assessment of students' acceptability ratings of teacher-initiated interventions for classroom misbehavior. *Journal of School Psychology*, *24*(3), 277–283.

Vogelgesang, K. L., Bruhn, A. L., Coghill-Behrends, W. L., Kern, A. M., & Troughton, L. C. W. (2016). A single-subject study of a technology-based self-monitoring intervention. *Journal of Behavioral Education*, *25*(4), 478–497. doi:10.1007/s10864-016-9253-4

Weber, J., Scheuermann, B., McCall, C., & Coleman, M. (1993). Research on self-monitoring as a behavior management technique in special education: A descriptive review. *Remedial and Special Education*, *14*(2), 38–56.

Wills, H. P., & Mason, B. A. (2014). Implementation of a self-monitoring application to improve on-task behavior: A high-school pilot study. *Journal of Behavioral Education*, *23*(4), 421–434. doi:10.1007/s10864-014-9204-x

Witt, J. C., & Martens, B. K. (1983). Assessing the acceptability of behavioral interventions used in classrooms. *Psychology in the Schools*, *20*(4), 510–517.

Witt, J. C., & Elliott, S. N. (1983). *Children's Intervention Rating Profile*. Lincoln, NE: University of Nebraska.

12

STORY MAPPING

Shobana Musti

Pace University, Pleasantville, NY, USA

Alana Oif Telesman

The Ohio State University, Columbus, OH, USA

Michele M. Nobel

Ohio Wesleyan University, Delaware, OH, USA

Introduction

Reading comprehension is an essential skill for students' success in the school and in the workplace. Experts contend that reading comprehension is the ultimate goal and essence of reading (NRP, 2000). This is especially true when students transition from the "learning to read" stage in early elementary grades to the "reading to learn" stage in upper elementary grades and beyond. Reading comprehension is a complex and active process of constructing meaning from words (Stagliano & Boone, 2009). According to the National Reading Panel (NRP, 2000), reading comprehension is the interaction between vocabulary knowledge, interaction with text, and application of reading comprehension strategies.

While good readers are known to use active strategies to interact with the text to make meaning, less-skilled readers, and students with learning disabilities (LD) have difficulties choosing comprehension strategies while reading. Students with poor comprehension often have difficulty understanding the different text structures and, in turn, have difficulty recalling relevant story information (Boon et al., 2015). As a result, these students are unable to extract meaning from texts and need explicit instruction in text comprehension.

According to the Institute of Education Sciences (Kamil et al., 2008), one strategy that has been effective in improving comprehension in narrative text structures is story mapping (SM). A story map is a graphic organizer with a visual-spatial display of story grammar elements such as main

DOI: 10.4324/9781003275749-12

character, setting, problem or conflict, major events, and resolution, typically found in narrative texts. SM is designed to direct students' attention to the story grammar elements before, during, and after reading a passage of text as they are explicitly taught to complete the graphic organizer. Educators considering this strategy, including teachers, intervention specialists, and school psychologists, can implement SM classwide or in 1:1, 2:1, or small-group formats. Supported by schema theory, SM facilitates activating students' background knowledge before reading and serves as a guide in recording relevant information during the reading process (Boulineau et al., 2004).

SM is an evidence-based strategy with over three decades of demonstrated evidence in improving reading comprehension in upper-elementary school students with LD (Davis, 1994; Idol & Croll, 1987), middle-school students with LD (Gardill & Jitendra, 1999), and secondary students with LD (Dimino et al., 1990; Gurney et al., 1990). Stagliano and Boon (2009) showed that SM can be effective in improving comprehension skills of expository texts for three fourth-grade students with LD. Studies support use of SM to improve comprehension scores in literal and inferential questions (Gardill & Jitendra, 1999; Taylor et al., 2002). Most of the studies used a direct instruction format that included the teacher modeling the use of the graphic organizer followed by giving students guided practice and then independent practice in the use of story maps.

Case Study

Background Information

Sabrina was a 12-year-old girl, enrolled in sixth grade in Walnut Middle School. Born in the United States to Spanish-speaking parents, Sabrina spoke both English and Spanish fluently. Sabrina was diagnosed with ADHD in elementary school and takes a low dose of prescription medication for inattention. Sabrina was referred to the student assistance team by her English language arts teacher, Mr. Evans, who observed Sabrina having difficulty finding the main idea in a story and often having trouble with following a sequence in math problems.

Results from cognitive and achievement tests completed as part of an educational evaluation served as a helpful tool in understanding Sabrina's abilities. In the *Woodcock Johnson Tests of Cognitive Abilities, Fourth Edition (WJ IV COG)*, Sabrina received a standard score of 98 (45th percentile) which placed her in the average range for her age. She scored in the average range on the Comprehension-Knowledge and Short-term Working Memory subtests. In the subtests on Processing Speed, Sabrina scored in the below-average range for her age. The test required the student to locate and circle two identical letter patterns in a row of six patterns. The WJ IV ACH Story Recall subtest that measures Long-Term Retrieval required the student to recall increasingly complex stories presented from an audio recording. Sabrina had difficulty recalling the facts from the stories, placing her in the below average range for her age.

Sabrina's academic skills were assessed with the *Wechsler Individual Achievement Test – Third Edition* (WIAT-III). In the area of reading, Sabrina developed grade-level foundational skills. She was able to apply phonics knowledge to decode unknown words (Pseudoword Decoding subtest) and grade-level sight words (Word Reading subtest) and scored in the average range for her age. Sabrina received a standard score of 91 (27th percentile) on the Oral Reading Fluency subtest with accuracy in the average range. Sabrina showed difficulty comprehending the passages she read. She scored in the below-average range for her age on the Comprehension subtest. She also showed difficulty with literal comprehension questions and making inferences within a story.

The school psychologist reviewed Sabrina's Beginning of the Year (BOY) Benchmark assessments in Oral Reading Fluency (ORF) and Maze Benchmark assessments for Grade 6 (DIBELS, 2020). As shown in Table 12.1, for ORF, Sabrina's scores indicated she was performing in an acceptable range for her grade level for Words Read Correct and Accuracy. Scores in the "green" or core support level indicate minimal risk of not meeting end of the year benchmark levels. About 80% of students who score at or

TABLE 12.1 Sabrina's Data on DIBELS ORF and Maze Beginning of Year (BOY) Benchmark

	Raw Scores	*Cut Scores*	*Benchmark Goal Details*
ORF – Words Read Correct	129	123	Green – Core Support – Minimal Risk
ORF – Incorrect	3	—	—
ORF – Total Words Read	132	—	—
ORF - Accuracy	97.7	96+	Green – Core Support – Minimal Risk
Maze - Correct	16	—	—
Maze - Incorrect	8	—	—
Maze - Adjusted	12	14.5	Red – Intensive Support – At Risk
	Composite Score	Cut Score	Benchmark Goal Details
Benchmark 1 Beginning	341.72	336	Green – Core Support – Minimal Risk

above the 40th percentile rank on this criterion measure fall in this range or above. On the maze assessment, which uses a cloze procedure to measure reading comprehension, Sabrina scored well below her same-grade peers. Sabrina's Adjusted Score of 12 is below the expected cut score of 14.5 and places her into the "red" level, indicating a need for Intensive Support and At-Risk for not meeting end of the year benchmarks. Despite the low score for the Maze, Sabrina's overall Composite Score of 341.7 was above the cut score for her grade and placed her into the "green," level indicating minimal risk. When determining a student's overall risk, the composite score is the best predictor of end of the year performance (DIBELS, 2020). However, risk on each subtest remains important for determining where to focus individualized instruction. For Sabrina, the low score on the Maze was commensurate with her difficulty on the WIAT-III Comprehension subtest and indicated a need for targeted intervention in reading comprehension.

Problem Identification

According to Sabrina's WIAT-III scores, Sabrina received a standard score of 91 (27th percentile) on the Oral Reading Fluency (ORF) subtest with accuracy in the average range and below average for her age on the Comprehension subtest. Sabrina showed difficulty comprehending the passages she read. Specifically, she had difficulty with literal comprehension questions and making inferences within a story. Sabrina was scoring lower on the Comprehension subtest than would be expected given her average cognitive abilities and her average scores on the ORF, Pseudoword Decoding, and Word Reading Subtests.

To gain additional information regarding Sabrina's below-average comprehension, DIBELS 8 Maze was administered. Sabrina's performance on the Maze was below her same-grade peers, indicating a need for targeted intervention to boost her skills in reading comprehension. The Maze assessment uses a cloze procedure, which indicates that Sabrina is not always able to determine which word best fits within the context of sentences she is reading silently. Of the 24 sentences that Sabrina read, she was able to correctly choose 16 words to fit within the cloze blanks. She made 8 errors, which, after weighted scoring, gave her an adjusted score of 12. It was unclear what contributing factors may be affecting Sabrina's ability to correctly select words for the blanks in the sentences where she made errors. The school psychologist noticed that Sabrina appeared to be attentive to the task, was working carefully, and continued to work until time expired.

Sabrina's teachers reported that Sabrina was often unable to make predictions or inferences when reading. She had difficulty summarizing what she read into 3–5 sentences or one main overarching theme. She occasionally struggled to sequence the events of a story, especially if the text was more complex with foreshadowing or story sequences that were out of chronological order. Her performance answering literal comprehension questions was inconsistent. Her teachers noted that her ability to decode was strong, but she seldom volunteered to read aloud when the opportunity was given. Her teachers believed she was unable to monitor the context of what she was reading while she focused on decoding.

From the information collected through various assessments and from her teachers' observations, it appeared that Sabrina was struggling in reading comprehension. While this area of deficit did not appear to be dramatically affecting her overall performance on the WIAT-III or DIBELS 8, deficits in reading comprehension likely affected Sabrina's daily performance in her academic courses, which could affect her ability to perform well on tests and quizzes. As the amount of required reading and the difficulty of the material increases for the sixth grade and beyond, Sabrina will need strong comprehension skills to navigate course material. It is vital that the reading comprehension difficulties she is experiencing are remediated to ensure she can be successful academically.

Problem Analysis

The school psychologist and Mr. Evans created CBM probes to better understand Sabrina's current levels of performance in comprehending narrative text structures. Based on observations and prior assessments, Mr. Evans hypothesized that Sabrina is primarily struggling to incorporate metacognitive strategies while reading such as monitoring her understanding, making inferences, applying prior knowledge, and integrating ideas from texts and passages.

Mr. Evans selected 20 fiction passages (i.e., probes) and standardized the difficulty level by including the same Lexile range and overall word count. The passages contained at least five story grammar elements: place/setting, who/what, a problem, at least three events that took place, and a solution or main idea. From there, he created a list of 8 comprehension questions that assessed student's basic recall, sequencing, and inferential skills. To keep consistency across passages, three questions focused on recall, four questions focused on sequencing of events in the story, and one question focused on making inferences.

Mr. Evans created story-map answer keys for each story. Each story contained five story grammar elements and all possible answers were displayed in the answer key. Answers were marked as either correct or incorrect with no partial credit. Each answer key included all possible answers to minimize the discrepancy between graders.

After consulting with the school psychologist, Mr. Evans decided that it would be a good idea to screen all students on their comprehension skills. This way students who scored similar in range to Sabrina could benefit from Tier 2 intervention with story mapping in a small group format. Mr. Evans administered three probes, on Monday, Wednesday, and Friday to all of students in his sixth-grade ELA class. To complete the probe, all students were given 10 minutes to read a passage aloud chorally and answer the comprehension questions. The choral reading allowed students of all reading abilities to keep pace with the reading. Mr. Evans scored the probes using the answer key and calculated the percentage of correct responses. Based on the initial three baseline probes, three other students in addition to Sabrina were identified to receive SM instruction in a small group setting as a Tier 2 intervention (see Table 12.2 for a breakdown of Sabrina's results for each CBM).

Intervention Goals

Mr. Evans used data to determine intervention goals such that the goals were reasonable given present levels and allotted time to meet the goal, and the intensity of intervention was matched to academic need. Sabrina's intervention goals were determined by using data from the CBM measures to ascertain her present levels of performance coupled with percentages for mastery and grade-level targets. For the first three weeks of intervention, Sabrina was expected to answer at least 80% of the comprehension correctly during the story-mapping phase and reach 90% accuracy at the end of six weeks of intervention. Mr. Evans and the school psychologist agreed to review data at the end of Week 3 to determine if any adjustments need to be made to the intervention.

For the Maze goal, the criterion for mastery was developed by using the End of Year minimum "green" level score established by DIBELS 8 (i.e., 26.5 corrects) and an expectation that Sabrina would be able to increase the number of correct responses per week by 1.5 additional attempted cloze sentences with no more than 8 incorrect responses. Careful data collection and plotting allow Mr. Evans and Sabrina to track her progress and adjust instruction accordingly.

Measurement of Target Reading Skill, Data Collection Strategies, and Progress Monitoring

The school psychologist and Mr. Evans measured Sabrina's overall comprehension using both CBMs and standardized Maze assessments. As stated, before beginning intervention, Sabrina completed three probes to

TABLE 12.2 Sabrina's Data on Comprehension Probes during Baseline and Intervention

Phase	*Probe*	*Correctly Answered Questions by Type*			*Correct Responses (8)*	*Overall Percentage Correct*
		Recall (3)	*Sequencing (4)*	*Inferential (1)*		
BL	1	1	1	0	3	37.5
BL	2	3	1	0	4	50
BL	3	2	1	0	3	37.5
SM	4	3	2	0	5	62.5
SM	5	2	2	1	5	62.5
SM	6	3	1	0	4	50
SM	7	2	2	0	4	50
SM + CL	8	3	3	0	6	75
SM + CL	9	3	3	1	7	87.5
SM + CL	10	3	4	0	7	87.5
SM + CL	11	3	4	1	8	100
SM + CL	12	2	4	0	6	62.5
SM + CL	13	3	4	1	7	87.5
SM + CL	14	3	4	1	8	100
SM + CL	15	3	3	1	7	87.5
SM + CL	16	3	4	1	8	100
SM + CL	17	3	4	0	7	87.5
SM + CL	18	3	4	0	7	87.5
SM + CL	19	3	4	1	8	100
SM + CL	20	3	4	1	8	100

Note: SM = Story Mapping; CL + Cooperative Learning.

assess her baseline performance. Results from baseline indicated that Sabrina correctly answered an average of 42% of comprehension questions across three different passages (see Table 12.2). This score in addition to other assessments highlighted the need for intervention.

Once intervention began, Sabrina completed 3–4 probes each week in her Tier 2 reading group. Similar to baseline, Mr. Evans calculated the total percentage of correct comprehension questions. Each probe had a total of eight possible comprehension questions. Questions were broken up as follows: three recall questions, four sequencing, and one inferential. Each probe had an accompanying answer key where the type of question was highlighted in a different color to clearly delineate under which category it would fall. Recall questions were highlighted in blue, sequencing in green, and inferential questions in red. Mr. Evans calculated Sabrina's percent correct by taking her correct responses, dividing this number by the total number of possible questions, and multiplying the number by 100. He also tracked the number of correct responses based on the question type to see if there were any patterns in Sabrina's responses.

Mr. Evans remembered learning about the importance of progress monitoring in his graduate classes. He realized that data-based decisions should be made after 3–5 data points. Mr. Evans reviewed his data collection after 4 intervention sessions and calculated an average percentage of 56.25% correct responses for Sabrina. This was similar performance to the other students who were receiving support. Although these data were higher than baseline performance, he wanted even better results for his students. Mr. Evans added an additional component to intervention—story mapping with cooperative learning (i.e., SM + CL). After adding this component, he was pleased to see a positive change in the level and slope of Sabrina's performance (see Figure 12.1).

In addition to assessing potential progress using teacher-designed probes, Sabrina also completed the Maze assessment once every two weeks. This way, Mr. Evans could easily conduct a normative comparison with her peers. In addition to collecting data in his table, Mr. Evans also graphed Sabrina's percentage of correct responses on both CBM and maze assessments so he could get a visual representation of her growth. Although no causal conclusions could be made from this type of graphical design, Mr. Evans could still see a positive trend in Sabrina's performance from baseline to intervention (see Figure 12.1).

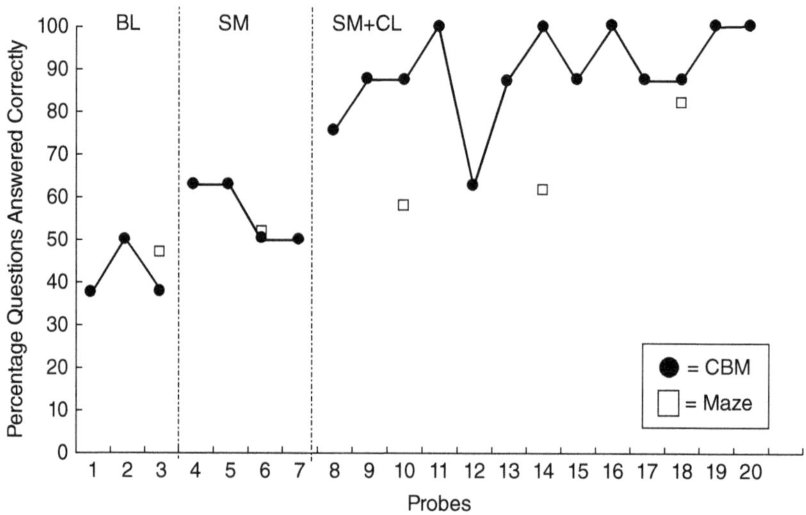

FIGURE 12.1 Sabrina's Percentage of Correct Responses

Intervention Plan

The school psychologist and Mr. Evans decided to provide Tier 2 instruction to four students (including Sabrina) in the use of story mapping. Following baseline, the students received Tier 2 instruction in a small-group setting three days a week during a regularly scheduled intervention period. A *Model-Lead-Test* format was used to introduce the story map to the students. On the first day, the teacher presented the students a copy of the story map (see Appendix A). The teacher explained the purpose of the story map as a helpful strategy that students can use to organize information in a passage and write down different story grammar elements. The teacher then discussed each of the five elements of story grammar: place/setting, who/what, a problem, at least three events that took place, and a solution or main idea. The teacher allowed students to ask questions about the story map and/or the story grammar elements.

The teacher then started each session with pre-reading activities. He probed students for background information or prior experience as it related to the story passage. He then went on to chorally read a story passage with the students and modeled how to complete the story map. He engaged the students by asking questions related to the story grammar elements, such as: "Where did this story take place? Who or what is this story about? Can you recall the events in the story? Do you think there was a problem in this story? What was the solution or the main idea for the story?" The students ended the session by completing their copy of the story maps and comparing their responses to the teacher's version. The teacher repeated the same modeling procedure on Day 2 with a new passage. He ended the session with modeling how to answer the comprehension questions that accompanied the passage.

On Days 3 and 4, the teacher engaged the students in the guided practice of completing the story maps. The students read the passage independently and tried to complete as many elements of the story map as they could. The teacher provided feedback on correct responses and engaged them in a discussion for incorrect or incomplete answers until the students were able to complete the story map. As in Stagliano and Boon (2009), students were encouraged to reread the passage, think aloud, and ask the teacher if they needed assistance or further explanation. After completing the story map, the students completed the comprehension questions with the help of the teacher.

Starting with Day 5, the students engaged in the process independently. Students read the passage, completed the story map and answered comprehension questions. At the end of three weeks of Tier 2 intervention, the teacher realized that students were having trouble with reading the passage independently and were asking each other and the teacher questions to complete the story map. The comprehension data were in the 50–60% accuracy range. After discussing with the school psychologist, the teacher decided to add a cooperative learning component to SM intervention (SM + Cooperative Learning). This added 10 minutes to the total intervention time resulting in 30-minute sessions which fit within the intervention period.

In the SM + Cooperative Learning period, the students continued to read the story independently. They were then encouraged to determine what they believed to be the best answers for the story elements. The teacher then followed a modified version of steps outlined in Mathes et al. (1997). Each week one student assumed the role of the leader for each element of story grammar. For example, if Sabrina was assigned leader for Place/Setting, then the other students assumed the role of leader for Who/What, the Problem, Events, and Main Idea/ Solution. The leader assignments were rotated each week such that each student was the leader for different story elements. Using a prompt card for each story element (see Appendix B), the leaders engaged the group in a cooperative learning session discussing the elements of the story, asking questions of students in the group, and gaining consensus on the answers to the SM elements. Once the students completed the story map, they proceeded to answer the comprehension questions independently.

Intervention Fidelity and Interobserver Agreement Plans

The school psychologist collected intervention fidelity data twice a week during the first two weeks of intervention when the teacher embedded the *Model-Lead-Test* format to train the students to use story mapping (see Appendix C for checklist). Once students started to use the story map independently, the school psychologist assessed intervention fidelity once a week. Percentage fidelity was calculated by calculating the number of steps the teacher completed divided by the total number of steps multiplying by 100. Fidelity was high at 100% for the six steps in Tier 2 intervention (SM) and at 100% for the five steps in the second phase of intervention (SM + Cooperative Learning).

The teacher served as the primary examiner and scored all the comprehension questions. For interrater reliability, the teacher made a copy of students' responses for one session each week and the school psychologist served as the second scorer. Percentage agreement was calculated by dividing the number of agreements by the total agreements and disagreements and multiplying by 100. Interobserver agreement was 100%. One reason for high agreement was because both scorers used the answer key when scoring the responses.

Intervention Outcome Data

Percentage correct responses on CBM comprehension probes. Figure 12.1 provides a visual representation of Sabrina's improvement on overall comprehension from baseline through intervention. When looking at Figure 12.1, intervention consisted of two phases – phase one (SM) included SM alone and phase two (SM + CL) added a cooperative learning phase to SM procedure. Sabrina's mean percentage of correct responses on three baseline probes was approximately 42% (range: 37.5% to 50%). Data were relatively stable at these low levels, which indicated the need to begin intervention. Once Sabrina started receiving intervention using story mapping, her data showed a positive change in level with an average percentage of 56.25% (range: 50% to 62.5%). Despite clear progress, her percentage of correct responses were still below an appropriate level to ensure she could successfully gain meaning from texts. Additionally, based on visual inspection of data, Sabrina's performance appeared to be declining in trend. Thus, the team decided to implement phase two to boost her performance. During phase two, Sabrina made another positive jump in level with an average percentage of 89.4% (range: 62.5% to 100%). Sabrina achieved perfect scores on more than five probes during intervention. Her performance during phase two suggests steady and stable progress on comprehension probes.

Percentage correct responses on maze comprehension probes. Sabrina's progress on bi-weekly maze probes mirrored her performance on CBM probes. When given a baseline maze probe, Sabrina correctly answered 46.4% of the questions. This was a similar result to her average performance on CBM probes. During phase one (SM), Sabrina's progress was limited as noted by the 51.8% correct responses on maze probe 2. Sabrina's attempts were the same as baseline (28) with one fewer incorrect item. As noted in Figure 12.1, her performance on the maze probe was commensurate with her CBM probes during this phase. SM alone was not producing the robust effects necessary for Sabrina to be more successful when comprehending. With the changes made during phase two (SM + CL), Sabrina's third maze probe showed additional improvements in her ability to comprehend with 57.8% correct responses—an increase of 6% over maze probe 2. Again, this maze probe is commensurate with her performance on CBM probes in phase two, as indicated on Figure 12.1. Sabrina's fourth maze probe showed another increase in correct responses, up to 61.4% correct responding. Also, as indicated by data shared in Table 12.3, Sabrina was increasing her overall attempts from 28 attempts in baseline to 35 attempts by maze probe 4. Sabrina's final maze probe showed marked improvement with 81.7% correct responses, increases in attempts (35 to 41),

TABLE 12.3 Sabrina's Data on Maze Progress Monitoring Probes

Phase (week)	*Probe*	*Corrects*	*Incorrects*	*Attempts*	*Adjusted*	*Difference Between Probes*	*Percent Correct (adjusted/ attempts)*
BL (1)	1	18	10	28	13	–	46.4
SM (3)	2	19	9	28	14.5	+1.5	51.8
SM + CL (5)	3	23	9	32	18.5	+4.0	57.8
SM + CL (7)	4	26	9	35	21.5	+3.0	61.4
Sm + CL (9)	5	36	5	41	33.5	+12.0	81.7

Note: SM = Story Mapping; CL = Cooperative Learning.

and a decrease in errors from 10 on the baseline maze probe to 5 on the final maze probe (see Table 12.3). The increase in overall percent correct on maze probes across phase two are commensurate with Sabrina's increasing performance on the CBM probes, as noted in Figure 12.1. Overall, the maze probes provide additional evidence that Sabrina's comprehension skills continued to improve as the SM intervention was boosted with cooperative learning in phase two.

Intervention Acceptability

An adapted version of Lane and Beebe-Frankenberger (2004)'s intervention acceptability forms for teachers and students were completed by Mr. Evans and the four students who participated in the Tier 2 intervention group (Appendix D). Mr. Evans strongly agreed that the SM intervention was effective in improving the comprehension skills of Sabrina and the three students in the small group. He believed that the addition of the cooperative learning component to discuss the elements of a story map was an efficient way to address the difficulty students were having at arriving at the answers on their own. He believed the discussion and the questioning techniques embedded as prompts for the leader of the group provided for the "think-aloud" needed to understand the sequences of events in the story. The students also rated the SM intervention as being easy to use and something that they would use in the future. All but one of the students liked the cooperative learning component added to the SM intervention. Sabrina agreed that the SM intervention improved her grades and made her feel good about herself.

Intervention Considerations

This case study outlines how SM could be utilized to improve reading comprehension for a middle-school student who needed to acquire additional metacognitive strategies. Story mapping has shown to be effective with elementary- and secondary-school students. At the elementary grades, Staal (2000) recommends the use of a Story Face instead of the typical story map graphic organizer. The main distinction between the two is that instead of the boxes seen in a story map, the story elements in a Story Face are arranged in the shape of a face that gives readers a context for the story. For example, the eyes are two circles that represent the setting and main characters, the nose in the shape of a triangle represents the problem, the mouth comprises of a series of circles representing the main events that lead to the solution. The circles for the mouth could be arranged in a lower arc for a happy face or an upward arc for a sad face depending on the overall theme of the story.

The SM strategy, as outlined in this chapter, illustrates use of a story map that requires students to fill in the details by handwriting the information onto a story map. However, there are an increasing number of school districts that have rolled out 1:1 devices to students. Especially at the middle- and high-school levels, teachers can consider using electronic formats of story maps so that students can directly enter the information on their laptop computers. Sharing the story maps with the teachers with cloud-sharing capabilities makes it an efficient way to receive teacher feedback. It also provides a space for storage for future review.

Although story mapping is often associated with narrative texts in Language Arts classes, it can also be integrated into other subject areas such as science and mathematics to support student comprehension. For example, teachers can use story maps to help students work through complicated multistep math problems. Story maps can help guide students in selecting the appropriate mathematical operation to use with different word problems that require higher level problem solving (Xin et al., 2008). Similar to mathematics, story maps can help students in Science classes to gain further understanding of complex processes (i.e., the water cycle) or capturing changes in phenomena over time. Across many different subject areas, story mapping can be a useful tool to support student learning.

Conclusion

SM is an effective strategy to increase students' comprehension skills at the elementary, middle, and high school levels. Sabrina's case study illustrates how SM can be used to improve the comprehension skills of a middle-school student with grade-level decoding ability but had difficulty with understanding the story details. Using curriculum-based measures, the school psychologist and teacher were able to select an intervention that best suited Sabrina's need to have a more systematic way to process the information in the text passages. Based on her scores on the comprehension probes, they were able to modify the SM intervention by adding the cooperative learning component. Although SM was implemented in a small group in this case study, teachers can consider thinking along the lines of universal design for learning and introduce SM to all students in their classes.

Appendix A: The Story Map

Story or Passage Title: ________________________________

Setting/Place

Who/What

Problem

Events (in order)

1. ____

____

2. ____

____

3. ____

____

____

4. ____

____

⬇

Solution/ Main Idea

Appendix B: Example of a Prompt Card for Leader

PROMPT CARD FOR SETTING/PLACE

Share: I think the Setting/Place for this passage is ____________ __________________because (point to the answer in the passage and read it for your group).

Ask: What did you write for Setting/Place? What is your evidence?

Discuss: *If your answers are the same, then move to next step. If your answers are different, then say* "Let's discuss the answers and decide on group's answer."

Record: I'm going to write ______________in the Setting/Place on the story map.

Report: Our group agreed the Setting/ Place for this passage was ________________

Appendix C: Intervention Fidelity Checklist – Story Mapping Intervention

Date: ____________________ Passage: ____________________

Step	*Procedure*			*Completed (Circle One)*
1	Prereading activity. Teacher engaged students in a discussion on background information or prior experience on topic of passage			Yes No
2	Reading story. Teacher reads the passage chorally with the students (during training phase) OR teacher allows students to read passage independently			Yes No
Use of Story Map				
	Model	**Lead**	**Independent (Test)**	
3	Teacher reviews each story element and thinks aloud the answers	Teacher reviews each story element and elicits students' response	Teacher allows students to respond to each story element	Yes No
4	Teacher models writing responses on story map	Teacher models writing responses along with students	Teacher allows students to write responses independently	Yes No
5	Teacher checks students' work on story map	Teacher checks students' work on story map	Teacher checks students' work on story map	Yes No
6	Recapitulates story details by walking through completed story map	Recapitulates story details by walking through completed story map	Recapitulates story details by walking through completed story map	Yes No
7	Administers comprehension probe			Yes No
Cooperative Story Mapping				
8	Teacher encourages students to take out their prompt cards and get started with discussing each of the story elements.			Yes No
9	Once students complete story maps, teacher recapitulates story details by walking through completed story map. (Provides corrective feedback as needed).			Yes No
10	Administers comprehension probe			Yes No
	Percentage integrity for SM (Tier 2) = steps completed (steps 1–7) /7 x 100			
	Percentage integrity for Cooperative SM (Tier 2b) = steps completed (steps 1 and 2) + (steps 8, 9, 10) /5 x 100			

Appendix D: Intervention Acceptability – Teacher Form

Please indicate the extent to which you agree or disagree with each statement below by circling the appropriate number.

	Strongly Disagree	*Disagree*	*Neutral*	*Agree*	*Strongly Agree*
The Story Mapping intervention:					
1. Fit into my regular schedule	1	2	3	4	5
2. Supplemented my current classroom interventions	1	2	3	4	5
3. Taught important skills	1	2	3	4	5
4. Was a fair way to handle the problem	1	2	3	4	5
5. Was suitable given the classroom culture	1	2	3	4	5
6. Will have lasting positive effects	1	2	3	4	5
7. Is one I will use again when needed	1	2	3	4	5
8. Is one I will permit to continue if taught by someone else	1	2	3	4	5
9. Is one I will recommend to others	1	2	3	4	5
10. In your opinion, rate the effectiveness of the intervention for:	Not at all Effective	Somewhat Effective	Neutral	Moderately Effective	Very Effective
Student 1	1	2	3	4	5
Student 2	1	2	3	4	5
Student 3	1	2	3	4	5
Student 4	1	2	3	4	5

Open-ended comments (if any):

Intervention Acceptability – Student Form

Please indicate the extent to which you agree or disagree with each statement below by circling the appropriate number.

	Strongly Disagree	*Disagree*	*Neutral*	*Agree*	*Strongly Agree*
The Story Mapping intervention:					
1. Was easy for me to stick with	1	2	3	4	5
2. Taught me important skills	1	2	3	4	5

		Strongly Disagree	*Disagree*	*Neutral*	*Agree*	*Strongly Agree*
3.	Helped me with my passage comprehension	1	2	3	4	5
4.	Quickly improved my skill	1	2	3	4	5
5.	Made a difference in my grades	1	2	3	4	5
6.	Helped me feel better about myself	1	2	3	4	5
7.	Is one I will use again when needed	1	2	3	4	5
8.	Is one I will tell other kids about	1	2	3	4	5
9.	Was better with the cooperative learning group	1	2	3	4	5
10.	Anything else you want to tell us about story mapping or the cooperative learning group?					

References

Boon, R. T., Paal, M., Hintz, A., & Cornelius-Freyre, M. (2015). A review of story mapping instruction for secondary students with LD. *Learning Disabilities: A Contemporary Journal*, *13*, 117–140.

Boulineau, T., Fore III, C., Hagan-Burke, S., & Burke, M. D. (2004). Use of story-mapping to increase the story-grammar text comprehension of elementary students with learning disabilities. *Learning Disabilities Quarterly*, *27*, 105–121.

Davis, Z. T. (1994). Effects of prereading story-mapping on elementary readers' comprehension. *Journal of Educational Research*, *87*, 353–360.

Dimino, J., Gersten, R., Carnine, D., & Blake, G. (1990). Story grammar: An approach for promoting at-risk secondary students' comprehension of literature. *The Elementary School Journal*, *91*, 19–32.

Gardill, M. C., & Jitendra, A. K. (1999). Advanced story-map instruction: Effects on the reading comprehension of students with learning disabilities. *The Journal of Special Education*, *33*, 2–17.

Gurney, D., Gersten, R., Dimino, J., & Carnine, D. (1990). Story grammar: Effective literature instruction for high school students with learning disabilities. *Journal of Learning Disabilities*, *23*, 335–343.

Idol, L., & Croll, V. J. (1987). Story-mapping training as a means of improving reading comprehension. *Learning Disability Quarterly*, *10*, 214–229.

Kamil, M. L., Borman, G. D., Dole, J., Kral, C. C., Salinger, T., & Torgesen, J. (2008). *Improving adolescent literacy: Effective classroom and intervention practices: A practice guide* (NCEE #2008-4027). Washington, DC: National Center for Education Evaluation and Regional Assistance, Institute of Education Sciences, U.S. Department of Education. Retrieved from https://ies.ed.gov/ncee/wwc/PracticeGuides

Lane, K. L., & Beebe-Frankenberger, M. E. (2004). *School-based interventions: The tools you need to succeed*. Boston: Allyn and Bacon.

Mathes, P. G., Fuchs, D., & Fuchs, L. S. (1997). Cooperative story mapping. *Remedial and Special Education*, *18*, 20–27.

National Reading Panel. (2000). *Report of the National Reading Panel – Teaching children to read: An evidence-based assessment of the scientific research literature on reading and its implications for reading instruction (report of the subgroups)*. Washington, DC: National Institute of Child Health and Human Development.

Staal, L. A. (2000). The story face: An adaptation of story mapping that incorporates visualization and discovery learning to enhance reading and writing. *The Reading Teacher*, *54*, 26–31.

Stagliano, C., & Boon, R. T. (2009). The effects of a story-mapping procedure to improve the comprehension skills of expository text passages for elementary students with learning disabilities. *Learning Disabilities: A Contemporary Journal*, *7*, 35–58.

Taylor, L. K., Alber, S. R., & Walker, D. W. (2002). The comparative effects of a modified self questioning strategy and story-mapping on the reading comprehension of elementary students with learning disabilities. *Journal of Behavioral Education*, *11*(2), 69–87.

University of Oregon. (2020). *8th Edition of Dynamic Indicators of Basic Early Literacy Skills* (DIBELS®). Eugene, OR: University of Oregon. Retrieved from https://dibels.uoregon.edu

Xin, Y. P., Wiles, B., & Lin, Y. Y. (2008). Teaching conceptual model—Based word problem story grammar to enhance mathematics problem solving. *The Journal of Special Education*, *42*(3), 163–178.

13

KNOW-WANT TO KNOW-LEARN

Mary E. Tusing

University of Wisconsin-Eau Claire, Eau Claire, WI, USA

Brian Orr

Communication Sciences and Disorders, University of Wisconsin-Eau Claire, Eau Claire, WI, USA

Angela Stokes

Eleva-Strum School District, Eleva, WI, USA

Introduction

The ability to comprehend and make meaning from written text is an essential skill and the primary goal of reading instruction. Classroom teachers spend a good deal of time planning instruction to support growth in students' literacy skills. Unfortunately, the most recent National Assessment of Education Progress (NAEP; National Center for Educational Statistics, 2022) data show significant stagnation in the literacy skills of our nation's youth, with one in three 4th-grade students lacking the reading comprehension skills necessary for college and career readiness. Many believe the COVID-19 pandemic has only exacerbated these longstanding deficits. School-based literacy teams need effective strategies for using reading data to design effective classwide and small-group interventions that support reading comprehension skills. In this chapter, we illustrate how one school team used the Know-Want to Know-Learn (K-W-L) comprehension strategy (Ogle, 1986) in a systematic, classwide intervention involving informational text linked to the science curriculum to address the reading needs of its 5th graders. First, we provide a brief overview of the RAND model of reading comprehension to illustrate the myriad factors influencing proficiency in reading comprehension, particularly the comprehension of informational text. Then, we describe K-W-L, its application, evidence base, and suitability for integrated literacy instruction within content-area learning.

DOI: 10.4324/9781003275749-13

RAND Model for Reading Comprehension

For older students, the ability to understand, make meaning, and learn from different types of reading material is influenced by a complex set of factors (Castles et al., 2018; Catts & Kamhi, 2014; Leach, Scarborough, & Rescorla, 2003; Oakhill et al., 2019). The RAND Reading Study Group's (2002) reading comprehension model is a useful framework for school-based teams planning literacy instruction. According to the RAND model, reading comprehension depends upon the dynamic interactions among variables in three primary dimensions: the *reader* who is doing the comprehending, the *text* that is to be comprehended, and the *activity* in which comprehension is a part. For example, each student in a classroom brings a unique set of cognitive skills (e.g., attention, memory, reasoning), language abilities, psychological attributes (e.g., motivation, interests, self-efficacy as a reader), and knowledge sources (e.g., vocabulary, topic, comprehension strategies) to the task of reading to learn. Of primary importance is the reciprocal relationship between students' background knowledge and their ability to understand and use what they read (Elleman et al., 2022; Kendeou et al., 2016). This is especially true for informational texts in content-areas like science, history, and social studies (Wexler, 2019). Prior knowledge allows students to make inferences necessary to fill in missing information not explicitly stated in the text. It also acts as a scaffold for students to make more robust and meaningful connections across their learning. Importantly, instructional practices that assist students in activating their background knowledge and vocabulary before reading are positively associated with enhanced learning (Cervetti & Wright, 2020; Gajria et al., 2007; Wanzek et al., 2010).

Regarding text and activity, texts vary in difficulty based on several factors (e.g., genre, subject matter, language complexity, text structure) and reading activities have a variety of instructional purposes, such as acquiring knowledge or evaluating an argument, that happen in different learning contexts. Informational texts, the primary genre for content-area instruction in later grades, are typically more challenging for students to comprehend because of the variability and complexity of their structure, their use of content-specific knowledge and vocabulary, and the reasoning and thinking demands they place on the reader (Best et al., 2008; Oudega & van den Broek, 2018). As noted, activities that strategically activate prior knowledge can help students better understand what they read. Unfortunately, activation strategies are of limited benefit when students have poor background knowledge to begin with (Catts, 2022: Cervetti & Wright, 2020; Compton et al., 2014), a challenge that may disproportionally impact students from culturally and linguistically diverse backgrounds. The importance of building student background knowledge to support comprehension is a key reason why the Common Core State Standards (2010) call for having students read widely and deeply. However, knowing how to engage with texts for different learning purposes also involves skills that often need to be taught explicitly (Duke & Martin, 2015). An integrated approach to literacy instruction leverages the reciprocal relationship between reading comprehension and background knowledge by embedding implicit comprehension instruction within content area study (Cervetti & Wright, 2020; Guthrie et al., 2004; Wexler, 2019). Integrated approaches have been found to boost reading comprehension abilities, vocabulary, and content-area learning more effectively than teaching content and skills in isolation (Catts, 2022; Hwang et al., 2023).

Know-Want to Know-Learn

Donna Ogle's (1986) Know-Want to Know-Learn (K-W-L) and K-W-L Plus (Carr & Ogle, 1987) framework is a longstanding set of reading comprehension strategies often employed with content-area reading. It is well suited for integrated literacy instruction because it teaches students how to build and refine content-area knowledge by practicing research-based reading comprehension strategies. It uses a graphic organizer to teach students steps for activating prior knowledge before reading, setting a purpose for reading, and reflecting on what they have read (see Figure 13.1). Key to K-W-L's utility is that it provides educators with a mental frame of the interactions among the reader, text, and activity dimensions of comprehension and how the dimensions vary based on the phase of reading (before, during, after). Typically, educators first guide students in K-W-L through explicit modeling. In the 'what do we Know' step, teachers have students discuss what they know about the text's topic. Their primary role is to model specific questioning that activates text-relevant background knowledge. For example, students can think about categories of information they expect to learn in the text or how the information is likely to be organized (e.g., text structure). During 'what do we Want to know' step, students establish purposes for reading a specific text by generating a set of questions they need and want to have answered. The 'what did we Learn' step has students strategically read and reflect on the information in the text. Students are taught to take notes on the reading by focusing on how it answers their pre-selected questions, noting new information germane to the subject area, and considering what they still need to learn about the topic. Finally, students use their K-W-L chart to produce a written summary of what they have learned.

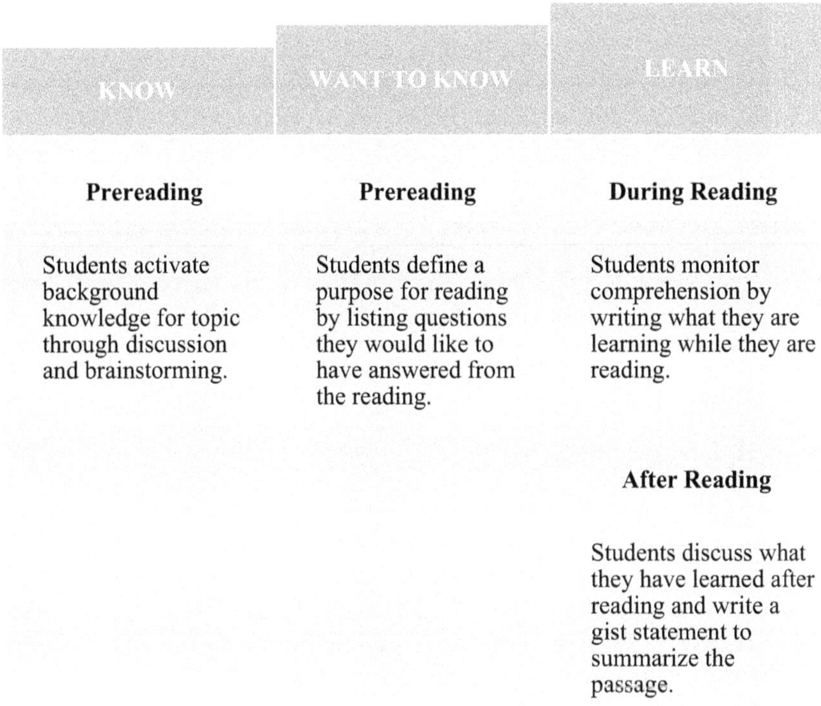

FIGURE 13.1 Steps for completion of K-W-L

K-W-L has been extensively referenced in peer-reviewed journals, trade publications, and academic textbooks (Alsalhi, 2020; Greenwood, 2019; Hilden & Jones, 2012; Jared & Jared, 1997; McAllister, 1994; Ogle, 2009; Spor & Schneider, 1999; Telaumbanua, 2019). Ogle's (1986, 1989; Carr & Ogle, 1987) original articles have been cited over 2,500 times, not including citations from international publications. Despite this ubiquity, there is a surprising paucity of empirical research directly assessing the effects of the K-W-L procedure on reading comprehension in K-12 classrooms (Hattan, 2019; Hattan & Lupo, 2020; Lupo et al., 2019; Stahl, 2008). Further, the many variations and adaptations of K-W-L described in professional publications (e.g., TWL: Akerson, 2001; KWWL: Bryan, 1998; KWL-THC: Crowther & Cannon, 2004; KWHHL: Szabo, 2006; KNL: Wallach et al., 2014; KLEW: Hershberger et al., 2006) make it difficult to synthesize the different levels of evidence for the purpose of forming a consensus regarding K-W-L's effectiveness. Instead, support for the use of K-W-L as a tool to teach reading comprehension skills stems from its consistency with current understandings of how reader, text, and activity factors interact during the reading process and its inclusion of a variety of instructional practices shown to positively influence reading comprehension such as knowledge activation, setting purposes, and comprehension monitoring (Duke & Martin, 2015; Edmonds et al., 2009; Kendeou et al., 2014; Pao & Williams, 2015; Scammacca et al., 2007). As with all local uses of research-based educational practices, evidence for the effectiveness of a program is best substantiated through purposeful methods of formative assessment that are regularly reviewed and acted upon to promote desired reading outcomes (Riley-Tillman, Burns, & Gibbons, 2013).

Case Study

Background Information

During data review meetings after the fall benchmarking period, 5th-grade teachers at Madison Elementary expressed concern that more than half (57%) of students performed below benchmark on the Star Reading (Renaissance Learning, 2020) assessment, which primarily focuses on reading comprehension. Teachers were challenged by the number of students who appeared to need additional support given that school resources for targeted small-group intervention in upper grades were limited. The literacy coach and school psychologist participate in all grade-level data reviews and had anticipated increased academic needs following pandemic-related school closures and the school's need to use virtual learning formats throughout much of the previous year. The literacy coach, Ms. Bryan, and the school psychologist, Mr. Nagle, had researched potential support strategies, including classwide intervention approaches (Burns et al., 2016). During a collaborative team meeting with the 5th-grade team, Ms. Bryan discussed the benefits of classwide intervention (e.g., reaching a large portion of students, reducing the number of students needing Tier 2 intervention, and improving content-area reading comprehension; Preast et al., 2019). The teachers were open to learning more about classwide approaches and agreed to do more collaborative problem-solving to determine their classes' needs.

Madison is part of a rural K-12 school district in a midwestern state. The school enrolls 330 students overall and 45% of those students qualify for free and reduced lunch. Given regional employment opportunities, the school has recently seen enrollment growth in the number of Latinx students (12%). There are two 5th-grade teachers, Mr. Bishop and Mrs. Cook, both of whom have over 15 years of teaching experience. For the past three years, the school has focused professional development efforts on the science of reading. Both 5th-grade teachers were Language Essentials for Teachers of Reading and Spelling (LETRS; Lexia LETRS, n.d.) trained. Madison was also in its third year of using EL (EL Education, n.d.) for English Language Arts instruction. In 5th grade, EL employs a two-hour literacy block to support reading fluency and comprehension development, language usage and mechanics, writing practice, and word study/vocabulary. Explicit instruction on close reading for informational texts is embedded in daily lessons and prompts students to read informational text in small chunks, think about the gist, use strategies to find the meaning of unknown words, and ask and find answers to questions about the text. Empower Reading (SickKids, n.d.) was the main Tier 3 intervention for older students; its primary focus is reading decoding and spelling.

Problem Identification

There were 24 5th graders in each class and only 41% of them scored at benchmark (i.e., 40th percentile) or higher on the fall Star Reading screener. This was significantly below the standard Multi-Level Systems of Support (MLSS) goal of having 80% of students at benchmark (Christ & Aranas, 2014). Further, the number of 5th graders needing additional reading support had increased by 20% relative to the previous year's class (see Figure 13.2). This notable difference made the 5th-grade needs more poignant and placed a greater burden on classroom teachers.

Problem Analysis

Ms. Bryan and Mr. Nagle hypothesized that the 5th-grade reading needs represented a classwide difficulty. Following strategies defined by Burns et al. (2015), they calculated the median Star Reading score for each class and compared the median to the benchmark standard. Each class's median was below the benchmark score of 555 (i.e., 40th percentile) confirming that a classwide approach would likely be the most efficient way to address students' needs. They also examined the distribution of 5th graders' screening scores more closely to better appreciate the severity of the group's needs. Most students not at benchmark on Star Reading at the beginning of 5th grade scored in the 'intervention' (i.e., 11th–25th percentile) range or higher, suggesting moderate reading risk. The group showed similar patterns of need at the end of 4th grade. The number of students in the 'urgent intervention' (i.e., below 10th percentile) category had not changed relative to 4th grade. These students were already known to teachers and had started more intensive intervention because of their IEP or English Learner needs.

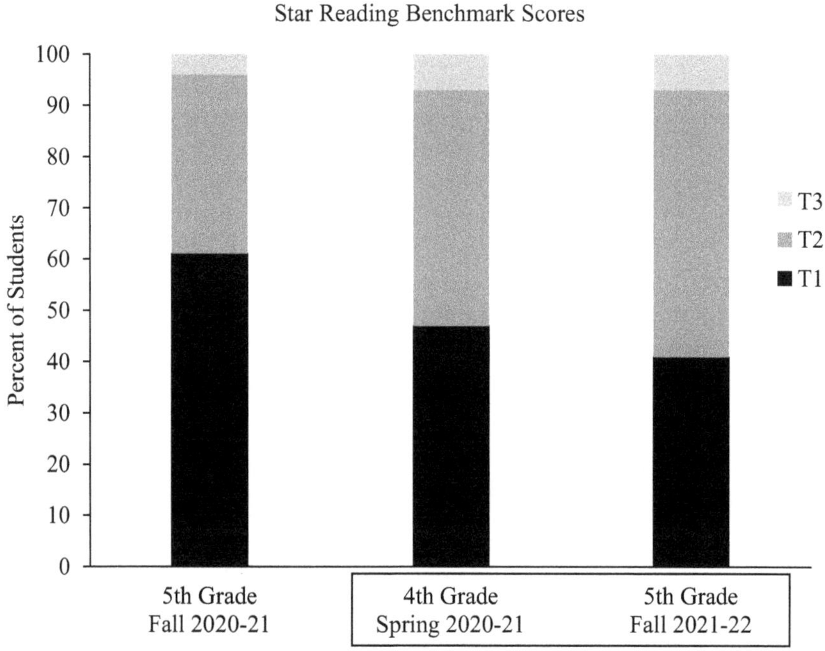

FIGURE 13.2 Longitudinal grade-wide benchmark reading scores

Given trends in the Star Reading data, Ms. Bryan believed the classwide intervention target should be comprehension. However, she agreed with Mr. Nagle that ruling out reading fluency as a primary factor in student performance was an important consideration. They collaborated to complete oral reading fluency (ORF) screeners with all 5th graders. Except for the Tier 3 students, most 5th graders had oral reading fluency scores at or above 110 WCPM. Further, classwide median scores were 131 and 127 WCPM. Reading guidance (Denton et al., 2012) suggests that an appropriate fluency target for older readers is 100–125 WCPM in grade-level material. Thus, classwide fluency data confirmed that reading fluency wasn't a primary concern for most 5th graders. Considering these data and the fact that the EL curriculum provided daily fluency practice anyway, Mr. Nagle and Ms. Bryan agreed it would be best to talk with the 5th-grade team about classwide strategies to support their students' reading comprehension.

At the next 5th-grade team meeting, Mrs. Cook and Mr. Bishop agreed that their students needed reading comprehension support. The considerable loss of instructional time the previous year meant that students had not consistently received comprehension instruction embedded in the EL curriculum. Ms. Bryan described K-W-L as a possible classwide intervention. She believed K-W-L was a good fit for the 5th-grade reading needs because it provided explicit teaching and practice with research-based strategies known to support comprehension, specifically activating background knowledge and vocabulary before reading and purposefully making connections between old and new learning after reading. Teachers had familiarity with K-W-L and saw that it complimented the "notice and wonder" strategies at the beginning of each EL module. However, they had reservations about giving up ELA time for an activity that was not a part of the curriculum. Given the lost instruction time that also occurred in science in social studies the prior year, the team brainstormed that increased reading practice in those subject areas might not only help reading but could also build students' content knowledge and vocabulary.

Measurement of Target Reading Skill, Data Collection Strategies, Progress Monitoring

Matching progress monitoring assessments to reading comprehension interventions is challenging because measures vary in their sensitivity to the complex array of reading comprehension skills that can be targeted in an intervention. They also vary in their focus on narrative versus informational text structures (Carlson, Seipel, & McMaster, 2014). The Madison teachers needed efficiently administered weekly assessments that would be sensitive enough to detect desired improvements in students' comprehension of informational texts following K-W-L practice. While an important marker of the overall reading health of 5th graders at the school, Star Reading was ruled out because it could only be given every two weeks and did not consistently include informational text. Taking these factors into consideration, Mr. Nagle brought three types of curriculum-based measurements to the 5th-grade team for consideration: maze (Shin, Deno, & Espin, 2000), reading comprehension rate (Neddenriep et al., 2007), and vocabulary-matching (Espin & Foegen, 1996) assessments. After review, the team agreed to use weekly maze assessments because reading comprehension rate and vocabulary-matching measures were more time-intensive in preparation. In addition, the maze assessments could be matched to the science concepts in passages that would be used for K-W-L practice.

The 5th-grade team decided to have students practice K-W-L with science readings. Like Preast et al. (2019), Ms. Bryan created maze passages for progress monitoring using free materials from ReadWorks.org. She selected informational passages related to the upcoming science unit on ecosystems. To ensure that the passages would be similar in difficulty level, she chose readings with Lexile ratings between 900–980. Mr. Nagle converted the passages to maze assessments using an online maze passage generator (http://www.interventioncentral.org/teacher-resources/test-of-reading-comprehension). Each passage was at least 300 words in length. When converted to a maze assessment, every seventh word in the passage was replaced with an array of three words. Only one of the words was correct for the context of the passage. Students were to select the correct word that fit in the sentence. Mr. Nagle modeled how to administer the three-minute probes by completing baseline maze assessments in each classroom the week before intervention. Teachers then completed maze assessments every Thursday during the intervention period. Mr. Nagle scored weekly assessments, calculated each class's median word selections (WS) score, and provided teachers with classwide graphs and student-level data for Friday collaboration meetings.

In addition to maze passages, Mr. Nagle suggested that the team also consider teacher-completed goal attainment scales (GAS) to monitor students' ability to apply the K-W-L technique. According to Roach and Elliott (2005), GAS serves as a criterion-referenced measure that, when defined to reflect baseline performance and desired work quality, can be sensitive to growth in academic performance. Mr. Nagle saw that GAS could provide teachers with an agreed-upon scoring rubric to monitor the desired outcomes for student-generated K-W-L charts. After reviewing several GAS examples, the school psychologist and teachers co-constructed GAS scales. First, they had to clarify the learning targets of the K-W-Ls and what they wanted to see in student work. They identified two key targets: references to science knowledge and concepts and use of science vocabulary. These targets were chosen with the hypothesis that strategic reading of science passages would grow students' content-specific background knowledge and science vocabulary. Thus, as K-W-L practice progressed, the knowledge students activated before reading and the connections made while reading should be reflected in K-W-L entries that had increased references to science concepts and terms. To practice GAS, each teacher scored their own and their colleagues' students' first K-W-L worksheets. Mr. Nagle assisted them in reviewing their scoring consistency. Inconsistencies were discussed and the GAS was refined (see Figure 13.3). Teachers then used the GAS scale to score and graph the K-W-Ls student dyads produced each week. The percent of students achieving scores of +2 was also calculated and graphed.

Intervention Plan

First, materials were needed for the K-W-L intervention. For informational passages, teachers agreed to use readings from the EL Life Science Module for whole class K-W-L instruction. For students' K-W-L practice with

K-W-L GAS Rubric

Student Partners: <u>Gael and Aislyn</u> **Teacher:** <u>Cook</u>

Goal: Students will activate science background knowledge before reading.
Target: K and W column entries reference science unit topics.
Examples: conservation of energy, organisms interact in ecosystems, ecosystems cycle energy, balanced ecosystems are healthy

GAS Rating: SCIENCE CONCEPT References													
+2	> 60% reference science concepts										X	X	
+1	50% reference science concepts					X	X		X	X			X
0	30% reference science concepts			X	X			X					
-1	< 30% reference science concepts	X	X										
-2	no reference to science concepts												
	Date:												

Goal: Students will use science vocabulary before and after reading.
Target: K and column entries and gist include science vocabulary.
Examples: ecosystem, matter (solid, liquid, gas), energy, photosynthesis, producer, decomposer, consumer, food web, boreal/temperate/tropical forest, estuaries, biodiversity

GAS Rating: VOCABULARY References													
+2	5+ different vocabulary words												
+1	3-4 different vocabulary words						X	X	X	X	X	X	X
0	2 different vocabulary words		X	X	X	X							
-1	1 vocabulary word	X											
-2	no vocabulary words												
	Date:												

FIGURE 13.3 Goal attainment scale for K-W-L worksheets completed by students

independent reading, Ms. Bryan selected informational passages from ReadWorks.org that were related to the science unit. Lexiles for the passages ranged from 750–1020, which was consistent with suggested text complexity bands for 5th grade (Common Core Standards Initiative, 2010). Topics included ecosystems in forests, rainforests, estuaries, and oceans; food webs and living environments of insects and animals; and the impacts of acid rain. Teachers agreed that the passages expanded on topics covered in the science unit. A review of the readings showed they included many vocabulary words germane to the science unit. Most passages were 200 to 500 words in length. They were organized in paragraph form and either pictures or charts of supporting information. Ms. Bryan also created a K-W-L worksheet for students to record responses to pre-reading, during-reading, and post-reading comprehension prompts (see Appendix A).

Next, support staff and the 5th-grade team planned the intervention steps collaboratively. Ms. Bryan provided teachers with coaching on how to use K-W-L as a comprehension strategy. She emphasized the importance of the pre-reading, during-reading, and after-reading components of K-W-L and their connection to evidence-based strategies for comprehension instruction. Then she modeled the key steps of K-W-L with a selected science passage and the K-W-L worksheet (see Appendix B). Teachers anticipated how students might respond. Using ideas from other K-W-L resources found through a Google search, strategies in the EL curriculum, and their own experience, they discussed methods for eliciting student discussion for each K-W-L phase. Mr. Bishop and Mrs. Cook wanted students to do more with the Learned column for the K-W-L, so they added the requirement that students write a one-sentence summary of the reading (Carr & Ogle, 1987). To be consistent with the language arts curriculum, they referred to the summary statement as the 'gist' of the reading.

Teachers agreed to have students practice K-W-L for 30 minutes, four times per week during the upcoming month-long science block. To form reading partner dyads, student scores on Star Reading were ordered from highest to lowest and divided in half. The top student in the top half of the class was paired with the top student in the bottom half of the group, the second highest with the second highest, and so on (Burns et al., 2016). Mr. Nagle's practicum student made K-W-L binders for each student including science passages, K-W-L worksheets and directions, and weekly maze assessments. Materials were organized to minimize daily class transitions and provide quick access to work products for progress monitoring. Mrs. Cook and Mr. Bishop had the K-W-L activities mirror existing classroom routines in the ELA block so behavior expectations would be clear. Before the initial K-W-L whole-group lesson, Mrs. Cook and Mr. Bishop first talked with students about the purpose of the K-W-L strategy and their expectations for student learning. They let the students know that they would practice K-W-L strategies during science. Then, they defined what the letters K-W-L stood for and showed students a completed K-W-L. Teachers let students see how K-W-L added to reading strategies that they practiced during ELA. Mrs. Cook and Mr. Bishop expressed confidence in the students' ability to learn how to use K-W-L and let them know that their goal was for all 5th-graders to improve their weekly maze scores and their next Star Reading score through this targeted reading practice.

During a whole-group lesson on Monday of each week, teachers modeled K-W-L with students, including questioning and writing information on the worksheet. For the remaining three days of the week, students practiced doing K-W-Ls in pairs. They were to complete three additional science readings per week. Reading partners took turns being the recorder and writing information on the K-W-L worksheet. For the Learned column, students read each paragraph of a passage to themselves. Then, they stopped to discuss what they learned and what to write on the K-W-L worksheet. After reading, they reviewed the Learned column and together wrote a 'gist' statement for the passage. To support implementation, Mr. Nagle or Mrs. Bryan monitored K-W-L partner work once per week. This gave teachers time to score completed K-W-L worksheets using the GAS rubric. To build in corrective feedback at the beginning stages of group K-W-L practice, teachers showed students an exemplar from completed worksheets and highlighted why it was a strong K-W-L. During collaboration time, teachers reviewed GAS rubric scores and maze graphs and used the data to plan teaching points for the following week's whole group K-W-L practice.

Intervention Fidelity and Interobserver Agreement Plans

Because he recognized that using intervention scripts can improve treatment integrity and intervention outcomes (Hawkins et al., 2008), Mr. Nagle took notes throughout intervention planning and incorporated them into a step-by-step K-W-L checklist (see Appendix B) for the team. Mrs. Cook and Mr. Bishop reviewed the checklist and found it acceptable. Ms. Bryan observed K-W-L time in each class on the first day of implementation. Both teachers completed 100% of the steps on the K-W-L checklist. On the subsequent days, Mr. Nagle and Ms. Bryan noted the quality of classwide academic engagement when they monitored partner work during the intervention. Teachers agreed with their observations that students were actively engaged with the K-W-L practice. At the next collaboration meeting, the team reviewed students' K-W-L charts and GAS scores. In Mrs. Cook's class, 97% of the students correctly completed K-W-L charts for the two readings for the week; 99% of Mr. Bishop's students had correctly completed charts. Correct completion was defined as writing relevant information in each chart column.

Given strong fidelity to K-W-L procedures in the first week and recognition that high-stakes decisions were not being made from the data, the team agreed that teacher report on their own adherence to K-W-L procedures would be an adequate ongoing marker of implementation fidelity. Mr. Nagle also provided teachers with an Intervention Log (see Appendix C) to record relevant details for each day with the recognition that their own self-monitoring would likely support intervention fidelity (Roach & Elliott, 2008). Last, student work products and the teacher-completed GAS rubrics provided natural secondary measures of intervention fidelity.

Intervention Outcome Data and Summary of Effects Relative to Stated Goals

Visual analysis of weekly class median maze scores (see Figure 13.4) showed positive upward trends following baseline, suggesting positive gains in students' comprehension of informational text. Mr. Nagle assisted the team in contextualizing the data further. Because the maze passages were developed from ReadWorks.org readings, specific norms for performance did not exist. Mr. Nagle referenced previous research that suggested 18 correct word selections (WS) within the 3-minute assessment was a meaningful fall benchmark (Graney et al., 2009). 5th-graders in a similar classwide intervention had baseline scores ranging from 4 to 17 WS when reading informational text (see Preast et al., 2019). Madison's 5th-grade data were similar. The median baseline WS for each class was below fall benchmark expectations. After one month of K-W-L practice, Mr. Bishop's class's median maze score exceeded the fall benchmark and Mrs. Cook's class approached it. The mean rate of improvement for Mr. Bishop's class was 2.12 and Mrs. Cook's was 1.89. Both classes showed accelerated rates of growth relative to typical expectations (see Graney et al., 2009).

Visual analysis of session-by-session gains in K-W-L GAS scores also showed positive upward trends. Teachers first noted an immediate increase in the percentage of students earning GAS scores of +1 in each class for both

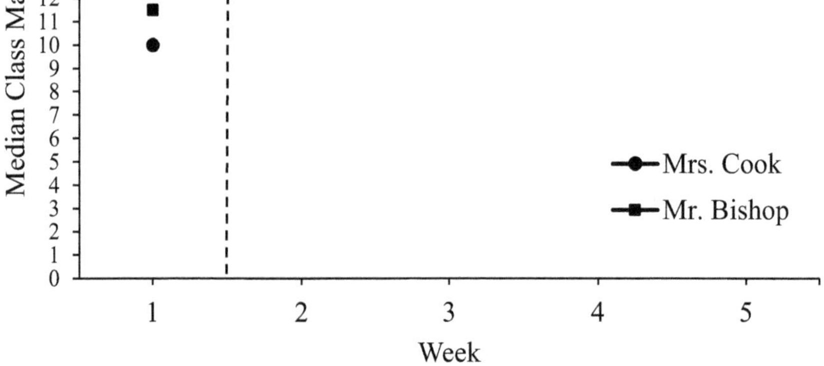

FIGURE 13.4 5th-grade classwide Maze data

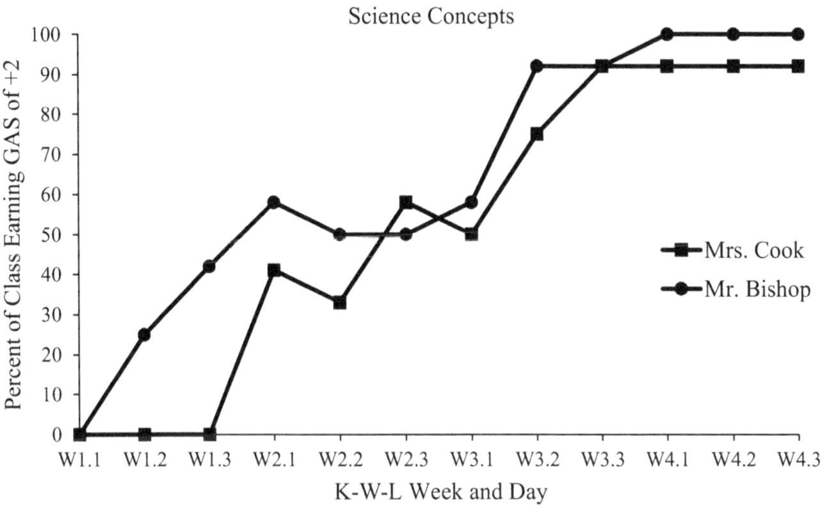

FIGURE 13.5 5th-grade Science Concepts GAS data

references to science concepts and science vocabulary use. Because none of Mrs. Cook's students earned +2 GAS scores on either target during week one, she provided more explicit modeling of how to use science concepts and vocabulary in K-W-L statements in the following Monday's lesson. Ms. Bryan also joined her for the lesson and both teachers provided corrective feedback on the student's K-W-L's to reinforce how to earn a score of +2. By week two, the percentage of students earning +2 for references to science concepts in both classes was gradual and followed a steady trend upward. Each class met the goal of having 90% of students achieve GAS scores of +2 for science concepts by the 4th week of intervention (see Figure 13.5). This means that students consistently referenced science concepts germane to the science unit over 60% of the time when activating background knowledge (K) and identifying their purposes for reading (W) on the K-W-L chart.

The 90% goal for science vocabulary was not met by either class (see Figure 13.6). However, there was a positive and steady trend upward for +1 GAS scores. The team was pleased with this growth and concluded that the 5+ word target for a GAS +2 score may have been too steep relative to the number of different science vocabulary terms prompted in the K-W-L passages. Positively, 100% of students in both classes earned +1 GAS scores or higher by the end of intervention. Considered together, the team determined the K-W-L classwide intervention was successful. They saw it as an effective way to boost students' reading comprehension skills after pandemic-related gaps in educational opportunities for students at their school.

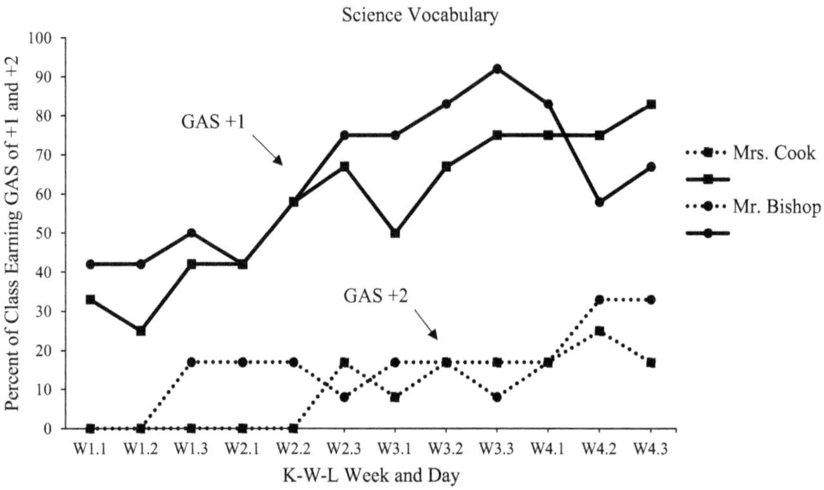

FIGURE 13.6 5th-grade Science Vocabulary GAS data

Intervention Acceptability

Collaborative discussions at team meetings provided informal data on teacher acceptability for the classwide intervention. After four weeks of intervention, Mr. Nagle asked teachers to reflect on the intervention's feasibility in terms of time and materials, acceptability, and effectiveness (Hawkins, et al., 2008). He asked questions such as "Is K-W-L easy to use in your classroom?," "Are the materials like the K-W-L chart and the informational passages acceptable?," "Do you think K-W-L is supporting your students' reading comprehension skills?," and "Do you think other teachers would use K-W-L with their students?" Mrs. Cook and Mr. Rhodes found K-W-L easy to integrate within existing classroom routines. They were impressed with how students grasped and readily participated in the intervention. As a result, they observed that students increased the amount of informational text reading typically completed in a science unit. In addition to supporting students' comprehension strategies for reading, Mrs. Cook and Mr. Rhodes believed student gains in content knowledge for science and science vocabulary positively enhanced learning during the science unit. They thought other teachers would use K-W-L as a classwide intervention. Both teachers planned to use K-W-L with future science and social studies units.

Given the evidence that student perspectives on academic interventions are also important (Forman et al., 2013; Nagle & Gagnon Glover, 2014), Mr. Nagle suggested that the 5th-grade students also be asked social-acceptability questions. Student responses to a modified version of the Kids

TABLE 13.1 Average Students' KIP Responses by Teacher

	Teacher	
Question	*Cook*	*Bishop*
1. How much did you like talking about the reading before you read?	4.3	4.1
2. How much did you like writing what you knew before reading?	3.8	3.3
3. How much did you like writing questions for reading before you read?	3.3	3.0
4. How much did you like writing answers to your questions when reading?	3.4	3.3
5. Were there times when you didn't want to do K-W-L in class?	2.1	2.3
6. Were there times when you wished you could do more K-W-L in class?	3.5	3.4
7. How much did K-W-L help you understand what you read?	4.1	3.9
8. Do you think your reading has improved?	4.8	4.3
9. Do you think your reading has gotten worse?	1.1	1.2

Intervention Profile (Eckert et al., 2017) are in Table 13.1. The KIP uses a 5-point Likert scale where 1 = not at all, 2 = a little bit, 3 = some, 4 = a lot, 5 = very, very much. In general, students like using K-W-L and believed it helped them get better at reading about science, but they didn't rate the writing requirements for K-W-L as favorably.

Intervention Considerations

Ogle (2009) recognized that K-W-L effectiveness depends largely on the teacher's ability to use it as both an instructional strategy and a diagnostic tool. As illustrated with this case study, student-completed K-W-Ls can serve as a formative assessment that guides refinements in instruction or intervention in a multitude of ways. Decision-making is optimized when teachers have well-defined ways of measuring goals for what they want students to show in their work. We offer three important K-W-L intervention considerations, each of which can be guided by systematically reviewing student work products. The considerations are relevant for student or group-level intervention planning. First, explicit teacher modeling and multiple opportunities for student practice with K-W-L steps are essential when teaching it as a comprehension strategy (Hilden & Jones, 2012). While the goal is for students to naturally and independently use the metacognitive strategies embedded in K-W-L when reading (e.g., activating prior knowledge, identifying purposes for reading, and monitoring comprehension), getting to that point requires purposeful gradual release on the part of the teacher. Teachers can use the quality of students' K-W-L entries to gauge when specific modeling and guided feedback can be faded. As an example, Madison teachers began fading emphases on science concepts and vocabulary in their K-W-L modeling after 75% of the class earned GAS scores of +1 for each domain. Second, when incorporated as part of an integrated approach to literacy instruction, the information in students' K-W-Ls helps teachers appreciate student understanding and facility with content-area knowledge as well as domain-specific and domain-general vocabulary (Townsend et al., 2020). Observations can guide refinements and clarifications needed during content instruction. Last, monitoring what students can or cannot generate when activating prior knowledge (**K**now) and setting a purpose for reading (**W**ant to know) also has diagnostic utility. If an individual student struggles with the K and W stages of K-W-L despite high doses of teacher modeling of its implicit thinking strategies, then student-specific problem analysis may be in order. Significant gaps in background knowledge for a topic may be one reason for a student's difficulty. In this case, more explicit pre-teaching of content and vocabulary may be called for. Another reason for poor knowledge activation may be weaknesses in the cognitive processes needed to access and articulate one's knowledge. Students with these types of needs may benefit from more structured approaches to knowledge activation that support the processes important for inferencing (Barth & Elleman, 2017; Cain et al., 2001; Elbro & Buch-Iversen, 2013), such as concept mapping and categorizing (Carr & Ogle, 1987) or think-alouds (Wanzek, Al Otaiba, & McMaster, 2020).

Conclusion

K-W-L is a commonly referenced strategy for supporting reading comprehension of informational texts. Most published applications of K-W-L involve implementing it as a whole-group teaching strategy to promote content-area learning. There is limited research evaluating its effectiveness as a targeted reading intervention, but research-based instructional methods known to promote reading comprehension are foundational to each phase of the K-W-L procedure. This case study demonstrates how K-W-L can be used as a classwide intervention when classwide deficits are evident in benchmark screening data. By strategically practicing K-W-L with informational passages related to the class's science unit, classwide improvements in reading comprehension were achieved and students increased the frequency of their use of science terms.

Appendix A: Implementation Checklist

K-W-L Whole-Group Instruction

Student Materials: Binder with K-W-L worksheets, pencil, reading passage for the day

Teacher Preparation: Preview reading passage for the day. Consider science concepts and vocabulary.

Before Reading:

1. Activate background knowledge by identifying what students KNOW about the topic.

Read the title of the passage and name the key concept. Be sure to be specific when naming concepts (e.g., consumers, not animals in forests). Facilitate group discussion about what students **KNOW** about the topic and record it in the K column. In the discussion, remind students of the key learning topics for the unit (e.g., healthy ecosystems, how energy is cycled).

Today we will read about ___. I want you to talk with a partner about what you know about ___. Since we are reading this for science, we should think about things that may be related to what we've already learned in our unit. Let students discuss the topic for 1–2 minutes. **Now, let's discuss what we know about ___. I'll keep track of our ideas in the "know" column of this K-W-L chart. You should write these things on your chart too. Let's come up with at least five things.**

Additional facilitators:

- As students say what they know, encourage them to state how they know that information, what made them think about that fact, or how they could prove it.
- Have students think about science concepts and vocabulary associated with the topic.
- If there are unanswered questions, save them for the Want to Know column.
- If misconceptions arise, either correct false information or leave the misconceptions so that students correct misconceptions on their own as they read.

2. Define a purpose for reading by having students state what they WANT TO KNOW.

Facilitate a discussion of what the students **WANT TO KNOW** about the topic. Use references to science unit identified in step 1, disagreements or conflicting information generated by students, and any other questions the students generate to write questions in the W column.

Given what we already know about ___, what kinds of things do we want or need to learn from the article we will read? Great, I will write these questions in the "want to know" column of the K-W-L chart. Model spacing. **Let's try to identify three things we want to know.**

Additional facilitators:

- Are there other things you *think* you will learn about this topic when you read? Think about the kinds of information we are learning in this science unit.
- Were there some things we weren't sure about or disagreed on that we want to know?
- [Choose ideas from K column.] What more would you like to know about ___?

Now, star the questions that you are most interested in getting answers to. You can star as many questions as you would like.

During Reading:

1. Prompt comprehension monitoring by having students write what they LEARN while reading.

a) Model reading and notating **LEARNED** information in the L portion of the K-W-L chart with the first 1–2 paragraphs of the passage.

Now I want you to read the first (or first two) **paragraphs. Think about whether what you read answers any of our questions about ___.** Give students time to read the designated portion of the passage. **Now, let's discuss what we learned from that part of the reading. We will write what we learned in the "learned" column of the chart. When we answer one of our questions, we write the answer right next to the question.** Facilitate discussion while modeling completion of K-W-L chart.

Additional facilitators:

- Did we answer any of our questions about ___?
- Did we learn any other things?
- Given what we've read so far, does anyone have any new questions that we should add to the "want to know" column?

b) Have students complete the reading independently.

Great work everyone! Now, I want you to finish reading the passage. As you read, write what you are learning in the "learned"

column. You will probably want to stop after every paragraph or two to think about what you have read. If you have new questions, write those in the W column. When you can, be sure to use your science vocabulary.

After Reading:

1. Reinforce comprehension by discussing and summarizing information LEARNED.

a) Discuss what students learned while reading. Questions developed before and during reading should be reviewed to see if they were answered. Reinforce student use of science vocabulary and references to science concepts. If questions were not answered, students can be encouraged to recognize more reading on the topic might help them find the answer.

Let's talk about what you learned. I'll write what you learned on our K-W-L chart. As we talk, check if you have the same ideas on your chart. If you don't, add them to what you have already written.

Additional facilitators:

- Did we answer our questions about ___? What else did we learn? Was anything particularly surprising?
- Great. That's a science term from our vocabulary wall. Were there any other terms?
- Nice work. That's a concept from our science unit.
- If there were unanswered questions about a topic, maybe someone will want to do some reading on their own to find out the answer.

b) Summarize what the students learned from reading. Have students discuss in pairs first, then model writing a gist statement. Use terms and references to 'gist' that are consistent with teaching from ELA instruction.

Now, we will write a gist statement for what we've read in this article. Do a quick pair and share with the person next to you and tell each other what you think the gist of the article is? Give the students time to discuss. **___ tell us what you said about the gist of the article.** Repeat the ideas. **Nice. We would write that as a gist statement that says, ___** (paraphrase and model writing a gist statement based on the student contribution.

Adapted from Ogle (1986); Carr and Ogle (1987); Mather and Jaffe (2002).

Appendix B: K-W-L Worksheet and Example

Names: ______________________ *Date:* __________

K KNOW	W WANT TO KNOW	L LEARN
1. Talk about the topic and write what you know about it.	2. Write what you want to know when you read.	3. Read each paragraph to yourself. Then, talk about what you learned and write it.
Remember to talk about how you know the fact or what made you think about it.	Are there things you think you will learn when you read?	If you answer one of your W questions, write the answer right next to the question.
Think about science vocabulary you know that is related to the topic.	Think about the kinds of things you've already learned from reading about this topic.	If you learn more things, write keywords for your learning.
Think about how what we are learning in science might be related to this topic.	Did you disagree on anything that you want to get the answers to when you read?	4. When you are finished reading, talk about what you learned. Think about these things. • Did you answer your questions? • What else did you learn? • Were you surprised by anything? • Was there any science vocabulary? • How does this relate to what we are learning in science?

5. Together, write a gist statement for the reading.

____

Names: ______________________ Date: __________

K KNOW	W WANT TO KNOW	L LEARN
Ecosystems have producers and consumers.	What are the producers in oceans?	zooplankton, sea snow, algae.
Organisms in ecosystems interact to live.	Does photosynthesis happen under water?	only near the top where there is light.
Fish are consumers.	Do all fish eat plants?	
There are coral reefs in oceans.	What are foodwebs in oceans?	
Pollution is bad for oceans.	How are underwater ecosystems different?	?
		the ocean has many ecosystems – coral reefs, mangroves, estuaries
		ecosystems change as the water gets deeper
		there is a sunlit zone, twilight zone, dark zone and abyss
		fish come to the sunlit zone to feed

Gist:
Most of the energy in ocean ecosystems is made where there is sunlight.

Appendix C: Intervention Log

Teacher: ________________ Week: ____________

Date: _____ Start Time: _____ End Time: _____ To what degree were you able to carry out the intervention as designed? 1 2 3 4 5 6 7 8 9 Not at all Somewhat Fully	Students Absent: Comments:
Date: _____ Start Time: _____ End Time: _____ To what degree were you able to carry out the intervention as designed? 1 2 3 4 5 6 7 8 9 Not at all Somewhat Fully	Students Absent: Comments:
Date: _____ Start Time: _____ End Time: _____ To what degree were you able to carry out the intervention as designed? 1 2 3 4 5 6 7 8 9 Not at all Somewhat Fully	Students Absent: Comments:
Date: _____ Start Time: _____ End Time: _____ To what degree were you able to carry out the intervention as designed? 1 2 3 4 5 6 7 8 9 Not at all Somewhat Fully	Students Absent: Comments:

References

Akerson, V. (2001). Teaching science when your principal says "teach language arts". *Science and Children*, *38*(7), 42–47.

Alsalhi, N. R. (2020). The effects of the use of the Know-Want-Learn Strategy (KWL) on fourth grade students' achievement in science at primary stage and their attitudes towards it. *EURASIA Journal of Mathematics, Science and Technology Education*, *16*(4), 1305–8223.

Barth, A. E., & Elleman, A. (2017). Evaluating the impact of a multistrategy inference intervention for middle-grade struggling readers. *Language, Speech & Hearing Services in Schools*, *48*(1), 31–41.

Best, R., Floyd, R., & McNamara, D. (2008). Differential competencies contributing to children's comprehension of narrative and expository texts. *Reading Psychology*, *1445*, 137–164.

Bryan, J. (1998). K-W-W-L: Questioning the known. *The Reading Teacher*, *51*(7), 618–620.

Burns, M. K., Karich, A. C., Maki, K. E., Anderson, A., Pulles, S. M., Ittner, A., et al. (2015). Identifying classwide problems in reading with screening data. *Journal of Evidence Based Practices in Schools*, *14*, 186–204.

Burns, M. K., Pulles, S. M., Helman, L., & McComas, J. J. (2016). Intervention based assessment frameworks: An example of a tier 1 reading intervention in an urban school. In S. L. Graves & J. Blake (Eds.), *Psychoeducational assessment and intervention for ethnic minority children: Evidence-based approaches* (pp. 165–182). Washington, DC: American Psychological Association.

Cain, K., Oakhill, J. V., Barnes, M. A., & Bryant, P. E. (2001). Comprehension skill, inference-making ability, and their relation to knowledge. *Memory and Cognition*, *29*(6), 850–859.

Carlson, S. E., Seipel, B., & McMaster, K. (2014). Development of a new reading comprehension assessment: Identifying comprehension differences among readers. *Learning and Individual Differences*, *32*, 40–53.

Carr, E., & Ogle, D. (1987). K-W-L Plus: A strategy for comprehension summarization. *Journal of Reading*, *30*(7), April, 626–631.

Castles, A., Rastle, K., & Nation, K. (2018). Ending the reading wars: Reading acquisition from novice to expert. *Psychological Science in the Public Interest*, *19*(1), 5–51.

Catts, H. W. (2022). Rethinking how to promote reading comprehension. *American Educator*, *45*(4), 26.

Catts, H. W., & Kamhi, A. G. (2014). Prologue: Reading comprehension is not a single ability. *Language, Speech, and Hearing Services in Schools*, *45*(3), 73–76.

Cervetti, G. N., & Wright, T. S. (2020). The role of knowledge in understanding and learning from text. In E. B. Moje, P. P. Afflerbach, P. Enciso, & N. K. Lesaux (Eds.), *Handbook of reading research, Volume V* (pp. 237–260). Milton Park, Abindon, Oxon; New York, NY: Routledge.

Christ, T. J., & Aranas, Y. A. (2014). Best practices in problem analysis. In P. L. Harrison & A. Thomas (Eds.), *Best practices in school psychology: Data-based and collaborative decision making* (pp. 87–98). Bethesda, MD: National Association of School Psychologists.

Compton, D. L., Miller, A. C., Elleman, A. M., & Steacy, L. M. (2014). Have we forsaken reading theory in the name of "quick fix" interventions for children with reading disability? *Scientific Studies of Reading*, *18*, 55–73.

Crowther, D. T., & Cannon, J. (2004). Strategy makeover. *Science and Children*, *42*(1), 42–44.

Denton, C. A., Vaughn, S., Wexler, J., Bryan, D., & Reed, D. (2012). *Effective instruction for middle school students with reading difficulties: The reading teacher's sourcebook*. Baltimore, MD: Brookes Publishing.

Duke, N. K., & Martin, N. M. (2015). Best practices for comprehension instruction in the elementary classroom. In S. R. Parris & K. Healey (Eds.), *Comprehension instruction: Research-based best practices* (pp. 211–223). New York, NY: Guilford Press.

E.L. Learning. (n.d.). *Expeditionary learning*. Retrieved from https://eleducation.org

Eckert, T. L., Hier, B. O., Hamsho, N. F., & Malandrino, R. D. (2017). Assessing children's perceptions of academic interventions: The Kids Intervention Profile. *School Psychology Quarterly*, *32*(2), 268–281.

Edmonds, M. S., Vaughn, S., Wexler, J., Reutebuch, C. K., Cable, A., Tackett, K. K., & Schnakenberg, J. W. (2009). A synthesis of reading interventions and effects on reading comprehension for older struggling readers. *Review of Educational Research*, *79*, 262–300.

Elbro, C., & Buch-Iversen, I. (2013). Activation of background knowledge for inference making: Effects on reading comprehension. *Scientific Studies of Reading*, *17*(6), 435–452.

Elleman, A. M., Steacy, L. M., Gilbert, J. K., Cho, E., Miller, A. C., Coyne-Green, A., Pritchard, P., Fields, R. S., Schaeffer, S., & Compton, D. L. (2022). Exploring the role of knowledge in predicting reading and listening comprehension in fifth grade students. *Learning and Individual Differences*, *98*, 102182.

Espin, C. A., & Foegen, A. (1996). Validity of three general outcome measures for predicting secondary students's performance on content-area tasks. *Exceptional Children*, *62*, 497–514.

Forman, S. G., Shapiro, E. G., Codding, R. S., Gonzales, J.E., Reddy, L. A., Rosenfield, S. A., Sanetti, L. M. H., & Stoiber, K. C. (2013). Implementation science and school psychology. *School Psychology Quarterly*, 28(2), 7–100.

Gajria, M., Jitendra, A. K., Sood, S., & Sacks, G. (2007). Improving comprehension of expository text structures in students with LD: A synthesis. *Journal of Learning Disabilities*, *40*, 210–255.

Graney, S. B., Missall, K. N., Martinez, R. S., & Bergstrom, M. (2009). A preliminary investigation of within-year growth patterns in reading and mathematics curriculum-based measures. *Journal of School Psychology*, *47*, 121–142.

Greenwood, R. (2019). Pupil involvement in planning topics using KWL grids: Opinions of teachers, student teachers, and pupils. *Educational Studies*, *45*(4), 497–519.

Guthrie, J. T., Wigfield, A., Barbosa, P., Perencevich, K. C., Taboada, A., Davis, M. H., Scafiddi, N. T., & Tonks, S. (2004). Increasing reading comprehension and engagement through concept-oriented reading instruction. *Journal of Educational Psychology*, *96*(3), 403.

Hattan, C. (2019). Prompting rural students' use of background knowledge and experience to support comprehension of unfamiliar content. *Reading Research Quarterly*, *54*(4), 451–455.
Hattan, C., & Lupo, S. M. (2020). Rethinking the role of knowledge in the literacy classroom. *Reading Research Quarterly*, *55*(S1), S283–S298.
Hawkins, R. O., Morrison, J. Q., Musti-Rao, S., & Hawkins, J. A. (2008). Treatment integrity for academic interventions in real-world settings. *School Psychology Forum*, *2*(3), 1–15.
Hershberger, K., Zembal-Saul, C., & Starr, M. L. (2006). Evidence helps the KWL get a KLEW. *Science and Children*, *43*(5), 50–53.
Hilden, K., & Jones, J. (2012). Comprehension and authentic reading: Putting the power back in K-W-L. *Reading Today*, December 2011/January 2012.
Hwang, H., Cabell, S. Q., & Joyner, R. E. (2023). Does cultivating content knowledge during literacy instruction support vocabulary and comprehension in the elementary school years? A systematic review. *Reading Psychology*, *44*(2), 145–174.
Jared, E. J., & Jared, A. H. (1997,). Launching into improved comprehension: Integrating the KWL model into middle level courses. *The Technology Teacher*, *56*(3), 24–31.
Kendeou, P., McMaster, K. L., & Christ, T. J. (2016). Reading comprehension: Core components and processes. *Policy Insights from the Behavioral and Brain Sciences*, *3*(1), 62–69.
Kendeou, P., van den Broek, P., Helder, A., & Karlsson, J., (2014). A cognitive view of reading comprehension: implications for reading difficulties. *Learning Disabilities Research & Practice*, *29*, 1–16.
Leach, J., Scarborough, H., & Rescorla, L. (2003). Late-emerging reading disabilities. *Journal of Educational Psychology*, *95*, 211–224.
Lexia LTRS. (n.d.). *Lexia language essentials for teachers of reading and spelling*. Retrieved from https://www.lexialearning.com/letrs
Lupo, S. M., Tortorelli, L., Invernizzi, M., Ryoo, J. H., & Strong, J. Z. (2019). An exploration of text difficulty and knowledge support on adolescents' comprehension. *Reading Research Quarterly*, *54*(4), 457–479.
Mather, N., & Jaffe, L. (2002). *Woodcock-Johnson III: Reports, recommendations, and strategies*. Hoboken, NJ: John Wiley & Sons.
McAllister, P. (1994). Using K-W-L for informal assessment. *The Reading Teacher*, *47*, 510–511.
Nagle, R. J., & Gagnon Glover, S. (2014). Best practices in designing and conducting needs assessment. In P. L. Harrison & A. Thomas (Eds.), *Best practices in school psychology: Foundations* (pp. 315–327). Bethesda, MD: National Association of School Psychologists.
National Center for Educational Statistics. (2022). *National Assessment of Educational Progress (NAEP), 2022 Reading Assessment*. U.S. Department of Education.
National Governors Association Center for Best Practices, & Council of Chief State School Officers. (2010). *Common core state standards for English language arts*. Retrieved from https://learning.ccsso.org/common-core-state-standards-initiative

Neddenriep, C. E., Hale, A. D., Skinner, C. H., Hawkins, R. O., & Winn, B. (2007). A preliminary investigation of the concurrent validity of reading comprehension rate: A direct, dynamic measure of reading comprehension. *Psychology in the Schools*, *44*, 373–388.

Oakhill, J., Cain, K., & Elbro, C. (2019). Reading comprehension and reading comprehension difficulties. In D. A. Kilpatrick, R. M. Joshi, & R. K. Wagner (Eds.), *Reading development and difficulties* (pp. 83–115). New York, NY: Springer.

Ogle, D. M. (1986). K-W-L: A teaching model that develops active reading of informational text. *The Reading Teacher*, *39*, 564–570.

Ogle, D. M. (1989). The know, want to know, learn strategy. In K. D. Muth (Ed.), *Children's comprehension of text: Research into practice* (pp. 205–223). Newark, DE: International Reading Association.

Ogle, D. (2009). Creating context for inquiry: From KWL to PRC2. *Knowledge Quest*, *38*(1), 56–61.

Oudega, M., & van den Broek, P. (2018). Standards of coherence in reading: Variations in processing and comprehension of text. In K. Millis, D. L. Long, J. P. Magliano, & K. Wiemer (Eds.), *Deep comprehension* (pp. 41–51). New York, NY: Routledge.

Pao, L. S., & Williams, J. P. (2015). Improving comprehension of informational texts in the elementary classroom. In S. R. Parris & K. Headly (Eds.), *Comprehension instruction: Research-based best practices* (pp. 238–253). New York, NY: Guilford Press.

Preast, J. L., Burns, M. K., Brann, K. L., Taylor, C. N., & Aguilar, L. (2019). Classwide partner reading intervention for science comprehension. *School Psychology Forum*, *13*(1), 29–40.

RAND Reading Study Group. (2002). *Reading for understanding: Toward an R&D program in reading comprehension*. Santa Monica, CA: RAND.

Renaissance Learning. (2020). *Research foundation for Star adaptive assessments*. Wisconsin Rapids, WI: Author.

Riley-Tillman, C. T., Burns, M. K., & Gibbons, K. (2013). *RTI applications: Assessment, analysis, and decision making*. New York, NY: Guilford Press.

Roach, A. T., & Elliott, S. N. (2005). Goal attainment scaling: An efficient and effective approach to monitoring student progress. *Council for Exceptional Children*, *37*(4), 8–17.

Roach, A. T., & Elliott, S. N. (2008). Best practices in facilitating and evaluating intervention integrity. In A. Thomas & J. Grimes (Eds.), *Best practices in school psychology V* (pp. 195–208). Bethesda, MD: National Association of School Psychologists.

Scammacca, N., Roberts, G., Vaughn, S., Edmonds, M., Wexler, J., Reutenbuch, C. K., & Torgesen, J. K. (2007). *Interventions for adolescent struggling readers: A meta-analysis with implications for practice*. Atlanta, GA: Research Corporation.

Shin, J., Deno, S. L., & Espin, C. (2000). Technical adequacy of the maze tasks for curriculum-based measurement of reading growth. *Journal of Special Education*, *34*, 164–172.

SickKids (n.d.). *Empower reading*. Retrieved from https://www.sickkids.ca/en/learning/empower-reading/

Spor, M. W., & Schneider, B. K. (1999). Content reading strategies: What teachers know, use, and want to learn. *Reading Research and Instruction*, *38*(3), 221–231.
Stahl, K. A. D. (2008). The effects of three instructional methods on the reading comprehension and content acquisition of novice readers. *Journal of Literacy Research*, *40*, 359–393.
Szabo, S. (2006). KWHHL: A student-driven evolution of the KWL. *American Secondary Education*, *34*, 57–67.
Telaumbanua, S. (2019). The implementation of Know Want Learn method to improve student's reading skill. *Journal of Humanistic and Social Studies*, *10*(2), 111–122.
Townsend, D., Barber, A. T., & Carter, H. (2020). Learning academic language, comprehending text. In E. B. Moje, P. Afflerbach, P. Enciso, & N. K. Lesaux (Eds.), *Handbook of reading research, volume V* (pp. 345–364). New York, NY: Routledge.
Wallach, G., Charlton, S., Bartholomew, J., Stone, C., Silliman, E., & Ehren, B. (2014). The spoken–written comprehension connection: Constructive intervention strategies. In C. A. Stone, E. R. Silliman, B. J. Ehren, & G. P. Wallach (Eds.), *Handbook of language and literacy: Development and disorders* (pp. 485–501). New York, NY: Guilford Press.
Wanzek, J., Wexler, J., Vaughn, S., & Ciulla, S. (2010). Reading interventions for struggling readers in the upper elementary grades: A synthesis of 20 years of research. *Reading and Writing*, *23*, 889–912.
Wanzek, J., Al Otaiba, S., & McMaster, K. L. (2020). *Intensive reading interventions for the elementary grades*. New York, NY: Guilford Press.
Wexler, N. (2019). *The knowledge gap: The hidden cause of America's broken education system and how to fix it*. New York, NY: Avery.

14

STRATEGIC NOTETAKING AND FLASHCARDS

Shawna Petersen-Brown

Minnesota State University, Mankato, MN, USA

Matthew K. Burns

University of Missouri, Columbia, MI, USA

Introduction

Students in the secondary grades are expected to read and comprehend more complex text with increasingly technical vocabulary. Although a student's decoding skills and vocabulary knowledge interact to impact reading comprehension (Hoover & Gough, 1990), vocabulary may be particularly influential on reading comprehension for older students (Elleman et al., 2009) and writing activities such as notetaking also lead to consistent effects on comprehension (Hebert et al., 2013). Therefore, providing instructional supports in both vocabulary and notetaking may be helpful to increase learning for secondary students with reading deficits.

Vocabulary

Effective vocabulary instruction includes direct and indirect methods (National Reading Panel [NRP], 2000). Direct vocabulary instruction entails explicitly teaching specific words, while indirect methods include wide reading and exposure to words in a variety of contexts (Beck et al., 2002; NRP, 2000). Pre-teaching words and their meanings may be particularly effective for increasing reading comprehension by improving vocabulary and decoding. Incremental rehearsal (IR) is a flashcard intervention that has been used to pre-teach unknown words to increase reading fluency and comprehension (Burns et al., 2004, 2011), and including word definitions when implementing IR increased maintenance and generalization (Petersen-Brown & Burns, 2011, 2019). IR uses a high percentage of known

DOI: 10.4324/9781003275749-14

items (e.g., seven to nine) to practice one unknown item (Tucker & Burns, 2016). An unknown item is introduced and practiced, then one known item is presented. The unknown item is presented again, followed by two known items. This process continues, with increased spacing in between presentations of the unknown item, until the unknown item has been presented along with all seven to nine knowns. After practicing the unknown item, the last known in the sequence is removed, the first unknown item becomes the first known, a new unknown is introduced, and the process repeats. In general, IR has large effects on learning a variety of information types across grade levels, ability levels, and information, including words (Burns et al., 2012). IR provides many opportunities to respond to unknown items (Szadokierski & Burns, 2008) and facilitates behavioral momentum through the inclusion of known items (Burns et al., 2009).

Notetaking

Students in the secondary grades are often expected to take notes during instruction and while reading. Notetaking is defined as identifying and recording the most important information during an activity (Hartley, 2002). Research suggests that writing about what one is reading, including through notetaking, improves comprehension (Graham & Hebert, 2011) by serving as a means for both encoding and storing information (Faber et al., 2000). Students often report difficulties with notetaking and require instruction and support to take notes effectively (Boyle et al., 2015). However, some reviews have found a wide range of effects associated with notetaking in the research, resulting in null effects overall (Kobayashi, 2006). Thus, it is important to review the evidence for specific notetaking interventions and to closely monitor the effects of notetaking interventions.

Strategic notetaking is an adaptable approach in which students implement basic strategies before, during, and after a lecture or reading to facilitate comprehension (Boyle, 2001). Strategic notetaking requires less preparation time than other notetaking methods and accommodations and may be more acceptable to teachers (Boyle, 2007). Strategic notetaking has been found to be beneficial for notetaking productivity, comprehension, and retention, as well as being acceptable to students (Boyle, 2007, 2011; Boyle & Weishaar, 2001).

Case Study

Will was a 9th-grade white male student at Hillcrest High School. In November, he was referred to the Student Assistance Team by his English and social studies teachers, who shared concerns about Will's reading fluency, reading comprehension, and written expression. A general education teacher and special education paraprofessional were present each day during both classes. The general education teacher provided instruction and directed other activities. The special education paraprofessional provided direct support to special education students, and both staff provided additional support other students as needed. In both classes, there was a combination of teacher-led instruction, reading in content-area text, and completing activities and written assignments individually or in small groups.

Background Information

Will's teachers noted that he received supplemental small-group intervention (Tier 2 or targeted support) in reading in 2nd through 5th grades due to scores in the at-risk range on oral reading fluency benchmark assessments. Teachers and interventionists noted that Will struggled to apply decoding skills, which resulted in slow and inaccurate reading. In middle school (from 6th to 8th grade), Will continued to perform in the at-risk range on standardized reading assessments but in the average range on math assessments. Will's 8th-grade teachers indicated that he usually did not finish in time when students were asked to read independently from class materials. He struggled to identify main ideas and key details, define key terms, and make inferences from text. Will also struggled with written expression—when asked to write during class, he usually wrote less than peers and used simple and repetitive sentence structures, but his spelling and use of conventions were generally correct. In middle school, Will received accommodations and one-on-one support as needed. Will's teachers provided accommodations including preferential seating, access to teachers' notes, small-group testing, and tests read aloud. Will progressed well with targeted support; he remained in the at-risk range on benchmark and standardized assessments in reading but did not fall into the high-risk range.

Will's high school teachers indicated that they began implementing accommodations at the start of the school year, specifically preferential seating and small-group testing. They indicated that keeping up with course reading was challenging for Will. He did not usually complete reading assigned during class, and he was more likely to correctly answer comprehension questions when content was presented orally rather than read. Will's in-class writing production and sentence structure did not meet expectations. Will participated in a daily study hall, and he preferred to complete work for math, science, and art than reading or social studies. The paraprofessional who supervised the study hall helped Will and other students identify priorities during each study hall period, and they noted that Will was resistant to completing reading or writing and frequently talked to friends or was passively off-task when completing reading or writing tasks. Although Will completed most homework, he performed poorly on quizzes. Will was earning a C– in Social Studies and a B in English.

Will's parents did not indicate any current or previous diagnoses that would impact his learning. They also observed that reading quickly and accurately was difficult for Will. They reported that they sat next to Will when he completed work at home, and they used audiobooks or text-to-voice tools when available. These supports have supported his comprehension. They also observed that 9th grade had been more challenging for Will given the higher text difficulty and greater expectations for independent work completion.

Problem Identification

The school psychologist completed a problem identification interview with Will's social studies and English teachers. Will's greatest strengths included his participation in discussions; he provided interesting and on-topic ideas. He had good background knowledge and made connections between prior knowledge and new concepts. He was respectful and kind, and he responded well to redirection. Although Will did not enjoy reading or writing, he was willing to attempt tasks when prompted. Their biggest concerns were that Will read slowly, did not typically understand what he read, did not independently define key terms, and did not seem to like school. Will's teachers indicated that he appeared to stay on-task during reading time, but he did not usually take notes. When asked to highlight key ideas, he often highlighted complete sentences or paragraphs but was unable to state a reason for highlighting these portions.

Will's teachers indicated that the highest priority skill was to correctly read and define key terms and answer comprehension questions correctly. Will's teachers expected that he show a high level of mastery in each area. Specifically, he would correctly read and define key terms in content-area text. In addition, he would correctly answer comprehension questions on in-class quizzes based on content-area text. Because Will and his family hoped to improve his social studies grade in particular, the social studies teacher volunteered to participate further in the problem identification and analyses process.

Problem Analysis

There are several reasons as to why reading interventions are not successful. Burns (2021) suggested that the first three phases of the learning hierarchy (Haring & Eaton, 1978) could be used to analyze student difficulties because students could struggle to initially learn the information (acquisition phase), retain the information (proficiency phase), or apply the information (generalization phase). If students are not initially learning the information, then more modeling, scaffolding, and alignment with student needs are needed; if students are not retaining the information, then more dosage or repetition is needed; and if students are not applying the information than more attention to transfer is needed. Because Will consistently demonstrated difficulty with reading fluency while struggling to identify main ideas and key details, defining key terms, and making inferences from text, we hypothesized that he was not initially learning the information and required additional support based on his individual needs. More specifically, we hypothesized that he did not comprehend what he read because he did not read with sufficient fluency, did not know the meaning of keywords, and did not identify main ideas and key details while reading.

Intervention Goals

The school psychologist and social studies teacher identified that Will needed to increase his knowledge of the meanings of keywords and improve his skills in identifying main ideas and key details while reading. They decided to monitor growth in these skills based on his performance on brief daily quizzes in social studies class as well as a general outcome measure for reading comprehension. Two goals were identified. First, in 8 weeks, Will will correctly answer a median of 80% (4 out of 5 items) of quiz questions correctly over the prior week's quizzes, with no single quiz falling below 60%. For the second goal, 8th-grade Maze passages from DIBELS 8th Edition (University of Oregon, 2021) were used to monitor progress in reading comprehension. The school psychologist selected 8th-grade probes because they did not locate any that were specific to high school grades. The second goal indicated that in 8 weeks, Will will obtain 28 correct responses in the 3-minute probe, which was the end-of-the-year 8th-grade benchmark assessment score for proficiency.

Measurement of Target Reading Skill, Data Collection Strategies, and Progress

Monitoring

Will's progress was monitored in two ways: a goal-specific measure and a general outcome measure. To measure progress on the first goal, the school psychologist relied on data collected by Will's social studies teacher, who administered daily quizzes that consisted of five short-answer items based on the reading for the day. Quizzes included four questions that required students to provide, describe, or define either a key detail or key term, and one question that required inference related to a main idea. All questions required a written response of up to one sentence. The data consisted of the number of items answered correctly each day, and the goal was 4 out of 5 (80%) answered correctly. The teacher conducted the short-answer quiz at the start of each class period and scored them that same day. The number answered correctly was then reported to the school psychologist within 1 day of Will completing each quiz.

To measure progress on the second goal, the paraprofessional monitored progress with weekly 8th-grade Maze passages. The paraprofessional administered one Maze probe every Tuesday in the hallway during the during the last 5 minutes of social studies class. The data collection began 3 weeks prior to beginning the intervention to establish a stable baseline, and the data were evaluated with a simple A-B nonexperimental design.

Intervention Plan

The intervention consisted of two components that were implemented over two phases. The paraprofessional pre-taught keywords with flashcards to help facilitate knowledge of those important words, and the school psychologist taught Will to implement strategic notetaking while reading. The multicomponent intervention was tested over a 3-week experimental phase, during which strategic notetaking was used 3 days per week and not implemented 2 days per week (baseline). Next, strategic notetaking was implemented daily over an 8-week implementation phase.

Pre-teaching Keywords. Keywords were pre-taught with incremental rehearsal (IR; Tucker & Burns, 2016) because it was the most researched flashcard intervention that consistently led to large effects (Burns et al., 2012) and positive ratings (National Center on Intensive Intervention, 2021). The intervention occurred three times per week during a study hall period held prior to social studies. The intervention was implemented by a paraprofessional at a table in the back of the study hall classroom that was far enough away from the other students to provide a quiet setting for the intervention and to not disruptive to the other students.

The keywords were defined as words that appeared frequently and were central to the meaning of the text (Burns et al., 2011). Will's social studies teacher provided five keywords for each assigned reading the day before the reading was due, and these were taught using IR three times per week during the experimental phase. This allowed the school psychologist to examine the effect with a multielement design with a rapid transition between conditions. The conditions consisted of the treatment conditions—days that keywords were taught (and notetaking required, see below)—and baseline conditions—the 2 days per week that the keywords were not taught and notetaking was not required. The keywords were pre-taught with IR with the following procedure:

1. The social studies teacher provided five keywords for the reading that was due the next day.
2. Three days per week, each keyword was written on a 3 x 5 index card in black ink with a landscape orientation so that the word fit within the middle half of the card vertically.
3. Eight known words for each session were also written on a 3 x 5 index card in black ink with a landscape orientation in the same manner that the keywords were written. The known words were taken from the 601–699 Word Lists (Kress & Fry, 2016), which roughly equated 6th-grade level words and was selected to ensure that he could easily read them.
4. The teacher also provided a brief (one-phrase) definition of each keyword, which was written lightly in pencil on the back of the card.
5. Will sat at a small desk at the back of the room three times each week and the paraprofessional sat directly across from him.
6. The paraprofessional started by presenting the eight known words and asked Will to read each one. Words that were correctly read within 2 seconds were considered known and were used for the intervention. Those that were read incorrectly or were not read after 2 seconds were not considered known and were not used for the intervention.
7. Each keyword was then taught by (a) presenting the card with the word on it, (b) modeling how to say the word, (c) asking the student to repeat the pronunciation of the word, (d) stating the brief definition of the word, (e) asking the student to restate the definition, and then (f) asking the student to restate the word and its corresponding definition. Any error in this process resulted in the entire step being repeated.
8. After the keyword was initially taught, it was then rehearsed with the known words. Will was asked to state the word and its corresponding brief definition for the keyword, but only had to correctly read the known words. The rehearsal consisted of the following;
   Keyword 1, Known Word (KW) 1
   Keyword 1, KW 1, KW 2
   Keyword 1, KW 1, KW 2, KW3
   Keyword 1, KW 1, KW 2, KW 3, KW 4

Keyword 1, KW 1, KW 2, KW 3, KW 4, KW 5
Keyword 1, KW 1, KW 2, KW 3, KW 4, KW 5, KW 6
Keyword 1, KW 1, KW 2, KW 3, KW 4, KW 5, KW 6, KW 7
Keyword 1, KW 1, KW 2, KW 3, KW 4, KW 5, KW 6, KW 7, KW 8

9. After completing the sequence in Step 8, the keyword became the new KW 1, the previous KW 8 was removed, and the second keyword was modeled as in Step 7 and rehearsed as **Keyword** 1 as in Step 8. The process continued until all five keywords were taught. Any errors were immediately corrected and the step was started over again.
10. Will placed the cards in his social studies notebook so that he could continue to practice them if needed.
11. Each Friday, after the final IR session of the week, Will was asked to read and define all keywords (both taught and not taught, during the 3-week experimental phase) from the week as a review and to monitor progress.

Strategic Notetaking. The second component of the intervention plan included teaching Will to use the strategic notetaking strategy to identify main ideas and key details while reading. The school psychologist and social studies teacher adapted a strategic notetaking form to fit its intended purpose (see Appendix A). Strategic notetaking includes strategies implemented before, during, and after listening to a lecture or reading from a text (Boyle, 2001). After learning the topic, Will jotted down what he already knew about the topic. Then, he wrote down the keywords learned through IR in the bottom right. His goal was to include each of those keywords in his notes and underline them. While reading, Will wrote down main ideas and key details. The two-page notetaking form allowed for seven ideas and/or details, although additional pages could be added as needed. After completing a page of notes (i.e., three to four ideas and/or details), Will wrote a summary sentence before continuing to the next page. After reading, Will wrote the three most important points.

Prior to beginning the intervention, the school psychologist introduced strategic notetaking to Will in a training session during study hall, which lasted the full period. The school psychologist used an excerpt from the textbook which Will had recently read. First, the school psychologist explained the importance of using notes to help us learn and remember information we hear and read. Then the school psychologist prompted Will to read the textbook heading and write a brief note in the "Before you read" portion of the notetaking form (see Appendix A). Then the school psychologist provided flashcards with five keywords from the excerpt. The school psychologist briefly reviewed the words with Will and told him that, usually, he would have learned these words ahead of time from the paraprofessional. After he wrote the words in the "Flashcard words" space, the school psychologist told him that he should use and underline each of these keywords in his notes. Then the school psychologist told Will that he would read the passage while looking for main ideas (what the passage is mostly about) and key details (the most important things about the topic). The school psychologist prompted Will to read silently and to stop at the end of each paragraph. At the end of each paragraph, the school psychologist asked what the paragraph was about and whether a main idea or key detail was included in the paragraph. The school psychologist collaboratively completed the "While you read" section of the notetaking form (see Appendix A). After Will finished reading the excerpt, Will and the school psychologist worked together to complete the "After you read" section, identifying the three most important points.

Will's social studies teacher was asked to assist Will in using the strategic notetaking form during the three intervention days in the first week of the experimental phase. The school psychologist provided an eight-step fidelity checklist, applied by reviewing permanent products of notetaking pages. At the end of the first week, the social studies teacher indicated Will required very little assistance. The team agreed that the following week, the social studies teacher would check in once each period notetaking was required and encourage him to raise his hand to ask for help. The social studies teacher gave Will a blank notetaking form and encouraged him to show it to his parents so that they could help him with reading if he did not complete it at school. Will used his completed notetaking form on quizzes administered the following class period.

Intervention Fidelity and Interobserver Agreement Plans

The intervention sessions during the experimental phase were observed by a second person using the intervention protocols outlined in the Intervention Plan for 33% of the intervention sessions. The IR portion of the observation consisted of 15 items, from Steps 6 through 8 in the intervention plan, for all five items (total of 75 steps). The number of observed correctly implemented steps was divided by the total number of items and multiplied by 100 to calculate an intervention fidelity percentage, which resulted in 99.6% fidelity. During the first of three observations, the paraprofessional forgot to ask the student for the brief definition during the first presentation of the keyword during the first rehearsal, but it was immediately corrected.

During the experimental phase on Fridays, the social studies teacher randomly selected one of Will's notetaking forms from the week and completed an 8-step strategic notetaking checklist corresponding to the primary elements of the form (writing the topic, writing what is known about the topic, writing main points and key details on each page, writing a summary on each page, writing down the keywords, using the keywords in the notes, appropriately using additional pages, and writing the most important points). The social studies teacher provided feedback as needed. This resulted in 95.6% implementation fidelity. In the first sampled form, Will did not write the most important points in the "After you read" portion of the worksheet, and the social studies teacher provided feedback. Will did not appear to need any reteaching during the experimental or implementation phases.

The daily quizzes were also scored by the school psychologist to assess interobserver agreement (IOA) for the correctness of the short answers. The number of items consistently scored as correct or incorrect independently by both the teacher and school psychologist was divided by the total number of items and multiplied by 100 to calculate the percentage of IOA, which resulted in 95.6% IOA. The 8th-grade Maze probes were also scored by the school psychologist and social studies teacher and each answer was rated as correct or incorrect. The number of items consistently scored as correct or incorrect independently by both scorers was divided by the total number of items and multiplied by 100 to calculate the percentage of IOA, which resulted in a total of 100% IOA.

Intervention Outcome Data

As can be seen in Figure 14.1, during the experimental condition, Will performed better when he was required to use notetaking and pre-taught

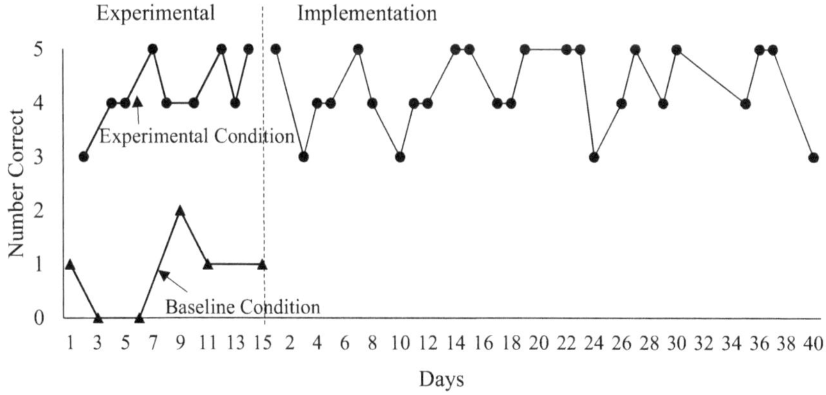

FIGURE 14.1 Number of Items Correct on Daily Social Studies Quizzes with (Experimental and Implementation) and without (Baseline) Notetaking and Preteaching Keywords with Flashcards

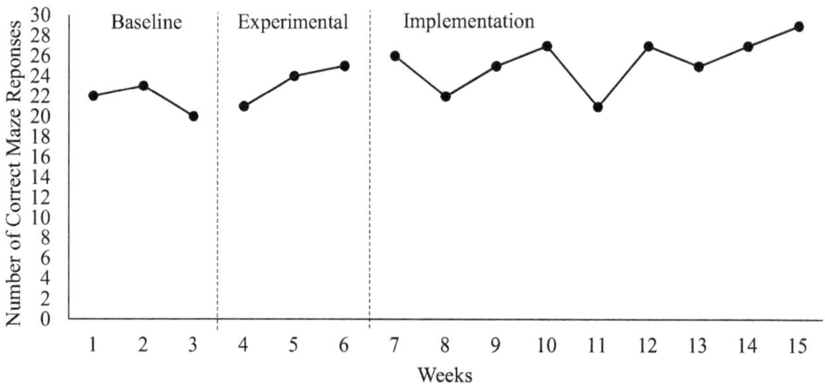

FIGURE 14.2 Number of Correct Maze Responses During the Baseline, Experimental, and Implementation Phases.

keywords with the IR flashcard technique. The mean number of correct responses increased from 0.83 (*SD* = 0.75) during the baseline condition to 4.22 (*SD* = 0.67), which resulted in an immediate change in level between the changing conditions. There was also 0% overlap between the baseline and experimental condition data. A total of 8 of the 9 data points in the experimental condition met or exceeded the goal of at least 80% (4 out of 5) correct.

During the implementation phase, the mean score for the daily quizzes remained 4.22 (*SD* = 0.70), which suggested that the effect continued once it was implemented without additional support. Moreover, 84.4% of the daily quizzes met or exceeded the goal of at least 80% correct.

As can be seen in Figure 14.2, Will made progress in his Maze scores once the intervention was implemented. There was an immediate and noticeable change in level and trend from baseline to experimental phases. The change to the implementation phase did not result in an immediate change in level, but the slope continued on a positive trend. The slope for the baseline phase was –1.0 correct answers increase per week, which increased to 2.0 correct answers increase per week for the experimental phase, and 0.5 growth in correct answers per week increase for the implementation phase. The slope in the experimental and intervention phases exceeded the average weekly ROI between the fall and spring 8th-grade benchmarks of 0.25 correct answers per week (University of Oregon, 2020). Will obtained the goal of 28 correct responses by the final week of intervention.

Intervention Acceptability

The social studies teacher and paraprofessional were asked to complete an intervention feedback questionnaire, which was modified from the Behavior Intervention Rating Scale (BIRS) to pertain to academic skills (see Appendix B; Von Brock & Elliott, 1987). The school psychologist sent a link to the survey in an online form. Both staff indicated a high level of acceptability; the social studies teacher's and paraprofessional's ratings resulted in scores of 104 and 109, respectively. BIRS scores of 84 and above are considered acceptable (Elliott & Treuting, 1991). There was minimal variation among items; both staff agreed or strongly agreed with all statements.

Intervention Considerations

This case study summarized how IR and strategic notetaking may be used to support reading comprehension and vocabulary for a secondary student in a general education social studies classroom. Specifically, this example illustrated how IR may be helpful in pre-teaching keywords and their definitions to facilitate reading comprehension. In this example, reading comprehension was further supported by strategic notetaking, an adaptable approach requiring little preparation. This strategy may be implemented for middle- and high-school students with varying levels of need and in a variety of academic domains.

This intervention may be adapted for use at the universal, targeted, and intensive levels. Strategic notetaking has been implemented in the research with students achieving in the average range (Boyle, 2011) and students with learning disabilities (Boyle, 2007, 2011; Boyle & Weishaar, 2001). Strategic notetaking has been shown in these studies to improve notetaking productivity and quality among students with and without learning disabilities. This is consistent with the broader body of research suggesting that students struggle with notetaking (Boyle et al., 2015). Adding in IR as a method for pre-teaching keywords may be effective for students needing targeted or intensive support, as demonstrated in this case study. Specifically, pre-teaching keywords has been shown to support reading fluency and reading comprehension (Burns et al., 2004, 2011). IR may be a particularly effective method given large effects demonstrated across student populations and information types (Burns et al., 2012).

The interventions implemented in this case study are adaptable to various purposes and content areas. For example, the research on strategic notetaking has been implemented in science classrooms (Boyle, 2007, 2011; Boyle & Weishaar, 2001), but it can easily be implemented in social studies classrooms and in English classrooms for some types of content (such as literary terms). Strategic notetaking has been primarily researched to improve listening comprehension of lecture information (Boyle, 2007, 2011; Boyle & Weishaar, 2001), but notetaking interventions are supported for supporting reading comprehension as well (Graham & Hebert, 2011).

Conclusion

IR and strategic notetaking were used together within this case study to support the reading comprehension of a 9th-grade student. Although implementing multiple interventions at once may be challenging, in this case, implementing either intervention alone may not have resulted in the observed benefits. IR was used to pre-teach key vocabulary words. This component was important because vocabulary knowledge is especially important for reading comprehension among older students (Elleman et al., 2009), and because students may experience frustration when they do not know keywords in text (Burns et al., 2004, 2011). However, effective strategies are also important for supporting reading comprehension (Graham & Hebert, 2011). In this case, strategic notetaking was taught as a comprehension strategy. In addition, many secondary students struggle to take effective notes, and strategic notetaking is an adaptable method that requires less teacher preparation (Boyle et al., 2015). Targeting vocabulary and comprehension strategies together using IR and strategic notetaking may effectively promote reading comprehension while also being efficient and acceptable.

Appendix A: Adapted Strategic Notetaking Form

Strategic Notetaking Form

Name: ______________________ Date: __________

BEFORE YOU READ

What is today's topic? ____

____

Describe what you know about the topic. (Write sentences or notes)

____

____

WHILE YOU READ

Write down main points and key details. Don't forget to use flashcard words.

1. ____

   ____
2. ____

   ____
3. ____

   ____
4. ____

   ____

Summarize your notes in 1 sentence before you turn the page.

____

____

____

____

Flashcard words:

1. ______________
2. ______________
3. ______________
4. ______________
5. ______________

WHILE YOU READ

Write down main points and key details. Don't forget to use your flashcard words.

1. ______________________________
____
2. ______________________________
____
3. ______________________________
____
4. ______________________________
____

Summarize your notes in 1 sentence before you turn the page.

____
____
____
____

Flashcard words:

1. __________
2. __________
3. __________
4. __________
5. __________

AFTER YOU READ

Write the 3 most important points from what you read, as notes sentences.

1. ______________________________
____
2. ______________________________
____
3. ______________________________
____

Appendix B: An empty social validity questionnaire shows the intervention acceptability survey with statements to agree and disagree with the help of a scale from 0 to 5

Intervention Acceptability Survey

Thank you for taking the time to complete this 24-item survey. Please evaluate the intervention by clicking on the oval which best describes your agreement or disagreement with each statement. Please respond to each statement.

The rating scale is as follows:
0 = Strongly Disagree; 1 = Disagree; 2 = Slightly Disagree; 3 = Slightly Agree; 4 = Agree; 5 = Strongly Agree

Note: On the Goole Form, each statement will be followed by the following response stimuli:
Mark only one oval.

	0	1	2	3	4	5	
Strongly Disagree	⬭	⬭	⬭	⬭	⬭	⬭	Strongly Agree

1. This would be an acceptacle intervention for the student's skill deficit.
2. Most teachers/interventionists would find this intervention appropriate for improving the student's skills.
3. This intervention shoud prove effective in improving the student's skill deficits.
4. I would suggest the use of this intervention to other teachers.
5. The student's skill deficit is servere enough to warrant the use of this intervention.
6. Most teachers would find this intervention suitable for the student's skill deficit.
7. I would be willing to use this intervention in the classroom setting.
8. The intervention would NOT result in negative side-effects for the student.
9. The intervention would be appropriate to use for a variety of students.
10. The intervention is consistent with others I have used in classroom settings.
11. The intervention was a fair way to address the student's skill deficits.
12. The intervention is reasonable for the student's skill deficits.
13. I like the procedures used in the intervention.
14. This intervention was a good way to address the student's skill deficits.
15. Overall, the intervention would be beneficial for the student.
16. The intervention would quickly improve the student's skills.
17. The intervention would produce a lasting improvement in the student's skills.
18. Using the intervention would improve the student's skills to the point that it would not noticeably deviate from oter classmates' skills.
19. Soon after using the intervention, the teacher would notice a positive change in the student's skills.
20. The student's skills will remain at an improved level even after the intervention is discontinued.
21. Using the intervention should not only improve the student's skills in the classroom, but also in other settings such as other classrooms.
22. When comparing this student to a student with average skills. the child's and the peer's skills woold be more alike after using the intervention.
23. The intervention should provide enough improvement in the child's skills so the skill no longer is a problem in the classroom.
24. Other skills related to the skill deficit are likely to be improved by the intervention.

Adapted from the Behavior Intervention Rating Scale (Von Brock & Elliott, 1987).

References

Beck, I. L., McKeown, M. G., & Kucan, L. (2002). *Bringing words to life: Robust vocabulary instruction*. New York: Guilford Press.

Boyle, J. R. (2001). Enhancing the note-taking skills of students with mild disabilities. *Intervention in School and Clinic*, *36*(4), 221–224.

Boyle, J. R. (2007). Strategic note-taking for middle-school students with learning disabilities in science classes. *Learning Disability Quarterly*, *33*, 93–109.

Boyle, J. R. (2011). Strategic note-taking for inclusive middle school science classrooms. *Remedial and Special Education*, *34*(2), 78–90.

Boyle, J. R., Forchelli, G. A., & Cariss, K. (2015). Note-taking interventions to assist students with disabilities in content area classes. *Preventing School Failure: Alternative Education for Children and Youth*, *59*(3), 186–195.

Boyle, J. R., & Weishaar, M. (2001). The effects of strategic notetaking on the recall and comprehension of lecture information for high school students with learning disabilities. *Learning Disabilities Research & Practice*, *16*(3), 133–141.

Burns, M. K., Ardoin, S. P., Parker, D. C., Hodgson, J., Klingbeil, D. A., & Scholin, S. E. (2009). Interspersal technique and behavioral momentum for reading word lists. *School Psychology Review*, *38*, 428–434.

Burns, M. K., Dean, V. J., & Foley, S. (2004). Preteaching unknown key words with incremental rehearsal to improve reading fluency and comprehension with children identified as reading disabled. *Journal of School Psychology*, *42*, 303–314.

Burns, M. K., Hodgson, J., Parker, D. C., & Fremont, K. (2011). Comparison of the effectiveness and efficiency of text previewing and preteaching keywords as small-group reading comprehension strategies with middle school students. *Literacy Research and Instruction*, *50*(3), 241–252.

Burns, M. K., Zaslofsky, A. F., Kanive, R., & Parker, D. C. (2012). Meta-analysis of incremental rehearsal using phi coefficients to compare single-case and group designs. *Journal of Behavioral Education*, *21*(3), 185–202. doi:10.1007/s10864-012-9160-2

Burns, M. K., (2021). Intensifying reading interventions through a skill-by-treatment interaction: what to do when nothing else worked learning hierarchy. *Journal of School Psychology*, *50*(4), 30–32.

Elleman, A., Lindo, E., Morphy, P., & Compton, D. (2009). The impact of vocabulary instruction on passage-level comprehension of school-age children: A meta-analysis. *Journal of Research on Educational Effectiveness*, *2*, 1–44.

Elliott, S. N., & Treuting, M. V. (1991). The behavior intervention rating scale: Development and validation of a pretreatment acceptability and effectiveness measure. *Journal School Psychology Review*, 29, 43–51.

Faber, J. E., Morries, J. D., & Lieberman, M. G. (2000). The effect of note taking on ninth grade students' comprehension. *Reading Psychology*, *21*, 257–270.

Graham, S., & Hebert, M. (2011). Writing to read: A meta-analysis of the impact of writing and writing instruction on reading. *Harvard Educational Review*, *81*(4), 710–744.

Gravois, T. A., & Gickling, E. (2008). Best practices in instructional assessment. In A. Thomas & J. Grimes (Eds.), *Best practices in school psychology* (Vol. IV, pp. 503–518). Bethesda, MD: National Association of School Psychologists.

Haring, N. G., & Eaton, M. D., (1978). Systematic procedures: An instructional hierarchy. In N. G. Haring, T. C. Lovitt, M. D. Eaton, & C. L. Hansen (Eds.), *The fourth R: Research in the classroom*. Columbus, OH: Charles E. Merrill Publishing Company.

Hartley, J. (2002). Notetaking in non-academic settings: A review. *Applied Cognitive Psychology*, *16*, 559–574.

Hebert, M., Gillespie, A., & Graham, S. (2013). Comparing effects of different writing activities on reading comprehension: A meta-analysis. *Reading and Writing: An Interdisciplinary Journal*, *26*, 111–138.

Hoover, W. A., & Gough, P. B. (1990). The simple view of reading. *Reading and Writing: An Interdisciplinary Journal*, 2, 127–160.

Kobayashi, K. (2006). Conditional effects of interventions in note-taking procedures on learning: A meta-analysis. *Japanese Psychological Research*, *48*(2), 109–114.

Kress, J. E., & Fry, E. B. (2016). *The reading teacher's book of lists*. Hoboken, NJ: John Wiley & Sons.

National Center on Intensive Intervention. (2021). *Academic intervention tools chart*. National Center on Intensive Intervention. Retrieved from https://charts.intensiveintervention.org/aintervention

National Reading Panel. (2000). *Report of the National Reading Panel*. National Institute of Child Health and Human Development. Retrieved from https://www.nichd.nih.gov/publications/pubs/nrp/findings

Petersen-Brown, S., & Burns, M. K. (2011). Adding a vocabulary component to incremental rehearsal to enhance retention and generalization. *School Psychology Quarterly*, *26*(3), 245–255.

Petersen-Brown, S., & Burns, M. K. (2019). Enhancing maintenance and generalization of sight words taught with incremental rehearsal: Applying the depth of processing and generalization frameworks. *School Psychology Quarterly*, *34*(3), 307–317.

Szadokierski, I., & Burns, M. K. (2008). Analogue evaluation of the effects of opportunities to respond and ratios of known items within drill rehearsal of Esperanto words. *Journal of School Psychology*, *46*, 593–609.

Tucker, J. A., & Burns, M. K. (2016). Helping students remember what they learn: An intervention for teachers and school psychologists. *Communiqué*, *44*(6), 23.

University of Oregon. (2020). *8th Edition of Dynamic Indicators of Basic Early Literacy Skills (DIBELS®): Benchmark goals*. Eugene, OR: University of Oregon. Retrieved from https://dibels.uoregon.edu

University of Oregon. (2021). *8th Edition of Dynamic Indicators of Basic Early Literacy Skills (DIBELS®): Administration and scoring guide* (2021 ed.). Eugene, OR: University of Oregon. Retrieved from https://dibels.uoregon.edu

Von Brock, M. B., & Elliott, S. N. (1987). Influence of treatment effectiveness information on the acceptability of classroom interventions. *Journal of School Psychology*, 25(2), 131–144.

15

READ, ASK, PARAPHRASE, QUESTION (RAP-Q)

Jessica L. Hagaman

University of Nebraska-Omaha, Omaha, NE, USA

Introduction

This chapter will discuss and provide an example of the RAP-Q strategy. The RAP-Q strategy is a broad reading comprehension strategy that incorporates several comprehension strategies within its steps, including paraphrasing and identifying main ideas while reading and then generating questions for self-study. First, this chapter will describe the RAP-Q strategy, including the steps, the intended target of intervention and evidence to support the intervention's effectiveness. Then, a case study is presented, including suggestions for how to teach the strategy, assessing strategy use, collecting data, and determining intervention acceptability. Finally, considerations for strategy use within the classroom will be discussed.

Reading Comprehension

Comprehension is the process of simultaneously extracting and constructing meaning from text (see Snow, 2002). This process is essential because the primary reason we read is to gain information, either for enjoyment or for specific purposes (e.g., learn new information; Shanahan et al., 2010). As students progress through school, comprehension becomes a primary way for them to gain access to information and becomes an essential skill in content-area classes (e.g., science, social studies). In order for students to be successful as they shift from developing foundational skills and teacher-supported instruction in earlier grades (e.g., decoding, sight words, word knowledge), students will need explicit teaching of cognitive

DOI: 10.4324/9781003275749-15

strategies in reading comprehension that can help them move towards the independent reading expected in secondary school (Vaughn et al., 2015) and that can be used in a variety of reading contexts.

Cognitive strategy instruction is an approach to teaching a variety of strategies that goes beyond simply teaching the steps of a strategy. This approach involves teaching students *how* and *when* to use a strategy, as well as *why* a strategy should be used. It involves identifying an appropriate strategy to teach students, discussion of the importance of the strategy, and explicit integration of self-regulation skills to support the use and maintenance of the strategy (see Sanders, Rollins, Mason, Shaw, & Jolivette, 2021; Sawyer, Graham, & Harris 1992). Specifically, this approach supports students in learning a strategy through explicit instruction in the steps, carefully scaffolded instructional supports, modeling of cognitive and metacognitive components, and explicit development of self-regulation to monitor and manage the reading process, reading strategies, and important behaviors associated with reading (e.g., Daly, Neugebauer, Chafouleas, & Skinner, 2015; Shanahan et al., 2010).

The RAP-Q Strategy

The RAP-Q strategy is one specific example of a reading comprehension strategy. The strategy is an acronym, where each letter represents a step in the reading comprehension process in which students should engage: *R*ead a paragraph, *A*sk yourself, "What were the main ideas and details of this paragraph?" *P*araphrase or *P*ut main ideas and details in your own words, and write *Q*uestions about the paragraph for self-study. RAP-Q can be most broadly categorized as a paraphrasing and self-questioning strategy that helps students engage in comprehension development while they are reading by actively identifying main ideas, supporting details, paraphrasing content, and developing questions for self-study. Through the act of reading and then paraphrasing, students engage in active processing while they are reading, facilitating deeper comprehension of text being read. In addition, RAP-Q helps students break the process of reading into smaller, more manageable units by using chunking and paraphrasing procedures to help students identify main ideas and details in text. Specifically, it requires students to break reading passages into smaller units or "chunks" (i.e., paragraphs) and process information from these smaller units of text (Schumaker, Denton, & Deshler, 1984). Breaking material into smaller units can facilitate processing, memory, and recall (Swanson, 1996). In addition, because it requires students to paraphrase material they read in their own words, students are actively involved in reading rather than passively approaching text (Hagaman,

Casey, & Reid, 2016). Research shows that students who engage in strategies that require a restatement or paraphrasing of text are more likely to recall text and understand main ideas (e.g., Best, Rowe, Ozuru, & McNamara, 2005).

The RAP-Q strategy can be considered a "combined" reading strategy (see Daly et al., 2015), as it involves both during-reading and post-reading steps that students complete. Specifically, during reading, students read paragraph-by-paragraph and then stop to identify main ideas and important details. Then, after reading, students paraphrase each paragraph and identify questions based on what they have read. These questions can then be used for self-study to increase comprehension and add additional processing because students must identify a question based on what they have read and find evidence to support the answer to their self-generated question. In addition, RAP-Q can also be used to help create the framework for important skills such as note-taking, by encouraging students to write about what they read (e.g., write the paraphrase or main ideas and details, highlight/underline main ideas in a reading) or create a framework for studying (e.g., write self-questions on note cards that can be used for studying later).

RAP-Q is based on *The Paraphrasing Strategy* (Ellis & Graves, 1990, Schumaker, Denton, & Deshler, 1984), sometimes called the RAP strategy. The RAP-Q extends the original three steps of the RAP strategy (i.e., *R*ead, *A*sk, *P*araphrase) by asking students to develop questions after reading each paragraph to use for self-study. Initial research demonstrated that students who were taught to use the RAP strategy increased their text recall from a baseline of 48% to 84% after a few short instructional sessions (Schumaker et al., 1984). Later studies on the RAP strategy found the strategy to be effective for middle-school students with learning disabilities (e.g., Ellis & Graves, 1990; Lauterbach & Bender, 1995) and students at-risk for reading failure (Hagaman & Reid, 2008) as well as high school students with and without disabilities (Katims & Harris, 1997). All studies resulted in increases in comprehension when participants were taught the three-step RAP strategy in a series of short lessons. These studies found increases on comprehension when measured by multiple-choice questions, but the RAP strategy has also resulted in increased text recall after reading (i.e., oral retell) and increases in correct responses to open-ended questions focused on main ideas and details in expository, social studies passages (e.g., Hagaman & Reid, 2008; Schumaker et al. 1984).

In addition to studies focused on teaching the RAP strategy to middle and secondary students, similar findings have been seen when the strategy is taught to younger, elementary-age students. Specifically, the effectiveness of the RAP strategy was noted with third-graders who were fluent readers but struggled with reading comprehension (Hagaman, Casey, & Reid, 2012), students with identified learning disabilities (LD) and concomitant language impairment or attention deficit hyperactivity disorder (ADHD; Kemp, 2017), and 4th graders at-risk for reading difficulties (Leidig, Grünke, Urton, Knaak, & Hisgen, 2018). In all cases, comprehension was measured by asking students to respond to questions based on the provided text and resulted in measured increases to comprehension for all students.

Several expansions of the RAP strategy have also been studied. One such expansion is the TRAP strategy, which adds a "before reading" strategy of predicting through the initial step "*Think* about what you are about to read—what do you already know? What do you want to know" to the existing three-step RAP strategy. The TRAP strategy has been found effective at improving reading comprehension in many settings. The strategy has been studied with elementary- and middle-school students (Ciullo, Mason, & Judd, 2021; Hagaman, Casey & Reid, 2012), has been paired with writing strategies to support persuasive quick-write procedures (Ciullo et al., 2021) and with students in more restrictive settings, such as within a secure juvenile justice setting (Sanders, Jolivette, & Harris, 2021). In all cases, after a few short lessons, the TRAP strategy resulted in higher amounts of text recalled (i.e., oral retell), increases in correct responses to open-ended explicit questions, and, when paired with writing strategies to support persuasive quick-write procedures (Ciullo et al., 2021), the TRAP strategy increased the number of ideas directly cited from within a provided passage.

Together, these findings suggest that the RAP-Q strategy can have positive effects on student reading comprehension for students of varying ages and abilities. However, when teaching strategies, it's important to not only consider *what* strategy is taught, but to also consider *how* the strategy is taught. There are currently two instructional approaches to teach strategies have been validated and used to teach the RAP or TRAP strategies: the Strategy Instruction Model (SIM; see Faggella-Luby, Graner, Deshler, & Drew, 2012; Schumaker, Deshler, & Ellis, 1986) and self-regulated strategy development model (SRSD; see Graham & Harris, 2003). Both instructional approaches include procedures for teaching and supporting a strategy while also addressing self-regulation techniques (e.g., goal setting, self-monitoring, self-instruction, and self-reinforcement). In addition, when either instructional approach is paired with a specific strategy such as RAP-Q, they can help students to develop important strategic behaviors (e.g., motivation, sustained attention, self-regulation) important to reading comprehension.

Case Study

Background Information

This section provides an illustration of how a 5th-grade teacher used the SRSD model to teach the RAP-Q strategy. In this example, the RAP-Q strategy will be illustrated using the six flexible instructional stages of the SRSD model (*Develop Background Knowledge, Discuss It, Model It, Memorize It, Support It, and Independent Performance*; Graham & Harris, 2003). Table 15.1 includes a short explanation for the six stages of the SRSD model. In addition, suggestions for differentiated small group instruction for students who needed more support is highlighted.

Mr. Williams is a 5th-grade teacher in a public school. At the beginning of the school year, he noticed that several students in his class were already having some difficulty with some important Common Core State Standards (CCSS, 2010) related to reading comprehension. Specifically, students were struggling with standards that expect students to read text,

TABLE 15.1 The Instructional Stages of the SRSD Model

SRSD Stage	*Short Explanation*
1. Develop Background Knowledge	Make sure students know what strategies are and why we use them Ensure students have the necessary prerequisite stills to engage in all steps of the selected strategy Collect baseline data
2. Discuss it	"Sell" strategy as something that will help improve performance Introduce mnemonic and steps of the strategy Obtain a commitment from students to try using the strategy
3. Model it	Model the use of strategy steps using a "think-aloud" procedure – Demonstrate cognitive and metacognitive knowledge associated with the strategy
4. Memorize it	Teacher plans ways to facilitate student memorization of strategy steps Automaticity and fluency of strategy steps helps improve comprehension
5. Support it	Teacher plans ways to scaffold and support strategy use, gradual transfer of strategy use from teacher to student(s)
6. Independent Performance	Student can use the strategy on their own, OR predetermined threshold of strategy use is obtained by student and teacher primarily monitors strategy use, student performance, and cues use of strategy

identify important information such as main ideas and important details, and summarize or paraphrase after reading (e.g., CCSS.ELA-Literacy.R.5.2: *Determine two or more main ideas of a text and explain how they are supported by key details; summarize the text*; CCSS.ELA-Literacy.RL.5.1: *Quote accurately from text when explaining what the text says explicitly and when drawing inferences from the text*).

His inclusive classroom has 23 students of varying ability, including students with learning, attention, and behavioral disabilities who struggle with reading as well as typically achieving students who have difficulty with various skills associated with reading text. Several other professionals work with him in his classroom to meet student needs: a special education teacher, a speech-language pathologist, and a paraprofessional. All three of these professionals help with varying subjects (e.g., writing, reading) and student needs by providing small-group instruction, and this allows Mr. Williams to create flexible grouping when he provides reading instruction.

Currently, Mr. Williams uses the reading curriculum provided by his district that has been aligned with the CCSS. The curriculum provides a structure for the texts his students read, including various forms of fiction, poems, and informational texts and expects students to build on skills they developed in 4th grade by deepening their engagement with these texts. In addition, his curriculum expects students to be able to read various types of text and use direct quotes, facts, and examples from the text to develop their own opinions or to explain it. His students are also increasingly expected to write about the texts they read to demonstrate their understanding. However, because he has noticed so many students in need of more explicit instruction in specific reading comprehension skills, he begins to investigate ways to support his students. When he teaches writing, he already teaches specific instructional strategies to support writing genres (e.g., opinion, persuasive) and uses the SRSD model to teach those writing strategies, and so he begins to consider a few simple reading strategies to evaluate and determine which might be appropriate for his students based on their current performance.

Problem Identification

Because Mr. Williams' school has a multi-tiered framework that requires all students to be screened in various skills, including reading, three times per year (Beginning, Middle, End), he has access to several types of data on his students already this year. Specifically, he has access to the Beginning of Year (BOY) fluency benchmark, which provides him with some information on which students are already demonstrating some risk according to their fluency scores. Those students have been noted, and Mr. Williams can see that some students are already receiving additional supports to address their foundational reading skills through special education. In addition to a fluency benchmark, his student's reading comprehension is assessed using the district's web-based Curriculum Based Measurement (CBM) program that provides students with a reading passage followed by several multiple-choice questions that evaluate both literal and inferential comprehension.

When looking at the data provided to him in the BOY benchmark for comprehension, Mr. Williams is provided percentile ranks for all his students based on their responses to the multiple-choice questions they answered. Based on the cut-scores provided by the district's CBM, he can see that roughly 40% of his class had difficulty answering literal questions based on the passage(s) provided to them and are considered to be at-risk (i.e., some risk or high risk). He noted that while roughly 60% of his class was determined to be demonstrating "minimal risk" according to the BOY CBM benchmark cut-score for 5th grade, it was still likely that some of these students may have difficulty consistently identifying important information in the passages they read. See Table 15.2 for class benchmark data.

Problem Analysis

Given these data, it was clear that Mr. Williams needed to provide some type of explicit instruction related to reading comprehension. While there were several students in his class that had demonstrated skill deficits in reading fluency (as measured by Oral Reading Fluency [ORF]), which appeared to contribute to their lower comprehension scores, the majority of these students were already receiving special education services; several of them for reading or language-related needs. This meant that several students in his class were demonstrating deficits in some skill or set of skills associated with reading comprehension and were not receiving any specific instruction yet to address these skill deficits. In addition, Mr. Williams wondered if some of the students that scored below the 60th percentile but were not considered to be "at-risk" according to the benchmark may be scoring lower on comprehension because of a performance deficit. That is, they have the necessary skills related to comprehension but are not yet demonstrating those skills consistently.

Mr. Williams had been considering several reading comprehension strategies, but given the focus of the CCSS for reading in 5th grade and the current needs of his class, it seemed appropriate to select a strategy that would establish a framework for identifying main ideas and supporting

TABLE 15.2 Beginning of Year Benchmark Data

Student	*ORF-WC*	*Risk*	*Comprehension Percentile*	*Risk*	*Disability Status?*	*Overall Risk*
1.	81	Some	16th	Some		Some
2.	104	Minimal	30th	Some		Some
3.	110	Minimal	82nd	Minimal		
4.	109	Minimal	44th	Minimal		
5.	78	High	10th	Some		High
6.	138	Minimal	66th	Minimal		
7.	123	Minimal	51st	Minimal		
8.	90	Some	23rd	Some	Yes	High
9.	140	Minimal	96th	Minimal		
10.	137	Minimal	90th	Minimal		
11.	95	Some	16th	Some		Some
12.	107	Minimal	66th	Minimal		
13.	134	Minimal	51st	Minimal		
14.	73	High	10th	High	Yes	High
15.	138	Minimal	96th	Minimal		
16.	120	Minimal	90th	Minimal		
17.	115	Minimal	90th	Some		Some
18.	99	Some	58th	Minimal		
19.	104	Minimal	58th	Minimal		
20.	71	High	6th	High	Yes	High
21.	105	Minimal	51st	Minimal		
22.	77	High	30th	Some	Yes	High
23.	139	Minimal	90th	Minimal		

Note. These data are example data using ORF risk levels of 81–102 Words Correct (WC) Some Risk and 0–80 WC High Risk and comprehension risk of 12th–33rd percentile for Some Risk and 0–11th percentile for High Risk.

details in various types of text. In addition, an appropriate strategy should involve paraphrasing and additional steps that can encourage students to engage more deeply in the text through writing, notetaking, or self-study because these are skills that his students will need in 5th grade and later grades. He ultimately decided on the RAP-Q strategy, because it is a simple, flexible strategy that can support his students in a variety of text and can easily be differentiated to support all students in his class.

In order to determine the specific skills associated with the RAP-Q strategy, Mr. Williams conducts a task analysis. The task analysis identified the following skills that are essential for strategy use: (1) students need to be able to read fluently on or close to grade-level text; (2) students will need to know what main ideas are and how to find them in a variety of passages;

(3) students will need to know what supporting details are; (4) students will need to know the meaning of most words in a passage (i.e., basic comprehension); (5) students will need to understand how to paraphrase; (6) students should be able to generate questions, based on text they read; and (7) students should know how to self-question and/or study. See Table 15.3 for an example for using the task analysis steps to collect and analyze classroom data.

Using this task analysis, Mr. Williams knew that many students did not have all these skills yet, and the point of teaching the strategy is to help them systematically develop these skills. He planned to collect some specific baseline data on his class to help him confirm his current hypothesis; that many students in his class are unable to identify main ideas and details in a provided text. In addition, because he already had access to the BOY benchmark data for his class for fluency and comprehension, he could indicate which students are already identified as "at-risk" and he could use these data to plan his instruction, the partners he would use, and the small group instruction for each lesson.

Intervention Goals

Because all students in Mr. Williams' class can benefit from explicit instruction in reading comprehension strategies, all students will be taught the RAP-Q strategy as a framework for additional reading comprehension strategies in the future. Differentiated and small-group instruction will provide opportunities to support specific needs of students, but the goals for the intervention are broad and the same for the whole class. The goals for implementing the RAP-Q strategy to a 5th grade, general education class are as follows:

1. Students will be able to list and explain the steps of the RAP-Q strategy;
2. Students will be able to identify main ideas and supporting details for an entire passage (i.e., the overall focus of the passage);
3. Students will be able to identify main ideas of each paragraph of a provided passage;
4. Students will be able to summarize or paraphrase information from a provided text;
5. Students will develop at least one self-question per passage to use for studying and/or identifying where the correct answer is found in text;
6. Students will demonstrate an increase in reading comprehension as measured using a 10 question, multiple-choice pre-test and post-test.

TABLE 15.3 Example Task Analysis Data Collection for Class

Task Analysis for RAP-Q	*Example Student 1*	*2*	*3*	*4*	*5*	*6*	*7*	*8*	*9*	*10*	*11*	*12*	*13*	*14*	*15*
1. Fluency at grade level	132 WPM	92 WPM													
2. Main ideas	+[a]	–[b]													
	Date Observed														
3. Supporting details	–	–													
4. Meaning of words (basic comprehension)	+	+													
5. Paraphrase	–	–													
6. How to generate questions	–	–													
7. How to self-question/study	–	–													

Note: This table provides an example of how a task analysis might be used to keep track of progress data on a whole class while teaching a strategy.
a + = skill observed
b – = skill not yet observed

Measurement of Target Reading Skill, Data Collection Strategies, and Progress Monitoring

To measure the effects of the RAP-Q strategy, Mr. Williams used two types of assessments. First, based on assessments used in previous research with similar strategies (e.g., RAP, TRAP), he created 10 comprehension questions based on provided passages to determine the comprehension abilities of his students. He used two similar passages (e.g., similar in length, expository passages) to create a set of comprehension questions to use as a pre- and post- measure to determine the effects of teaching his class the RAP-Q strategy. Similar to the comprehension CBM used by his district, he created 5 multiple-choice questions based on information in the passages that would require students to refer back to the text to answer them correctly (i.e., explicitly in the text). In addition, he included 5 open-ended questions, such as "What was this passage mostly about?," to evaluate this student's knowledge of main ideas and details (e.g., "What details in the reading tell you more specific information about Elephants?"). This allowed Mr. Williams to see the baseline performance of his class, while also measuring any change in the mean scores following instruction in the RAP-Q strategy. He was also able to see specific questions the class missed, and whether there was a pattern related to types of questions the class got incorrect (e.g., information based on details versus main ideas).

Second, Mr. Williams also needed some formative data on student progress to indicate how much instruction and support his class needed on the RAP-Q strategy while he was planning and teaching the strategy. While he used the six stages of the SRSD model to teach the strategy, he knew that some students would require more support and time than others to master the steps of the strategy. Therefore, each lesson he taught included data for progress monitoring. He collected data on: (1) student strategy use (e.g., evidence of using the strategy through highlighting/underlining main ideas or details in a passage, completing provided graphic organizers); (2) the accuracy of written paraphrases; (3) the questions students generate for each paragraph; and (4) their knowledge of the strategy steps.

Baseline Data. Before beginning instruction, Mr. Williams used the "pre-test" he created to collect baseline data on his students and asked them identify main ideas and details on a short, 3-paragraph informational text. Students were provided the text, written at grade level, and asked to identify the main idea of the overall passage. They were also asked to identify the main idea of each paragraph of the 3 paragraphs in the passage as well as examples of supporting details in each paragraph. Finally, students were asked to paraphrase the content of the passage by writing a response to the question "In your own words, what was this passage mostly about?" In addition to these open-ended questions, they were asked several basic multiple-choice comprehension questions, similar to those asked in district comprehension testing (e.g., Benchmark assessments). Together, the assessment had 5 multiple-choice questions and 5 short-answer questions for a total of 10 questions.

After collecting student responses, Mr. Williams reviewed his students' work. Mr. Williams first looked at the overall number of correct scores for his students (i.e., score out of 10 questions). The scores ranged from 3–9, with the average score for the class of 6.4 out of 10. Because short-answer questions can be more difficult, since they require response generation (e.g., writing, spelling), Mr. Williams also analyzed just the multiple-choice questions. Of the 5 multiple-choice questions given to his class, roughly 75% of the class (n = 17) answered 3 or fewer questions correctly. He noted that most students could identify the main idea of the entire passage when asked. However, not all students could identify the main ideas of individual paragraphs even when selecting from a list of possible answers; roughly half of his class did not correctly identify main ideas in each paragraph. In addition, most students could not identify relevant supporting details for the main ideas they identified. He also realized that several students could not summarize or paraphrase the content they read. In most cases, his students directly copied the title of the passage or copied the first sentence of the first paragraph rather than summarizing or paraphrasing information in their own words. Mr. Williams also noted that his students with identified disabilities had greater difficulties with the task and the act of writing responses to the open-ended questions (e.g., writing the main ideas, details, summary) was difficult for many of them; their responses were short, sometimes including only one word.

Based on these data and his previously conducted Task Analysis, Mr. Williams determined it was appropriate for him to begin instruction on the RAP-Q strategy by teaching all of his students the easier steps of the strategy first. This meant he began teaching them how to identify the main ideas and supporting details in a provided passage. Then he moved onto more difficult skills by instructing them in how to summarize or paraphrase, and then finally how to identify and create questions for self-study. For his instruction, Mr. Williams taught the RAP-Q strategy by following the SRSD model. Mr. Williams believed that the RAP-Q strategy would help his students with reading comprehension and planned his instructional lessons for the whole class and supplementary support for small-group instruction for his struggling readers.

Intervention Plan

Day One

Introducing the strategy. The first day of whole-class instruction started with developing the background knowledge and skills needed to be a good reader (SRSD stage: *Develop Background Knowledge*). Mr. Williams first reviewed and discussed why reading comprehension is important. He solicited feedback from his students by asking them to list all the things they read in the day (e.g., text on a computer/iPhone, posters, menus). Then, he asked the students to consider how important it is to understand all of those things. The students were able to eventually identify that understanding what they read is really important, and is the reason why people read. Finally, he asked the students to generate some things they think good readers do (e.g., look at the title of a book, look at the picture on a cover of a book, sound out and read words, ask for help when they don't know a word) and helped the students understand that good readers often use *strategies* to help them understand what they read.

Mr. Williams defined what a strategy was, to ensure students were clear on what strategies are in general. He defined a strategy as "something you might do to help you be faster, or better, or maybe more efficient at a task." He asked students to discuss some ways they have used or heard about strategies and then asked them to share ideas with the class. Several students identified that they use strategies in sports or when playing games and that these strategies helped them win, get faster, or score more points. Mr. Williams asked the class what a reading comprehension strategy would do and then discussed with students how a reading strategy would help them be better readers, remember more of what they read, potentially score better on quizzes and tests, and be better prepared for middle and high school in the future.

He then introduced the RAP-Q strategy to the class and explained to students that they would learn how to use the strategy. He introduced the steps of the strategy and the reasons for each step (e.g., why might a reader stop after each paragraph to identify main ideas and details?) and also discussed what an acronym is (each letter stands for a step to complete). He made sure there was a visual of the strategy and steps available for students to reference. See Figure 15.1.

After introducing the strategy, Mr. Williams established reading partners. Reading partners would provide each other support by being able to verbally summarize, paraphrase, and practice questioning each other as students learned the strategy. Mr. Williams had carefully selected partners based on student performance. Mr. Williams asked the student partners to

R – Read a paragraph

A – Ask yourself "What was the main idea of what I just read?"

- Can you find details that support that main idea?

P- Paraphrase or Put the main idea and details into your own words

- Paraphrasing is when you put material that you read into your own words.
- When you paraphrase the main ideas, try to think of other words to say what you read in the text

Q – Question- based on what you just read, can you rephrase the paraphrase into a question?

- Based on your paraphrase, write a question and an answer on the back of a notecard so that you can use this for studying later
  - *Example Paraphrase: There are 2 types of elephants*
  - *Example question: "how many types of elephants are there?"*

FIGURE 15.1 The RAP-Q Strategy

practice memorizing the RAP-Q strategy by pairing up and listing and naming the steps of RAP-Q and explaining why each was important (SRSD stage: *Memorize It*). To end this lesson, Mr. Williams emphasized the goals of becoming better readers and how using the RAP-Q strategy would help them be better readers (SRSD Stage: *Discuss It*) The class then established goals for learning the strategy, and made a commitment to learn it.

Day Two

Identifying main ideas and details. The next day, Mr. Williams asked student partners to verbally review the RAP-Q strategy (SRSD Stage: *Memorize It*) as a way to practice remembering the steps before learning how to use the strategy. He told the class that in his review of students' work from the prior day, he found that most students were able to identify the main idea of the passage that was given; but not everyone was able to identify the main ideas in each paragraph or to identify supporting details for the main idea. In addition, paraphrasing the passage was difficult for many students (SRSD Stage: *Develop Background Knowledge*). Mr. Williams made it clear that learning the RAP-Q strategy would help students, and asked if they were ready to start using the strategy.

Mr. Williams then displayed a short, grade-level passage (and provided copies for all students) and read aloud the passage while students followed along on their copy. Students raised their hands when they identified the main idea of the first paragraph. After identifying the main idea, students underlined it on their copy; with the help of Mr. Williams, they circled supporting details. Then Mr. Williams explained some ways to identify the main idea. He discussed how the main idea can sometimes be in the title of the passage or in the first sentence of a paragraph. He reminded students that paragraphs have several sentences. He also told students that a main idea might be a word or phrase that repeats in a paragraph and that it should be the overarching theme of the paragraph. Then he discussed the details of the paragraph and how to identify details (e.g., they support the main idea, they add more specific information about the topic) and let students know that some paragraphs might have a few supporting details and some might have many more. He told students that they had just completed the first two steps of the RAP-Q Strategy: *R*ead a paragraph and *A*sk yourself what the main idea was a identify supporting details (SRSD Stage: *Support it*).

Then Mr. Williams modeled the final two steps of the strategy by performing a short *think-aloud* (SRSD Stage: *Model it*) where he voiced aloud the steps he performed, the reasons for performing them, and other thoughts. For example, he voiced things like "I'm looking back at the paragraph and the main idea I underlined to remind me what this paragraph was about. And I remember that paraphrasing should not copy this, but be in my own words." He continued to think aloud and modeled how to paraphrase and then how to identify a question based on the paragraph and how to write this question on a note-card by saying "I can rephrase my paraphrase as a question, and then I can use this question to help me check my understanding later." He also included examples of self-statements in his modeling, such as "Wow, that took a long time, but I also feel pretty good about using this strategy!," as well as an example of a self-statement about problem definition ("What do I need to do next?"), planning ("First, I need to read a paragraph"), self-evaluation ("Does this look like the main idea of this paragraph?"), self-reinforcement ("Only two more paragraphs to go!"), and coping/persistence ("I can do this, I'm almost done").

After modeling, Mr. Williams asked students what they noticed about the paraphrasing (e.g., it was in his own words, short, about the paragraph, included the details and main idea that were underlined, he looked back at the paragraph while he paraphrased) and why paraphrasing can help with comprehension. Then, he did the same with the questions for self-study by asking students what they noticed about how he came up with a question (e.g., wrote it on a note-card/scratch paper, based on information in the paragraph, rephrased the summary as a question).

Then Mr. Williams moved to the second paragraph of the passage and read it aloud and told students that they would start to practice using the strategy with their partners or in their groups. He asked students to work with their partners to underline the main idea in what he had just read and circle some details. Then he asked them to practice paraphrasing. He gave them enough time to do these activities and then asked the group to generate questions together and Mr. Williams wrote two examples on the board and discussed with the class what made these good questions for self-study (SRSD Stage: *Support it*).

Finally, Mr. Williams now prompted students to work with their reading partners on the remaining paragraphs to underline the main idea, circle details, and paraphrase aloud. He provided some note-cards and scratch paper and encouraged the partners to also write questions based on each paragraph if they were ready. While the reading partners worked on this, Mr. Williams took the opportunity to check with some partners that needed additional support, in a small group.

Small-group instruction and differentiation. Based on student needs, Mr. Williams was prepared to first provide additional practice on the memorization of the RAP-Q mnemonic (SRSD Stage: *Memorize It*) or remind ers of the strategy steps. Next, he continued to support and instruct students, as needed, on how to identify the main idea or details and prompted them to identify those elements within their passage. He guided pairs to paraphrase the paragraph, with his help. Some students were given a supporting worksheet that prompted each step of the strategy and provided places for them to write responses (see Figure 15.2).

End of lesson. To end the second lesson, the whole class generated a few questions based on the remaining paragraphs and Mr. Williams used those questions to help students see how they could use the questions to "test themselves" on the passage they just read. He posed the questions to the class and had them answer the questions, orally, with their reading partners. He asked students to turn in their passages, so he could later analyze the main ideas and details they identified, to determine the next steps he should take for instruction and how much additional instruction and support the class might need on the RAP-Q strategy.

Day Three

Additional practice with paraphrasing and self-questioning. To begin, Mr. Williams asked student partners to "quiz" each other on the steps of the RAP-Q strategy (SRSD Stage: *Memorize It*) and then asked them to write

Title of Passage: ____

Paragraph 1 Main Idea: ____
Detail Detail Paraphrase in your own words: Question about the paragraph:

Paragraph 2 Main Idea: ____
Detail Detail Paraphrase in your own words: Question about the paragraph:

Paragraph 3 Main Idea: ____
Detail Detail Paraphrase in your own words: Question about the paragraph:

Use your questions from each paragraph (above) to "quiz" yourself!

Your response to question 1 ______________________________________
Your response to question 2 ______________________________________
Your response to question 3 ______________________________________

FIGURE 15.2 Graphic Organizer

the steps of the strategy on a paper to submit to him (this would allow him to see how many students have the strategy and steps memorized). Then, he told students they would be working with their partners after they completed the initial steps of the RAP-Q strategy on their own (SRSD Stage: *Support It*). Specifically, students were asked to individually read each paragraph, identify main ideas and details, and paragraph while using the *R, A, P* steps of the strategy. He provided all students with another informational passage written at grade level that contained several paragraphs.

He prompted students to remember the steps of the RAP-Q strategy and told students that he should see evidence of them using each step of the strategy (e.g., underlining or highlighting the main ideas of each paragraph) and provided another graphic organizer that helped walk students through the steps of the strategy and provided space for them to write a short paraphrase after each paragraph and a place to write their self-questions. He told students that once they had completed the graphic organizer, they would work with their partner to ask each other their self-generated questions and try to find the answers in the passage or in their notes (i.e., the paraphrasing written on their graphic organizer).

Small-group instruction and differentiation. Mr. Williams met with specific pairs, individuals, or small groups of students who required additional support and discussed and remodeled aspects of the paraphrasing and question-generating process. Depending on student needs, some students also needed continued support and prompting about main ideas and details in each paragraph of a passage. In some cases, Mr. Williams worked with students to help them develop positive self-reinforcement and coping statements when discouraged or frustrated with reading (e.g., what could you say to yourself to stay motivated?).

End of lesson. After all students had the opportunity to practice using the RAP-Q strategy, with varying amounts of support (e.g., working alone, with partner, supported by Mr. Williams), the whole class practiced answering a few comprehension questions based on the content of the passage. Mr. Williams showed the comprehension questions on the board and read the questions aloud before allowing the reading partners to discuss as needed to provide some processing think-time for students. Then he asked students to raise their hand if they knew the answer to the question, called on students to share responses and discussed whether the answer was correct (including discussion of how they found the answer, whether the RAP-Q strategy helped them remember more, etc). He repeated this process until all comprehension questions were answered as a class and congratulated the class on using the RAP-Q strategy to correctly answer comprehension questions similar to those they find in quizzes or tests in his class.

Day Four and Beyond

Evaluate and provide continued support. The next class sessions consisted of more collaborative practice with using the strategy. Based on student performance, not all students still required explicit instruction in strategy steps. Data from the previous lesson showed that most students had the strategy memorized and were able to correctly underline the main idea in all paragraphs. In addition, most students were also able to correctly identify details. There were still some students who struggled with paraphrasing more than a single word and students that struggled to consistently generate questions for self-study based on information in a passage. Mr. Williams continued to provide reading passages of various lengths and difficulty (e.g., topics on which students had prerequisite knowledge versus passages based on newer content) and encouraged students to use their reading partners as necessary. He also continued to monitor student progress and individualize support and instruction based on their needs. At this point, it was appropriate for Mr. Williams to fade some of the instructional supports he had been providing (i.e., peer support, shorter passages, guiding worksheets) and so he taught students how to take notes on a blank piece of paper by writing the main idea and a supporting detail from a paragraph. He also showed students how they could monitor their own strategy use by writing the letters RAP-Q next to each paragraph and crossing them off as they completed each paragraph. Some students were eager to try these techniques during the next few class sessions, while other students continued to use the graphic organizer(s) Mr. Williams provided (SRSD Stage: *Support it*). Mr. Williams repeated this lesson and various levels of support as necessary, with some students still requiring additional support, cues for strategy use, and individualized support.

Fading support and independent practice. Once the students in Mr. Williams' class were able to list and describe all the steps of the RAP-Q strategy, could consistently identify the main idea and details in a provided passage, paraphrase each paragraph, and generate questions on provided note-cards, Mr. Williams ended his instruction on RAP-Q and began working on generalization and transfer tasks that would encourage his students to use the RAP-Q strategy in other settings and make the strategy their own (SRSD Stage: *Independent Practice*). The class discussed places where they had already used the RAP-Q strategy, other than with Mr. Williams. In some cases, students were excited to share that they had been using the strategy on their own or that they liked "taking notes" like their older siblings did at home when they were studying or doing homework. In addition, as a class they discussed times that using the RAP-Q strategy might help them (e.g., when they were reading in other classes, when they were taking a test). Some students in class continued to require support to use the strategy, such as a graphic organizer or scratch paper with the steps of the strategy written at the top as a reminder. Mr. Williams knew that some students would require these supports for a longer period of time, but that the use of the strategy would still likely improve their comprehension skills.

As a final reading activity and "post-test" for this short unit focused on the RAP-Q strategy, the class was provided another passage with 10 multiple-choice and short-answer questions to measure their comprehension. Before students were given the passage, Mr. Williams asked students to write down the steps of the RAP-Q strategy and an explanation for what they do at each step. Then students were given a copy of the article and the following prompt, "Read this passage to yourself. You should remember to use your strategy when you're reading. Once you're done, you can work with your partner to quiz each other using the questions you develop for each paragraph before you take a short quiz." After being given time to read, partners were given a few more minutes and encouraged to work together in quizzing each other using the self-questions generated before they individually answered the comprehension questions about the passage. Students took the comprehension "post-test" and submitted their responses for Mr. Williams to analyze later. After this, the class celebrated their success in learning a new strategy and improving their comprehension. They agreed they were excited to learn more strategies in the future, and to continue using this strategy.

Intervention Fidelity and Interobserver Agreement Plans

While teaching the RAP-Q strategy, Mr. Williams evaluated his fidelity of instruction in two ways. First, an instructional checklist accompanied each lesson plan. Mr. Williams used this checklist to check off each lesson component after it was taught. This type of checklist was meant to reduce the possibility of the teacher missing a critical step during instruction and to be able to determine a percentage for Intervention Fidelity achieved by the teacher. Second, the fidelity checklist was used by outside observers to establish an inter-observer agreement (IOA). In Mr. Williams' classroom, he asked the paraeducator and the special education teacher to observe lessons using the instructional checklist. Based on published research on similar strategies to the RAP-Q strategy, Mr. Williams determined that treatment fidelity and IOA needed to meet a predetermined threshold of 90%. If not, additional instruction or repeating of a lesson was necessary to ensure all intervention components were provided to students. To see an example of a fidelity checklist for the first lesson, see Figure 15.3.

Intervention Outcome Data

When Mr. Williams had given students their pre-test, prior to beginning instruction on the RAP-Q strategy, the class had an average score of 6.4 out of 10 on the comprehension questions, with 52% (n = 12) of his class getting 7 or more (i.e., 70%) questions correct. Following several targeted lessons on the RAP-Q strategy, his post-test showed a small increase in the overall comprehension scores of his students. Specifically, the class average

RAP-Q Lesson 1: Introduce RAP-Q

Date: ____________
Length of lesson (time):

Components	Observed Yes	No
Set context for student learning		
Discussed importance of remembering what you read		
Introduced students to their current performance in reading comprehension		
Develop background knowledge		
Addressed why it is good to use strategies		
Discussed what good readers do		
Introduced steps of the RAP-Q strategy		
Discuss RAP-Q steps		
Described each step		
Gave examples of how to complete each step		
Obtaining commitment		
Encouraged students to use the RAP-Q strategy		
Discussed when it would be a good time to use the strategy		
Obtained verbal commitment		
Set a goal		
Discussed why it is important to set goals		
Prompted students to set a goal		
Assisted students in creating realistic goals		
Memorization		
Worked on memorization		
Allowed students time to practice memorizing with partner		
Prerequisites		
Explained to students how to identify main ideas and details		
Allowed students opportunity practice identifying main ideas and details		
Practiced paraphrasing		
Wrap-up/Generalization		
Reminded to practice		
Reminded to memorize		
Teacher behavior		
Materials ready for each activity		
Instruction delivered with enthusiasm		
Maintained appropriate pace during instruction		
Monitored and checked for understanding		

Treatment Fidelity:

Total Yes	
Total	24
% Fidelity	

FIGURE 15.3 Fidelity Checklist

was now 7.3 out of 10, with roughly 70% (n = 16) of his class scoring 7 or more correct on the 10 multiple-choice questions.

During instruction, Mr. Williams also collected data on student progress that he used to inform the amount or support he provided to students while teaching the strategy. With these data, Mr. Williams was also able to determine the effects of the RAP-Q strategy relative to the instructional goals he set for his class. Specifically, following instruction, all students in his class were able to correctly list and explain the steps of the RAP-Q strategy (Intervention Goal 1). Some of his students still relied on a visual reminder of the RAP-Q acronym (e.g., poster on the wall, bookmark), but could explain the steps using the acronym as a guide. Second, following instruction, all students were be able to identify main ideas and supporting details for an entire passage (Intervention Goal 2). Third, when provided a graphic organizer and instructor support, all students were able to identify main ideas of each paragraph of a provided passage (Intervention Goal 3). Some students were provided passages that were shorter in length (e.g., 4 paragraphs versus 6) or on topics that they were more familiar with to scaffold support across the students in his class, but with varying amounts of support, all students could correctly identify the main idea and at least two supporting details in the paragraphs of a provided text.

In the final two, most advanced steps of the RAP-Q strategy, roughly 70% of the class were able to achieve the intervention goals of paraphrasing (Intervention Goal 4) and developing self-questions (Intervention Goal 5) with various amounts of support. Most students still preferred to use a graphic organizer (see Figure 15.2) to support their paraphrasing and to generate questions and still relied on Mr. Williams to prompt their use of self-questions to find information in the text once they finished reading a passage. However, after several days of explicit instruction, the majority of the class was now ready to use the strategy with various supports or simple prompts from Mr. Williams or other professionals (e.g., paraeducator). Now, Mr. Williams felt it was appropriate to encourage students to make the strategy their own while cueing opportunities to use the strategy and continuing to monitor their comprehension and strategy use.

Intervention Acceptability

In addition to measuring the intervention's impact on student performance, following instruction, it's important to consider the intervention's acceptability to students. Students in Mr. Williams' class answered four questions in writing to share their perceptions about the intervention. These questions were based on previous peer-reviewed studies that investigated the effects of similar strategies (see Ciullo et al., 2021). The questions were: (1) Has the RAP-Q strategy helped you be a better reader? How? (2) If you were the teacher, would you make any changes to the lessons we did? What? (3) Have you used RAP-Q in other classes or in other places (like at home)? (4) Do you think the RAP-Q strategy would help other students? Overall, students reported that the intervention was beneficial, and a few indicated they had tried using the reading strategy in other settings. Students also wrote that they did not suggest any specific changes to the instruction and that they liked the strategy.

Intervention Considerations

This case study provides broad suggestions on how to effectively support the development of reading comprehension in a whole-class setting using a specific strategy. The RAP-Q strategy is an intervention that is relatively simple, low in cost, and requires no specific curricula or materials. Because the strategy is so simple, it is easily incorporated to many existing classroom structures or curricula in as little as 20–30-minute instructional sessions, a few times per week. Depending on the students in a given class, positive impacts on reading comprehension should be seen in as few as 4 instructional sessions (see Hagaman & Casey, 2017; Hagaman, Casey, & Reid, 2016). However, it is important to note that when teaching any strategy, practitioners should use a validated instructional model, such as the SRSD or SIM model, to ensure that key features such as modeling, guided practice, and support for self-regulation and executive functions are included. When using these models, the amount and type of support provided through scaffolding activities will vary based on student needs. Specifically, some students might require weeks of instructional support while others may only require a few short sessions followed by reminders in order to use the strategy. This highlights the importance of teachers collecting frequent and useful data on student progress in order to determine the point at which students require fewer supports. In addition, the strategy is highly flexible and can be used on various types and lengths of text, the steps of the strategy can be independently taught (i.e., main idea, detail, paraphrasing) before being put together, and the strategy can be paired with other strategies (e.g., writing strategies) once introduced. This flexibility is one of the most desirable features of this strategy.

Conclusion

Reading comprehension is a complex task and one that can be difficult for many students. The RAP-Q strategy is an example of a specific reading comprehension strategy that incorporates the identification of main ideas and details, paraphrasing, self-questioning, and self-monitoring to help students improve their comprehension. By using an instructional model, such as the SRSD instructional approach to teach the RAP-Q strategy, teachers combine explicit instruction in the steps of the strategy with the important development self-regulation skills to help students improve their reading comprehension while also developing strategic behaviors. As a result, they are giving students the necessary tools to be successful in school and beyond.

References

Best, R. M., Rowe, M., Ozuru, Y., & McNamara, D. S. (2005). Deep-level comprehension of science texts: The role of the reader and the text. *Topics in Language Disorders*, *25*, 65–83. doi:10.1097/00011363-200501000-00007

Ciullo, S., Mason, L. H., & Judd, L. (2021). Persuasive quick-writing about text: Intervention for students with learning disabilities. *Behavior Modification*, *45*(1), 122–146.

Daly, E. J., III, Neugebauer, S. R., Chafouleas, S. M., & Skinner, C. H. (2015). *Interventions for reading problems: Designing and evaluating effective strategies* (2nd ed.). New York, NY: Guilford Press.

Ellis, E. S., & Graves, A. W. (1990). Teaching rural students with learning disabilities: A paraphrasing strategy to increase comprehension of main ideas. *Rural Special Education Quarterly*, *10*, 2–10.

Faggella-Luby, M. N., Graner, P. S., Deshler, D. D., & Drew, S. V. (2012). Building a house on sand: Why disciplinary literacy is not sufficient to replace general strategies for adolescent learners who struggle. *Topics in Language Disorders*, *32*(1), 69–84. doi:10.1097/TLD.0b013e318245618e

Graham, S., & Harris, K. (2003). *Students with learning disabilities and the process of writing: A meta-analysis of SRSD studies*. New York, NY: Guilford Press.

Hagaman, J. L., & Casey, K. J. (2017). Paraphrasing strategy instruction in content area text. *Intervention in School and Clinic*, *52*, 210–217. doi:10.1080/1045988X.2014.966802

Hagaman, J. L., & Reid, R. (2008). The effects of the paraphrasing strategy on the reading comprehension of middle school students at risk for failure in reading. *Remedial and Special Education*, *29*(4), 222–234. doi:10.1177/0741932507311638

Hagaman, J. L., Casey, K. J., & Reid, R. (2012). The effects of the paraphrasing strategy on the reading comprehension of young students. *Remedial and Special Education*, *33*(2), 110–123. doi:10.1177/0741932510364548

Hagaman, J. L., Casey, K. J., & Reid, R. (2016). Paraphrasing strategy instruction for struggling readers. *Preventing School Failure*, *60*, 43–52. doi:10.1080/1045988X.2014.966802

Katims, D. S., & Harris, S. (1997). Improving the reading comprehension of middle school students in inclusive classrooms. *Journal of Adolescent and Adult Literacy*, *41*, 116–123.

Kemp, S. E. (2017). RAP: A reading comprehension strategy for students with learning disabilities and concomitant speech-language impairments or ADHD. *Journal of Education and Training*, *4*, 58–72.

Lauterbach, S. L., & Bender, W. M. (1995). Cognitive strategy instruction for reading comprehension: A success for high school freshmen. *High School Journal*, *79*, 59–64.

Leidig, T., Grünke, M., Urton, K., Knaak, T., & Hisgen, S. (2018). The effects of the RAP strategy used in a peer-tutoring setting to foster reading comprehension in high-risk fourth graders. *Learning Disabilities: A Contemporary Journal*, *16*(2), 231–253.

National Governors Association Center for Best Practices & Council of Chief State School Officers (2010). *Common Core State Standards*. Washington, DC: Authors.

Sanders, S., Jolivette, K., & Harris, C. (2021). Improving the reading comprehension skills of systems-involved youth: A preliminary investigation of an underserved population. *Learning Disabilities Research & Practice*, *36*. doi:10.1111/ldrp.12254

Sanders, S., Rollins, L. H., Mason, L. H., Shaw, A., & Jolivette, K. (2021). Intesification and individualization of self-regulation components within self-regulated strategy development. *Intervention in School and Clinic*, *56*(3), 131–140.

Sawyer, R. J., Graham, S., & Harris, K. R. (1992). Direct teaching, strategy instruction, and strategy instruction with explicit self-regulation: Effects on the composition skills and self-efficacy of students with learning disabilities. *Journal of Educational Psychology*, *84*, 340–352. doi:10.1037/0022-0663.84.3.340

Schumaker, J. B., Denton, P. H., & Deshler, D. D. (1984). *The paraphrasing strategy*. Lawrence, KS: University of Kansas.

Schumaker, J. B., Deshler, D. D., & Ellis, E. S. (1986). Intervention issues related to the education of LD adolescents. In J. K. Torgeson & B. Y. L. Wong (Eds.), *Learning disabilities: Some new perspectives*. New York, NY: Academic Press.

Shanahan, T., Callison, K., Carriere, C., Duke, N. K., Pearson, P. D., Schatschneider, C., & Torgesen, J. (2010). *Improving reading comprehension in kindergarten through 3rd grade: IES Practice Guide, NCEE 2010-4038*. Washington, DC: National Center for Education Evaluation and Regional Assistance, Institute of Education Sciences, US Department of Education. Retrieved from whatworks.ed.gov

Snow, C. (2002). *Reading for understanding: Toward an R&D program in reading comprehension*. Santa Monica, CA: Rand Corporation.

Swanson, H. L. (1996). Information processing: An introduction. In D. K. Reid, W. Hresko, & H. L. Swanson (Eds.), *Cognitive approaches to learning disabilities* (pp. 251–285). Austin, TX: PRO-ED.

Vaughn, S., Roberts, G., Wexler, J., Vaughn, M. G., Fall, A. M., & Schnakenberg, J. B. (2015). High school students with reading comprehension difficulties: Results of a randomized control trial of a two-year reading intervention. *Journal of Learning Disabilities*, *48*(5), 546–558. doi:10.1177/0022219413515511

INDEX

Pages in *italics* refer to figures, pages in **bold** refer to tables, and pages followed by "n" refer to notes.

For Product Safety Concerns and Information please contact our EU
representative GPSR@taylorandfrancis.com
Taylor & Francis Verlag GmbH, Kaufingerstraße 24, 80331 München, Germany

www.ingramcontent.com/pod-product-compliance
Ingram Content Group UK Ltd.
Pitfield, Milton Keynes, MK11 3LW, UK
UKHW020132200926
475702UK00005B/717
* 9 7 8 1 0 3 2 2 2 7 5 7 3 *